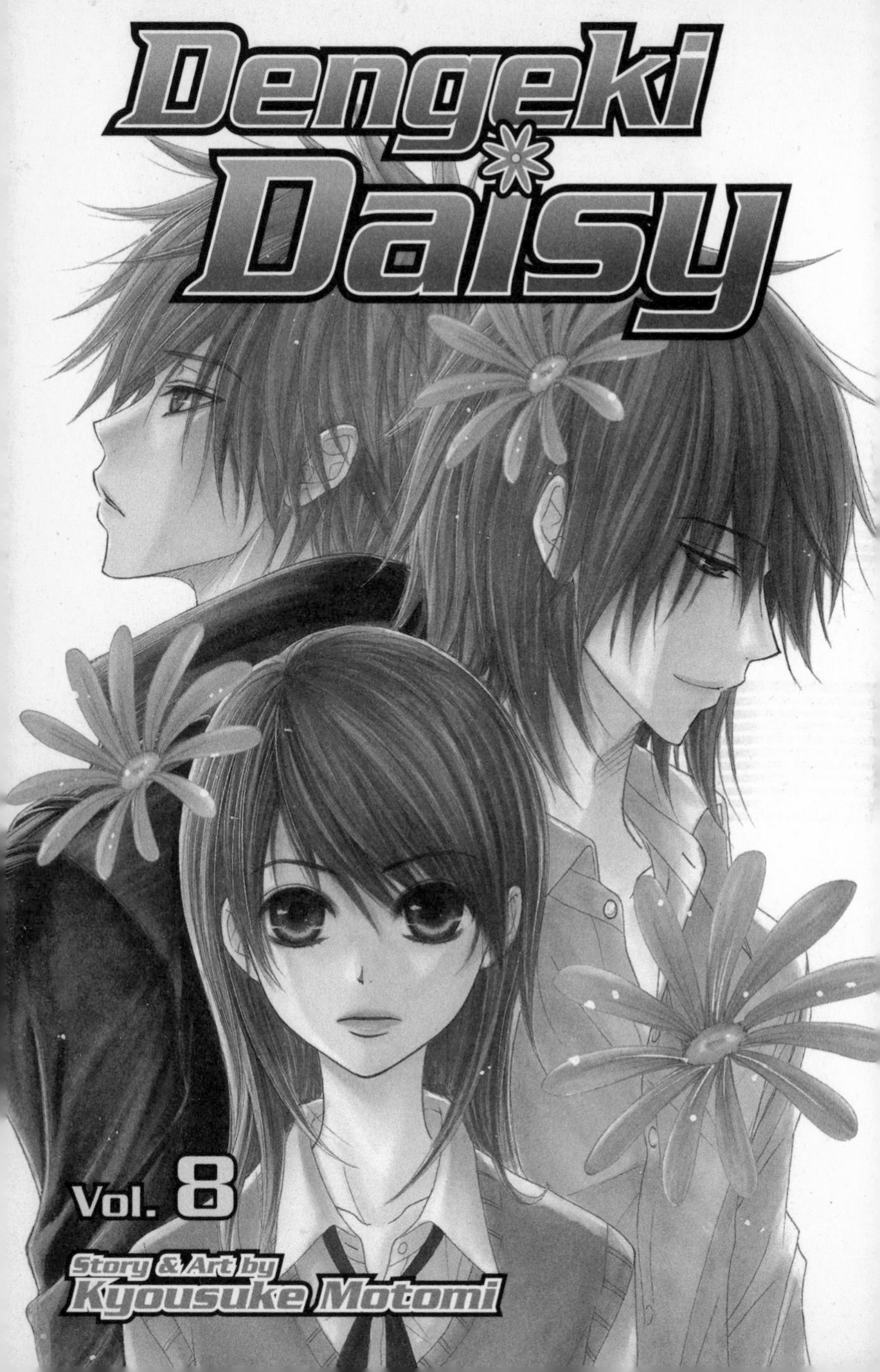
Dengeki Daisy
Vol. 8
Story & Art by
Kyousuke Motomi

Dengeki Daisy

Volume 8 CONTENTS

DAISY

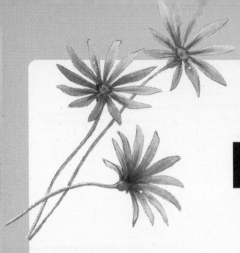

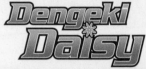

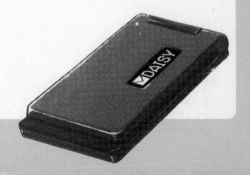

Dengeki Daisy Vol. 8

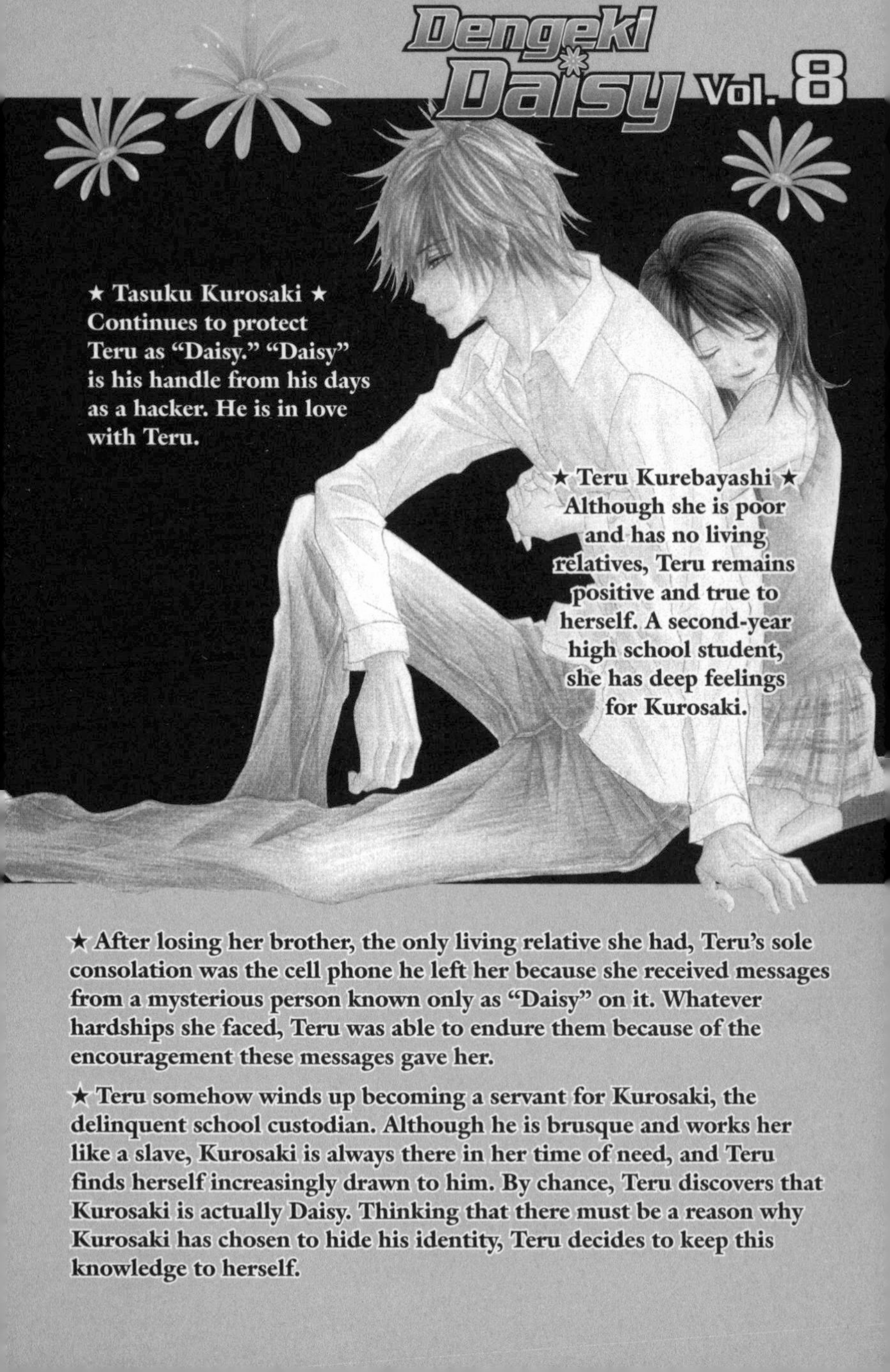
★ Tasuku Kurosaki ★
Continues to protect Teru as "Daisy." "Daisy" is his handle from his days as a hacker. He is in love with Teru.
★ Teru Kurebayashi ★
Although she is poor and has no living relatives, Teru remains positive and true to herself. A second-year high school student, she has deep feelings for Kurosaki.

★ After losing her brother, the only living relative she had, Teru's sole consolation was the cell phone he left her because she received messages from a mysterious person known only as "Daisy" on it. Whatever hardships she faced, Teru was able to endure them because of the encouragement these messages gave her.

★ Teru somehow winds up becoming a servant for Kurosaki, the delinquent school custodian. Although he is brusque and works her like a slave, Kurosaki is always there in her time of need, and Teru finds herself increasingly drawn to him. By chance, Teru discovers that Kurosaki is actually Daisy. Thinking that there must be a reason why Kurosaki has chosen to hide his identity, Teru decides to keep this knowledge to herself.

CHARACTERS...

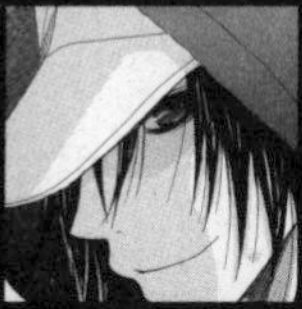

★ Akira ★
The culprit behind the Fake Daisy incident. Chiharu Mori's partner-in-crime.

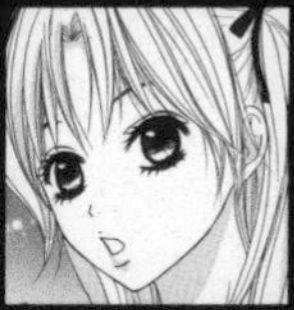

★ Rena ★
Teru's friend. She once was romantically involved with Arai.

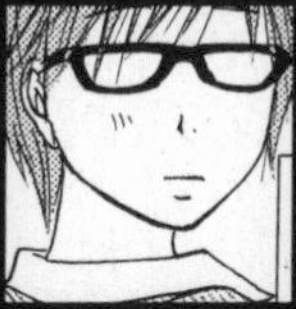

★ Kiyoshi Hasegawa ★
Teru's friend since grade school and Kurosaki's number two servant.

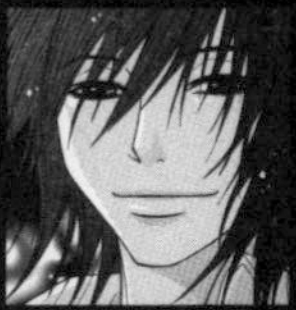

★ Soichiro Kurebayashi ★
Teru's older brother and a genius systems engineer. He died after leaving Teru in Kurosaki's care.

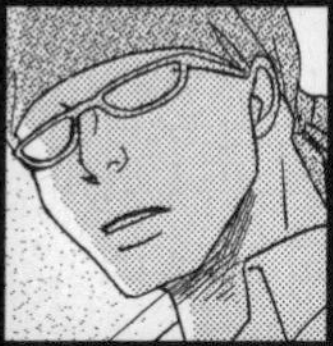

★ Boss (Masuda) ★
He used to work with Soichiro and currently runs the snack shop "Flower Garden."

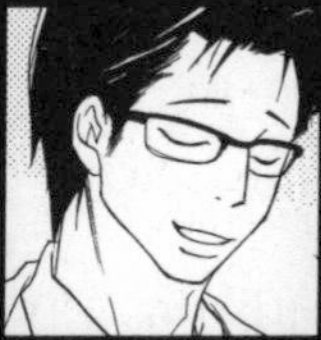

★ Takeda ★
Soichiro's former coworker. He is the owner of Kaoruko, a Shiba dog.

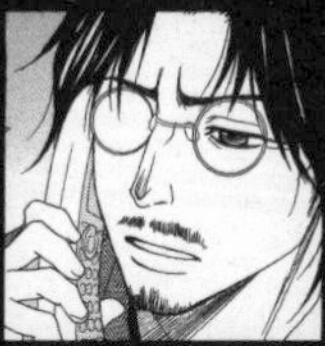

★ Director (Kazumasa Ando) ★
He used to work with Soichiro and is currently the director of Teru's school.

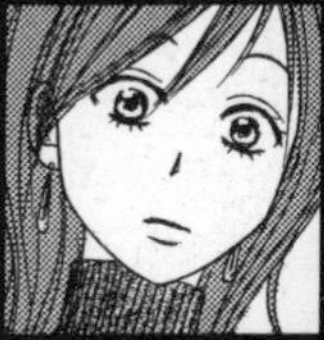

★ Riko Onizuka ★
She was Soichiro's girlfriend and is now a counselor at Teru's school.

STORY...

★ During this time, a fake Daisy appears, Teru's life is threatened, and strange incidents involving Teru and Kurosaki occur. Teru vows to stay close to Kurosaki, who has protected her at every turn. Meanwhile, Kurosaki begins to realize that in order to be with Teru, he will have to disclose the truth. The fake Daisy incident nears its climax, and it is learned that the real culprit behind it is Chiharu Mori, the school nurse and health teacher. After Mori manages to escape, Kurosaki makes up his mind to tell Teru everything.

★ Kurosaki and Teru enjoy their first date at the amusement park, but Mori's partner Akira snatches Teru away.

★ Akira tricks Teru into sending Kurosaki this message: "I can't forgive you for killing my brother. Please just disappear from my life." Kurosaki replies with, "It's true that I killed your beloved brother" and leaves her, but...?!

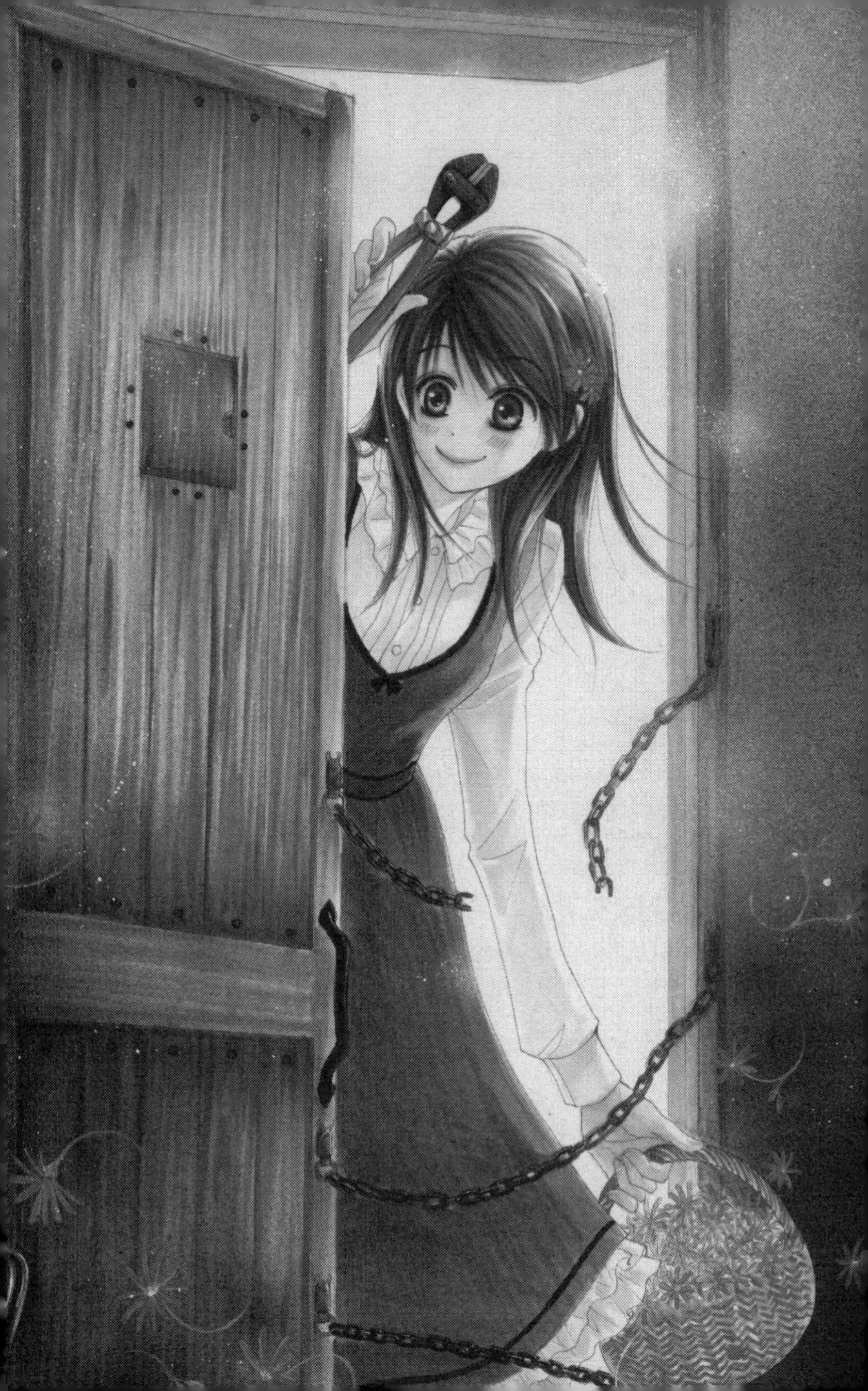

CHAPTER 35: BE HAPPY

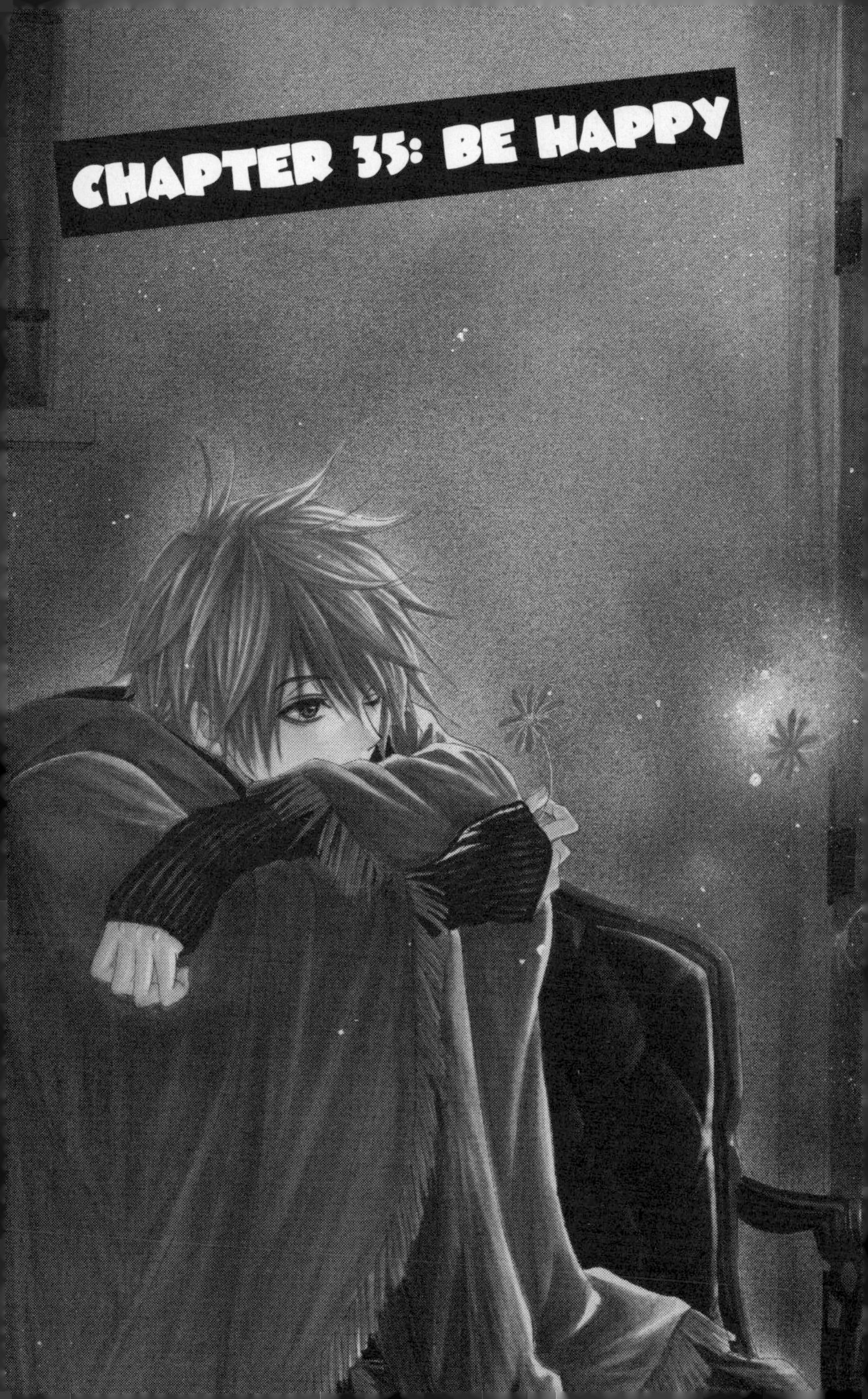

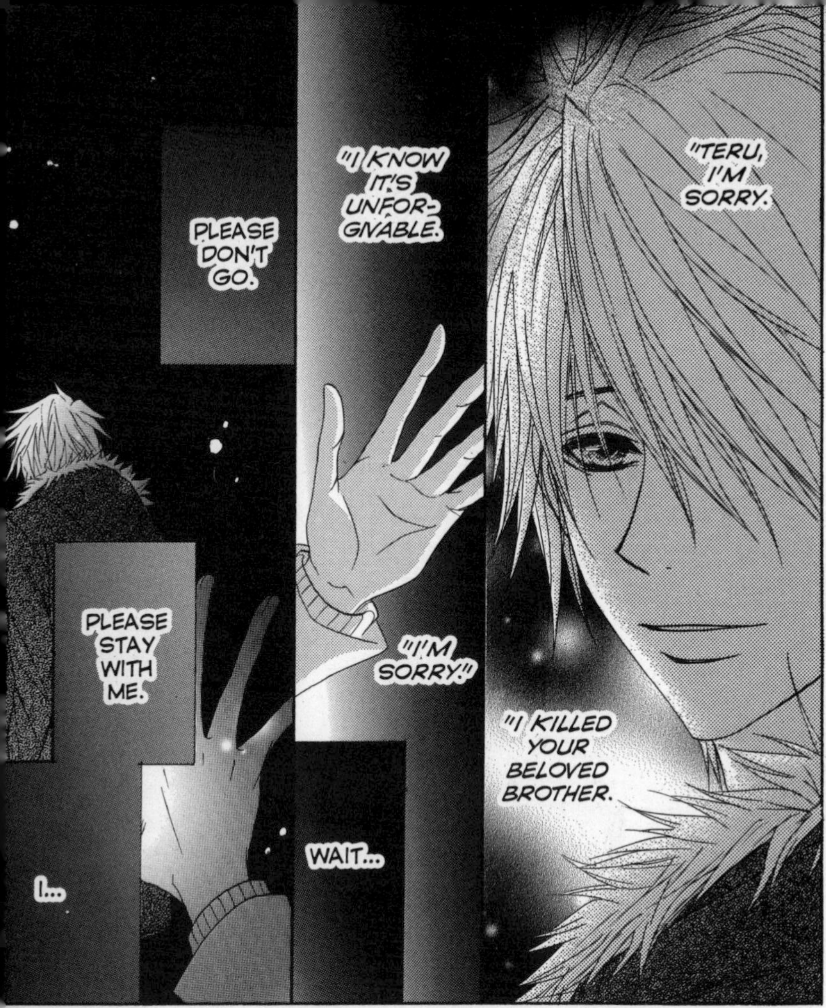
"TERU, I'M SORRY.
"I KILLED YOUR BELOVED BROTHER.
"I KNOW IT'S UNFORGIVABLE.
"I'M SORRY."
WAIT...
PLEASE DON'T GO.
PLEASE STAY WITH ME.
I...

THE BLUE DAISY SEEMS TO BE A SEMI-PERENNIAL PLANT. ONCE IT'S PLANTED, YOU CAN ENJOY IT FOR A LONG TIME.

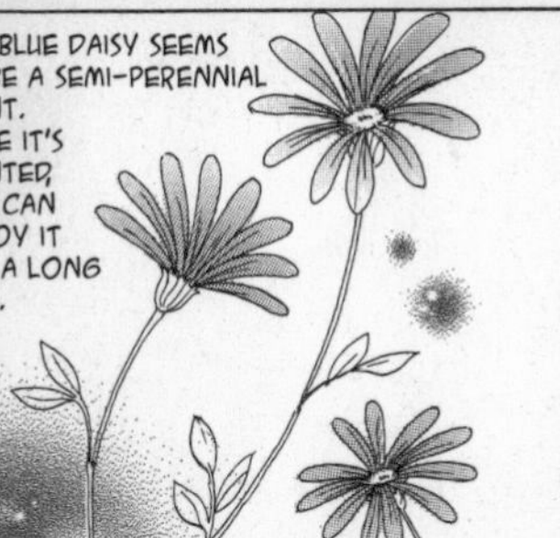

HELLO, EVERYONE!! IT'S KYOUSUKE MOTOMI. WE'VE ARRIVED AT VOLUME 8 OF *DENGEKI DAISY*.
I-I-IT'S A TOTAL SURPRISE. AND I OWE IT ALL TO YOU.
THANK YOU SO MUCH. THANK YOU FROM THE BOTTOM OF MY HEART.
THIS VOLUME IS WROUGHT WITH SLIGHTLY DIFFERENT TENSION THAN BEFORE, BUT I HOPE YOU'LL STICK WITH IT UNTIL THE LAST PAGE. I'M COUNTING ON YOU!!

※ THANK YOU TO ALL WHO WROTE LETTERS ADVISING ME ON HOW TO TAKE CARE OF A BLUE DAISY! I'LL TRY YOUR TIPS LIKE PRUNING.

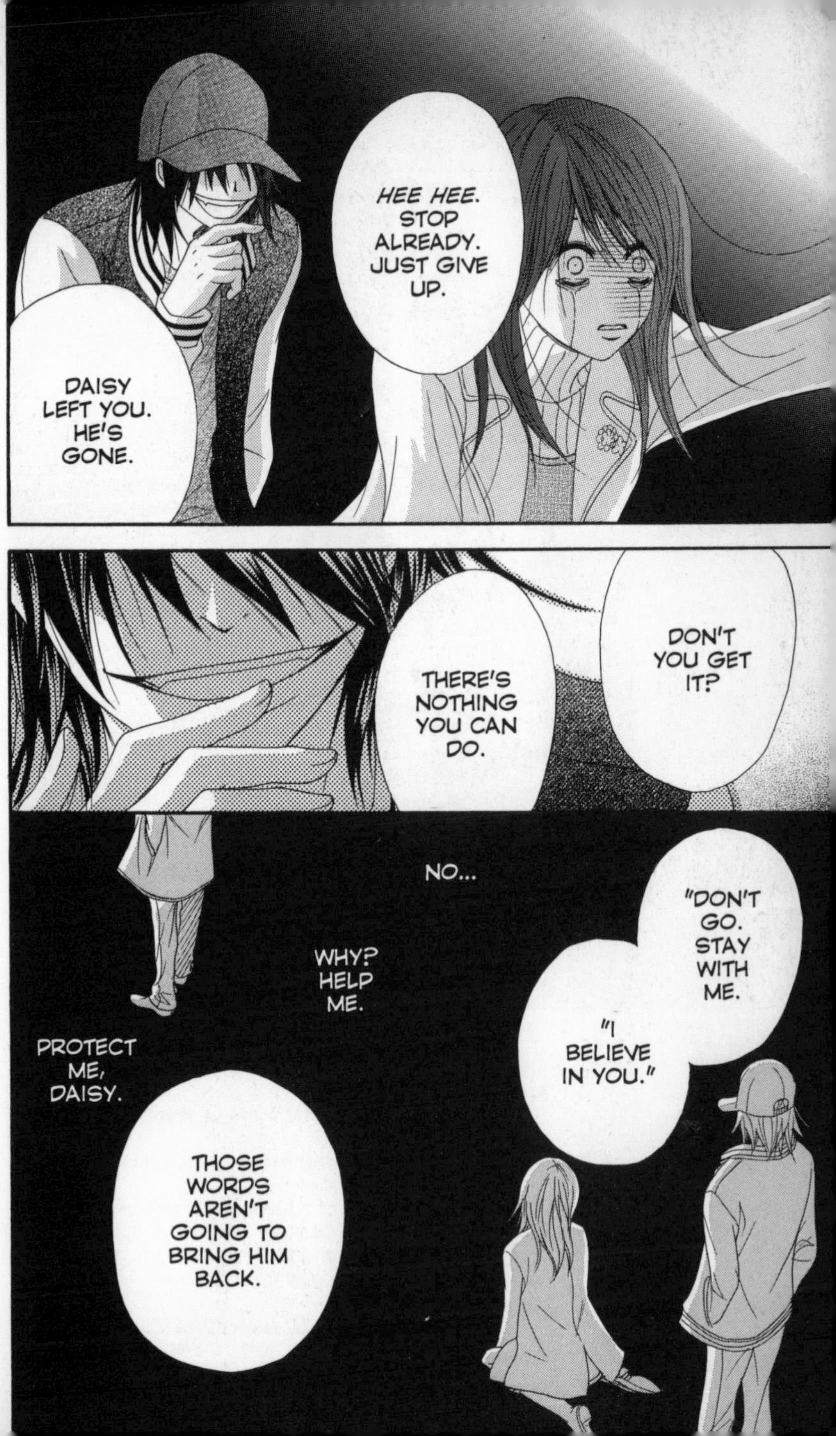
HEE HEE. STOP ALREADY. JUST GIVE UP.
DAISY LEFT YOU. HE'S GONE.
DON'T YOU GET IT?
THERE'S NOTHING YOU CAN DO.
"DON'T GO. STAY WITH ME.
"I BELIEVE IN YOU."
NO...
WHY? HELP ME.
PROTECT ME, DAISY.
THOSE WORDS AREN'T GOING TO BRING HIM BACK.

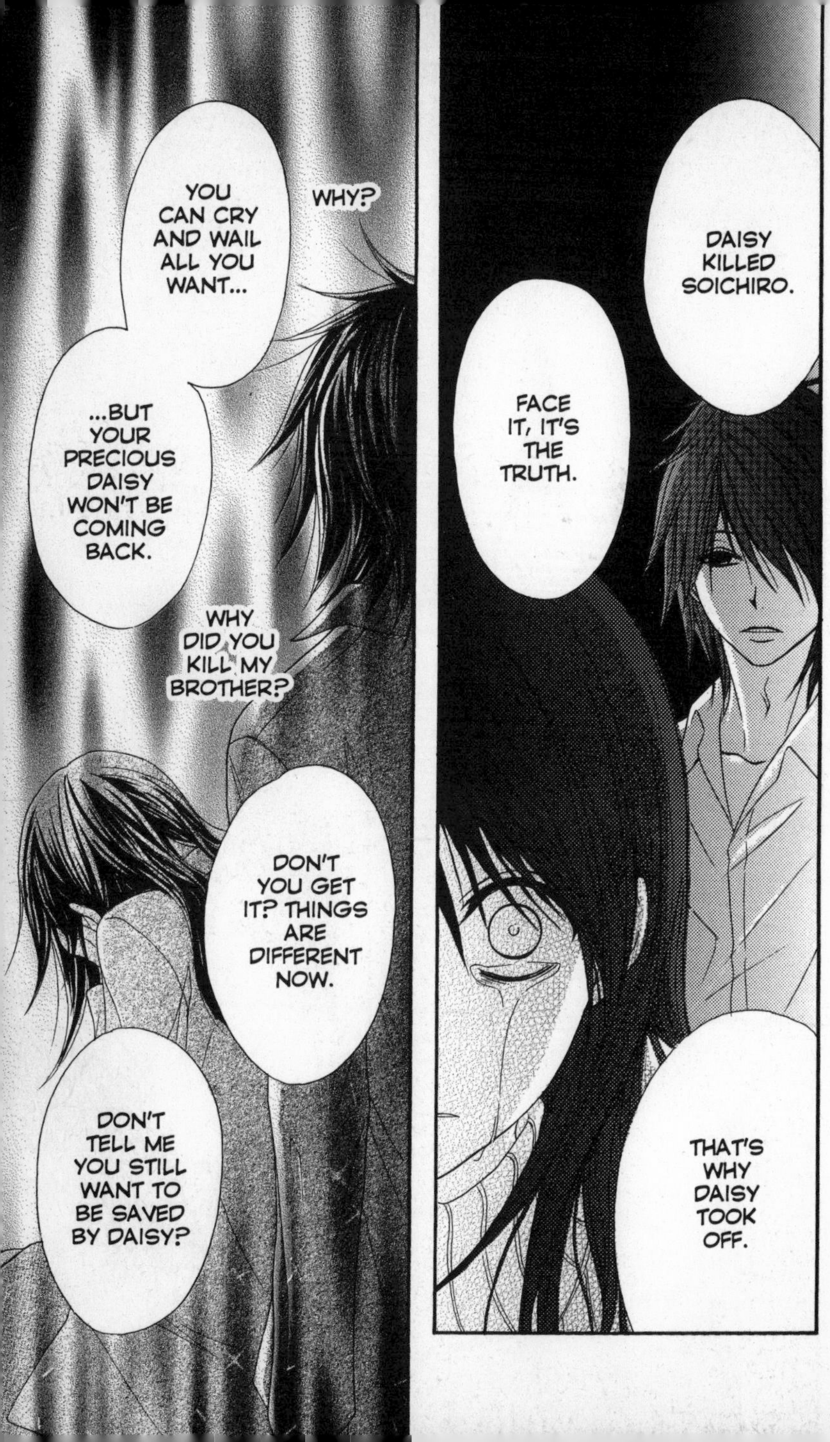
DAISY KILLED SOICHIRO.
FACE IT, IT'S THE TRUTH.
THAT'S WHY DAISY TOOK OFF.
WHY?
YOU CAN CRY AND WAIL ALL YOU WANT...
...BUT YOUR PRECIOUS DAISY WON'T BE COMING BACK.
WHY DID YOU KILL MY BROTHER?
DON'T YOU GET IT? THINGS ARE DIFFERENT NOW.
DON'T TELL ME YOU STILL WANT TO BE SAVED BY DAISY?

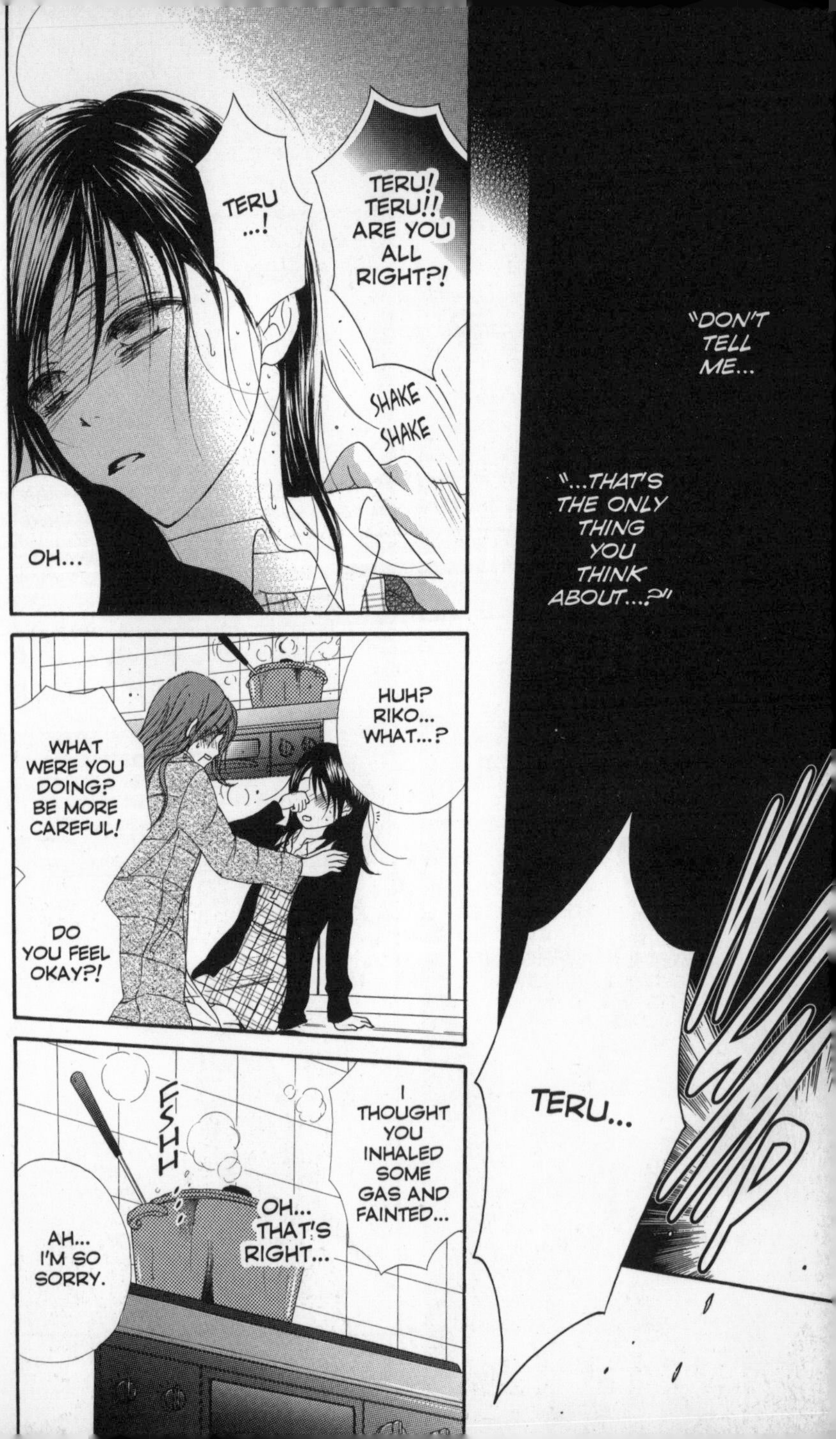
"DON'T TELL ME...
"...THAT'S THE ONLY THING YOU THINK ABOUT...?"
TERU...
TERU! TERU!! ARE YOU ALL RIGHT?!
SHAKE SHAKE
TERU ...!
OH...
HUH? RIKO... WHAT...?
WHAT WERE YOU DOING? BE MORE CAREFUL!
DO YOU FEEL OKAY?!
I THOUGHT YOU INHALED SOME GAS AND FAINTED...
FSHH
OH... THAT'S RIGHT...
AH... I'M SO SORRY.

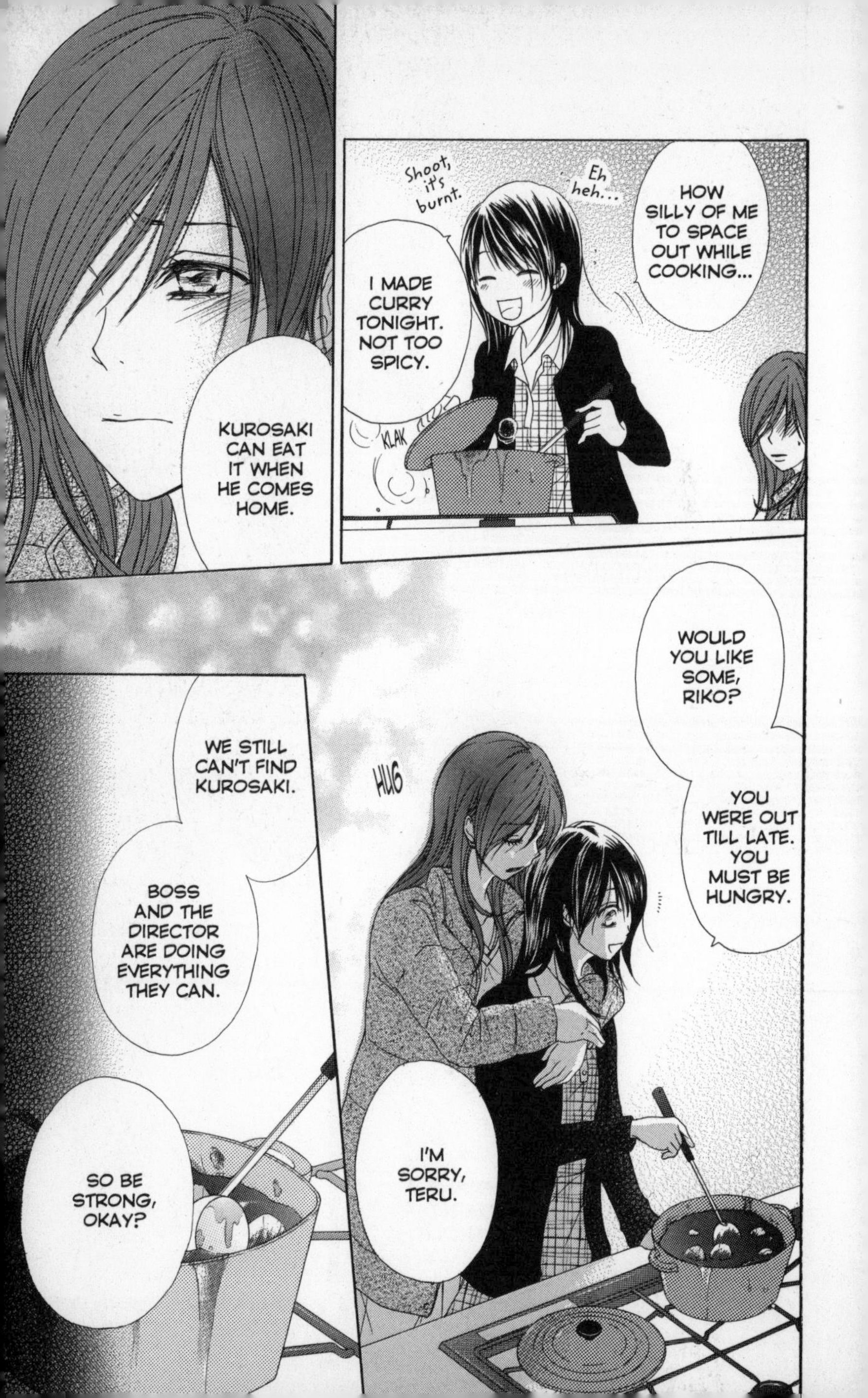
Eh heh...
HOW SILLY OF ME TO SPACE OUT WHILE COOKING...
Shoot, it's burnt.
I MADE CURRY TONIGHT. NOT TOO SPICY.
KLAK
KUROSAKI CAN EAT IT WHEN HE COMES HOME.
WOULD YOU LIKE SOME, RIKO?
YOU WERE OUT TILL LATE. YOU MUST BE HUNGRY.
HUG
WE STILL CAN'T FIND KUROSAKI.
BOSS AND THE DIRECTOR ARE DOING EVERYTHING THEY CAN.
I'M SORRY, TERU.
SO BE STRONG, OKAY?

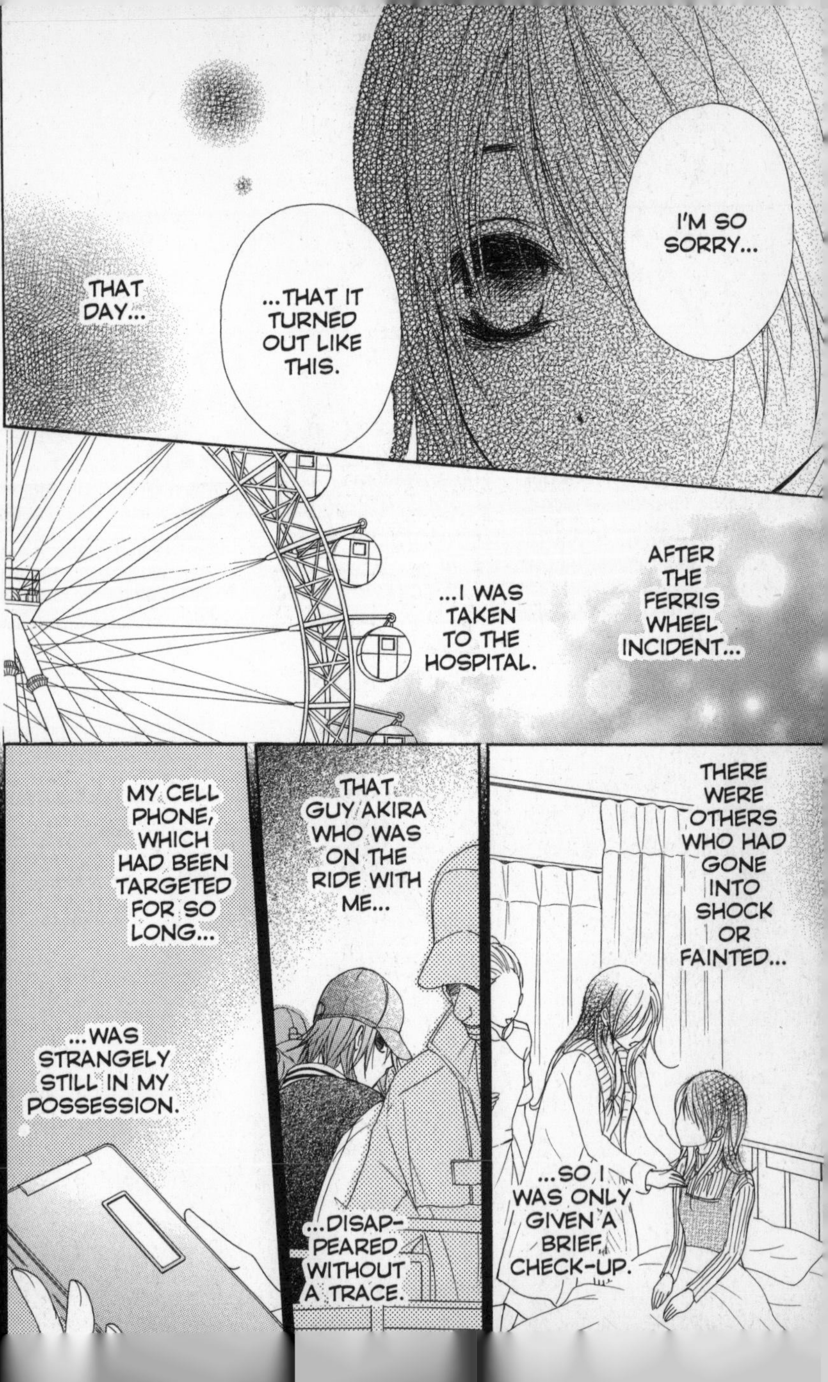
I'M SO SORRY...
...THAT IT TURNED OUT LIKE THIS.
THAT DAY...
AFTER THE FERRIS WHEEL INCIDENT...
...I WAS TAKEN TO THE HOSPITAL.
THERE WERE OTHERS WHO HAD GONE INTO SHOCK OR FAINTED...
...SO I WAS ONLY GIVEN A BRIEF CHECK-UP.
THAT GUY AKIRA WHO WAS ON THE RIDE WITH ME...
...DISAP-PEARED WITHOUT A TRACE.
MY CELL PHONE, WHICH HAD BEEN TARGETED FOR SO LONG...
...WAS STRANGELY STILL IN MY POSSESSION.

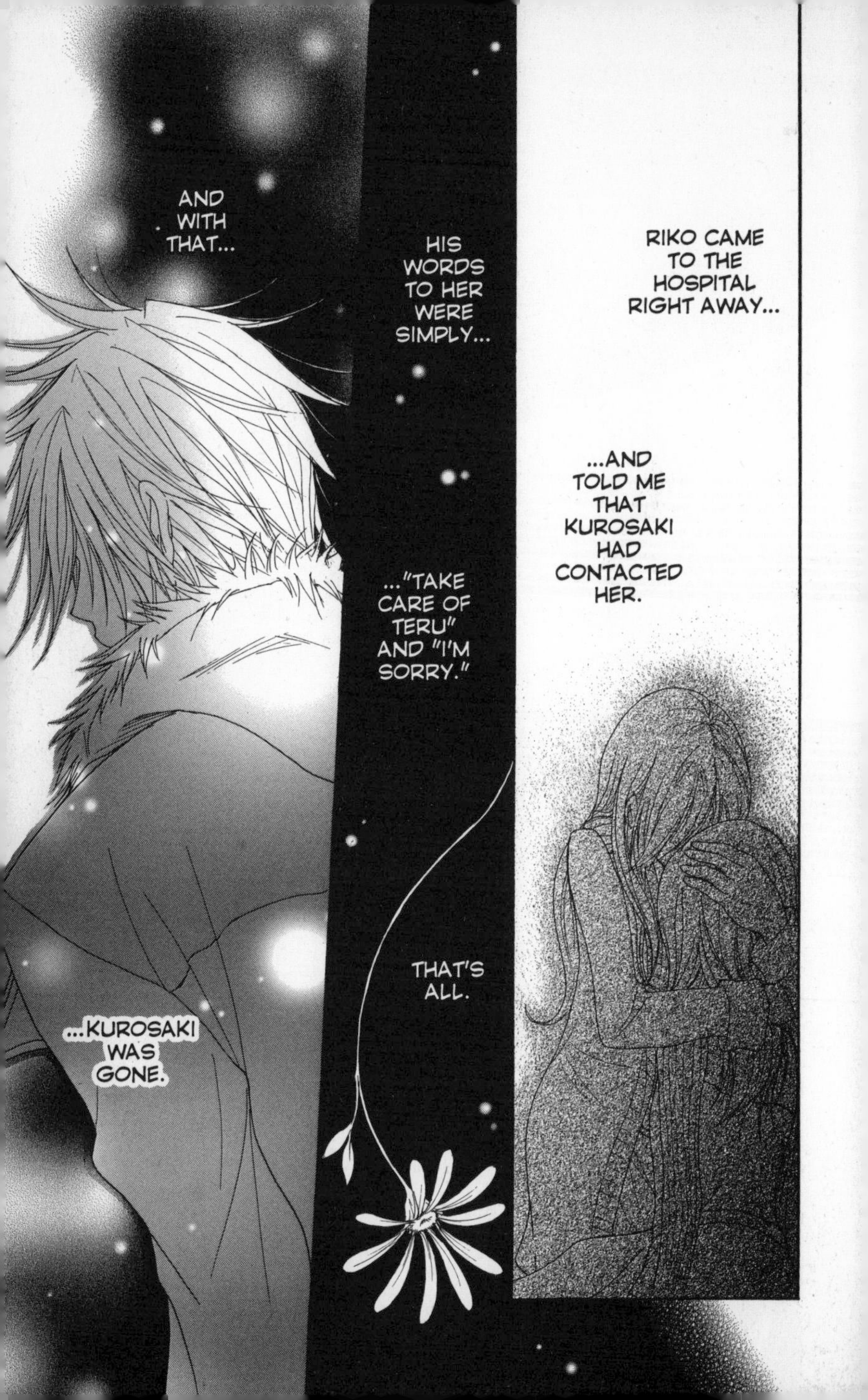
RIKO CAME TO THE HOSPITAL RIGHT AWAY...
...AND TOLD ME THAT KUROSAKI HAD CONTACTED HER.
HIS WORDS TO HER WERE SIMPLY...
..."TAKE CARE OF TERU" AND "I'M SORRY."
THAT'S ALL.
AND WITH THAT...
...KUROSAKI WAS GONE.

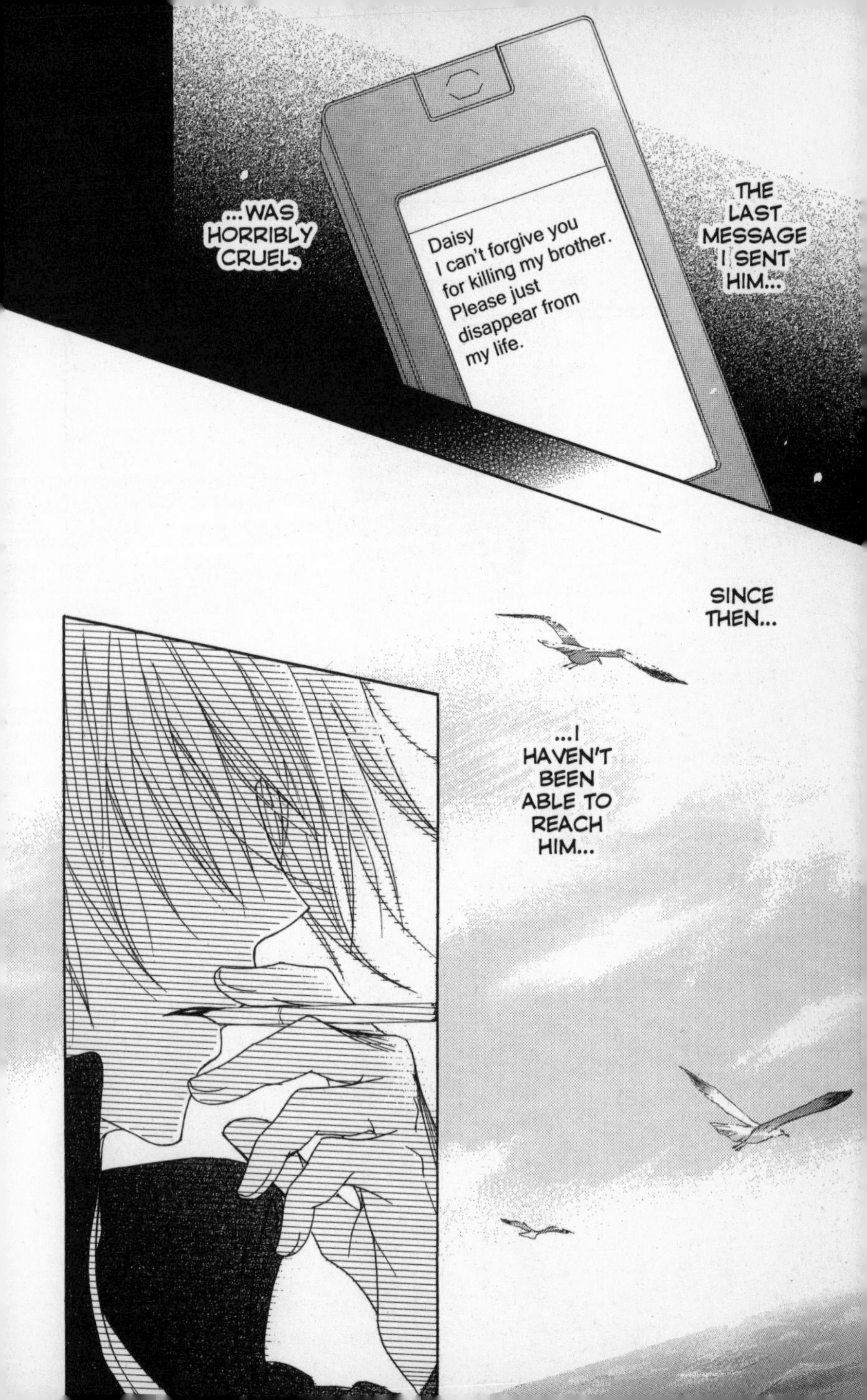
THE LAST MESSAGE I SENT HIM...
Daisy
I can't forgive you for killing my brother. Please just disappear from my life.
...WAS HORRIBLY CRUEL.
SINCE THEN...
...I HAVEN'T BEEN ABLE TO REACH HIM...

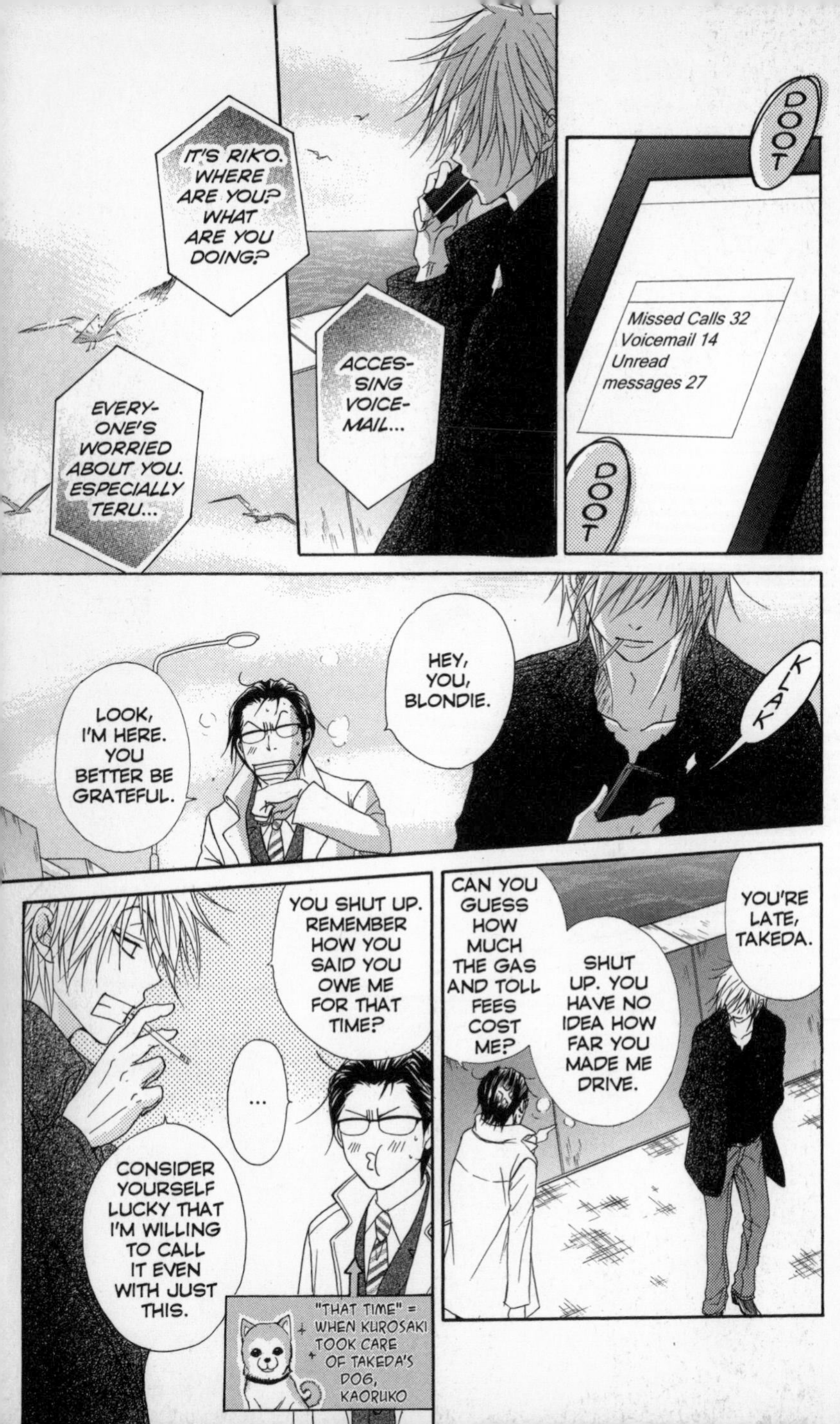
DOOT
Missed Calls 32
Voicemail 14
Unread messages 27
DOOT
ACCESSING VOICEMAIL...
IT'S RIKO. WHERE ARE YOU? WHAT ARE YOU DOING?
EVERYONE'S WORRIED ABOUT YOU. ESPECIALLY TERU...
KLAK
HEY, YOU, BLONDIE.
LOOK, I'M HERE. YOU BETTER BE GRATEFUL.
YOU'RE LATE, TAKEDA.
SHUT UP. YOU HAVE NO IDEA HOW FAR YOU MADE ME DRIVE.
CAN YOU GUESS HOW MUCH THE GAS AND TOLL FEES COST ME?
YOU SHUT UP. REMEMBER HOW YOU SAID YOU OWE ME FOR THAT TIME?
...
CONSIDER YOURSELF LUCKY THAT I'M WILLING TO CALL IT EVEN WITH JUST THIS.
"THAT TIME" = WHEN KUROSAKI TOOK CARE OF TAKEDA'S DOG, KAORUKO

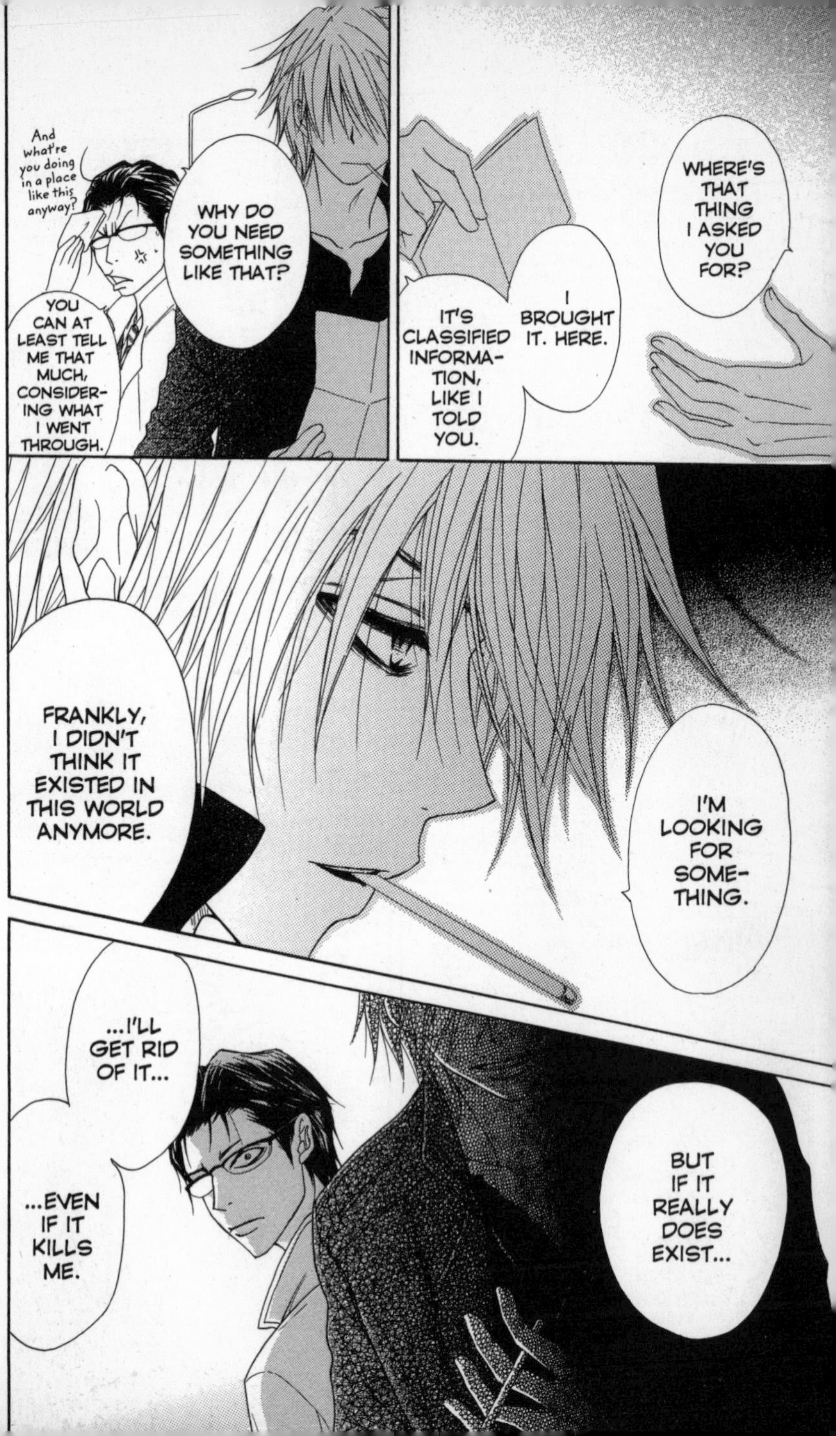
WHERE'S THAT THING I ASKED YOU FOR?
I BROUGHT IT. HERE.
IT'S CLASSIFIED INFORMATION, LIKE I TOLD YOU.
WHY DO YOU NEED SOMETHING LIKE THAT?
And what're you doing in a place like this anyway?
YOU CAN AT LEAST TELL ME THAT MUCH, CONSIDERING WHAT I WENT THROUGH.
I'M LOOKING FOR SOMETHING.
FRANKLY, I DIDN'T THINK IT EXISTED IN THIS WORLD ANYMORE.
BUT IF IT REALLY DOES EXIST...
...I'LL GET RID OF IT...
...EVEN IF IT KILLS ME.

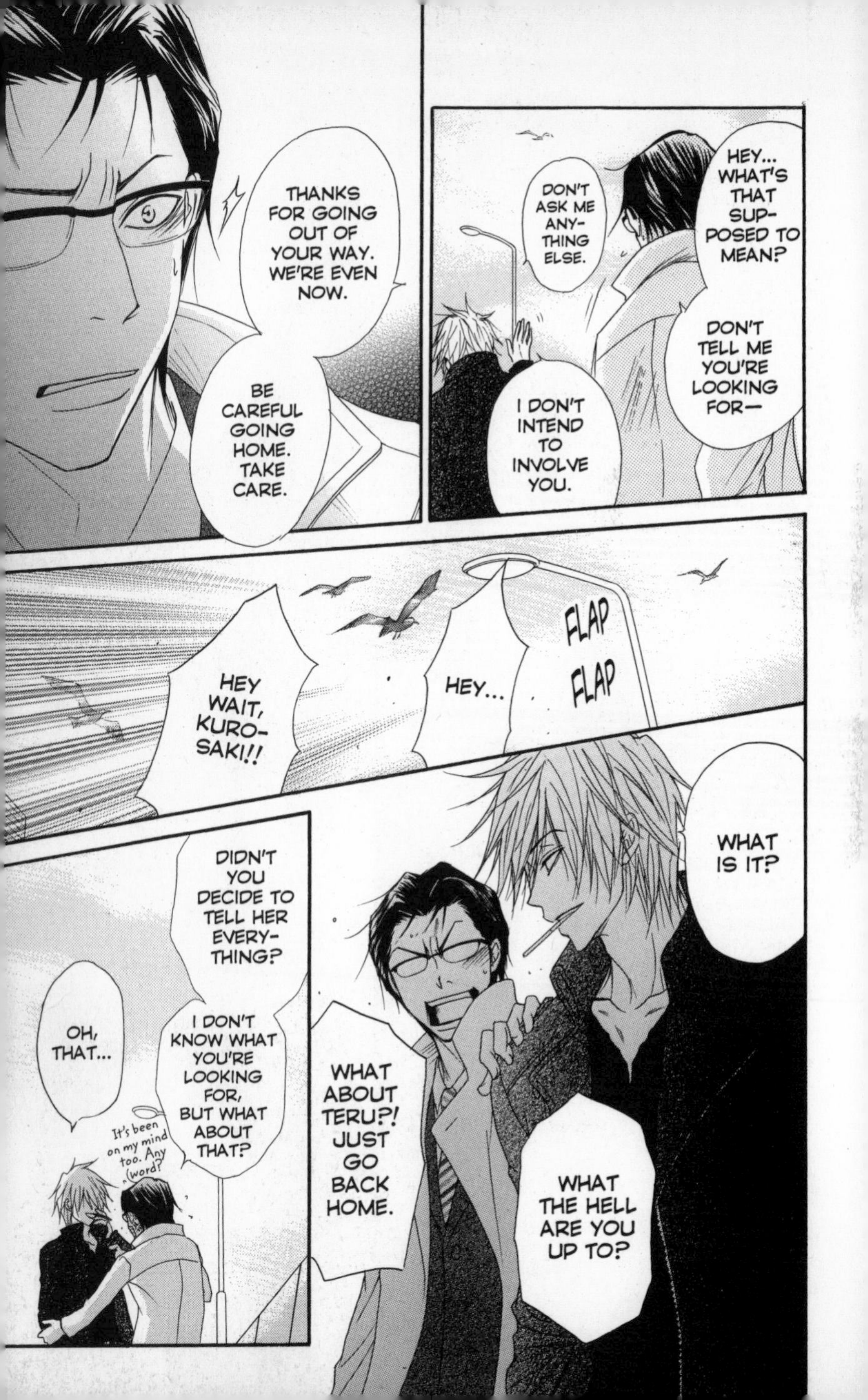
HEY... WHAT'S THAT SUP-POSED TO MEAN?
DON'T ASK ME ANY-THING ELSE.
DON'T TELL ME YOU'RE LOOKING FOR—
I DON'T INTEND TO INVOLVE YOU.
THANKS FOR GOING OUT OF YOUR WAY. WE'RE EVEN NOW.
BE CAREFUL GOING HOME. TAKE CARE.
FLAP FLAP
HEY...
HEY WAIT, KURO-SAKI!!
WHAT IS IT?
WHAT ABOUT TERU?! JUST GO BACK HOME.
WHAT THE HELL ARE YOU UP TO?
DIDN'T YOU DECIDE TO TELL HER EVERY-THING?
I DON'T KNOW WHAT YOU'RE LOOKING FOR, BUT WHAT ABOUT THAT?
OH, THAT...
It's been on my mind too. Any word?

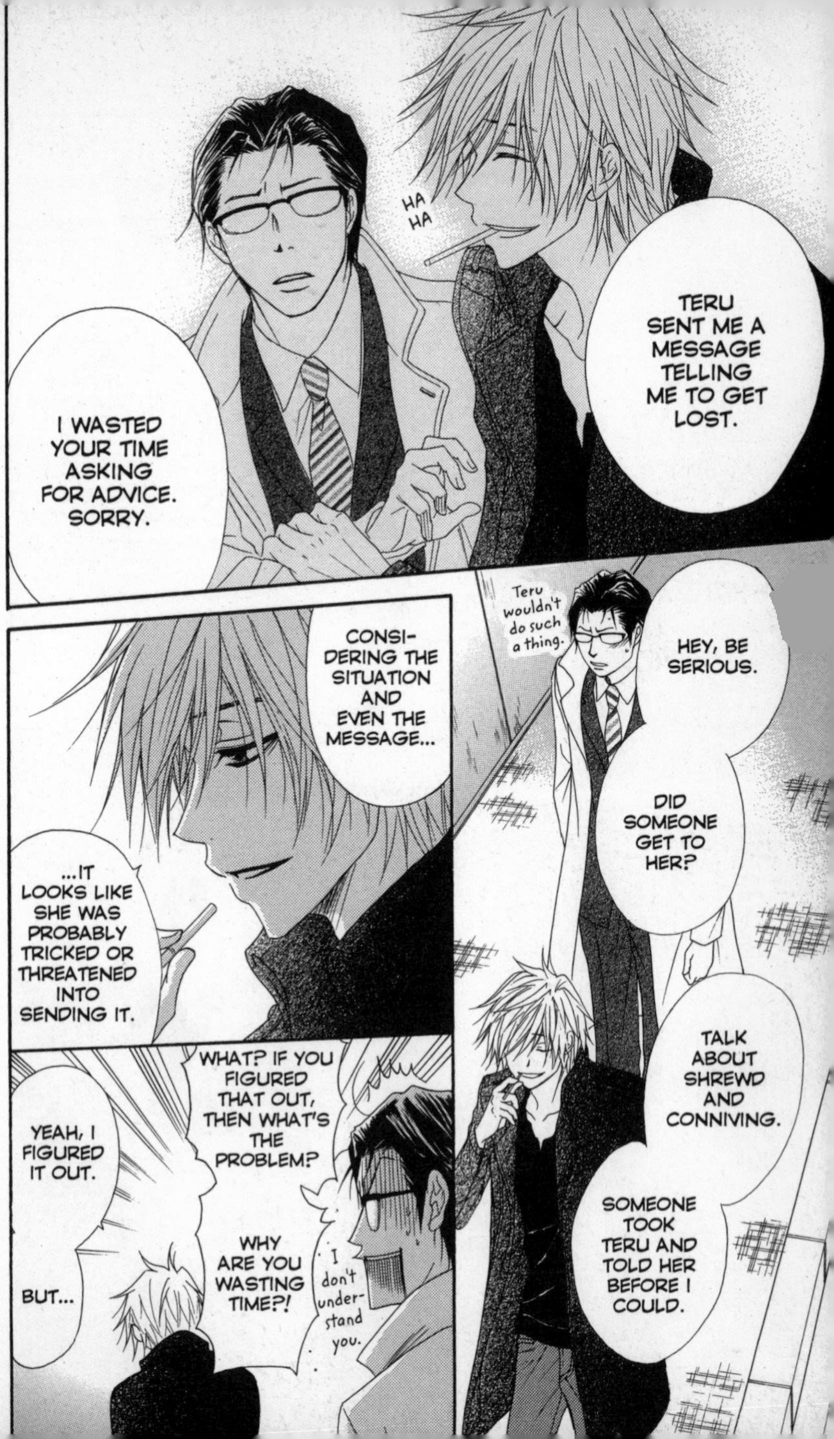
TERU SENT ME A MESSAGE TELLING ME TO GET LOST.
HA HA
I WASTED YOUR TIME ASKING FOR ADVICE. SORRY.
Teru wouldn't do such a thing.
HEY, BE SERIOUS.
DID SOMEONE GET TO HER?
TALK ABOUT SHREWD AND CONNIVING.
SOMEONE TOOK TERU AND TOLD HER BEFORE I COULD.
CONSI-DERING THE SITUATION AND EVEN THE MESSAGE...
...IT LOOKS LIKE SHE WAS PROBABLY TRICKED OR THREATENED INTO SENDING IT.
WHAT? IF YOU FIGURED THAT OUT, THEN WHAT'S THE PROBLEM?
YEAH, I FIGURED IT OUT.
WHY ARE YOU WASTING TIME?!
I don't under-stand you.
BUT...

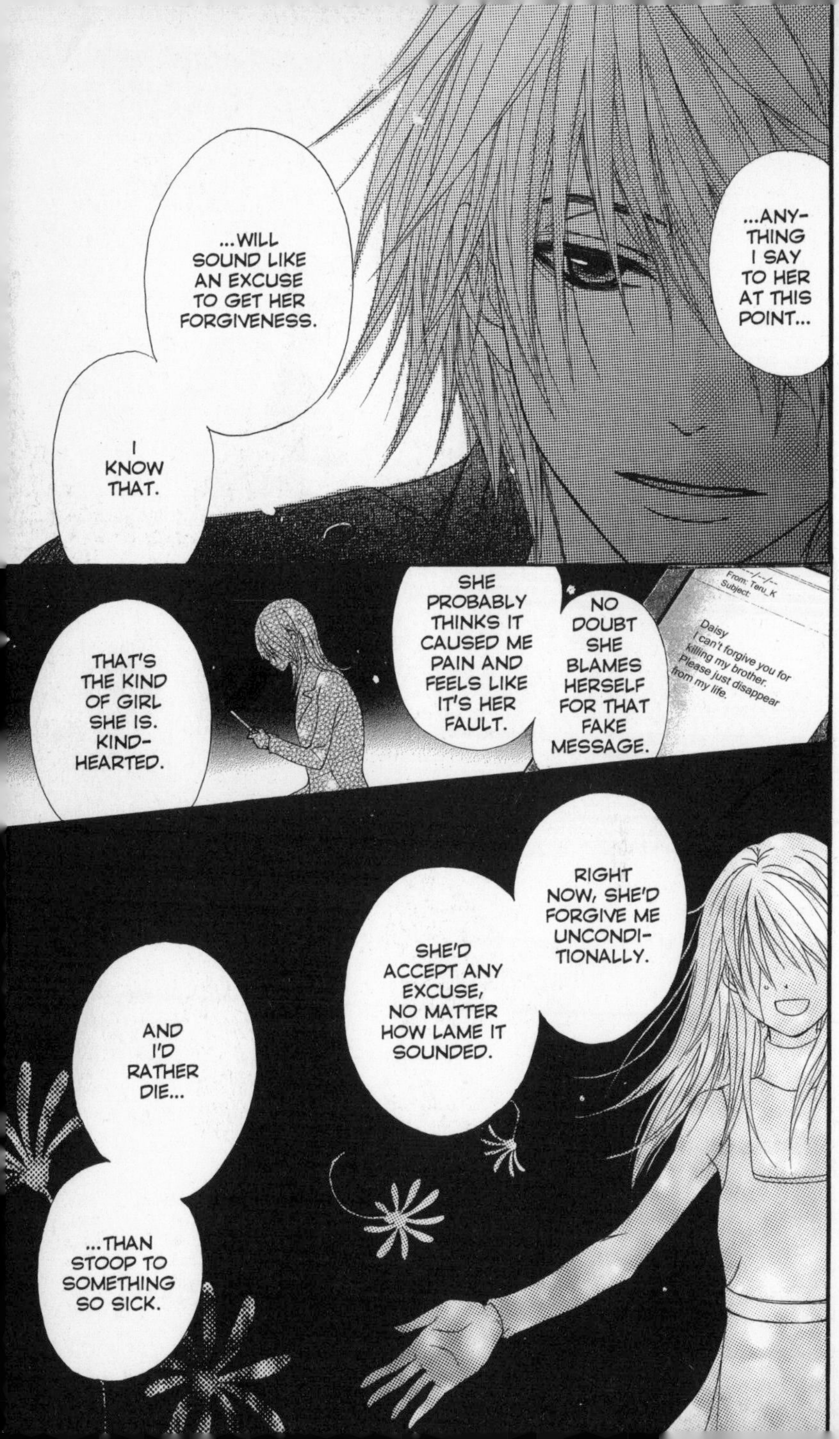
...ANYTHING I SAY TO HER AT THIS POINT...
...WILL SOUND LIKE AN EXCUSE TO GET HER FORGIVENESS.
I KNOW THAT.
From: Teru_K
Subject:
Daisy
I can't forgive you for killing my brother. Please just disappear from my life.
NO DOUBT SHE BLAMES HERSELF FOR THAT FAKE MESSAGE.
SHE PROBABLY THINKS IT CAUSED ME PAIN AND FEELS LIKE IT'S HER FAULT.
THAT'S THE KIND OF GIRL SHE IS. KIND-HEARTED.
RIGHT NOW, SHE'D FORGIVE ME UNCONDITIONALLY.
SHE'D ACCEPT ANY EXCUSE, NO MATTER HOW LAME IT SOUNDED.
AND I'D RATHER DIE...
...THAN STOOP TO SOMETHING SO SICK.

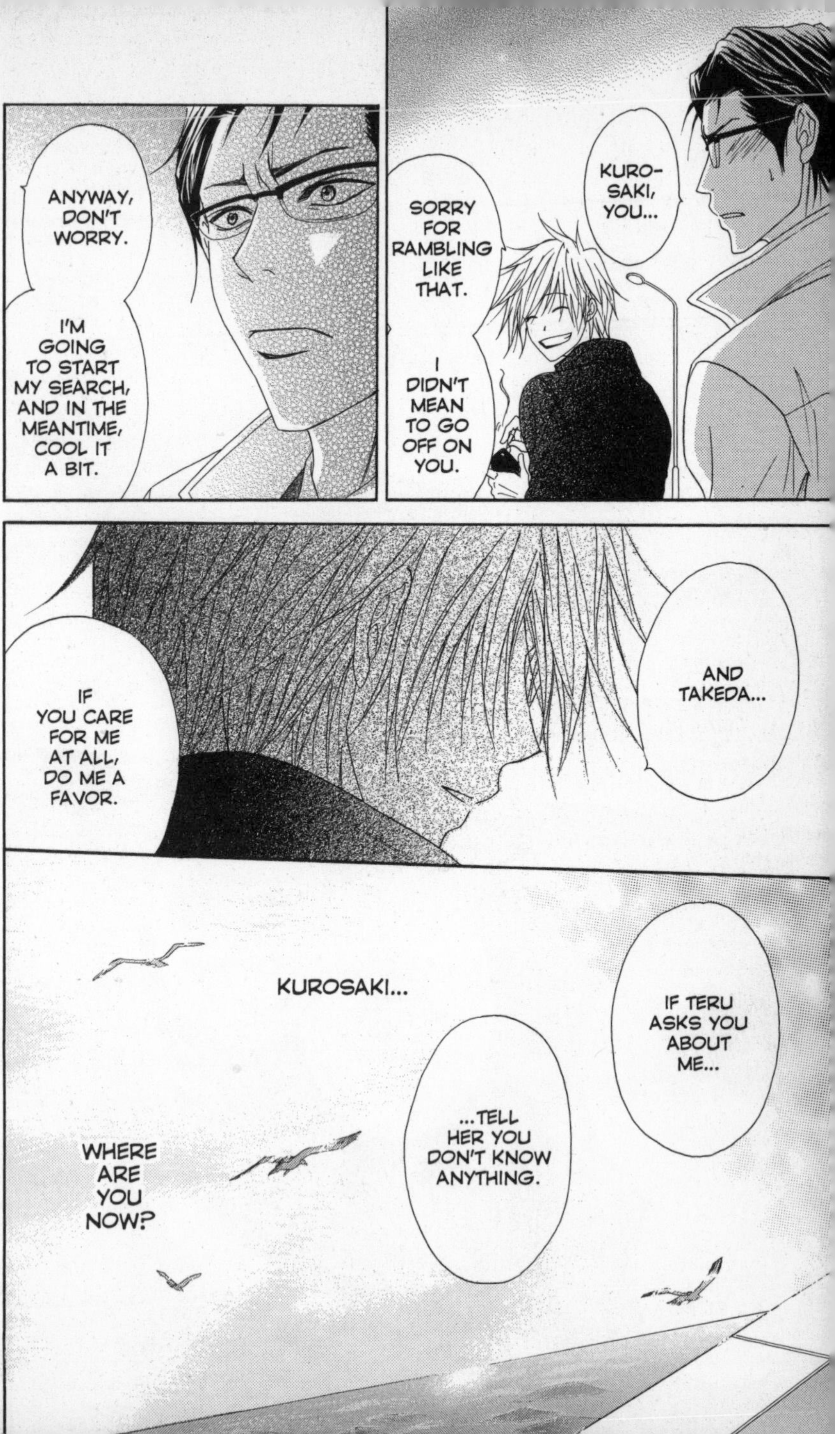
KURO-SAKI, YOU...
SORRY FOR RAMBLING LIKE THAT.
I DIDN'T MEAN TO GO OFF ON YOU.
ANYWAY, DON'T WORRY.
I'M GOING TO START MY SEARCH, AND IN THE MEANTIME, COOL IT A BIT.
AND TAKEDA...
IF YOU CARE FOR ME AT ALL, DO ME A FAVOR.
IF TERU ASKS YOU ABOUT ME...
...TELL HER YOU DON'T KNOW ANYTHING.
KUROSAKI...
WHERE ARE YOU NOW?

DENGEKI DAISY
QUESTION CORNER

BALDLY ASK!!

①

...HI! I'VE BROUGHT YOU THIS CORNER WHERE I ASK FOR YOUR KINDNESS AND UNDERSTANDING. THANK YOU FOR ALL THE QUESTIONS YOU SENT IN EVEN THOUGH WE DIDN'T HAVE MUCH TIME THIS TIME.

NOW, HERE WE GO!!!

Q.
IS KYOUSUKE MOTOMI A MALE?
(K.T., KANAGAWA PREFECTURE)

MOTOMI SENSEI, ARE YOU ♀ OR ♂?
IF YOU ARE ♀, DO YOU THINK YOU WILL GO BALD?
IF YOU ARE ♂, WHAT IS YOUR BUST SIZE?
THIS IS REALLY BOTHERING ME!!! SO PLEASE ANSWER!!!
(I.M., AICHI PREFECTURE)

A.
THIS IS THE SECOND MOST FREQUENTLY ASKED QUESTION I GET AFTER "WHEN WILL KUROSAKI GO BALD?" SO I'LL ANSWER. I REGRET TO INFORM YOU THAT KYOUSUKE MOTOMI IS, IN FACT, A WOMAN. MY APOLOGIES TO THE MANY WHO MAY BE THINKING, "HOW COULD A WOMAN PRODUCE SUCH ROUGH DRAWINGS?!" EVEN I THINK THAT IT'S STRANGE.
I'M A WOMAN, BUT I GET SO STRESSED WHEN I'M WORKING ON *DENGEKI DAISY* THAT I FEEL LIKE I'M LOSING MY HAIR.
AND I'M A WOMAN, BUT MY BUST SIZE IS ABOUT THE SAME AS TERU.
...HEH. I'M SORRY IF I CAUSED YOU SLEEPLESS NIGHTS OVER THIS. SORRY.

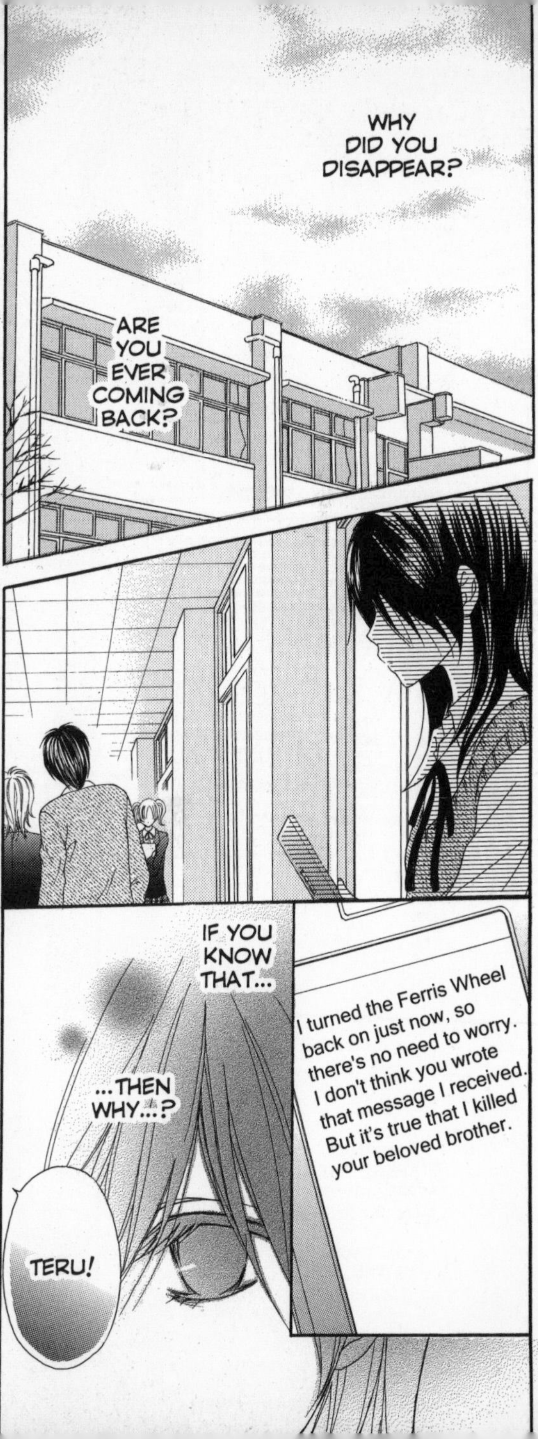
WHY DID YOU DISAPPEAR?
ARE YOU EVER COMING BACK?
I turned the Ferris Wheel back on just now, so there's no need to worry. I don't think you wrote that message I received. But it's true that I killed your beloved brother.
IF YOU KNOW THAT...
...THEN WHY...?
TERU!

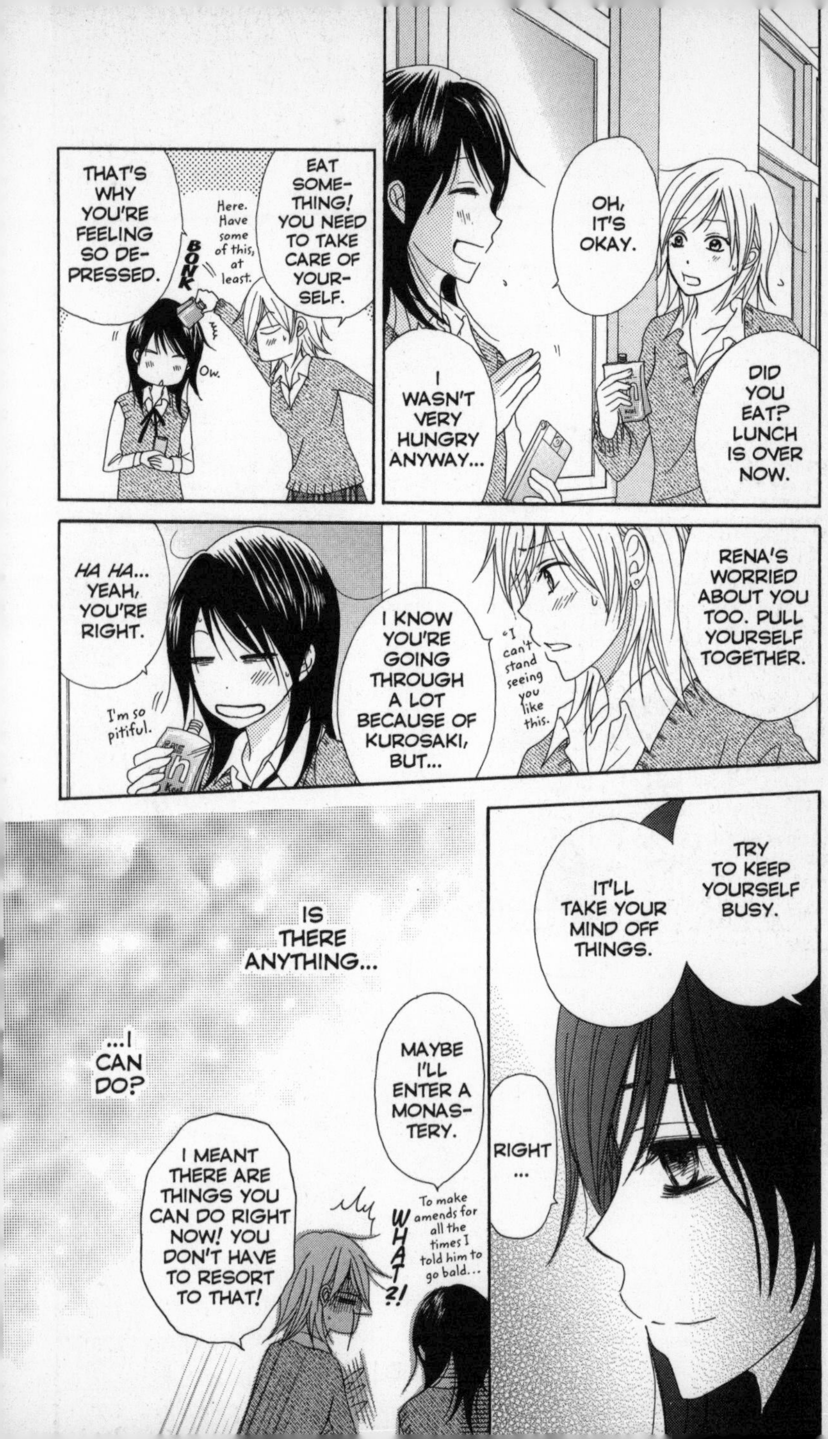
DID YOU EAT? LUNCH IS OVER NOW.
OH, IT'S OKAY.
I WASN'T VERY HUNGRY ANYWAY...
EAT SOME-THING! YOU NEED TO TAKE CARE OF YOUR-SELF.
Here. Have some of this, at least.
BONK
THAT'S WHY YOU'RE FEELING SO DE-PRESSED.
Ow.
RENA'S WORRIED ABOUT YOU TOO. PULL YOURSELF TOGETHER.
"I can't stand seeing you like this.
I KNOW YOU'RE GOING THROUGH A LOT BECAUSE OF KUROSAKI, BUT...
HA HA... YEAH, YOU'RE RIGHT.
I'm so pitiful.
TRY TO KEEP YOURSELF BUSY.
IT'LL TAKE YOUR MIND OFF THINGS.
RIGHT...
IS THERE ANYTHING...
...I CAN DO?
MAYBE I'LL ENTER A MONAS-TERY.
To make amends for all the times I told him to go bald...
WHAT?!
I MEANT THERE ARE THINGS YOU CAN DO RIGHT NOW! YOU DON'T HAVE TO RESORT TO THAT!

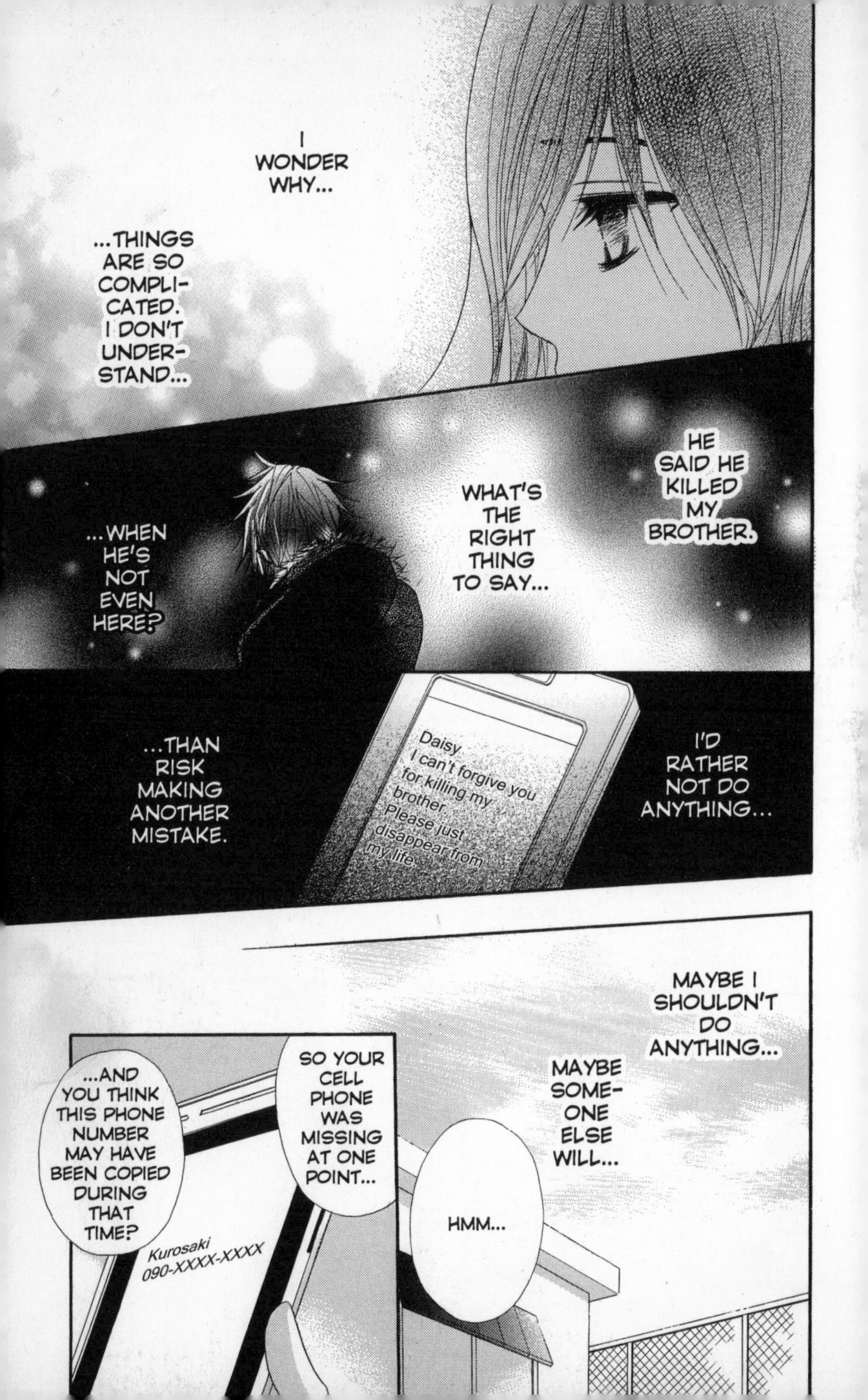
I WONDER WHY...
...THINGS ARE SO COMPLICATED. I DON'T UNDERSTAND...
HE SAID HE KILLED MY BROTHER.
WHAT'S THE RIGHT THING TO SAY...
...WHEN HE'S NOT EVEN HERE?
I'D RATHER NOT DO ANYTHING...
Daisy
I can't forgive you for killing my brother.
Please just disappear from my life.
...THAN RISK MAKING ANOTHER MISTAKE.
MAYBE I SHOULDN'T DO ANYTHING...
MAYBE SOMEONE ELSE WILL...
HMM...
SO YOUR CELL PHONE WAS MISSING AT ONE POINT...
...AND YOU THINK THIS PHONE NUMBER MAY HAVE BEEN COPIED DURING THAT TIME?
Kurosaki
090-XXXX-XXXX

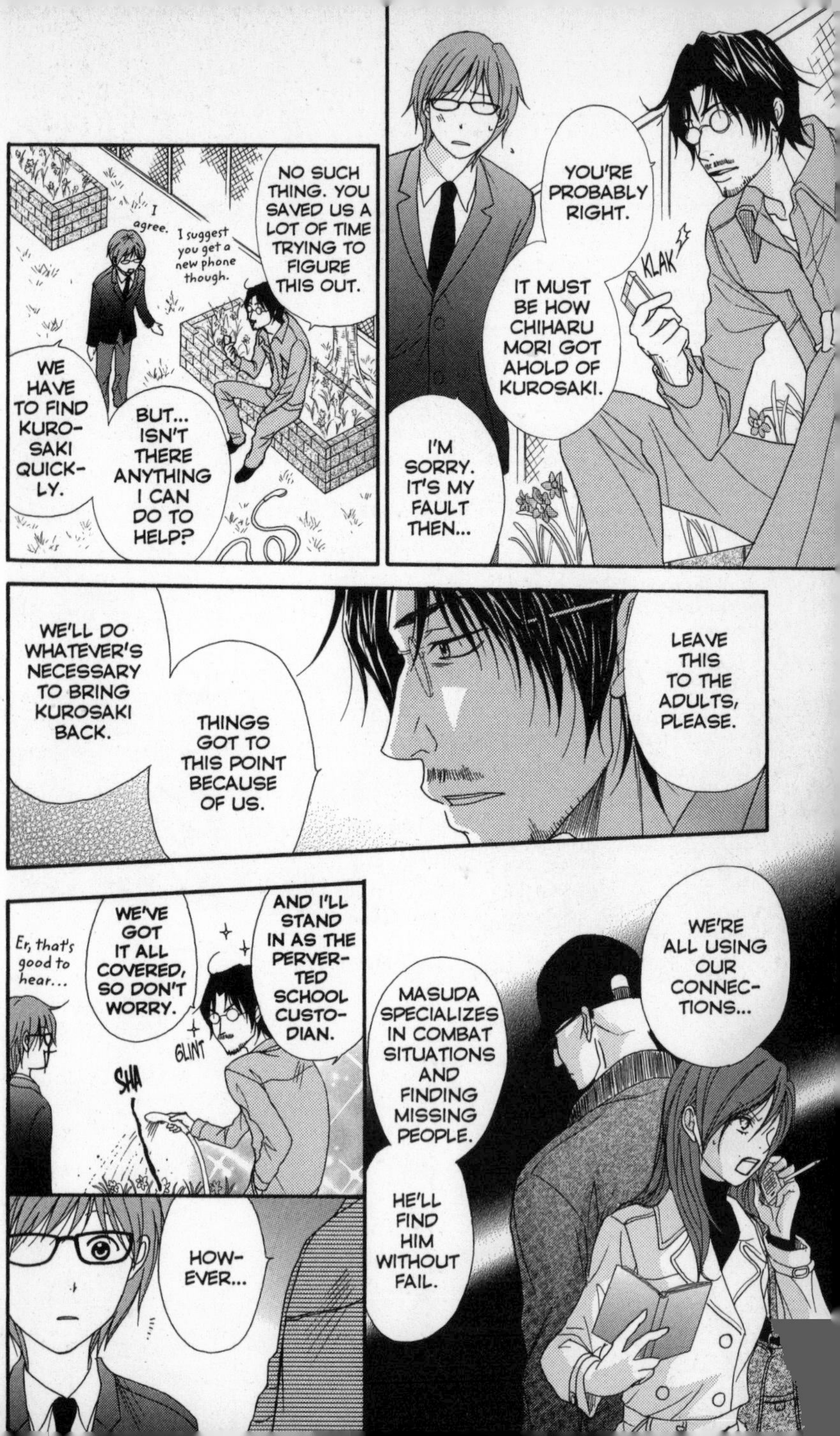

YOU'RE PROBABLY RIGHT.
KLAK
IT MUST BE HOW CHIHARU MORI GOT AHOLD OF KUROSAKI.
I'M SORRY. IT'S MY FAULT THEN...
NO SUCH THING. YOU SAVED US A LOT OF TIME TRYING TO FIGURE THIS OUT.
I suggest you get a new phone though.
I agree.
BUT... ISN'T THERE ANYTHING I CAN DO TO HELP?
WE HAVE TO FIND KURO-SAKI QUICK-LY.
LEAVE THIS TO THE ADULTS, PLEASE.
THINGS GOT TO THIS POINT BECAUSE OF US.
WE'LL DO WHATEVER'S NECESSARY TO BRING KUROSAKI BACK.
WE'RE ALL USING OUR CONNEC-TIONS...
MASUDA SPECIALIZES IN COMBAT SITUATIONS AND FINDING MISSING PEOPLE.
HE'LL FIND HIM WITHOUT FAIL.
AND I'LL STAND IN AS THE PERVER-TED SCHOOL CUSTO-DIAN.
WE'VE GOT IT ALL COVERED, SO DON'T WORRY.
GLINT
SHA
Er, that's good to hear...
HOW-EVER...

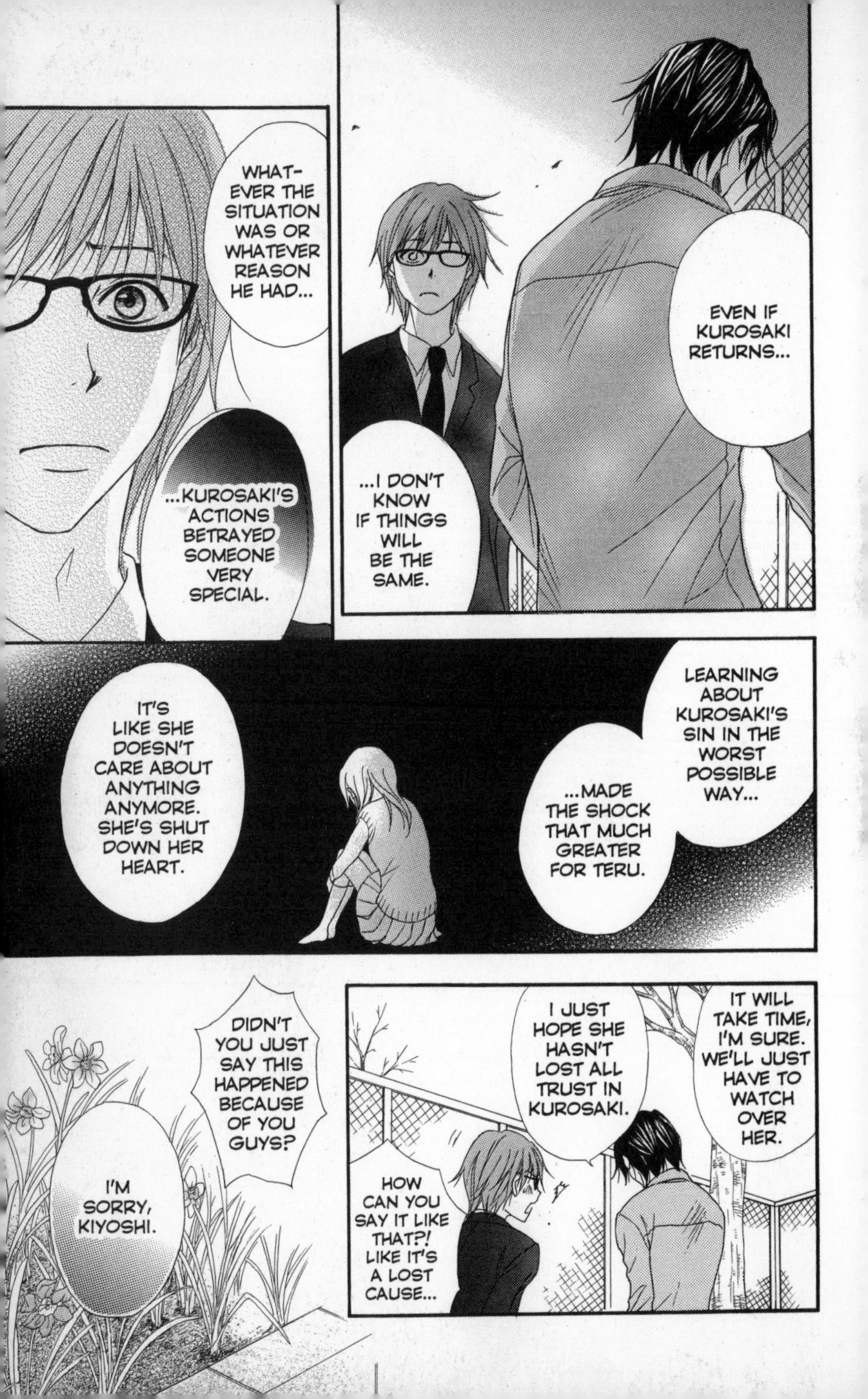
EVEN IF KUROSAKI RETURNS...
...I DON'T KNOW IF THINGS WILL BE THE SAME.
WHAT-EVER THE SITUATION WAS OR WHATEVER REASON HE HAD...
...KUROSAKI'S ACTIONS BETRAYED SOMEONE VERY SPECIAL.
LEARNING ABOUT KUROSAKI'S SIN IN THE WORST POSSIBLE WAY...
...MADE THE SHOCK THAT MUCH GREATER FOR TERU.
IT'S LIKE SHE DOESN'T CARE ABOUT ANYTHING ANYMORE. SHE'S SHUT DOWN HER HEART.
IT WILL TAKE TIME, I'M SURE. WE'LL JUST HAVE TO WATCH OVER HER.
I JUST HOPE SHE HASN'T LOST ALL TRUST IN KUROSAKI.
HOW CAN YOU SAY IT LIKE THAT?! LIKE IT'S A LOST CAUSE...
DIDN'T YOU JUST SAY THIS HAPPENED BECAUSE OF YOU GUYS?
I'M SORRY, KIYOSHI.

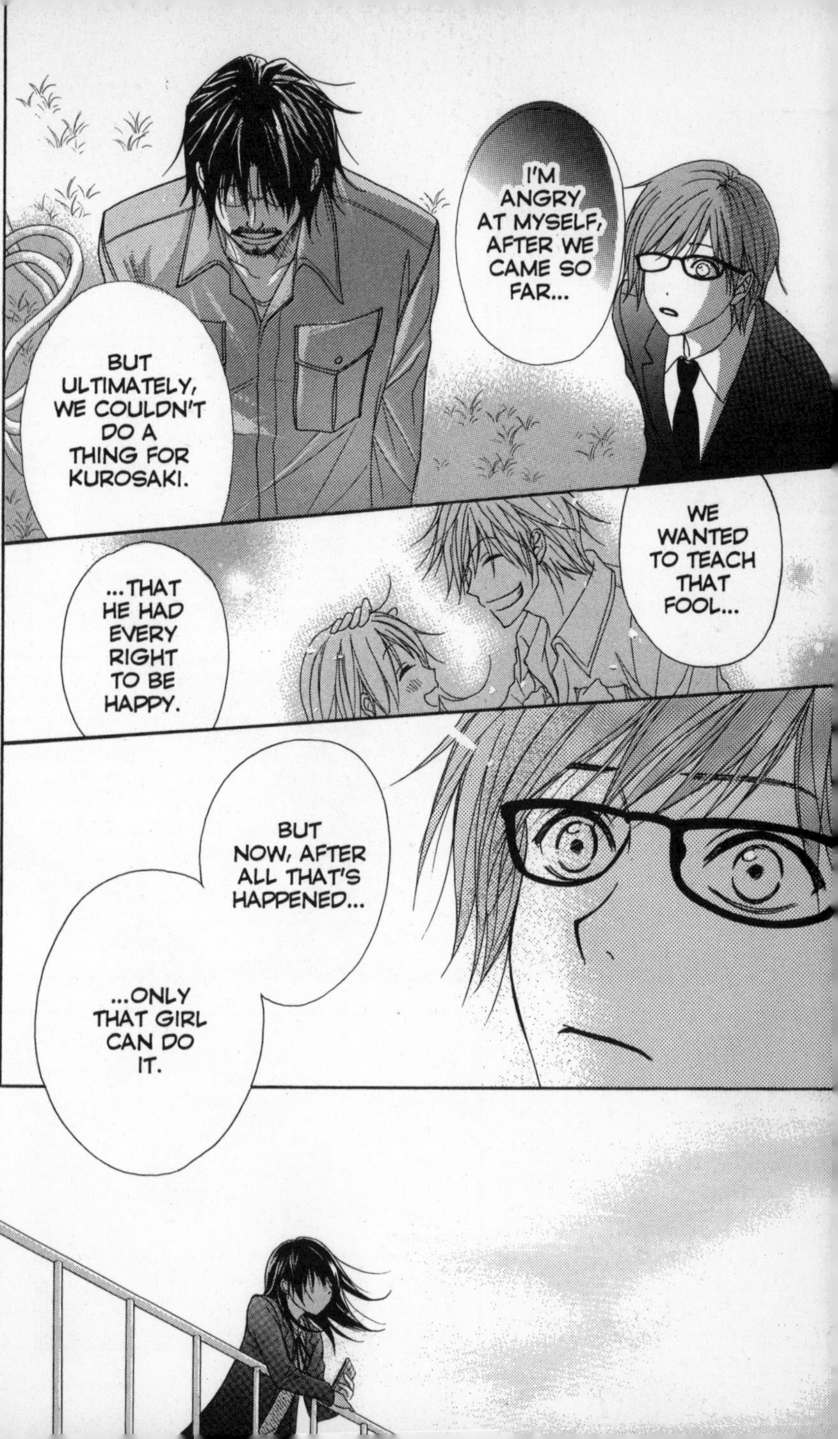
I'M ANGRY AT MYSELF, AFTER WE CAME SO FAR...
BUT ULTIMATELY, WE COULDN'T DO A THING FOR KUROSAKI.
WE WANTED TO TEACH THAT FOOL...
...THAT HE HAD EVERY RIGHT TO BE HAPPY.
BUT NOW, AFTER ALL THAT'S HAPPENED...
...ONLY THAT GIRL CAN DO IT.

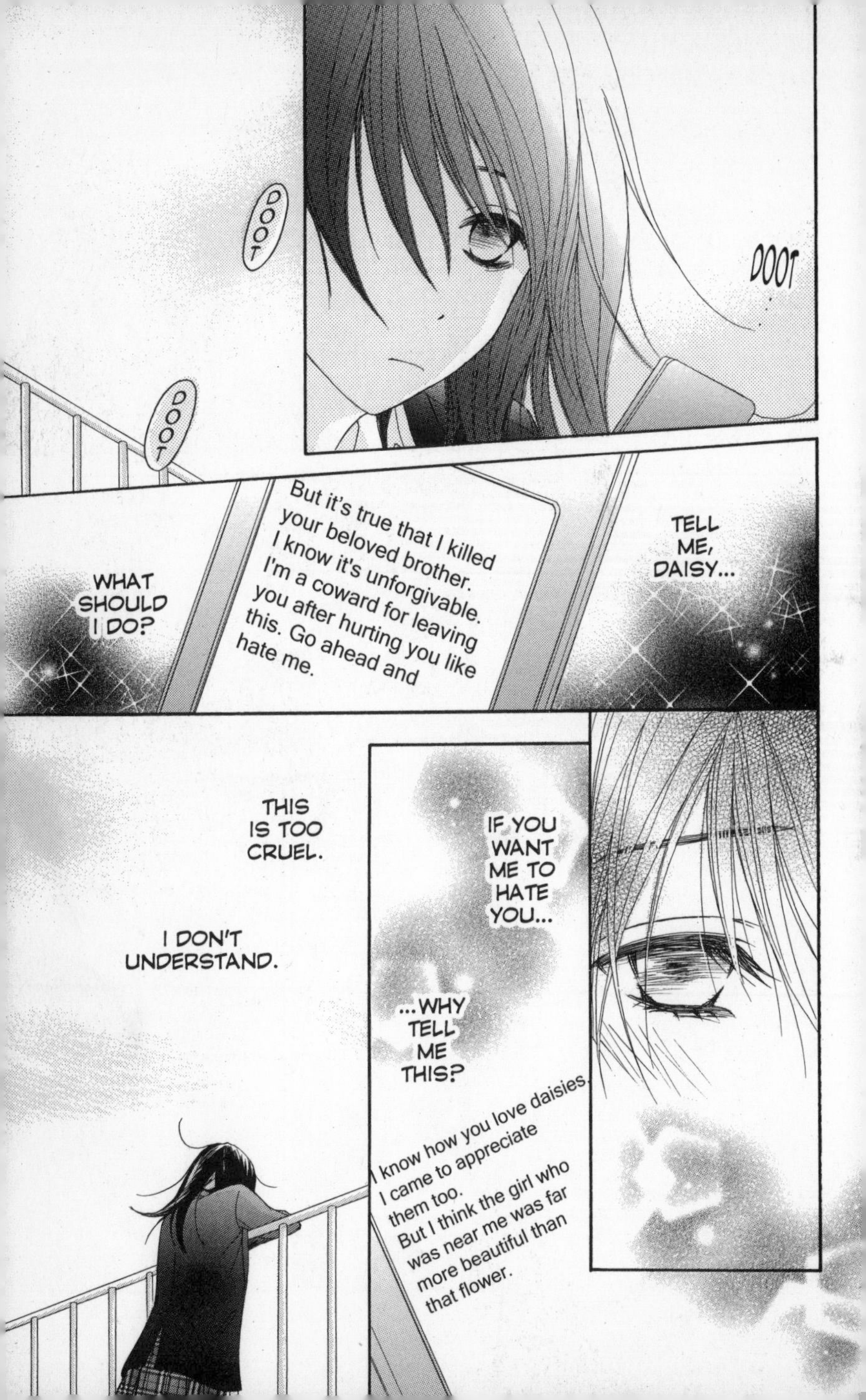
DOOT
DOOT
DOOT
TELL ME, DAISY...
But it's true that I killed your beloved brother. I know it's unforgivable. I'm a coward for leaving you after hurting you like this. Go ahead and hate me.
WHAT SHOULD I DO?
IF YOU WANT ME TO HATE YOU...
...WHY TELL ME THIS?
I know how you love daisies. I came to appreciate them too. But I think the girl who was near me was far more beautiful than that flower.
THIS IS TOO CRUEL.
I DON'T UNDERSTAND.

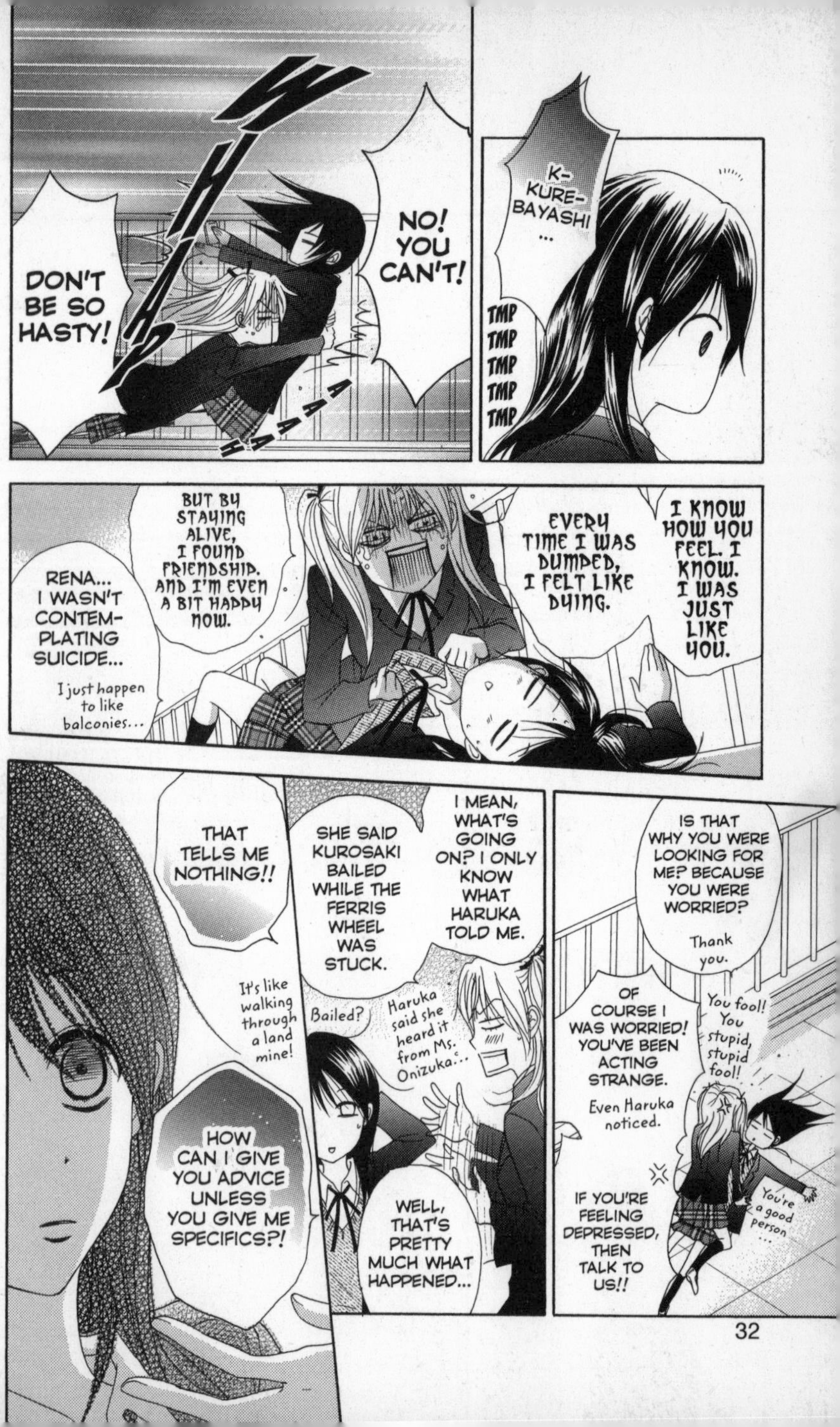
K-KUREBAYASHI...
TMP TMP TMP TMP TMP
NO! YOU CAN'T!
DON'T BE SO HASTY!
I KNOW HOW YOU FEEL. I KNOW. I WAS JUST LIKE YOU.
EVERY TIME I WAS DUMPED, I FELT LIKE DYING.
BUT BY STAYING ALIVE, I FOUND FRIENDSHIP. AND I'M EVEN A BIT HAPPY NOW.
RENA... I WASN'T CONTEMPLATING SUICIDE...
I just happen to like balconies...
IS THAT WHY YOU WERE LOOKING FOR ME? BECAUSE YOU WERE WORRIED?
Thank you.
OF COURSE I WAS WORRIED! YOU'VE BEEN ACTING STRANGE.
Even Haruka noticed.
You fool! You stupid, stupid fool!
IF YOU'RE FEELING DEPRESSED, THEN TALK TO US!!
You're a good person...
I MEAN, WHAT'S GOING ON? I ONLY KNOW WHAT HARUKA TOLD ME.
SHE SAID KUROSAKI BAILED WHILE THE FERRIS WHEEL WAS STUCK.
Bailed?
Haruka said she heard it from Ms. Onizuka...
WELL, THAT'S PRETTY MUCH WHAT HAPPENED...
THAT TELLS ME NOTHING!!
It's like walking through a land mine!
HOW CAN I GIVE YOU ADVICE UNLESS YOU GIVE ME SPECIFICS?!

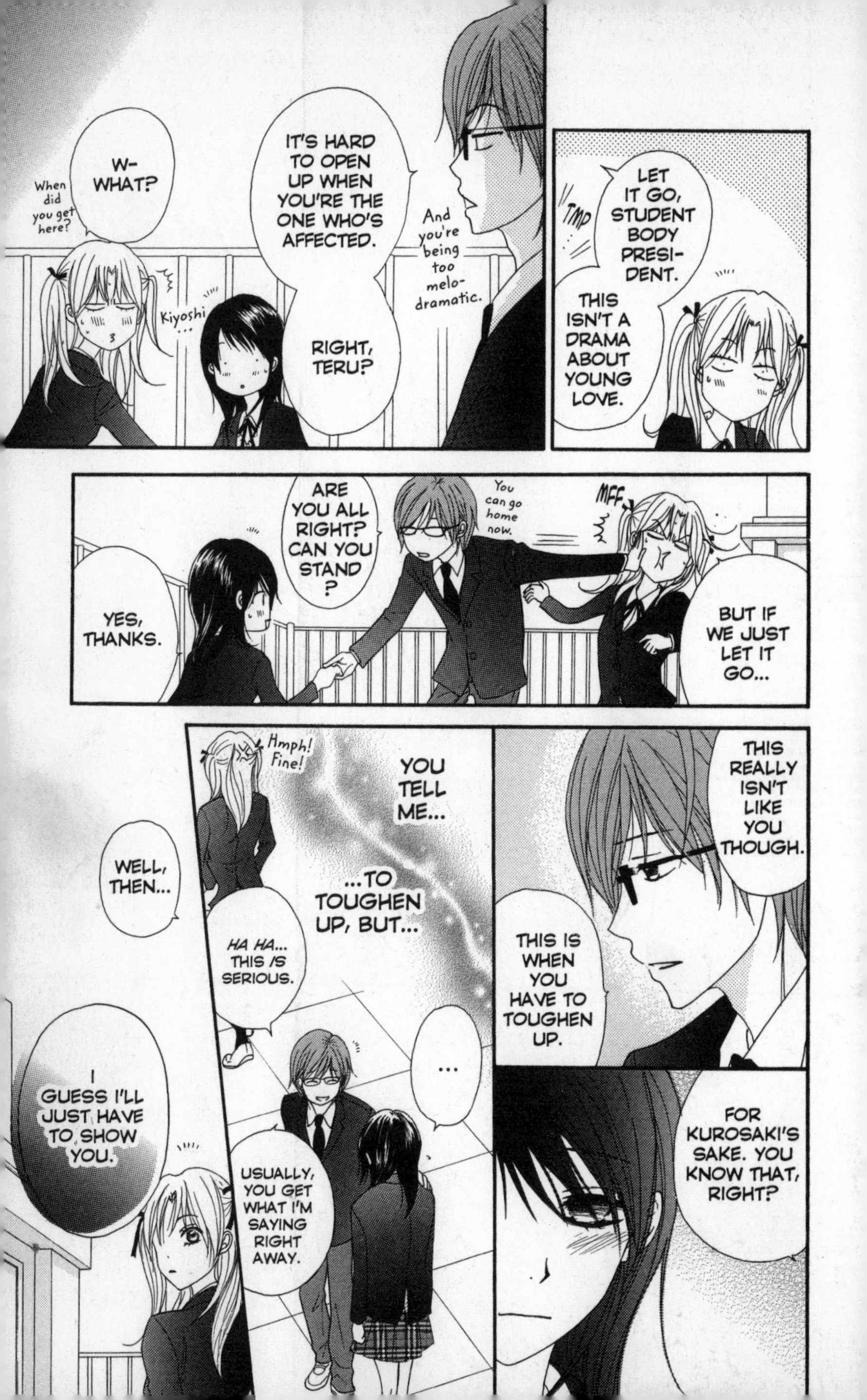
TMP
LET IT GO, STUDENT BODY PRESIDENT.
THIS ISN'T A DRAMA ABOUT YOUNG LOVE.
IT'S HARD TO OPEN UP WHEN YOU'RE THE ONE WHO'S AFFECTED.
And you're being too melo-dramatic.
W-WHAT?
When did you get here?
RIGHT, TERU?
Kiyoshi...
MFF
BUT IF WE JUST LET IT GO...
You can go home now.
ARE YOU ALL RIGHT? CAN YOU STAND?
YES, THANKS.
THIS REALLY ISN'T LIKE YOU THOUGH.
THIS IS WHEN YOU HAVE TO TOUGHEN UP.
FOR KUROSAKI'S SAKE. YOU KNOW THAT, RIGHT?
YOU TELL ME...
...TO TOUGHEN UP, BUT...
Hmph! Fine!
WELL, THEN...
HA HA... THIS IS SERIOUS.
...
USUALLY, YOU GET WHAT I'M SAYING RIGHT AWAY.
I GUESS I'LL JUST HAVE TO SHOW YOU.

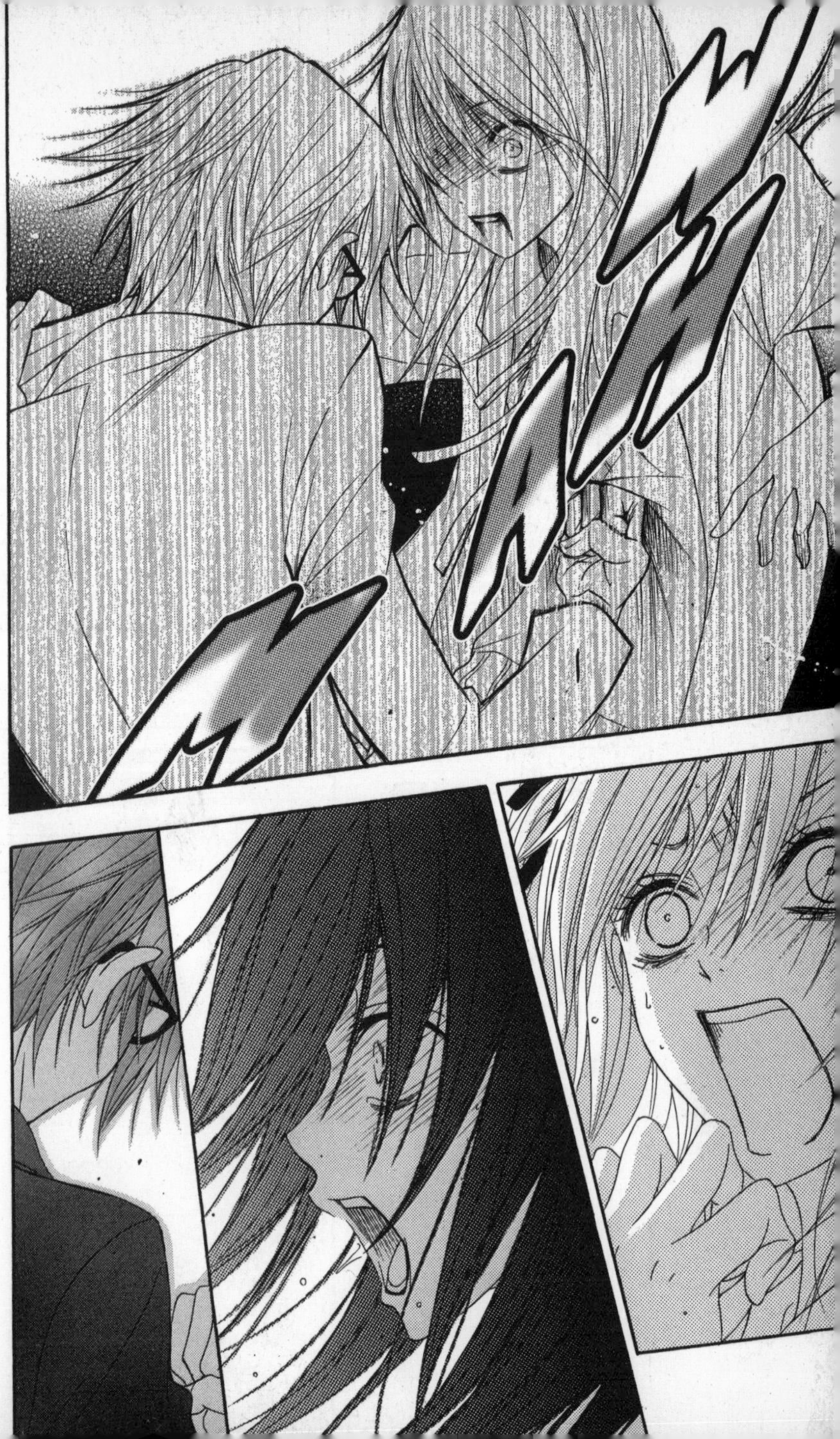

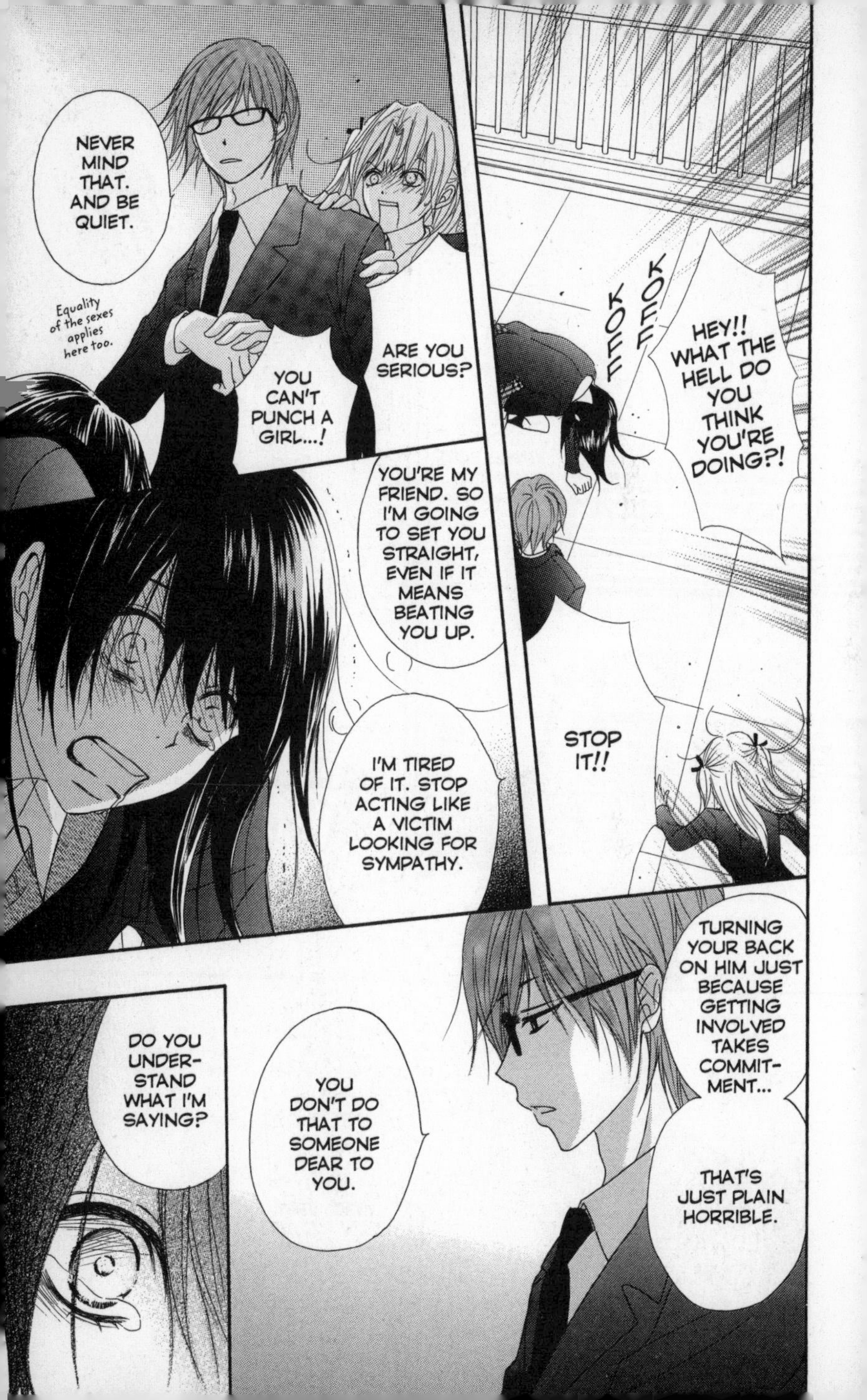
HEY!! WHAT THE HELL DO YOU THINK YOU'RE DOING?!
KOFF KOFF
STOP IT!!
ARE YOU SERIOUS?
YOU CAN'T PUNCH A GIRL...!
NEVER MIND THAT. AND BE QUIET.
Equality of the sexes applies here too.
YOU'RE MY FRIEND. SO I'M GOING TO SET YOU STRAIGHT, EVEN IF IT MEANS BEATING YOU UP.
I'M TIRED OF IT. STOP ACTING LIKE A VICTIM LOOKING FOR SYMPATHY.
TURNING YOUR BACK ON HIM JUST BECAUSE GETTING INVOLVED TAKES COMMIT-MENT...
THAT'S JUST PLAIN HORRIBLE.
YOU DON'T DO THAT TO SOMEONE DEAR TO YOU.
DO YOU UNDER-STAND WHAT I'M SAYING?

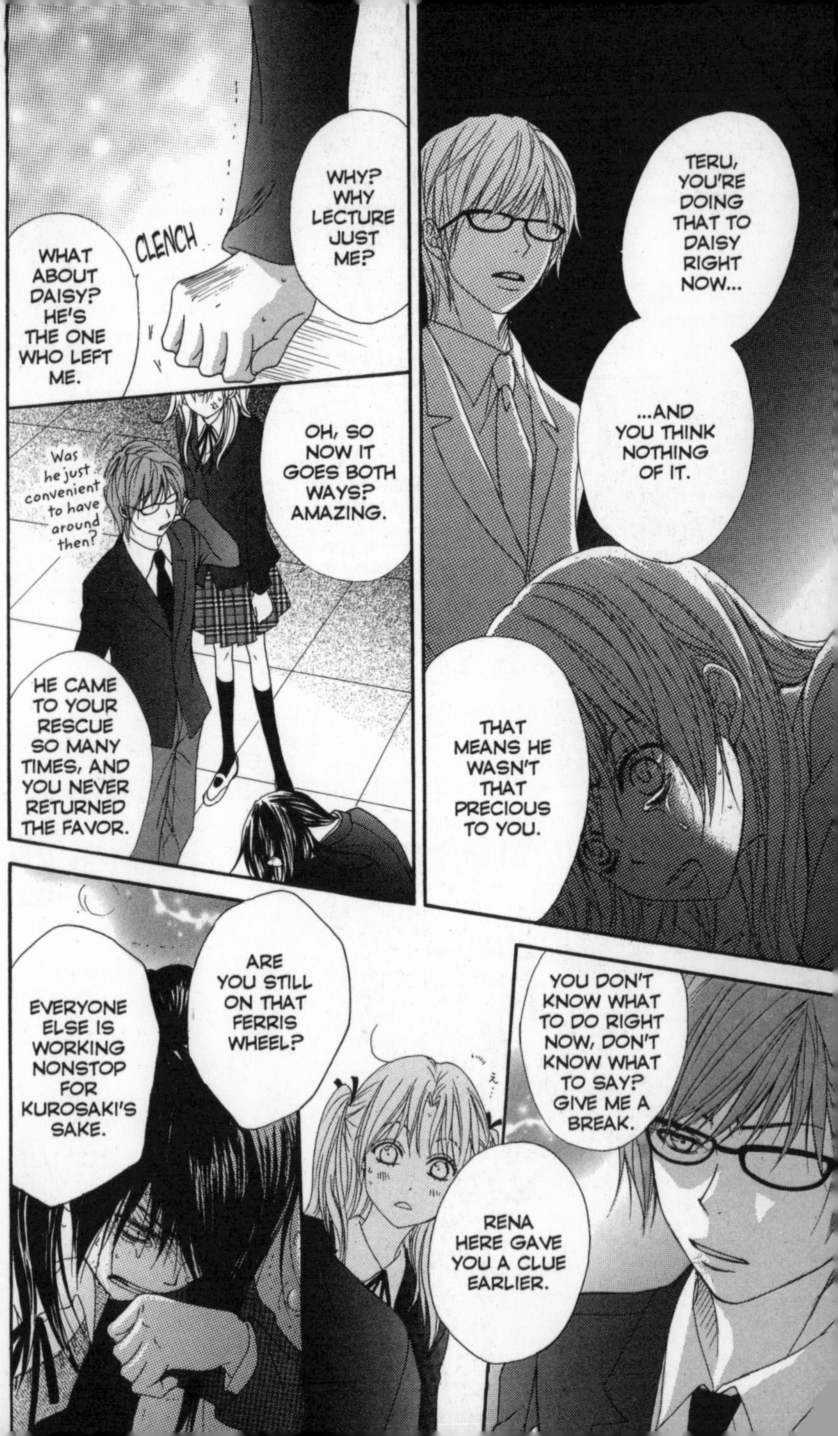
TERU, YOU'RE DOING THAT TO DAISY RIGHT NOW...
...AND YOU THINK NOTHING OF IT.
THAT MEANS HE WASN'T THAT PRECIOUS TO YOU.
WHY? WHY LECTURE JUST ME?
CLENCH
WHAT ABOUT DAISY? HE'S THE ONE WHO LEFT ME.
OH, SO NOW IT GOES BOTH WAYS? AMAZING.
Was he just convenient to have around then?
HE CAME TO YOUR RESCUE SO MANY TIMES, AND YOU NEVER RETURNED THE FAVOR.
YOU DON'T KNOW WHAT TO DO RIGHT NOW, DON'T KNOW WHAT TO SAY? GIVE ME A BREAK.
え…
RENA HERE GAVE YOU A CLUE EARLIER.
ARE YOU STILL ON THAT FERRIS WHEEL?
EVERYONE ELSE IS WORKING NONSTOP FOR KUROSAKI'S SAKE.

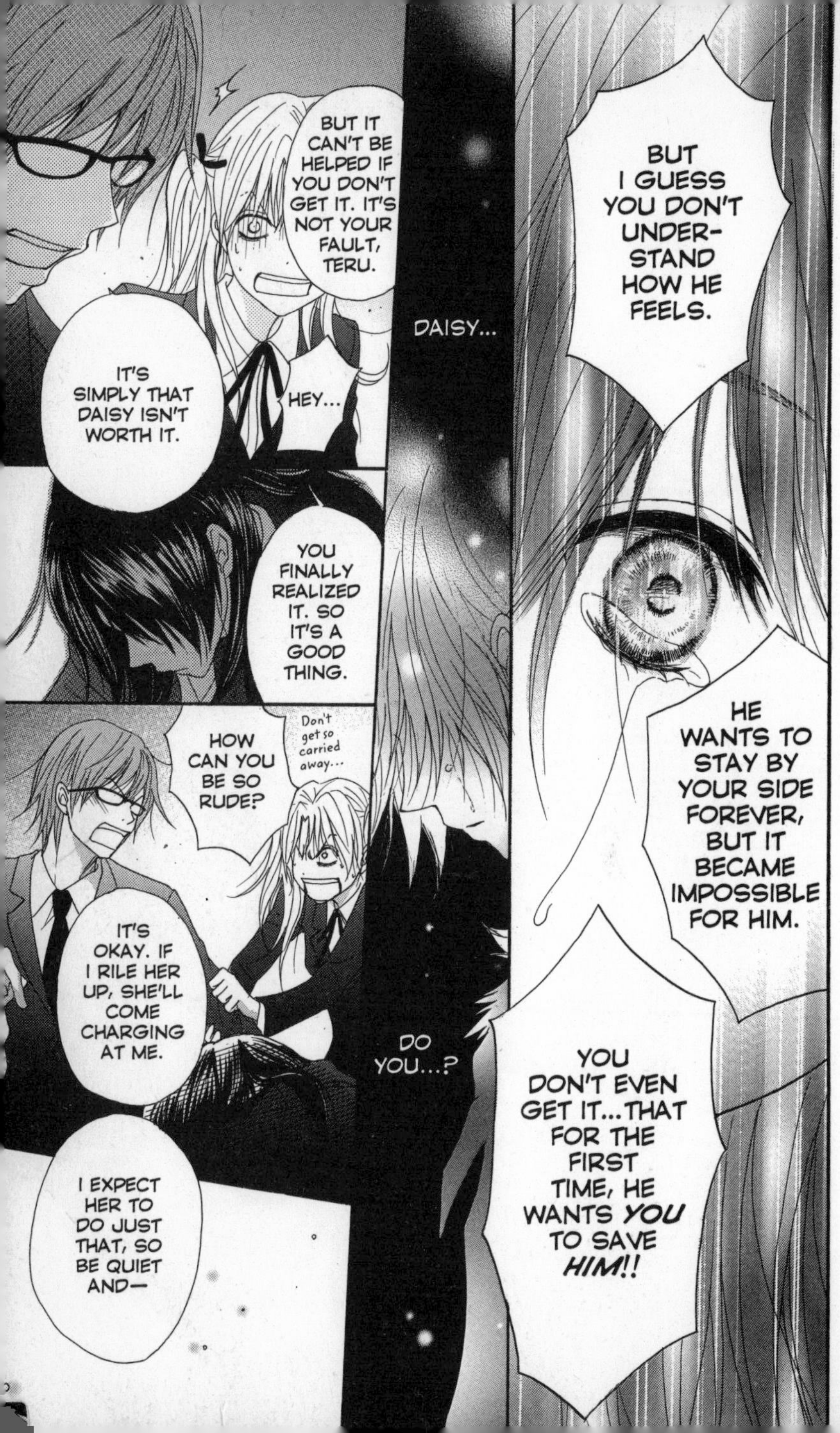
BUT I GUESS YOU DON'T UNDER-STAND HOW HE FEELS.
HE WANTS TO STAY BY YOUR SIDE FOREVER, BUT IT BECAME IMPOSSIBLE FOR HIM.
YOU DON'T EVEN GET IT...THAT FOR THE FIRST TIME, HE WANTS *YOU* TO SAVE ***HIM***!!
DAISY...
DO YOU...?
BUT IT CAN'T BE HELPED IF YOU DON'T GET IT. IT'S NOT YOUR FAULT, TERU.
HEY...
IT'S SIMPLY THAT DAISY ISN'T WORTH IT.
YOU FINALLY REALIZED IT. SO IT'S A GOOD THING.
Don't get so carried away...
HOW CAN YOU BE SO RUDE?
IT'S OKAY. IF I RILE HER UP, SHE'LL COME CHARGING AT ME.
I EXPECT HER TO DO JUST THAT, SO BE QUIET AND—

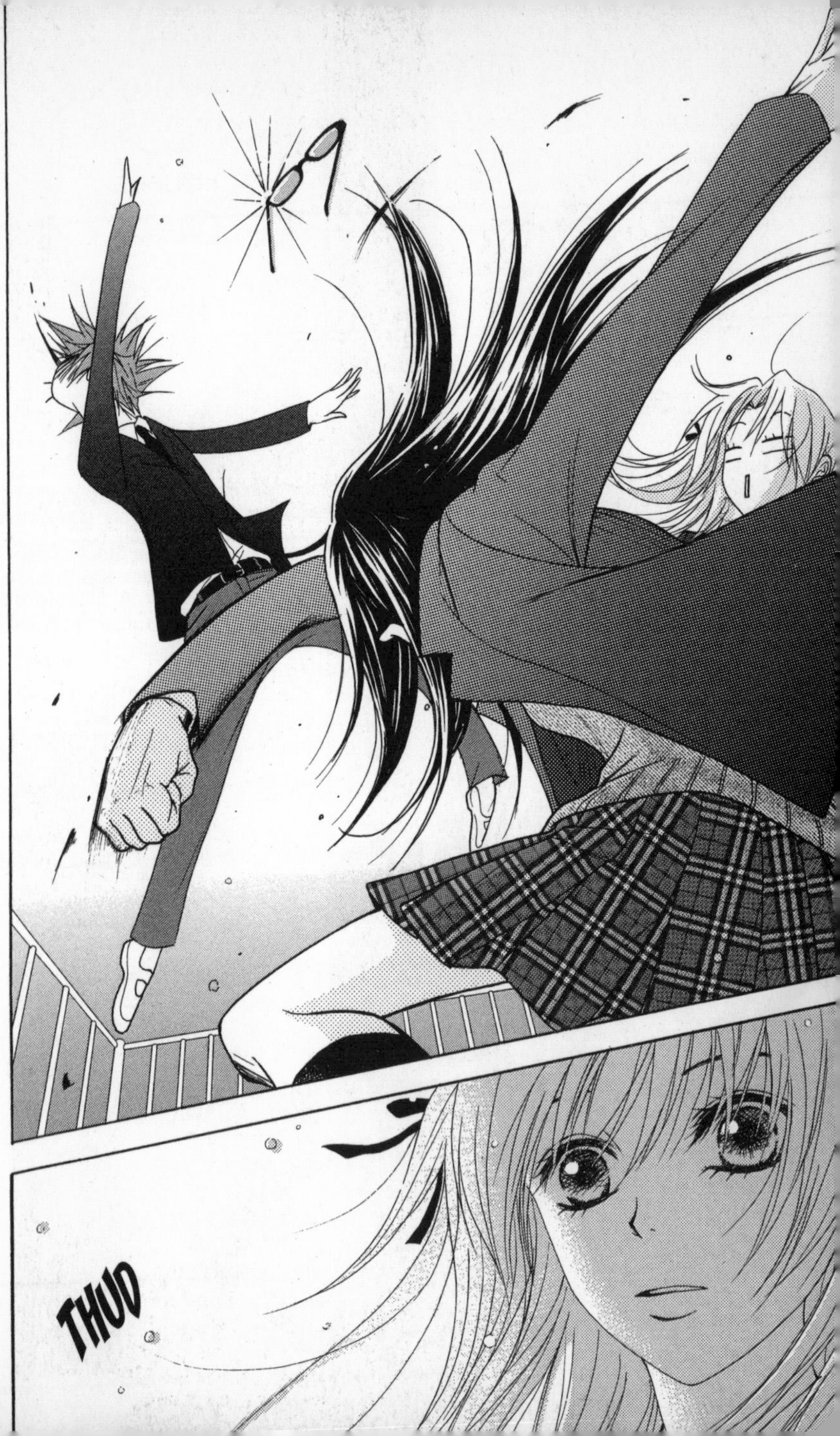
THUD

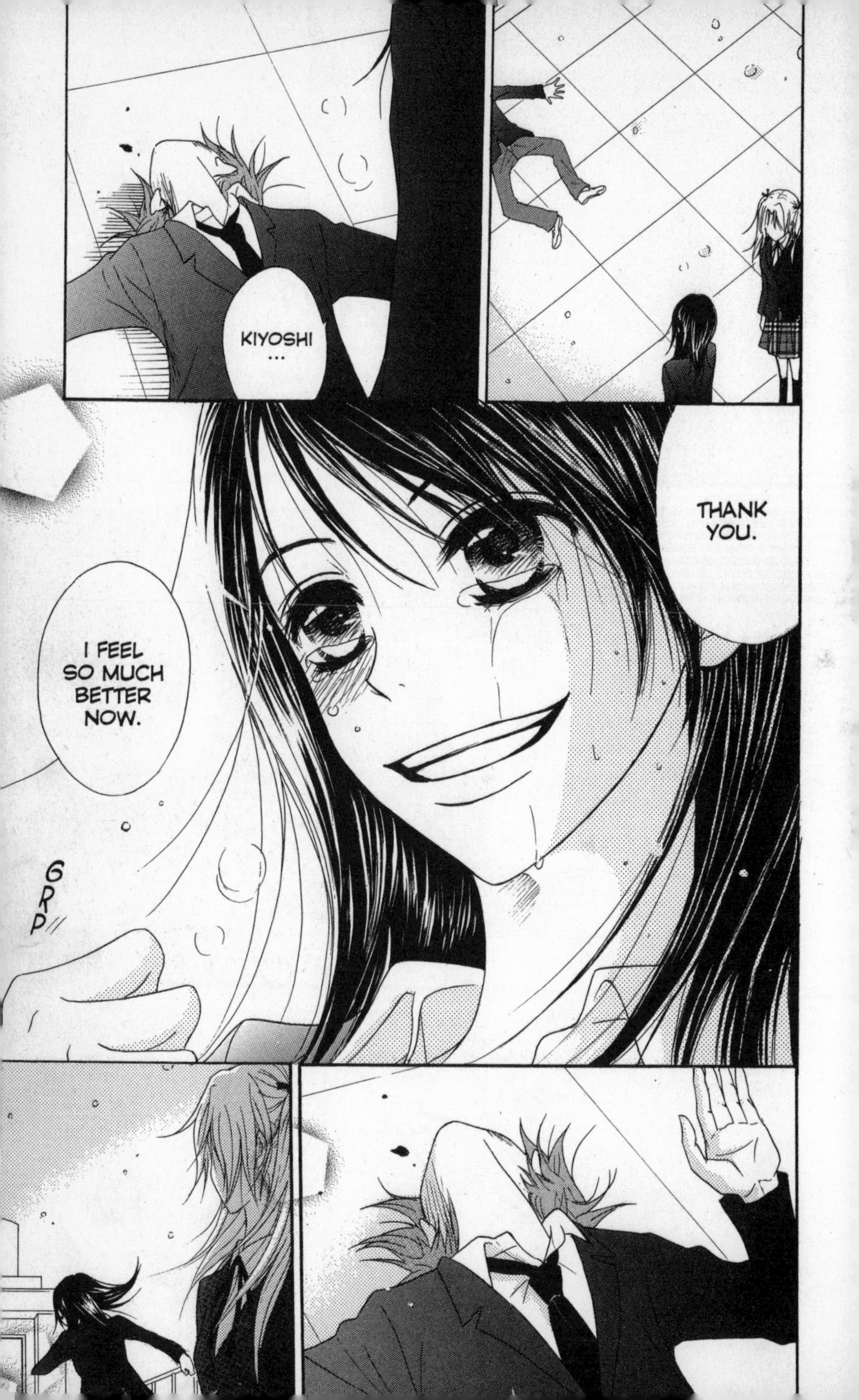
KIYOSHI ...
THANK YOU.
I FEEL SO MUCH BETTER NOW.
GRP

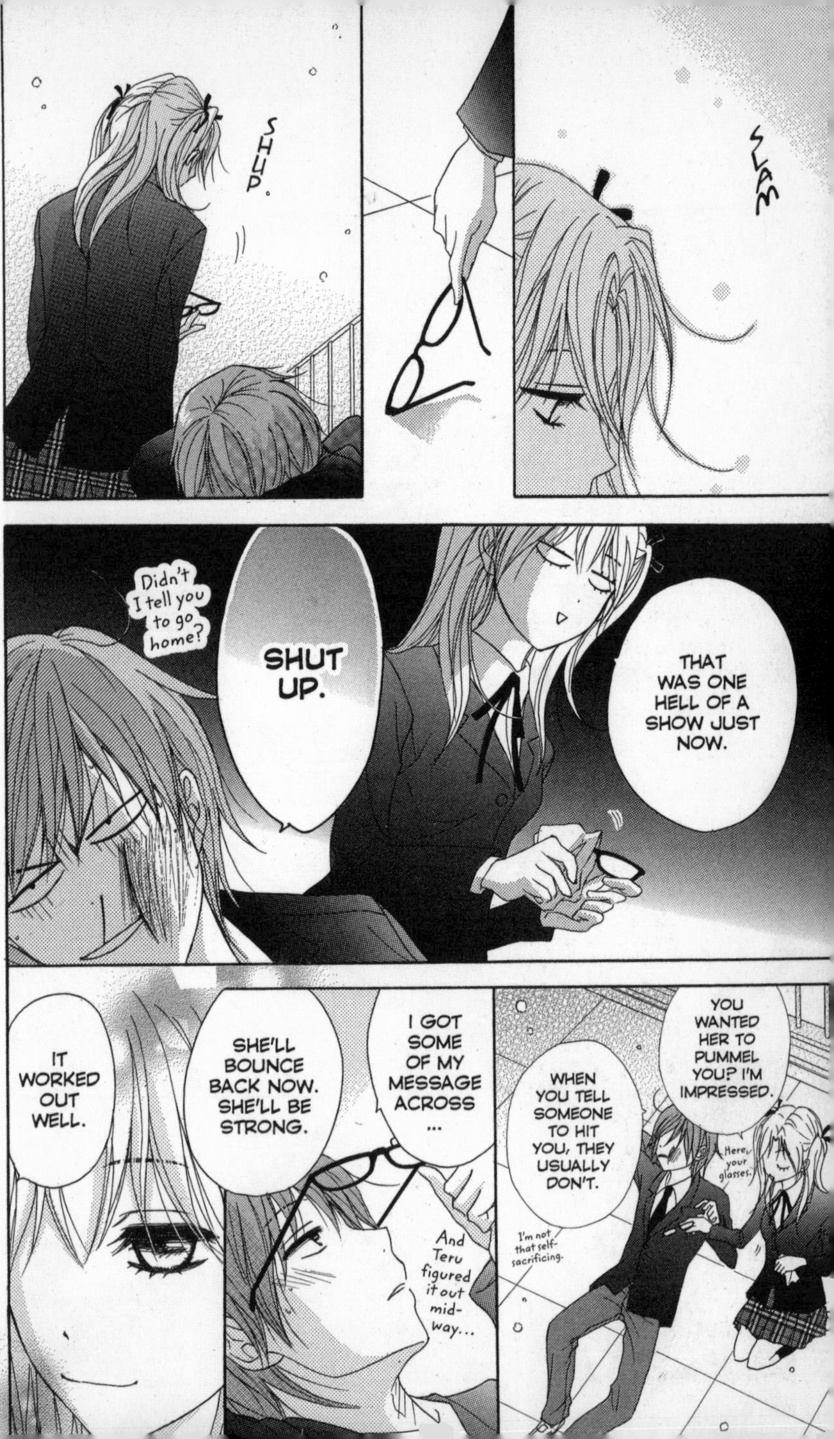
SLAM
SHUP
THAT WAS ONE HELL OF A SHOW JUST NOW.
SHUT UP.
Didn't I tell you to go home?
YOU WANTED HER TO PUMMEL YOU? I'M IMPRESSED.
Here, your glasses.
WHEN YOU TELL SOMEONE TO HIT YOU, THEY USUALLY DON'T.
I'm not that self-sacrificing.
I GOT SOME OF MY MESSAGE ACROSS...
And Teru figured it out mid-way...
SHE'LL BOUNCE BACK NOW. SHE'LL BE STRONG.
IT WORKED OUT WELL.

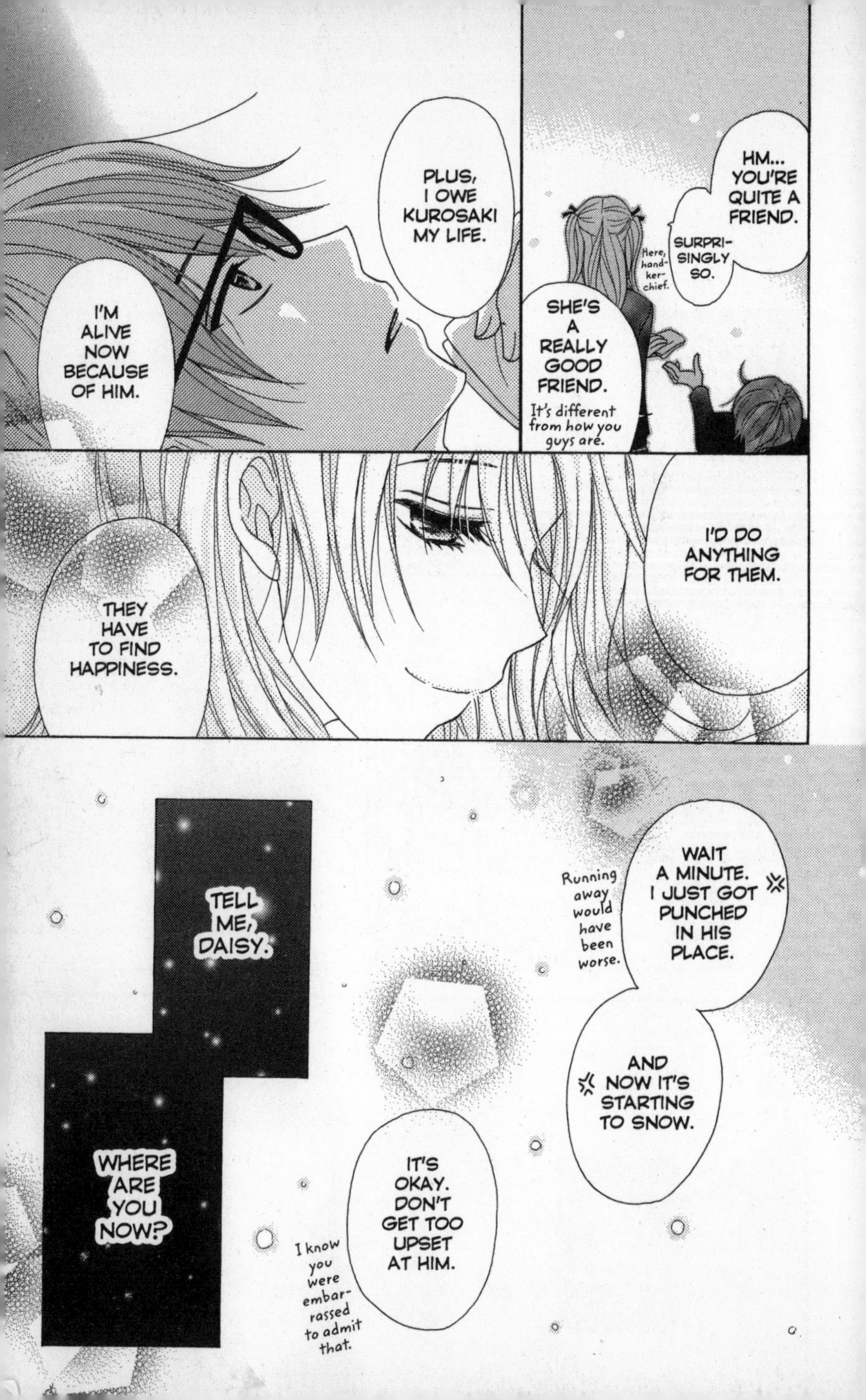
HM... YOU'RE QUITE A FRIEND.
SURPRI-SINGLY SO.
Here, hand-ker-chief.
SHE'S A REALLY GOOD FRIEND.
It's different from how you guys are.
PLUS, I OWE KUROSAKI MY LIFE.
I'M ALIVE NOW BECAUSE OF HIM.
I'D DO ANYTHING FOR THEM.
THEY HAVE TO FIND HAPPINESS.
WAIT A MINUTE. I JUST GOT PUNCHED IN HIS PLACE.
Running away would have been worse.
AND NOW IT'S STARTING TO SNOW.
IT'S OKAY. DON'T GET TOO UPSET AT HIM.
I know you were embar-rassed to admit that.
TELL ME, DAISY.
WHERE ARE YOU NOW?

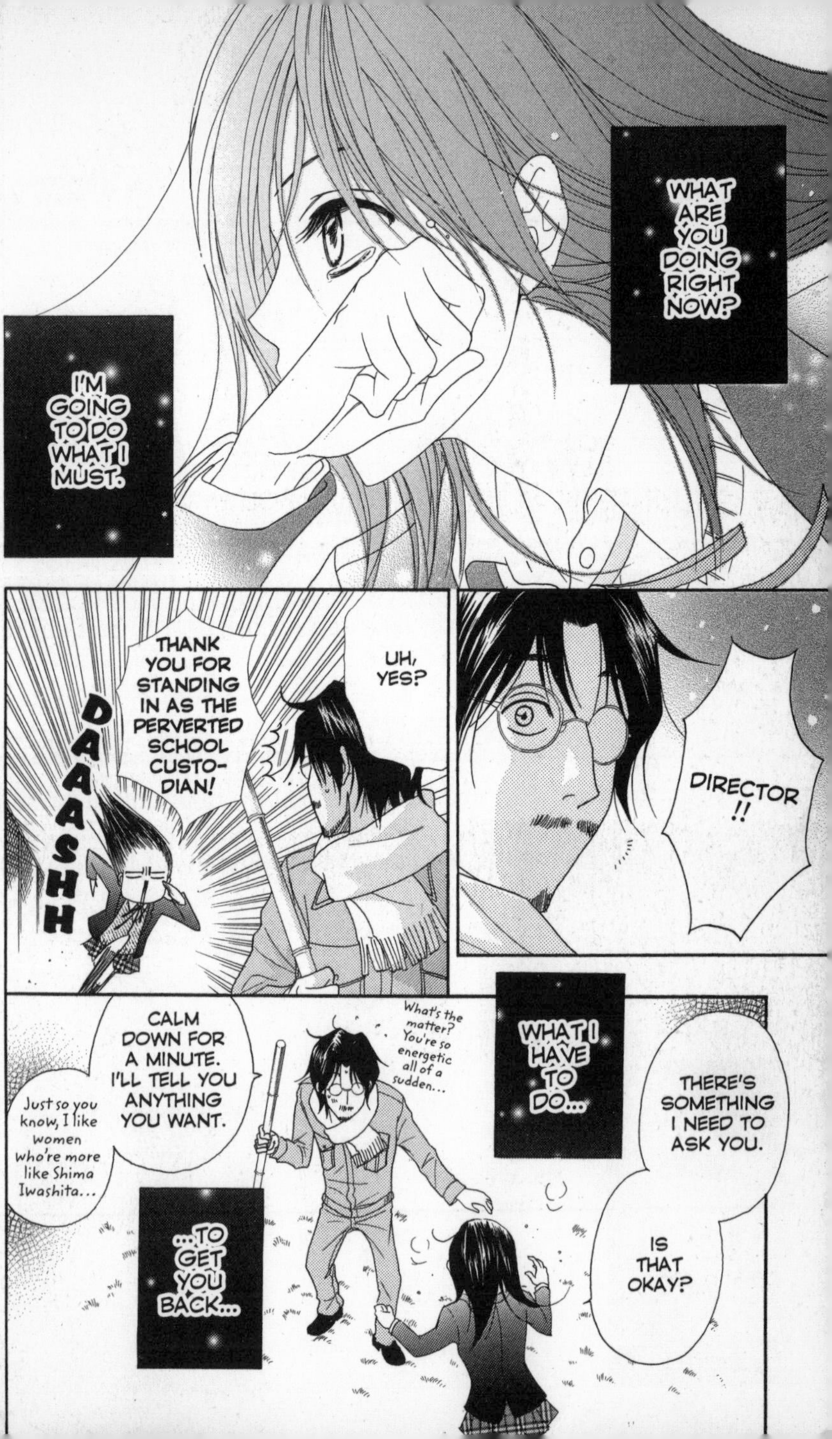
WHAT ARE YOU DOING RIGHT NOW?
I'M GOING TO DO WHAT I MUST.
DIRECTOR !!
UH, YES?
THANK YOU FOR STANDING IN AS THE PERVERTED SCHOOL CUSTO-DIAN!
DAAAASHH
WHAT I HAVE TO DO...
THERE'S SOMETHING I NEED TO ASK YOU.
What's the matter? You're so energetic all of a sudden...
CALM DOWN FOR A MINUTE. I'LL TELL YOU ANYTHING YOU WANT.
Just so you know, I like women who're more like Shima Iwashita...
IS THAT OKAY?
...TO GET YOU BACK...

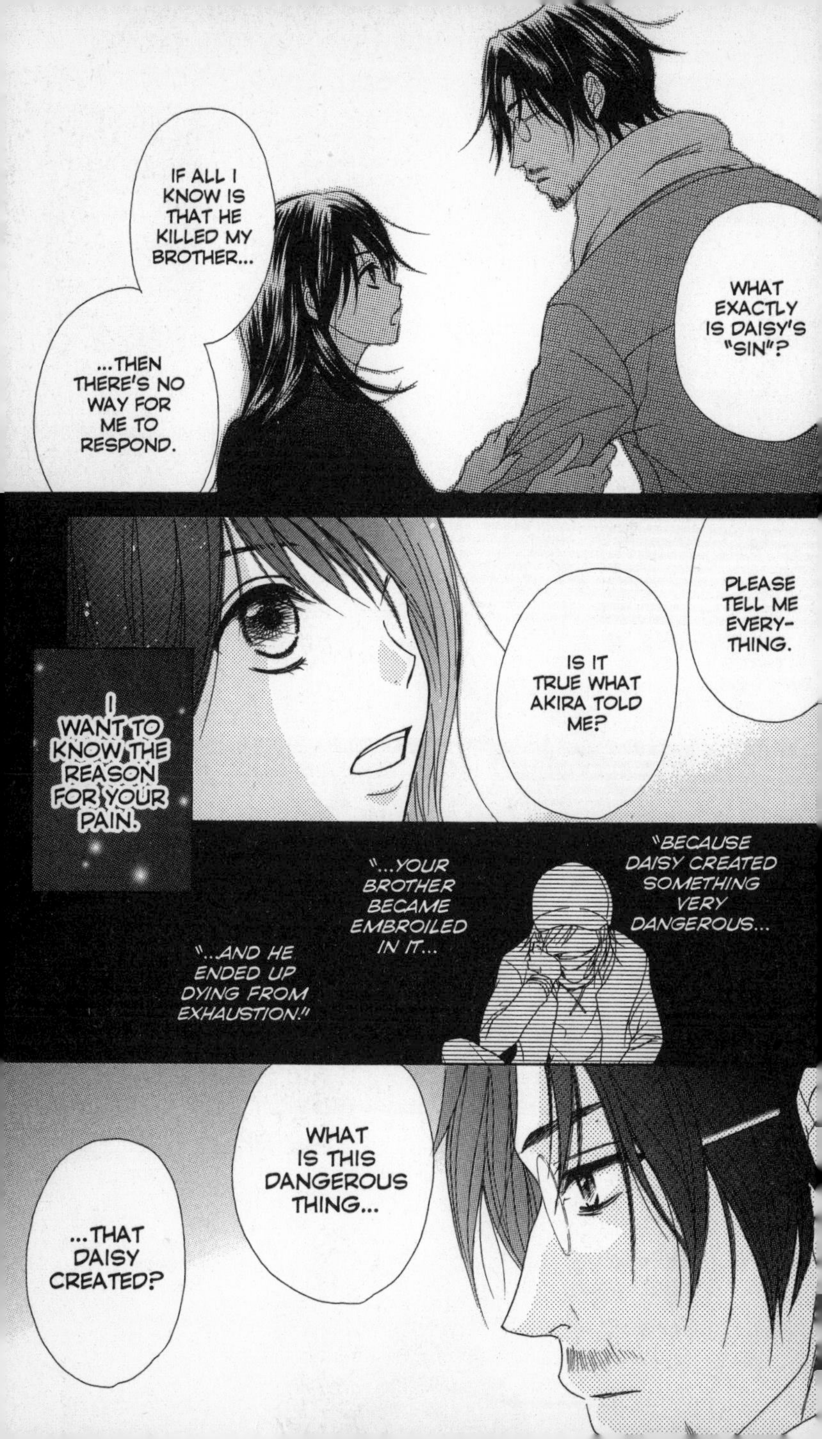
WHAT EXACTLY IS DAISY'S "SIN"?
IF ALL I KNOW IS THAT HE KILLED MY BROTHER...
...THEN THERE'S NO WAY FOR ME TO RESPOND.
PLEASE TELL ME EVERY-THING.
IS IT TRUE WHAT AKIRA TOLD ME?
I WANT TO KNOW THE REASON FOR YOUR PAIN.
"BECAUSE DAISY CREATED SOMETHING VERY DANGEROUS...
"...YOUR BROTHER BECAME EMBROILED IN IT...
"...AND HE ENDED UP DYING FROM EXHAUSTION."
WHAT IS THIS DANGEROUS THING...
...THAT DAISY CREATED?

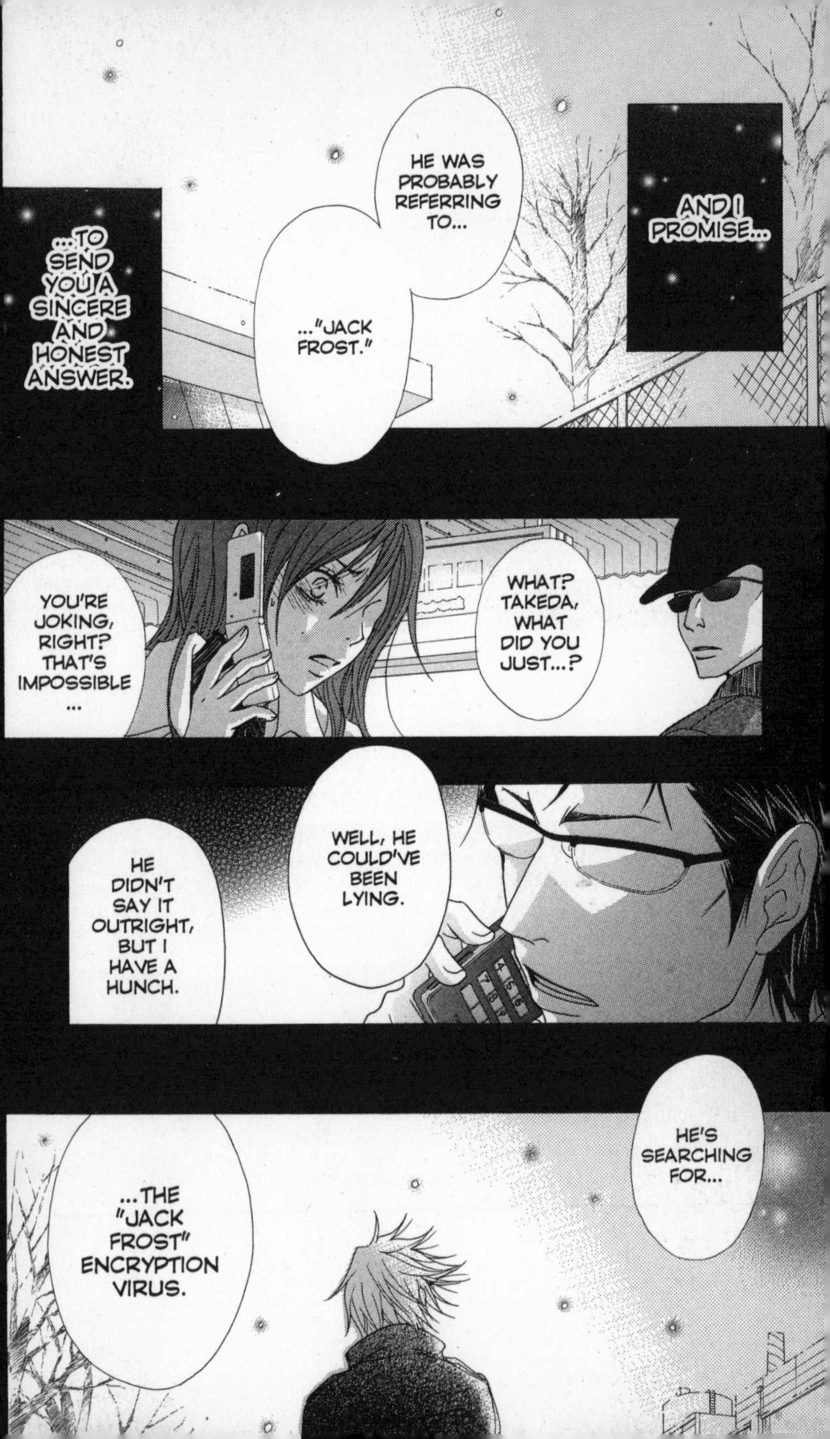
AND I PROMISE...
HE WAS PROBABLY REFERRING TO...
..."JACK FROST."
...TO SEND YOU A SINCERE AND HONEST ANSWER.
WHAT? TAKEDA, WHAT DID YOU JUST...?
YOU'RE JOKING, RIGHT? THAT'S IMPOSSIBLE...
WELL, HE COULD'VE BEEN LYING.
HE DIDN'T SAY IT OUTRIGHT, BUT I HAVE A HUNCH.
HE'S SEARCHING FOR...
...THE "JACK FROST" ENCRYPTION VIRUS.

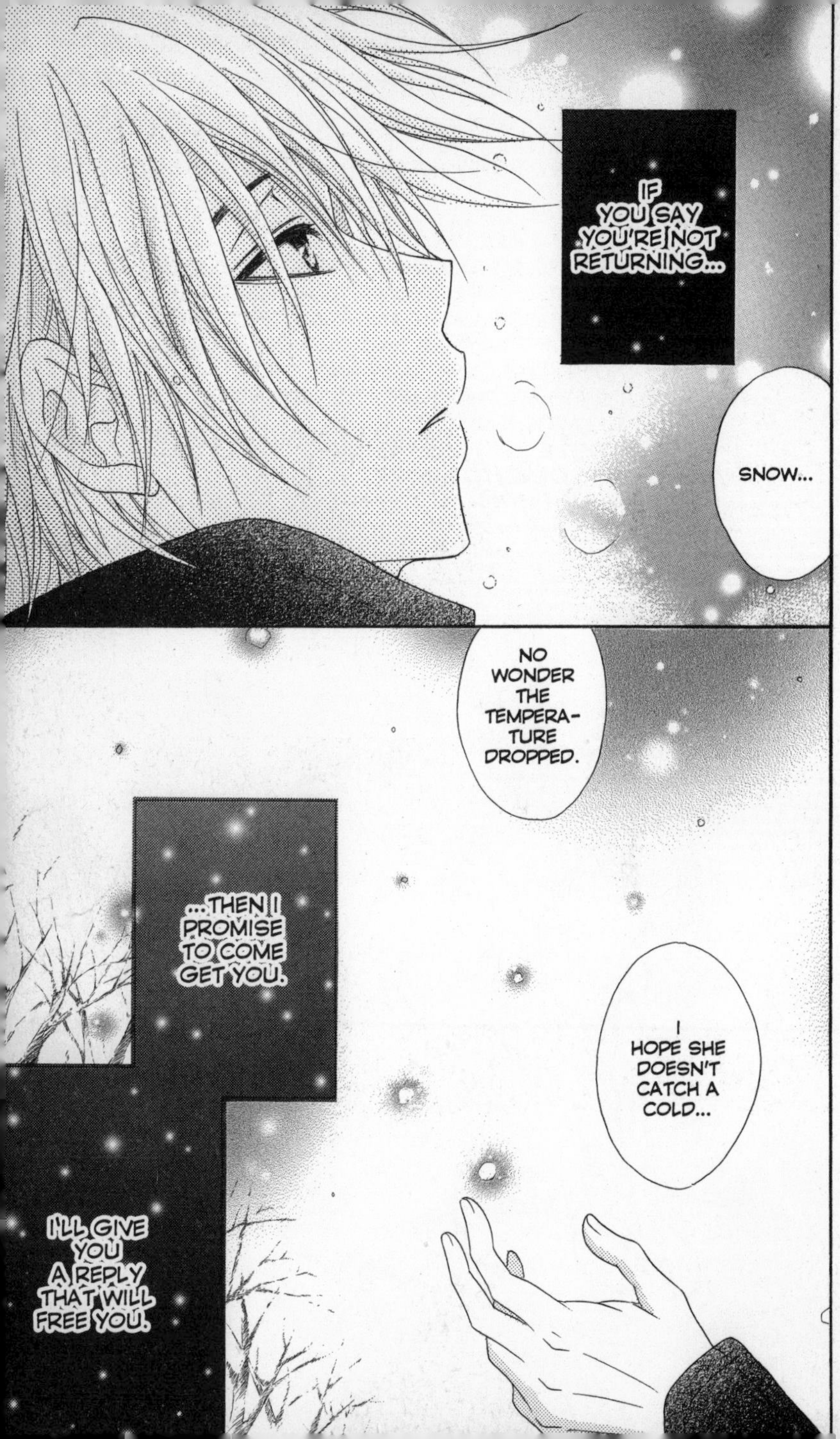
IF YOU SAY YOU'RE NOT RETURNING...
SNOW...
NO WONDER THE TEMPERA-TURE DROPPED.
...THEN I PROMISE TO COME GET YOU.
I HOPE SHE DOESN'T CATCH A COLD...
I'LL GIVE YOU A REPLY THAT WILL FREE YOU.

<SOME BAD LOVEY-DOVEY SKETCHES NO. ①>

DURING A MEETING WITH MY EDITOR, WE HAD A MEANINGLESS EXCHANGE. "WHEN THOSE LITTLE INTIMATE INTERLUDES USED TO HAPPEN EVERY TIME, IT GOT A LITTLE IRRITATING." "BUT DON'T YOU WANT TO MAKE THEM DO MORE OF THAT NOW?" "YES... ESPECIALLY SINCE THEY DON'T HAVE THE CHANCE TO." BEFORE I KNEW IT, I HAD A BUNCH OF SKETCHES. IT'S NOTHING MUCH, BUT I'D LIKE TO SHARE A FEW WITH YOU.

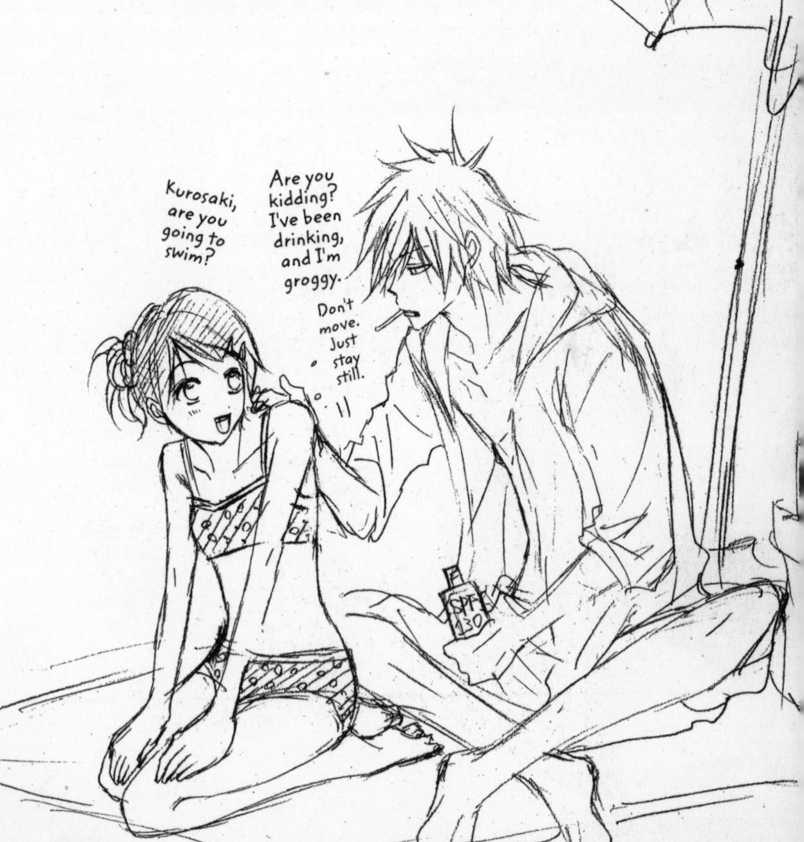
Kurosaki, are you going to swim?
Are you kidding? I've been drinking, and I'm groggy.
Don't move. Just stay still.
SPF 130

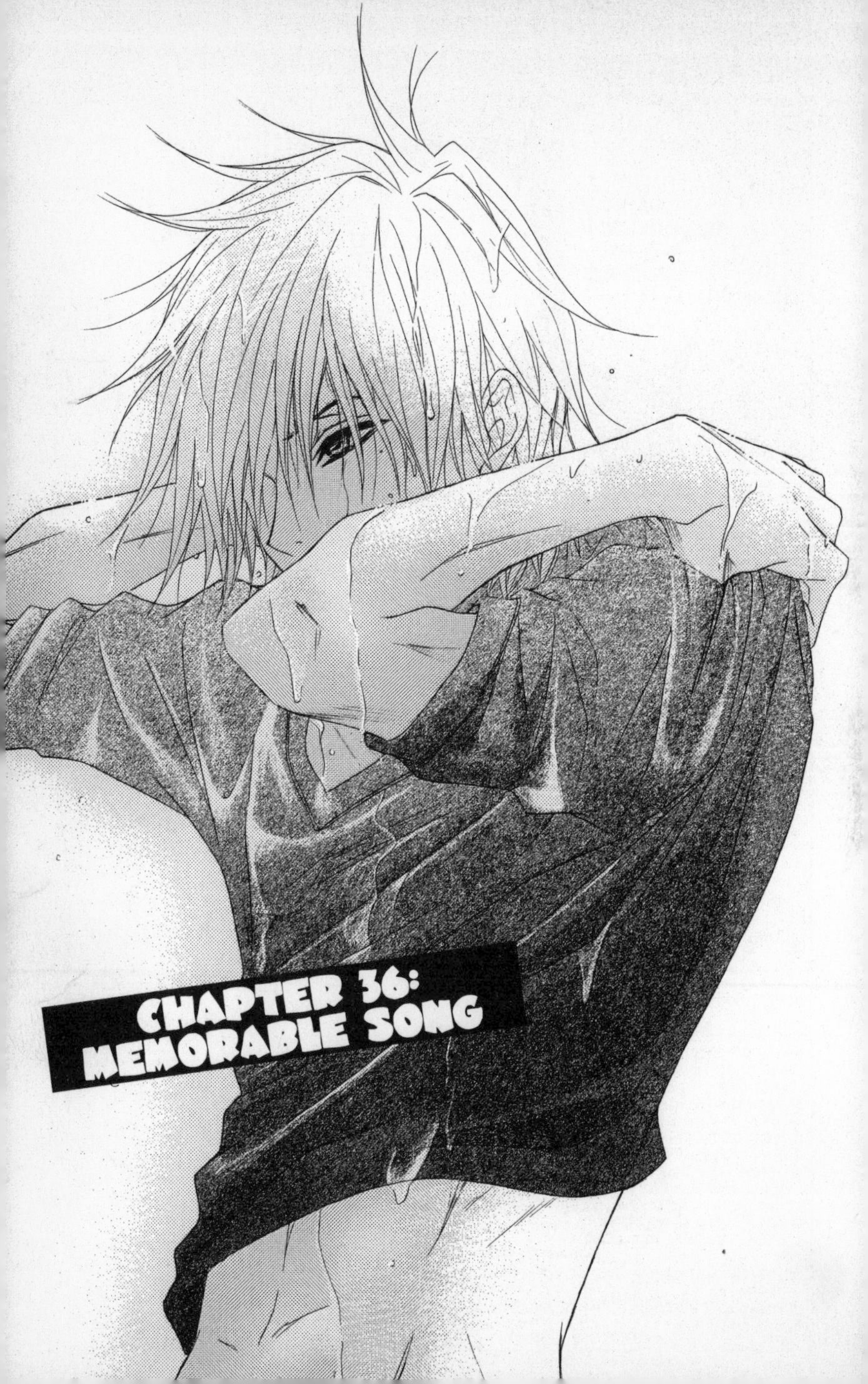
CHAPTER 36:
MEMORABLE SONG

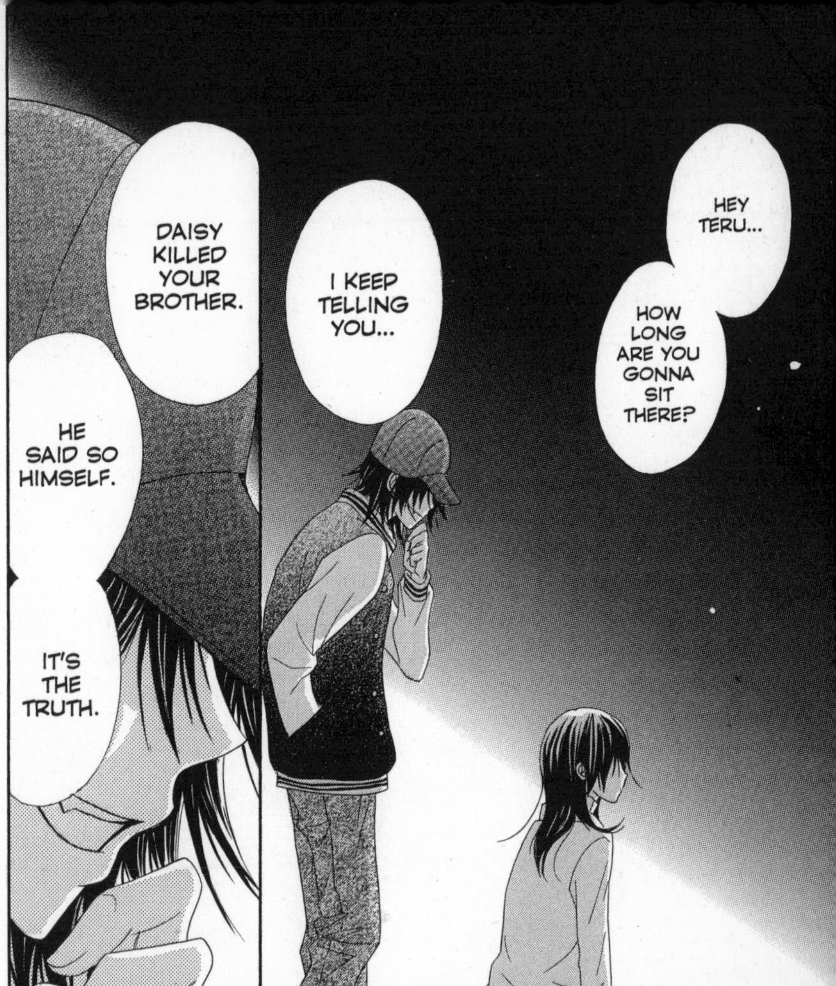
HEY TERU...
HOW LONG ARE YOU GONNA SIT THERE?
I KEEP TELLING YOU...
DAISY KILLED YOUR BROTHER.
HE SAID SO HIMSELF.
IT'S THE TRUTH.

ABOUT CHAPTER 35

CHOOSING TO BECOME THE VILLAIN IN ORDER TO LECTURE THE HEROINE (TERU) IS TO TAKE ON A MOST UNPLEASANT TASK FOR THE SAKE OF DIFFUSING A SITUATION... AND AS THE AUTHOR, IT'S MY PERSONAL BELIEF THAT THAT'S WHAT A TRUE HERO DOES. NOW THAT KUROSAKI IS TOTALLY GOOD FOR NOTHING, AND I LET KIYOSHI ACT COOL, I WAS NERVOUS THAT EVERYONE WOULD START SAYING, "KEEP KIYOSHI AS THE HERO, FORGET KUROSAKI ALREADY." (SERIOUSLY.)

HOWEVER, THAT DIDN'T HAPPEN.
YOU'RE LUCKY, KUROSAKI.
SORRY, KIYOSHI.

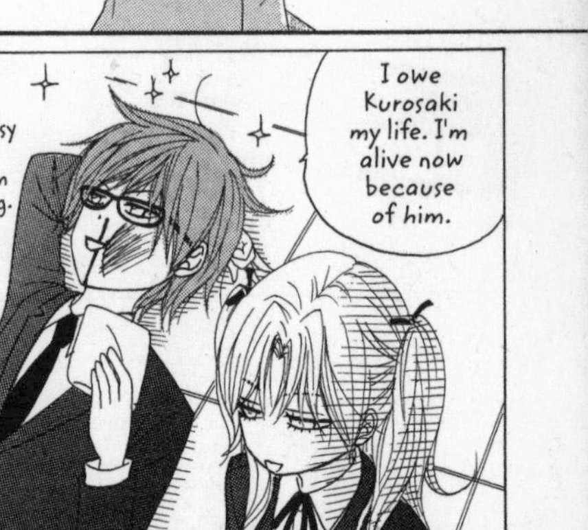
I owe Kurosaki my life. I'm alive now because of him.
Yes, that was a classy thing I said. I'm glowing.
Tell a lie, anything. I'd do anything. Heh.
Whatever. Can you please wipe your bloody nose?

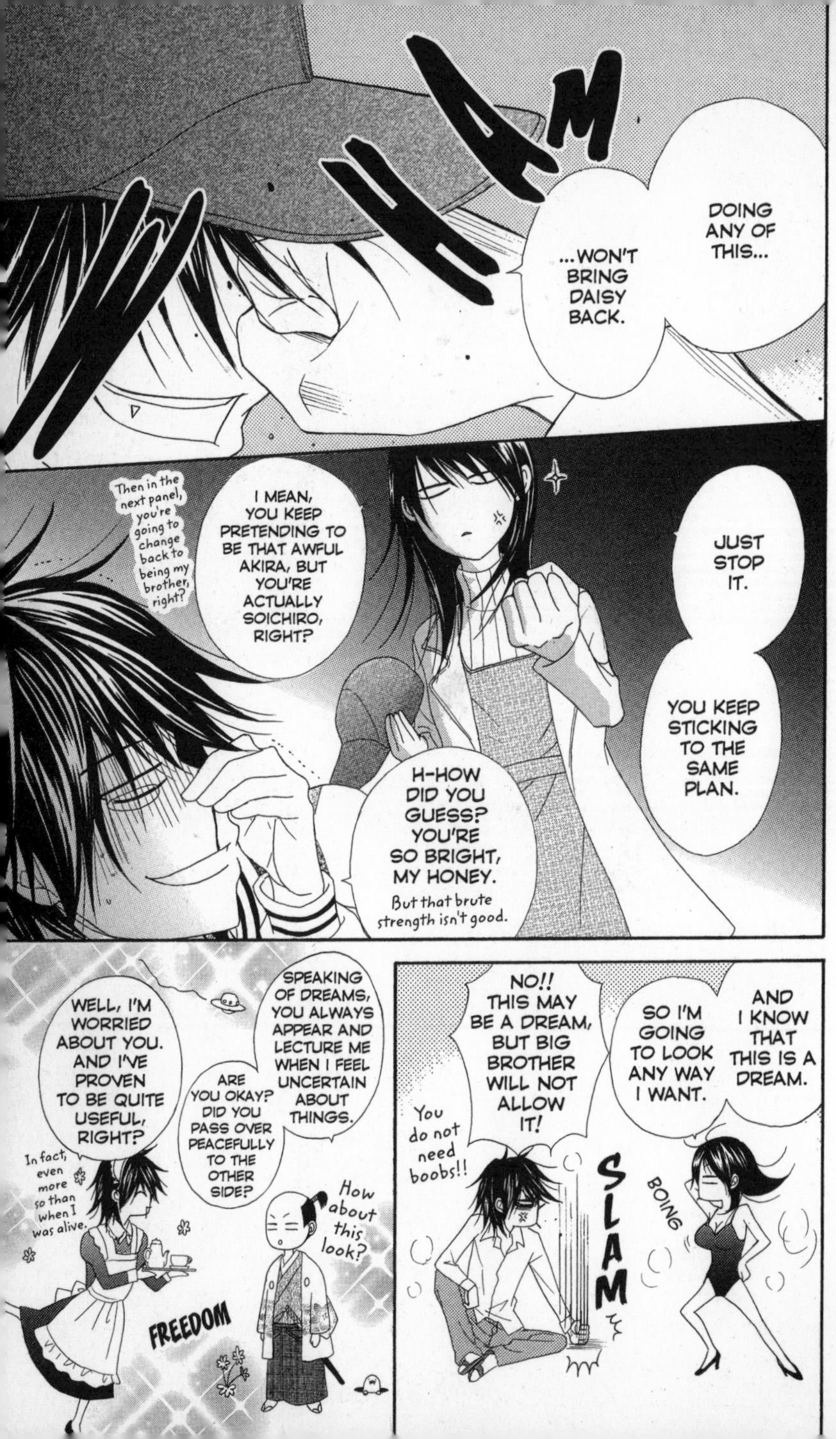
WHAM
DOING ANY OF THIS...
...WON'T BRING DAISY BACK.
JUST STOP IT.
YOU KEEP STICKING TO THE SAME PLAN.
I MEAN, YOU KEEP PRETENDING TO BE THAT AWFUL AKIRA, BUT YOU'RE ACTUALLY SOICHIRO, RIGHT?
Then in the next panel, you're going to change back to being my brother, right?
H-HOW DID YOU GUESS? YOU'RE SO BRIGHT, MY HONEY.
But that brute strength isn't good.
AND I KNOW THAT THIS IS A DREAM.
SO I'M GOING TO LOOK ANY WAY I WANT.
BOING
NO!! THIS MAY BE A DREAM, BUT BIG BROTHER WILL NOT ALLOW IT!
SLAM
You do not need boobs!!
SPEAKING OF DREAMS, YOU ALWAYS APPEAR AND LECTURE ME WHEN I FEEL UNCERTAIN ABOUT THINGS.
ARE YOU OKAY? DID YOU PASS OVER PEACEFULLY TO THE OTHER SIDE?
WELL, I'M WORRIED ABOUT YOU. AND I'VE PROVEN TO BE QUITE USEFUL, RIGHT?
How about this look?
In fact, even more so than when I was alive.
FREEDOM

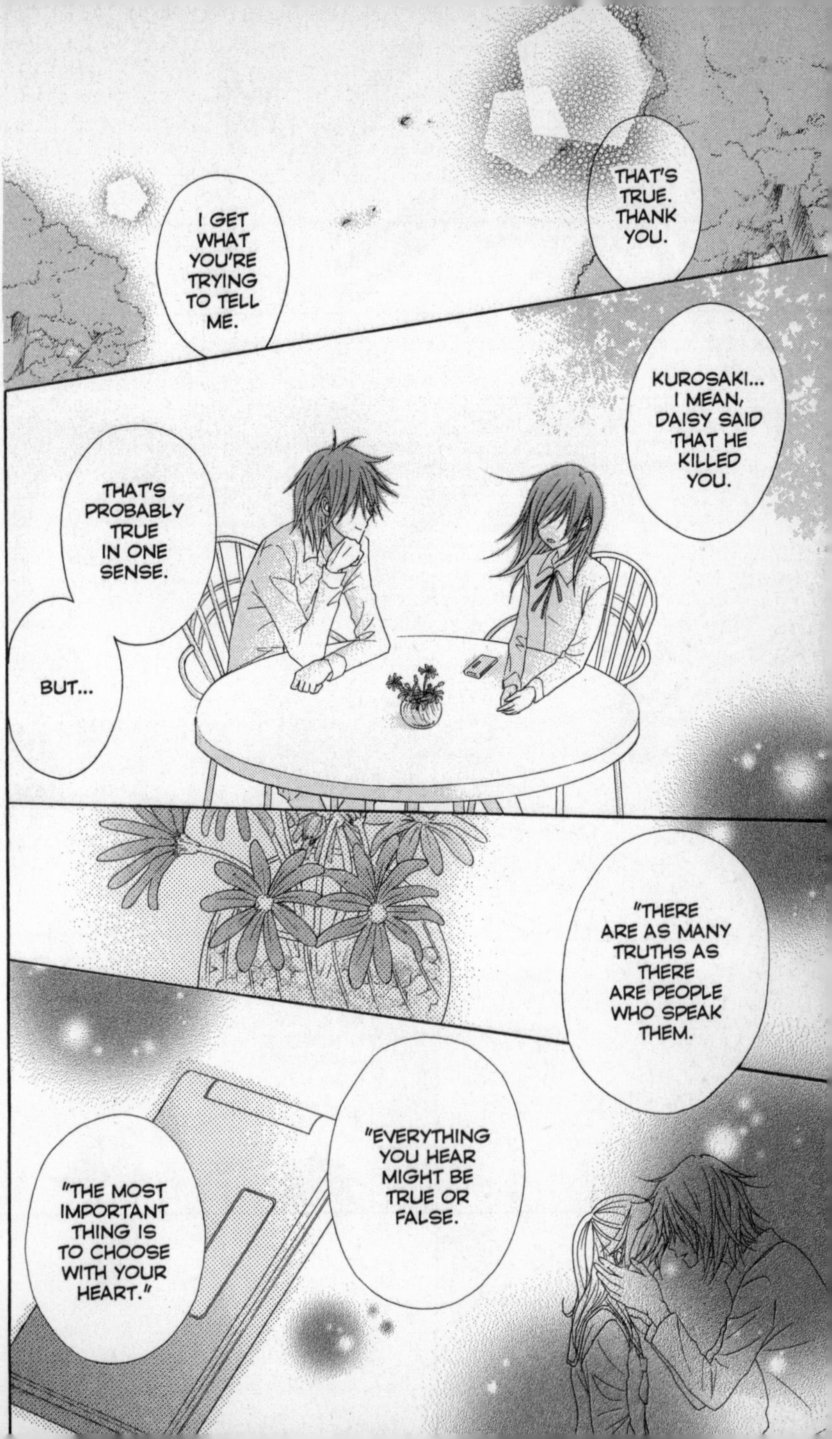
THAT'S TRUE. THANK YOU.
I GET WHAT YOU'RE TRYING TO TELL ME.
KUROSAKI... I MEAN, DAISY SAID THAT HE KILLED YOU.
THAT'S PROBABLY TRUE IN ONE SENSE.
BUT...
"THERE ARE AS MANY TRUTHS AS THERE ARE PEOPLE WHO SPEAK THEM.
"EVERYTHING YOU HEAR MIGHT BE TRUE OR FALSE.
"THE MOST IMPORTANT THING IS TO CHOOSE WITH YOUR HEART."

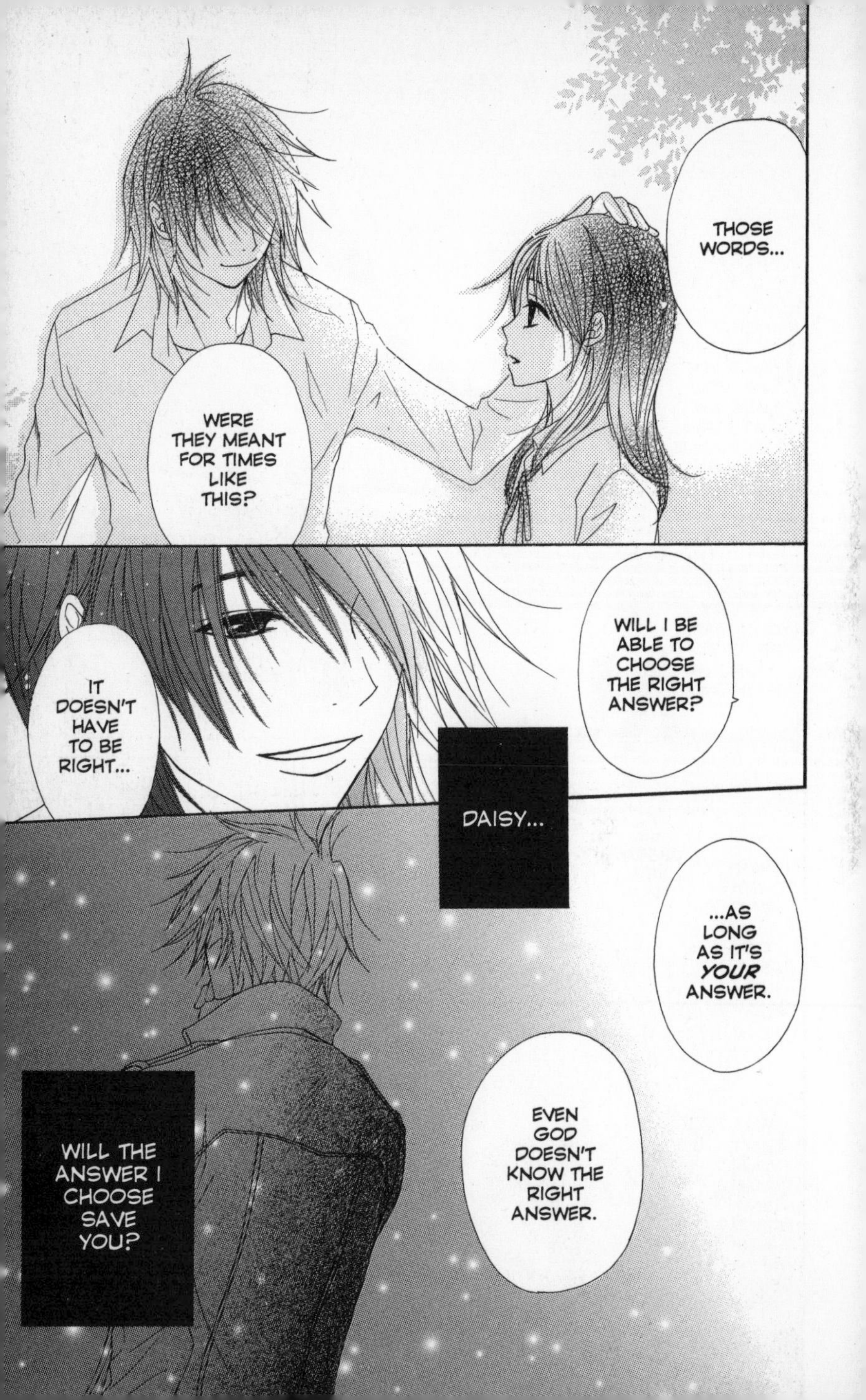
THOSE WORDS...
WERE THEY MEANT FOR TIMES LIKE THIS?
WILL I BE ABLE TO CHOOSE THE RIGHT ANSWER?
IT DOESN'T HAVE TO BE RIGHT...
...AS LONG AS IT'S *YOUR* ANSWER.
DAISY...
EVEN GOD DOESN'T KNOW THE RIGHT ANSWER.
WILL THE ANSWER I CHOOSE SAVE YOU?

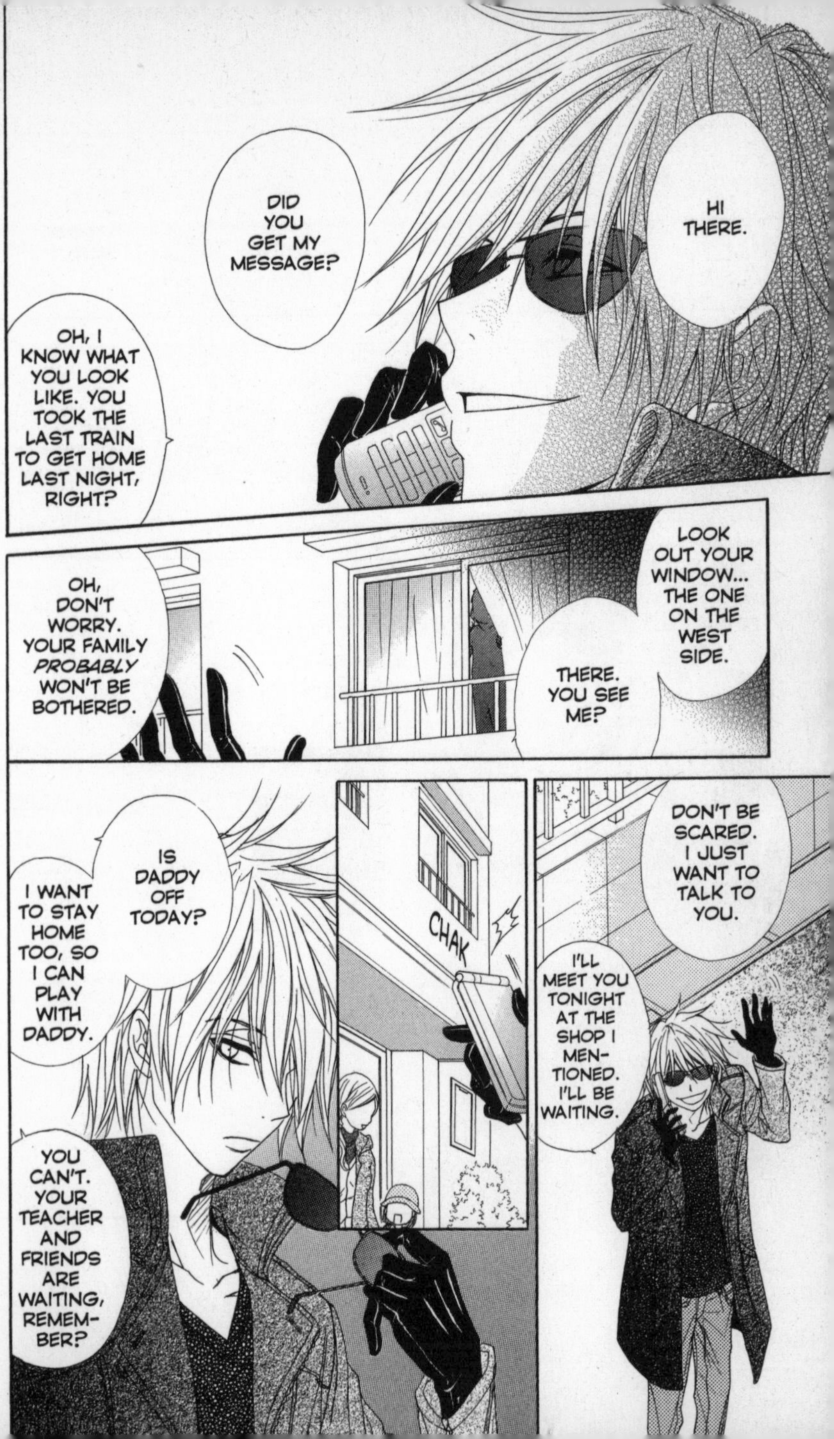
HI THERE.
DID YOU GET MY MESSAGE?
OH, I KNOW WHAT YOU LOOK LIKE. YOU TOOK THE LAST TRAIN TO GET HOME LAST NIGHT, RIGHT?
LOOK OUT YOUR WINDOW... THE ONE ON THE WEST SIDE.
THERE. YOU SEE ME?
OH, DON'T WORRY. YOUR FAMILY *PROBABLY* WON'T BE BOTHERED.
DON'T BE SCARED. I JUST WANT TO TALK TO YOU.
I'LL MEET YOU TONIGHT AT THE SHOP I MEN-TIONED. I'LL BE WAITING.
CHAK
IS DADDY OFF TODAY?
I WANT TO STAY HOME TOO, SO I CAN PLAY WITH DADDY.
YOU CAN'T. YOUR TEACHER AND FRIENDS ARE WAITING, REMEMBER?

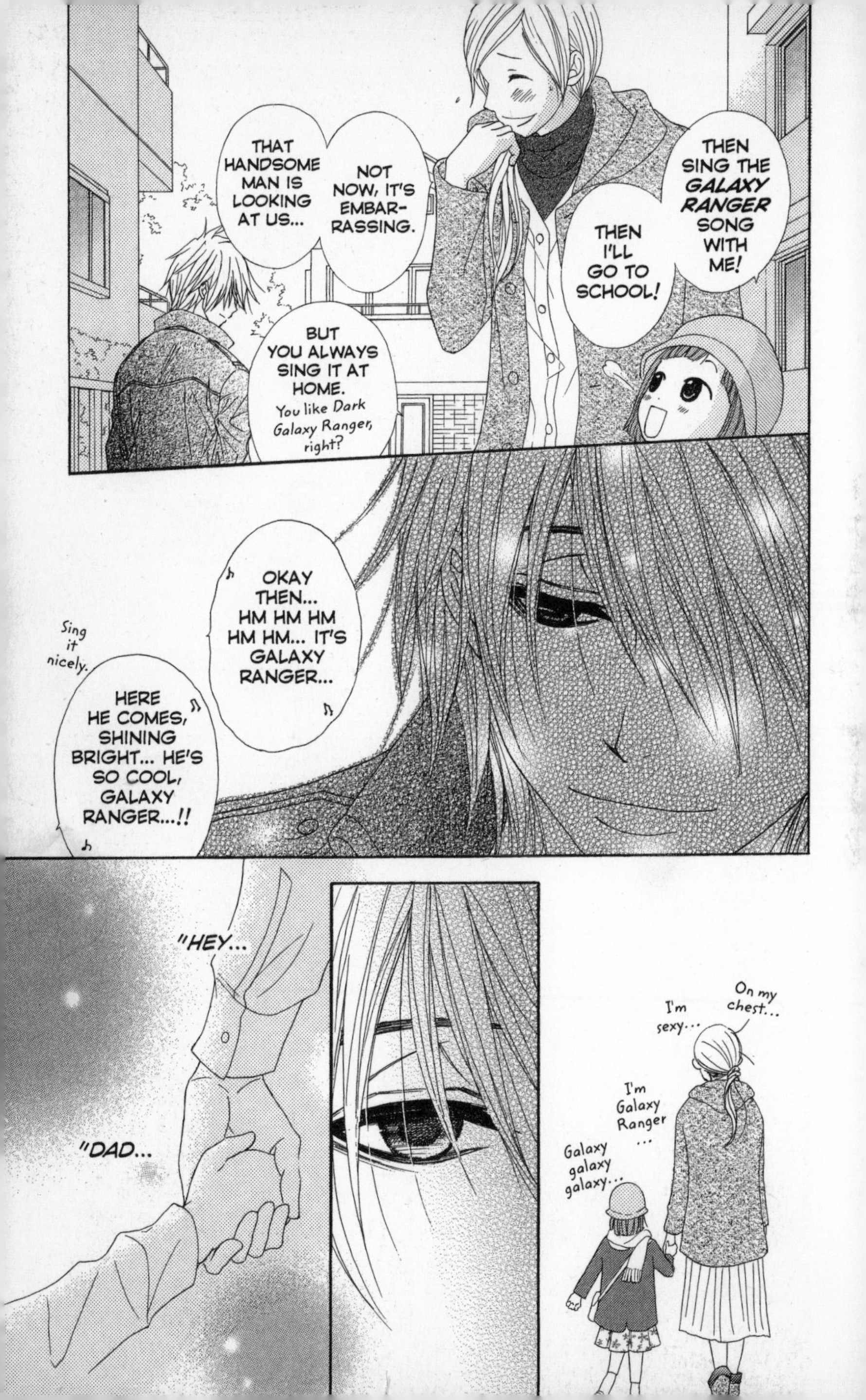
THEN SING THE GALAXY RANGER SONG WITH ME!
THEN I'LL GO TO SCHOOL!
NOT NOW, IT'S EMBARRASSING.
THAT HANDSOME MAN IS LOOKING AT US...
BUT YOU ALWAYS SING IT AT HOME. You like Dark Galaxy Ranger, right?
OKAY THEN... HM HM HM HM HM... IT'S GALAXY RANGER...
Sing it nicely.
HERE HE COMES, SHINING BRIGHT... HE'S SO COOL, GALAXY RANGER...!!
On my chest...
I'm sexy...
I'm Galaxy Ranger...
Galaxy galaxy galaxy...
"HEY...
"DAD...

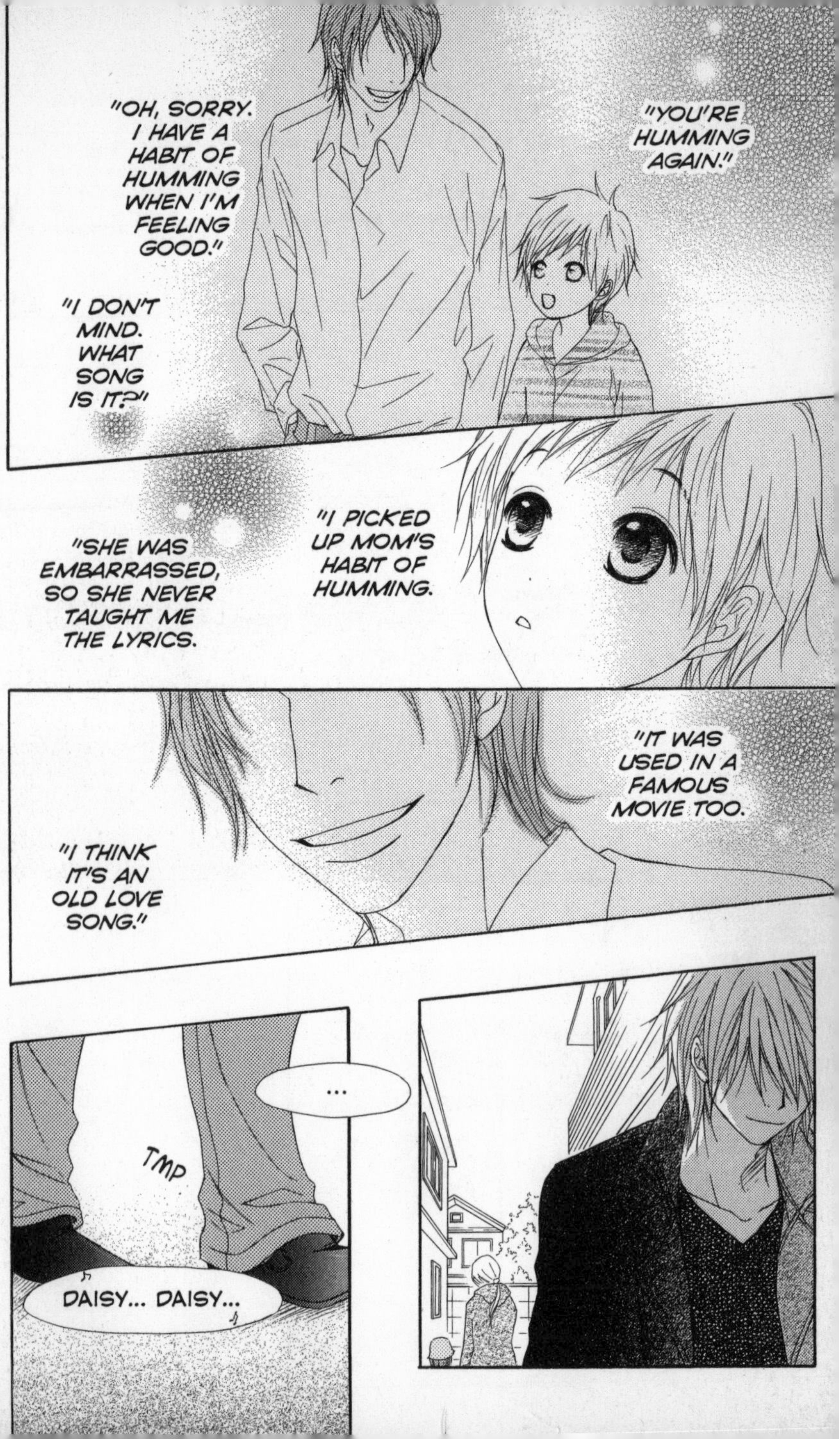
"YOU'RE HUMMING AGAIN."
"OH, SORRY. I HAVE A HABIT OF HUMMING WHEN I'M FEELING GOOD."
"I DON'T MIND. WHAT SONG IS IT?"
"I PICKED UP MOM'S HABIT OF HUMMING.
"SHE WAS EMBARRASSED, SO SHE NEVER TAUGHT ME THE LYRICS.
"IT WAS USED IN A FAMOUS MOVIE TOO.
"I THINK IT'S AN OLD LOVE SONG."
...
TMP
DAISY... DAISY...

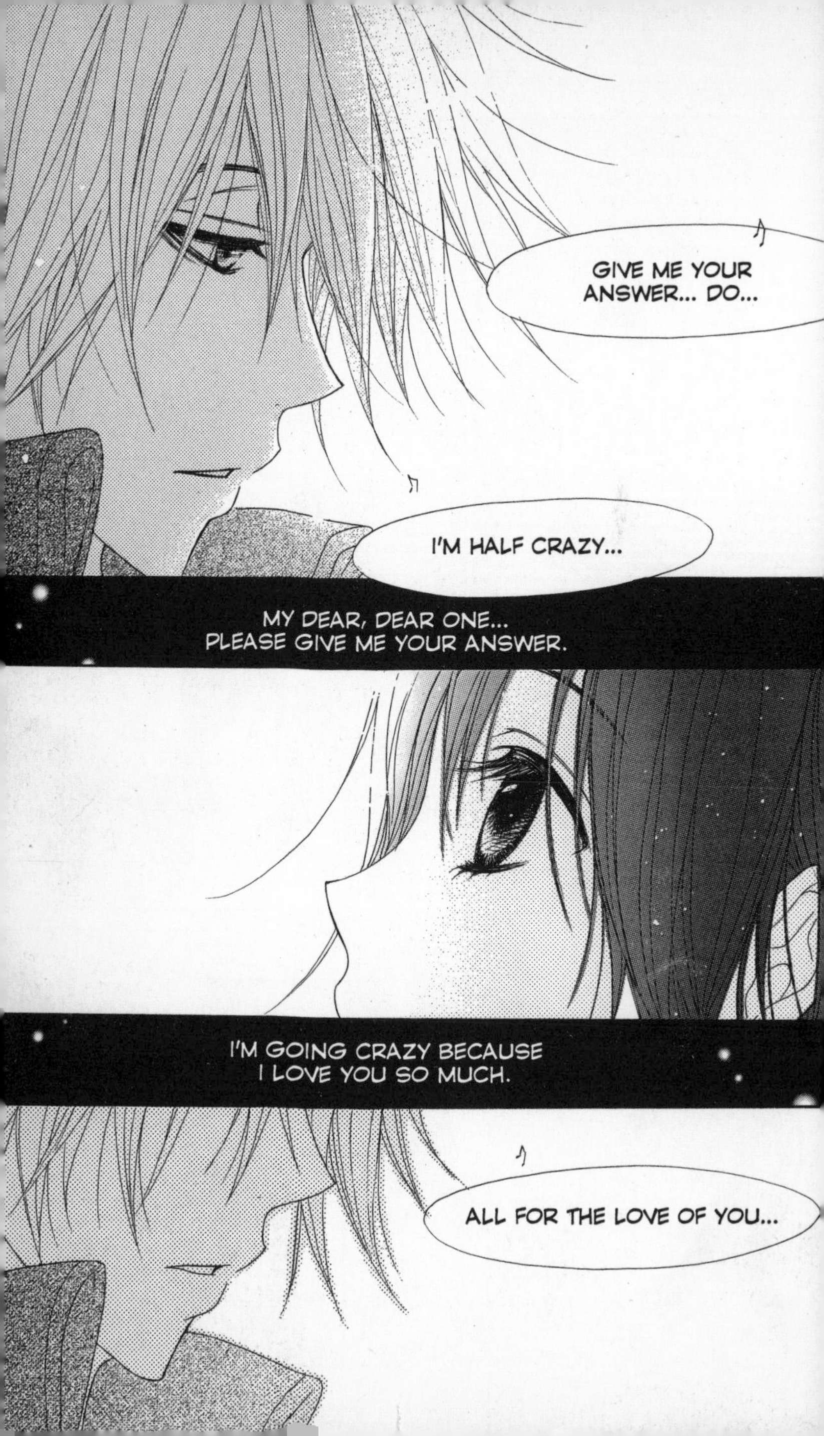
GIVE ME YOUR ANSWER... DO...
I'M HALF CRAZY...
MY DEAR, DEAR ONE... PLEASE GIVE ME YOUR ANSWER.
I'M GOING CRAZY BECAUSE I LOVE YOU SO MUCH.
ALL FOR THE LOVE OF YOU...

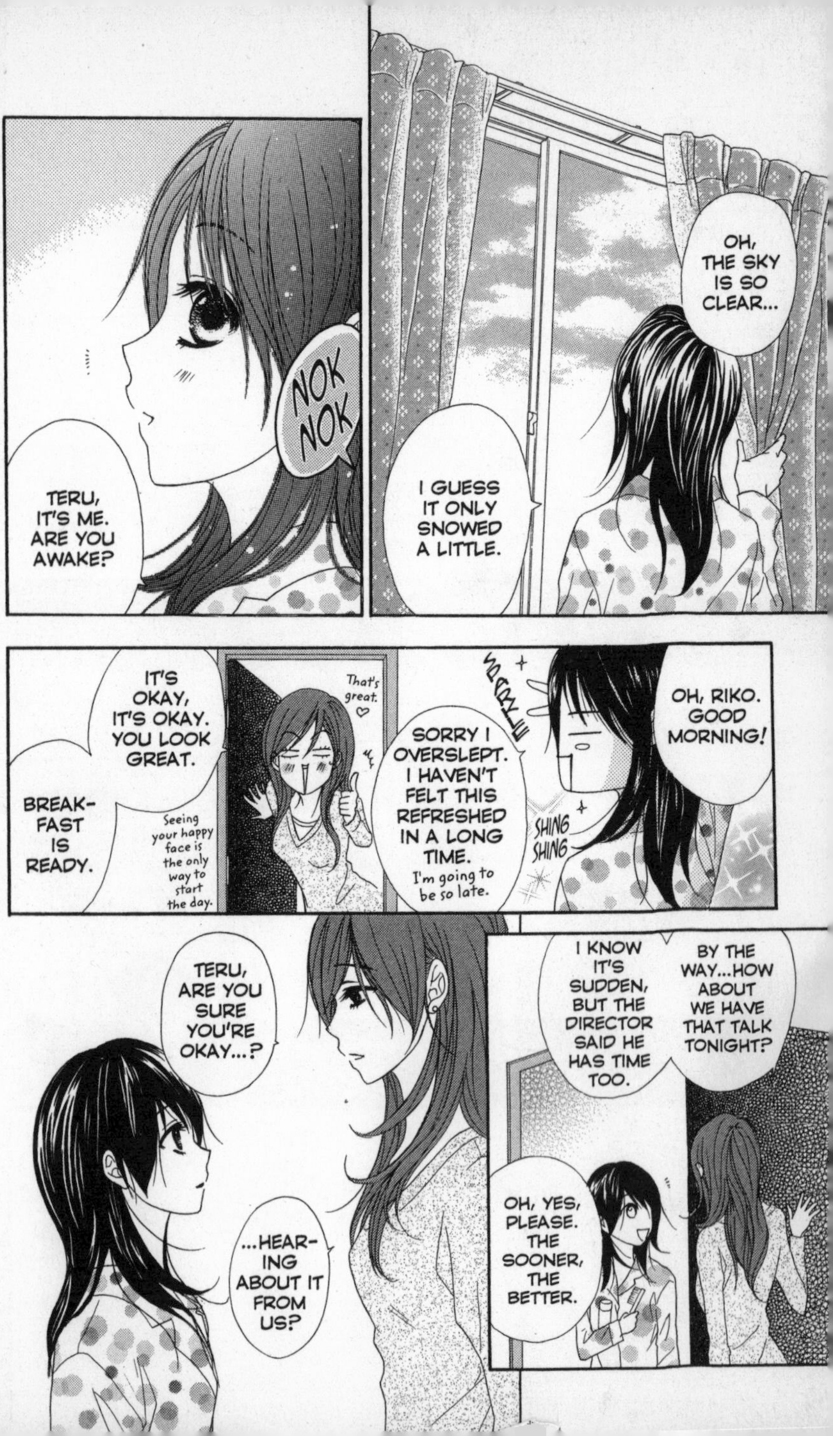
OH, THE SKY IS SO CLEAR...
I GUESS IT ONLY SNOWED A LITTLE.
NOK NOK
TERU, IT'S ME. ARE YOU AWAKE?
OH, RIKO. GOOD MORNING!
SHING SHING
SORRY I OVERSLEPT. I HAVEN'T FELT THIS REFRESHED IN A LONG TIME.
I'm going to be so late.
That's great.
IT'S OKAY, IT'S OKAY. YOU LOOK GREAT.
Seeing your happy face is the only way to start the day.
BREAK-FAST IS READY.
BY THE WAY...HOW ABOUT WE HAVE THAT TALK TONIGHT?
I KNOW IT'S SUDDEN, BUT THE DIRECTOR SAID HE HAS TIME TOO.
OH, YES, PLEASE. THE SOONER, THE BETTER.
TERU, ARE YOU SURE YOU'RE OKAY...?
...HEAR-ING ABOUT IT FROM US?

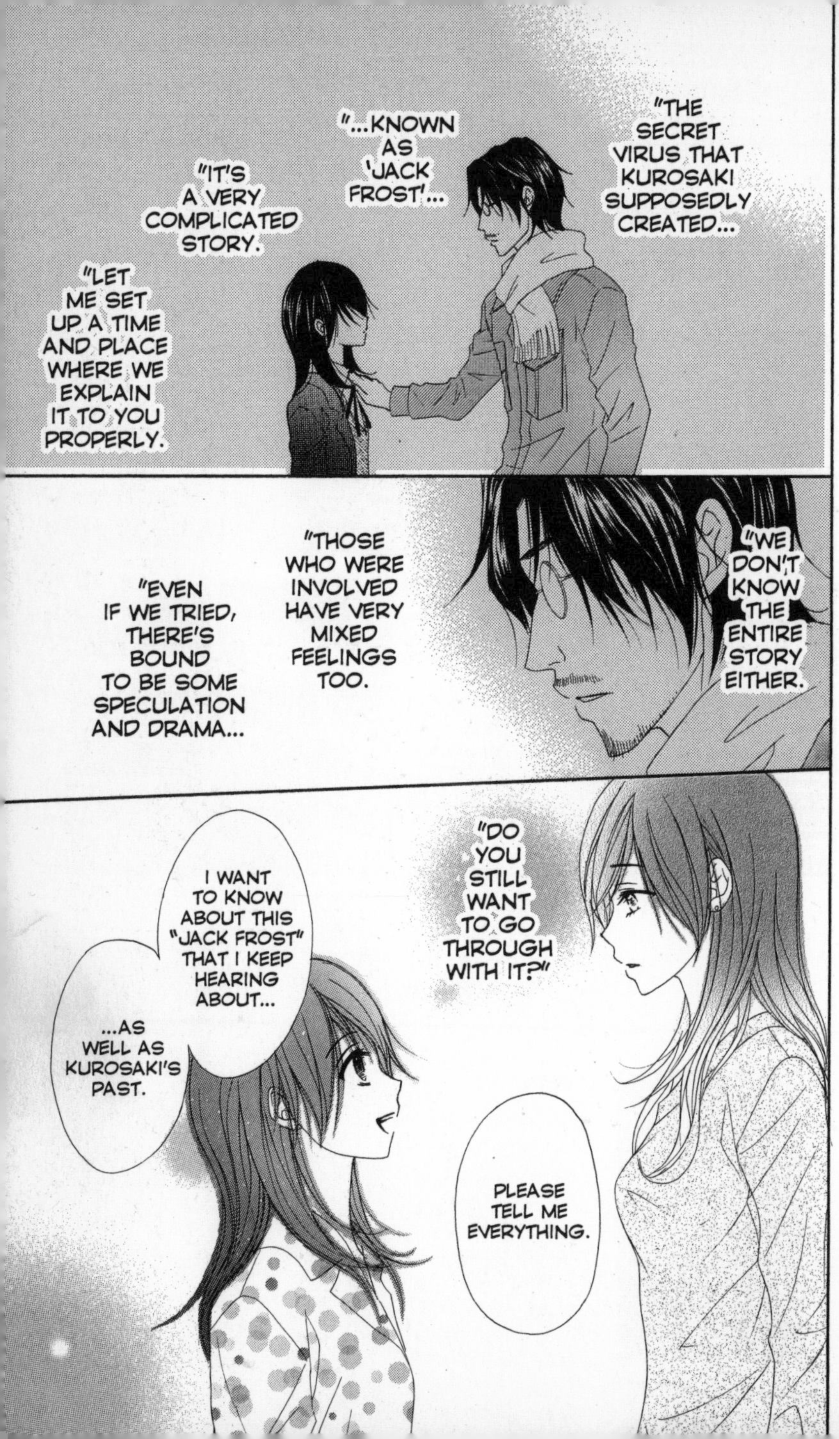
"THE SECRET VIRUS THAT KUROSAKI SUPPOSEDLY CREATED...
"...KNOWN AS 'JACK FROST'...
"IT'S A VERY COMPLICATED STORY.
"LET ME SET UP A TIME AND PLACE WHERE WE EXPLAIN IT TO YOU PROPERLY.
"WE DON'T KNOW THE ENTIRE STORY EITHER.
"THOSE WHO WERE INVOLVED HAVE VERY MIXED FEELINGS TOO.
"EVEN IF WE TRIED, THERE'S BOUND TO BE SOME SPECULATION AND DRAMA...
"DO YOU STILL WANT TO GO THROUGH WITH IT?"
I WANT TO KNOW ABOUT THIS "JACK FROST" THAT I KEEP HEARING ABOUT...
...AS WELL AS KUROSAKI'S PAST.
PLEASE TELL ME EVERYTHING.

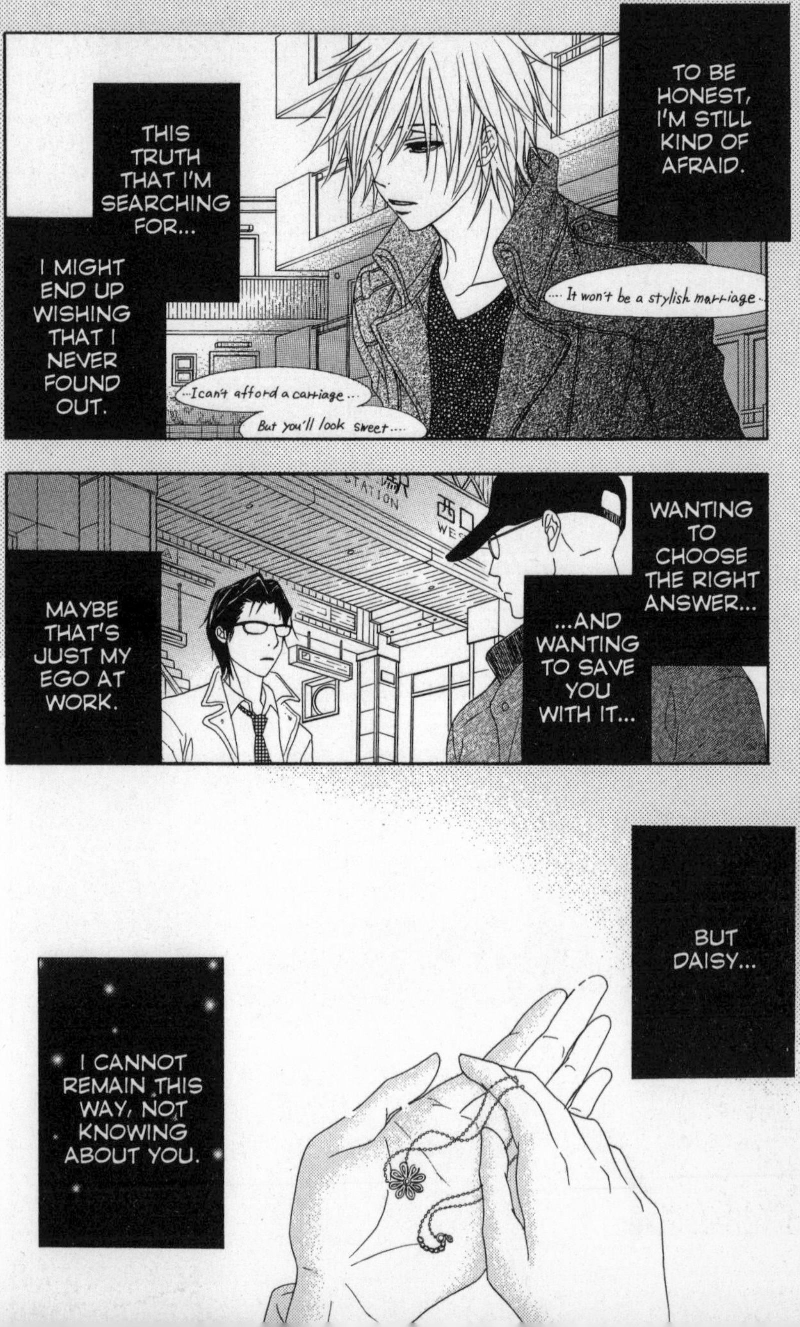
TO BE HONEST, I'M STILL KIND OF AFRAID.
THIS TRUTH THAT I'M SEARCHING FOR...
I MIGHT END UP WISHING THAT I NEVER FOUND OUT.
.... It won't be a stylish marriage...
...I can't afford a carriage...
But you'll look sweet....
STATION
WANTING TO CHOOSE THE RIGHT ANSWER...
...AND WANTING TO SAVE YOU WITH IT...
MAYBE THAT'S JUST MY EGO AT WORK.
BUT DAISY...
I CANNOT REMAIN THIS WAY, NOT KNOWING ABOUT YOU.

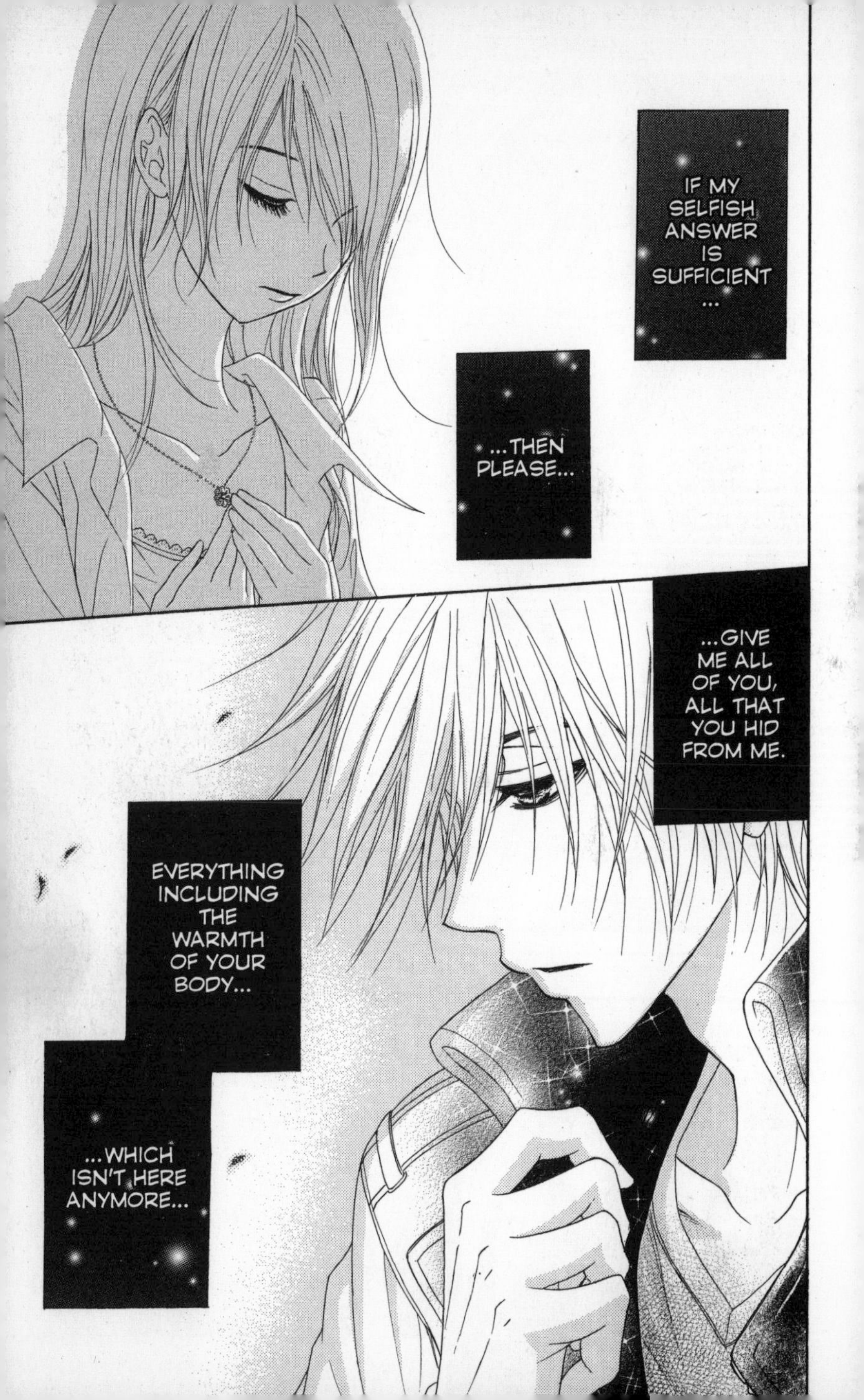
IF MY SELFISH ANSWER IS SUFFICIENT...
...THEN PLEASE...
...GIVE ME ALL OF YOU, ALL THAT YOU HID FROM ME.
EVERYTHING INCLUDING THE WARMTH OF YOUR BODY...
...WHICH ISN'T HERE ANYMORE...

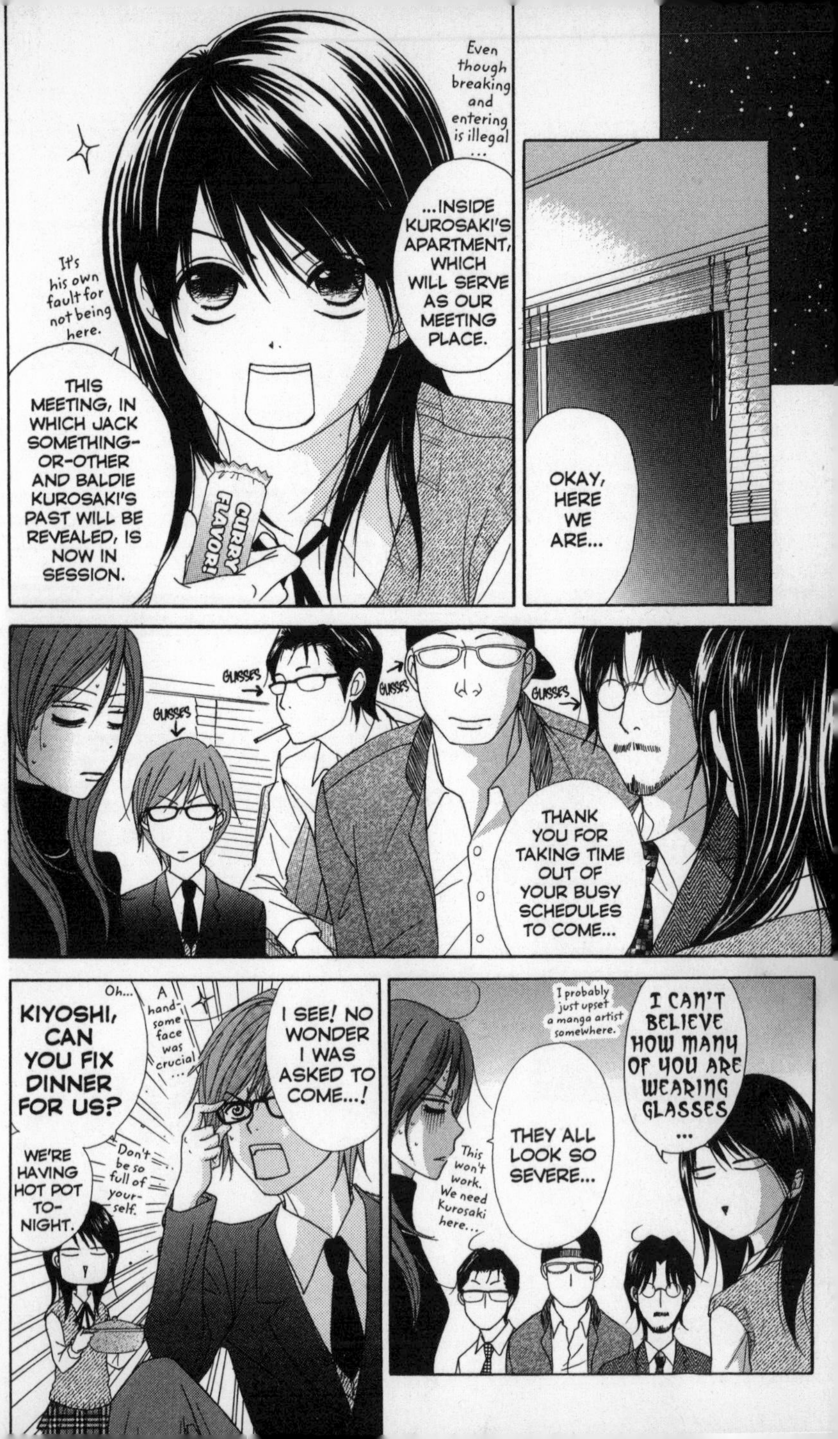
OKAY, HERE WE ARE...
Even though breaking and entering is illegal...
...INSIDE KUROSAKI'S APARTMENT, WHICH WILL SERVE AS OUR MEETING PLACE.
It's his own fault for not being here.
THIS MEETING, IN WHICH JACK SOMETHING-OR-OTHER AND BALDIE KUROSAKI'S PAST WILL BE REVEALED, IS NOW IN SESSION.
CURRY FLAVOR!
GLASSES
GLASSES
GLASSES
GLASSES
THANK YOU FOR TAKING TIME OUT OF YOUR BUSY SCHEDULES TO COME...
I CAN'T BELIEVE HOW MANY OF YOU ARE WEARING GLASSES...
I probably just upset a manga artist somewhere.
THEY ALL LOOK SO SEVERE...
This won't work. We need Kurosaki here...
I SEE! NO WONDER I WAS ASKED TO COME...!
A handsome face was crucial...
Oh...
KIYOSHI, CAN YOU FIX DINNER FOR US?
Don't be so full of yourself.
WE'RE HAVING HOT POT TONIGHT.

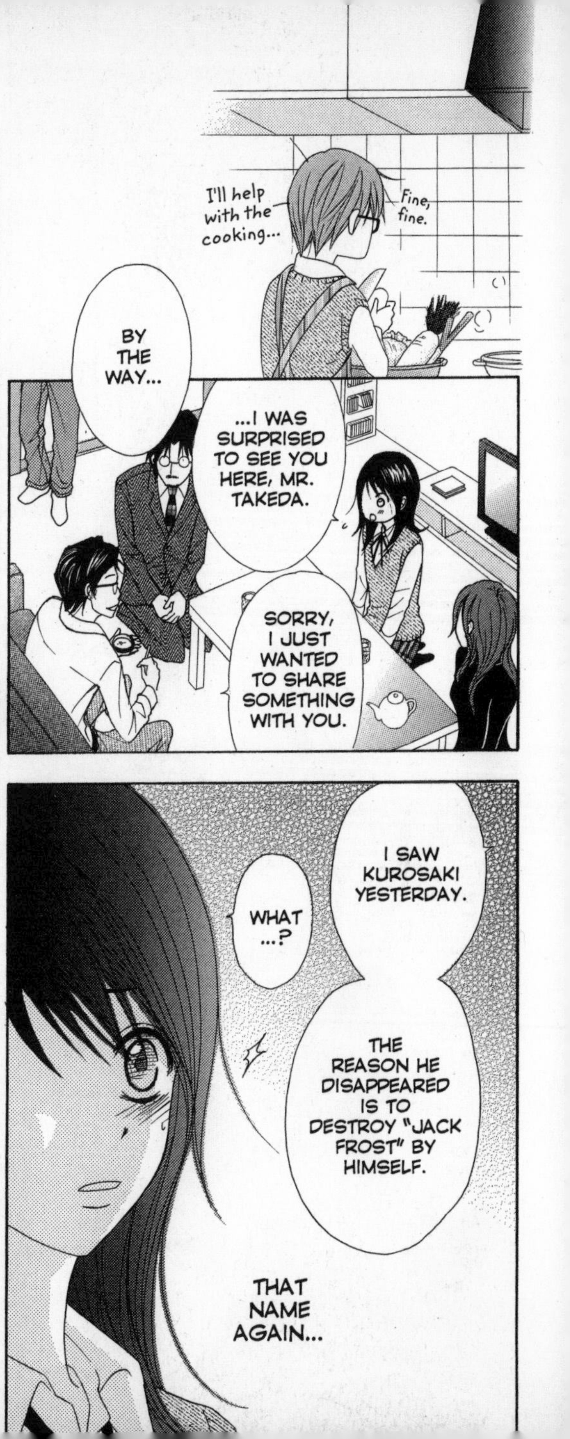
I'll help with the cooking...
Fine, fine.
BY THE WAY...
...I WAS SURPRISED TO SEE YOU HERE, MR. TAKEDA.
SORRY, I JUST WANTED TO SHARE SOMETHING WITH YOU.
I SAW KUROSAKI YESTERDAY.
WHAT ...?
THE REASON HE DISAPPEARED IS TO DESTROY "JACK FROST" BY HIMSELF.
THAT NAME AGAIN...

DENGEKI DAISY QUESTION CORNER

BALDLY ASK!! ②

Q. WHAT PERCENT OF KUROSAKI'S THOUGHTS IS OCCUPIED WITH TERU?

(AYAMI, KYOTO)

A. ABOUT 85 PERCENT OF HIS THOUGHTS ARE ON TERU. THE REMAINING 15 PERCENT IS ON TERU'S PANTIES.

Q. IF THERE WAS A SAFE, WHAT WOULD BE INSIDE?

(A. O., AICHI PREFECTURE)

A. TERU IS THE TYPE TO KEEP HER MOST VALUABLE POSSESSIONS CLOSE TO HER. IF SHE WERE TO PUT ANYTHING IN A SAFE, IT WOULD PROBABLY BE HER BANK PASSBOOK (SHE'D KEEP ANY REMAINING CASH).
KUROSAKI WOULD PUT TERU'S SCHOOL SWIMSUIT INSIDE.

Q. WHY DOES KUROSAKI ALWAYS GO FOR "BAIMAN" IN MAHJONG? IS THAT BECAUSE HE DOESN'T PAY ATTENTION?

(JOHN SMITH, NIIGATA PREFECTURE)

A. ...YOU ARE WELL-INFORMED... YOU ARE ABSOLUTELY RIGHT. KUROSAKI DOESN'T PAY ATTENTION, AND HE'S LAZY, SO HE'S NOT SUITED FOR GAMBLING. THAT'S WHY HE DOESN'T DELVE INTO SERIOUS GAMBLING LIKE HORSERACING OR PACHINKO.

(GAMES AND PLAYING MAHJONG WITH FRIENDS DOESN'T COUNT.)

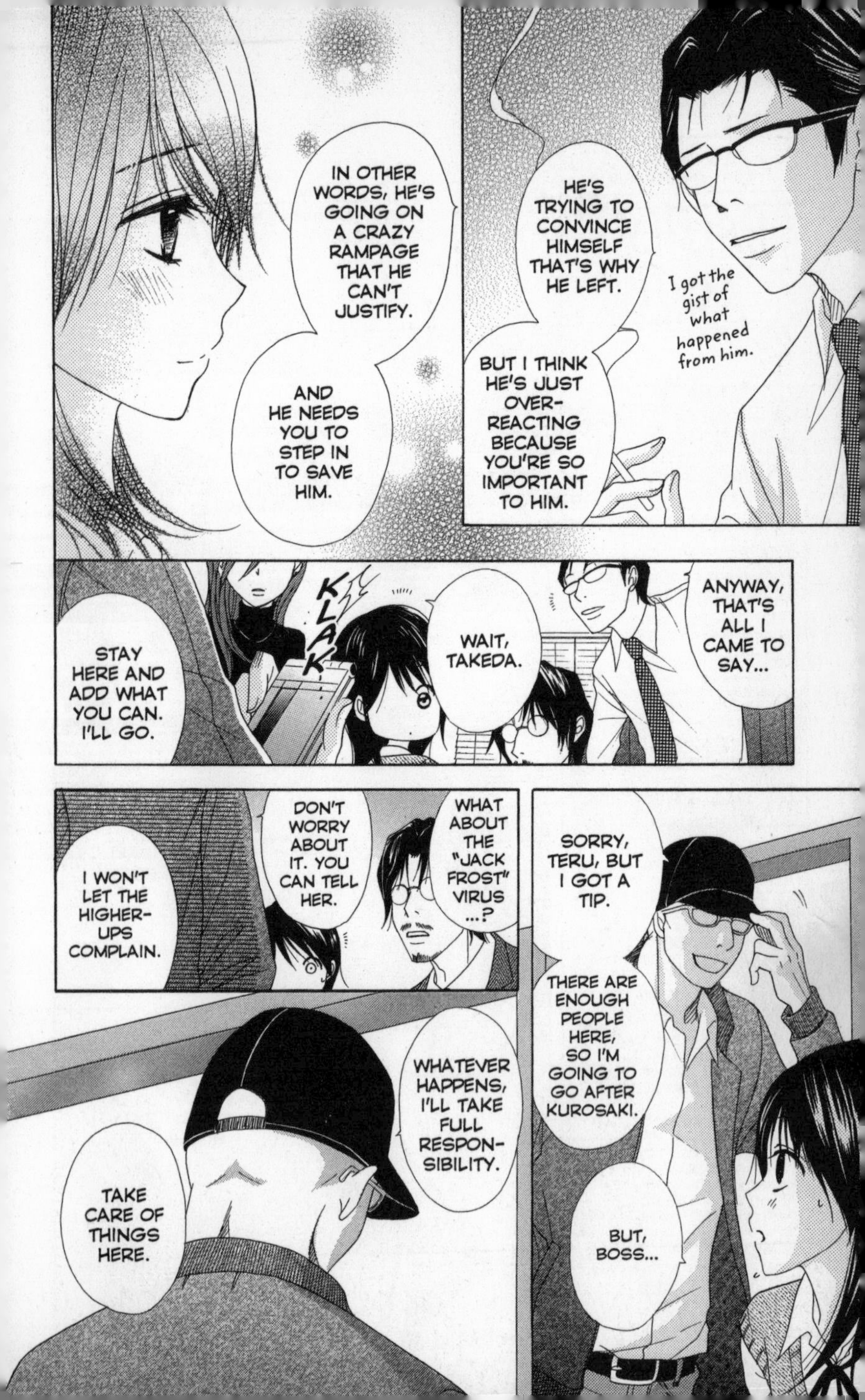
I got the gist of what happened from him.
HE'S TRYING TO CONVINCE HIMSELF THAT'S WHY HE LEFT.
BUT I THINK HE'S JUST OVER-REACTING BECAUSE YOU'RE SO IMPORTANT TO HIM.
IN OTHER WORDS, HE'S GOING ON A CRAZY RAMPAGE THAT HE CAN'T JUSTIFY.
AND HE NEEDS YOU TO STEP IN TO SAVE HIM.
ANYWAY, THAT'S ALL I CAME TO SAY...
WAIT, TAKEDA.
KLAK
STAY HERE AND ADD WHAT YOU CAN. I'LL GO.
SORRY, TERU, BUT I GOT A TIP.
THERE ARE ENOUGH PEOPLE HERE, SO I'M GOING TO GO AFTER KUROSAKI.
BUT, BOSS...
WHAT ABOUT THE "JACK FROST" VIRUS ...?
DON'T WORRY ABOUT IT. YOU CAN TELL HER.
I WON'T LET THE HIGHER-UPS COMPLAIN.
WHATEVER HAPPENS, I'LL TAKE FULL RESPON-SIBILITY.
TAKE CARE OF THINGS HERE.

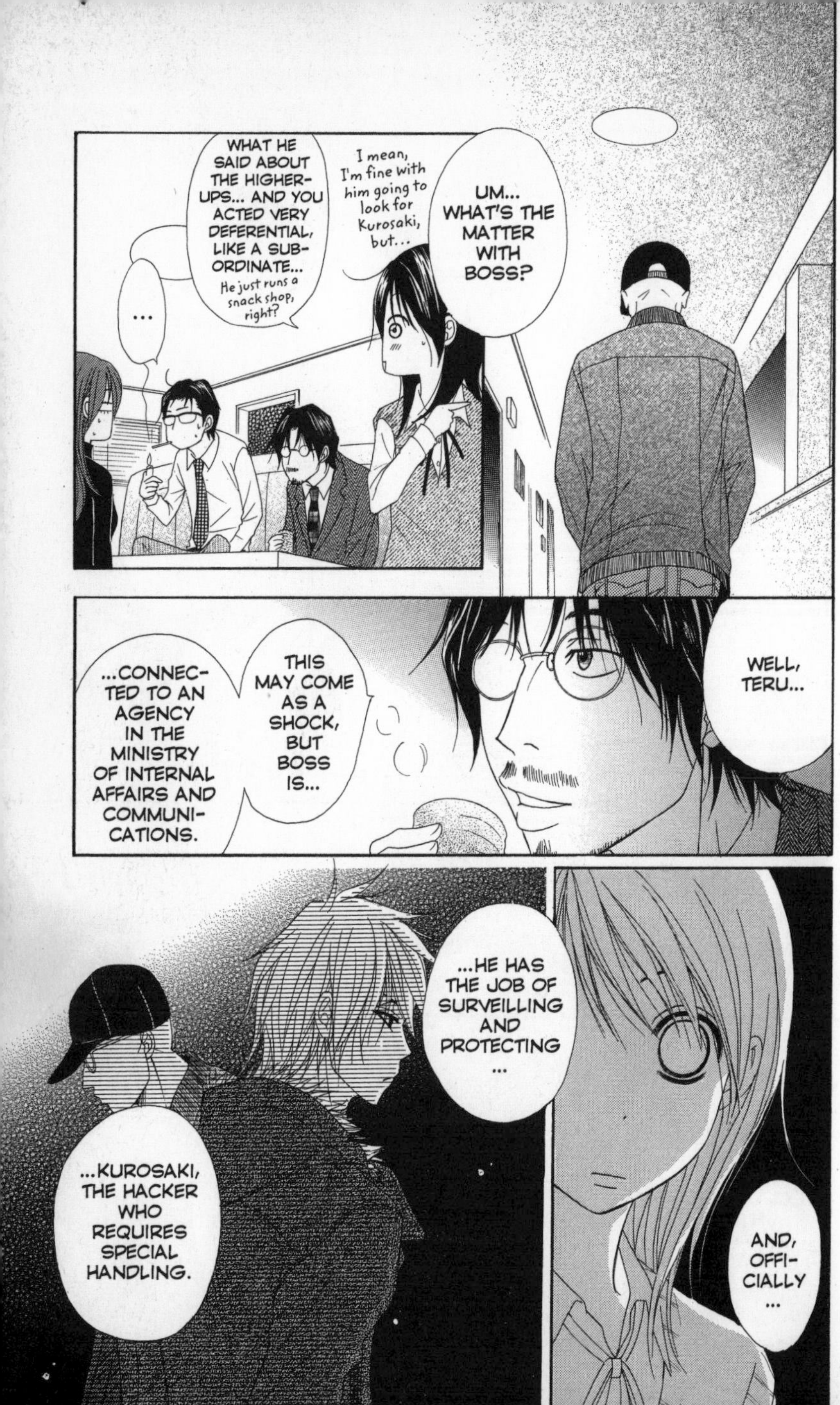
UM... WHAT'S THE MATTER WITH BOSS?
I mean, I'm fine with him going to look for Kurosaki, but...
WHAT HE SAID ABOUT THE HIGHER-UPS... AND YOU ACTED VERY DEFERENTIAL, LIKE A SUB-ORDINATE...
He just runs a snack shop, right?
...
WELL, TERU...
THIS MAY COME AS A SHOCK, BUT BOSS IS...
...CONNECTED TO AN AGENCY IN THE MINISTRY OF INTERNAL AFFAIRS AND COMMUNICATIONS.
AND, OFFICIALLY...
...HE HAS THE JOB OF SURVEILLING AND PROTECTING...
...KUROSAKI, THE HACKER WHO REQUIRES SPECIAL HANDLING.

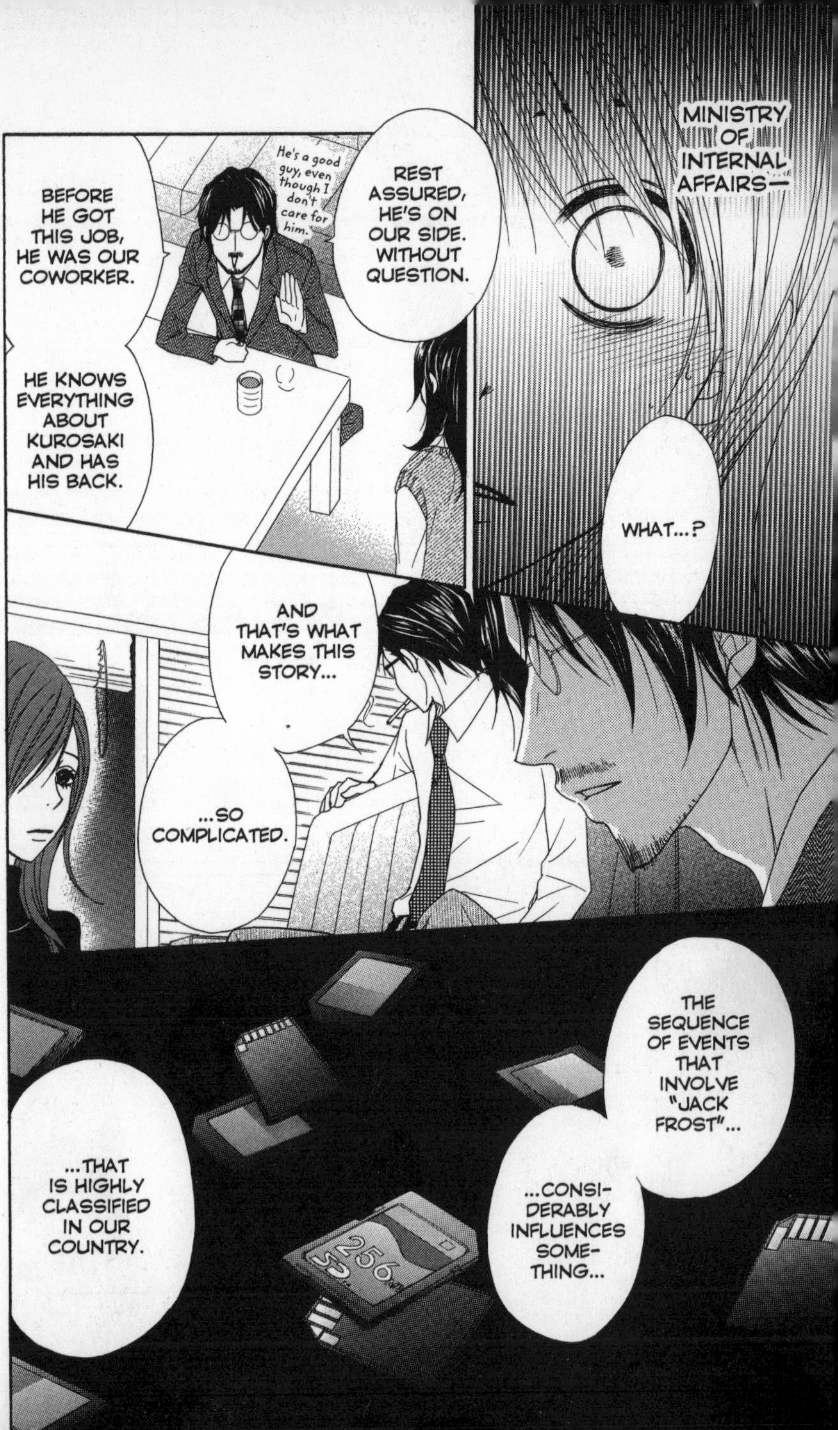
MINISTRY OF INTERNAL AFFAIRS—
WHAT...?
REST ASSURED, HE'S ON OUR SIDE. WITHOUT QUESTION.
He's a good guy, even though I don't care for him.
BEFORE HE GOT THIS JOB, HE WAS OUR COWORKER.
HE KNOWS EVERYTHING ABOUT KUROSAKI AND HAS HIS BACK.
AND THAT'S WHAT MAKES THIS STORY...
...SO COMPLICATED.
THE SEQUENCE OF EVENTS THAT INVOLVE "JACK FROST"...
...CONSI-DERABLY INFLUENCES SOME-THING...
...THAT IS HIGHLY CLASSIFIED IN OUR COUNTRY.

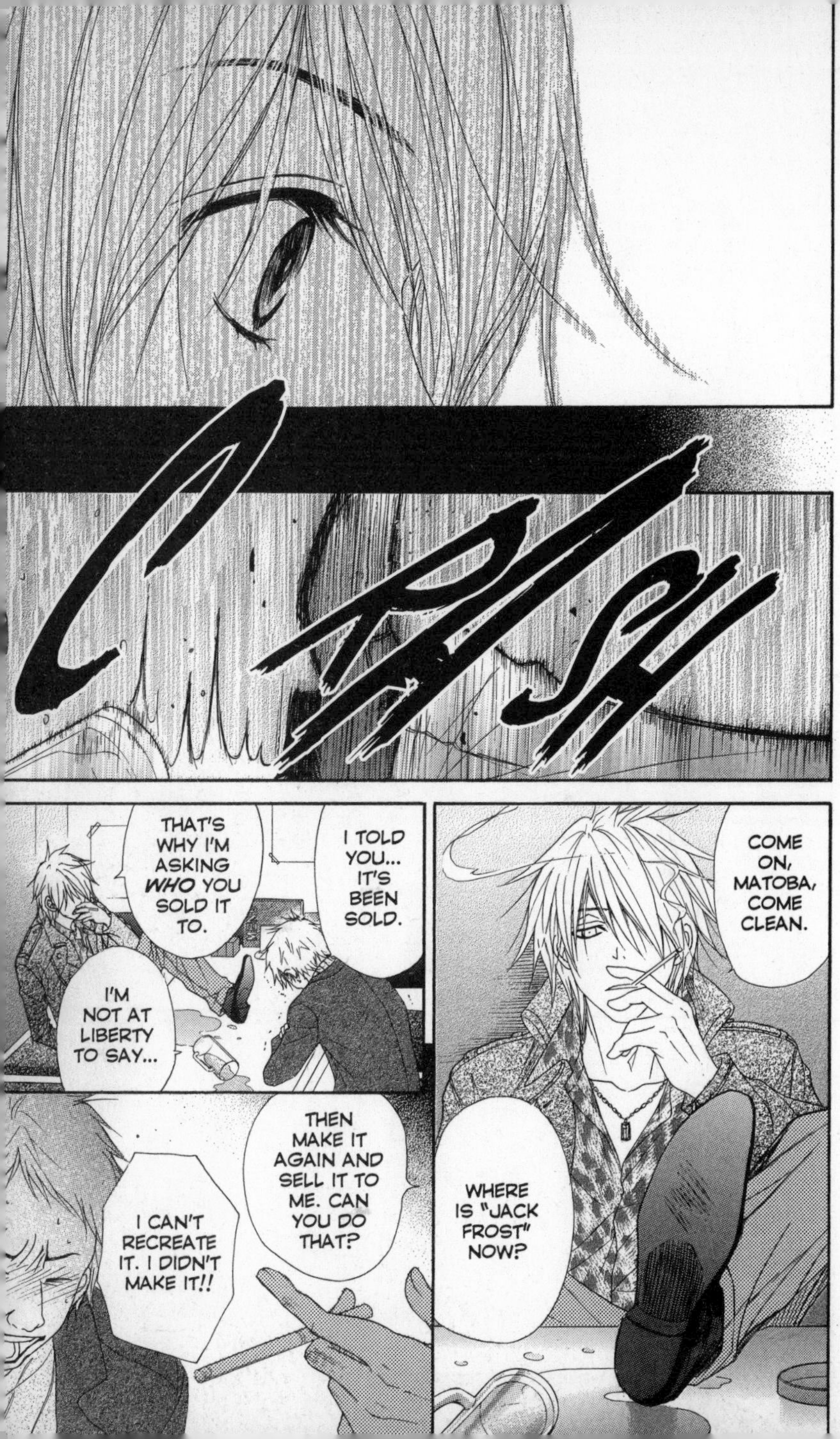
CRASH
COME ON, MATOBA, COME CLEAN.
WHERE IS "JACK FROST" NOW?
I TOLD YOU... IT'S BEEN SOLD.
THAT'S WHY I'M ASKING *WHO* YOU SOLD IT TO.
I'M NOT AT LIBERTY TO SAY...
THEN MAKE IT AGAIN AND SELL IT TO ME. CAN YOU DO THAT?
I CAN'T RECREATE IT. I DIDN'T MAKE IT!!

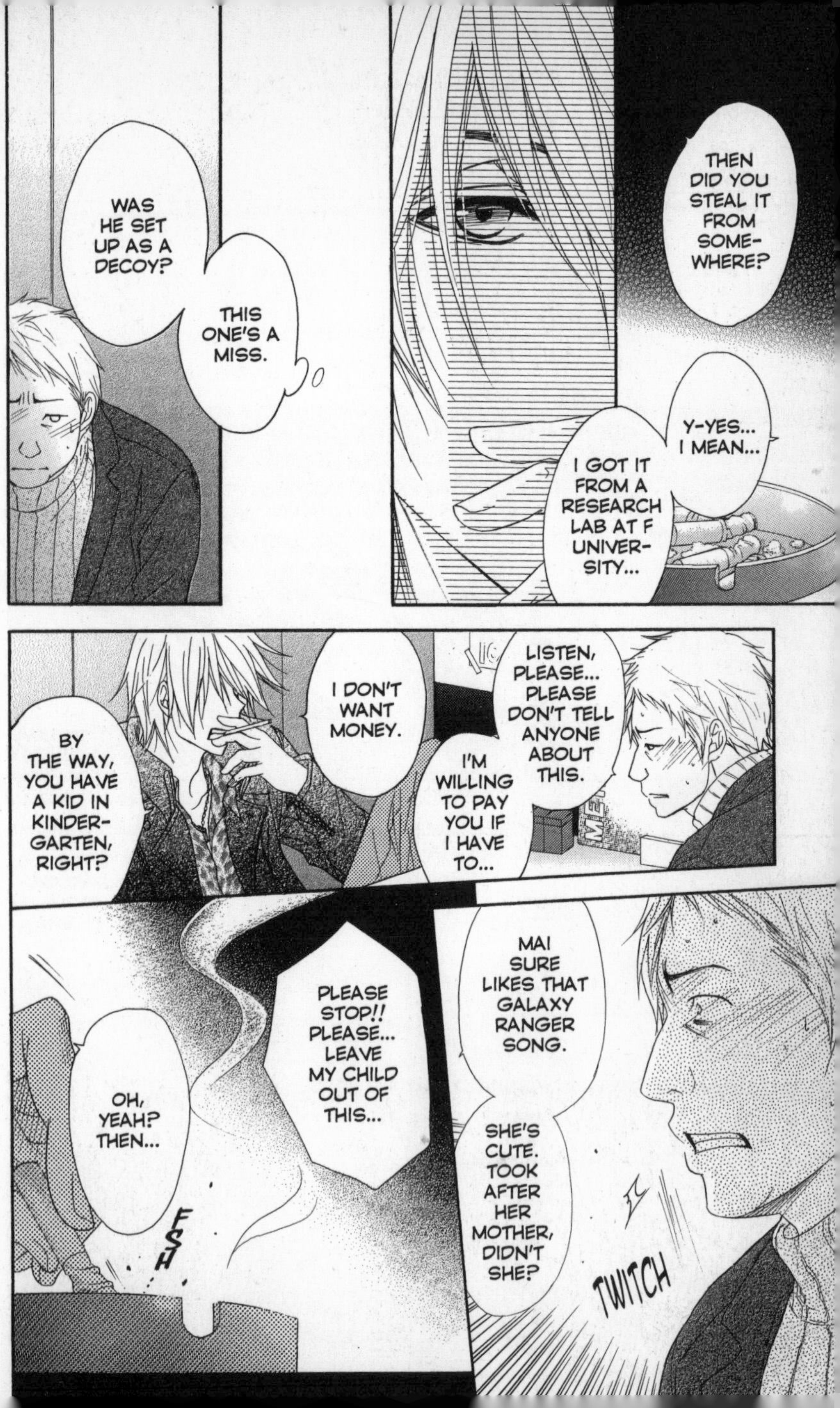
THEN DID YOU STEAL IT FROM SOME-WHERE?
Y-YES... I MEAN...
I GOT IT FROM A RESEARCH LAB AT F UNIVER-SITY...
WAS HE SET UP AS A DECOY?
THIS ONE'S A MISS.
LISTEN, PLEASE... PLEASE DON'T TELL ANYONE ABOUT THIS.
I'M WILLING TO PAY YOU IF I HAVE TO...
I DON'T WANT MONEY.
BY THE WAY, YOU HAVE A KID IN KINDER-GARTEN, RIGHT?
MAI SURE LIKES THAT GALAXY RANGER SONG.
SHE'S CUTE. TOOK AFTER HER MOTHER, DIDN'T SHE?
TWITCH
PLEASE STOP!! PLEASE... LEAVE MY CHILD OUT OF THIS...
OH, YEAH? THEN...
FSH

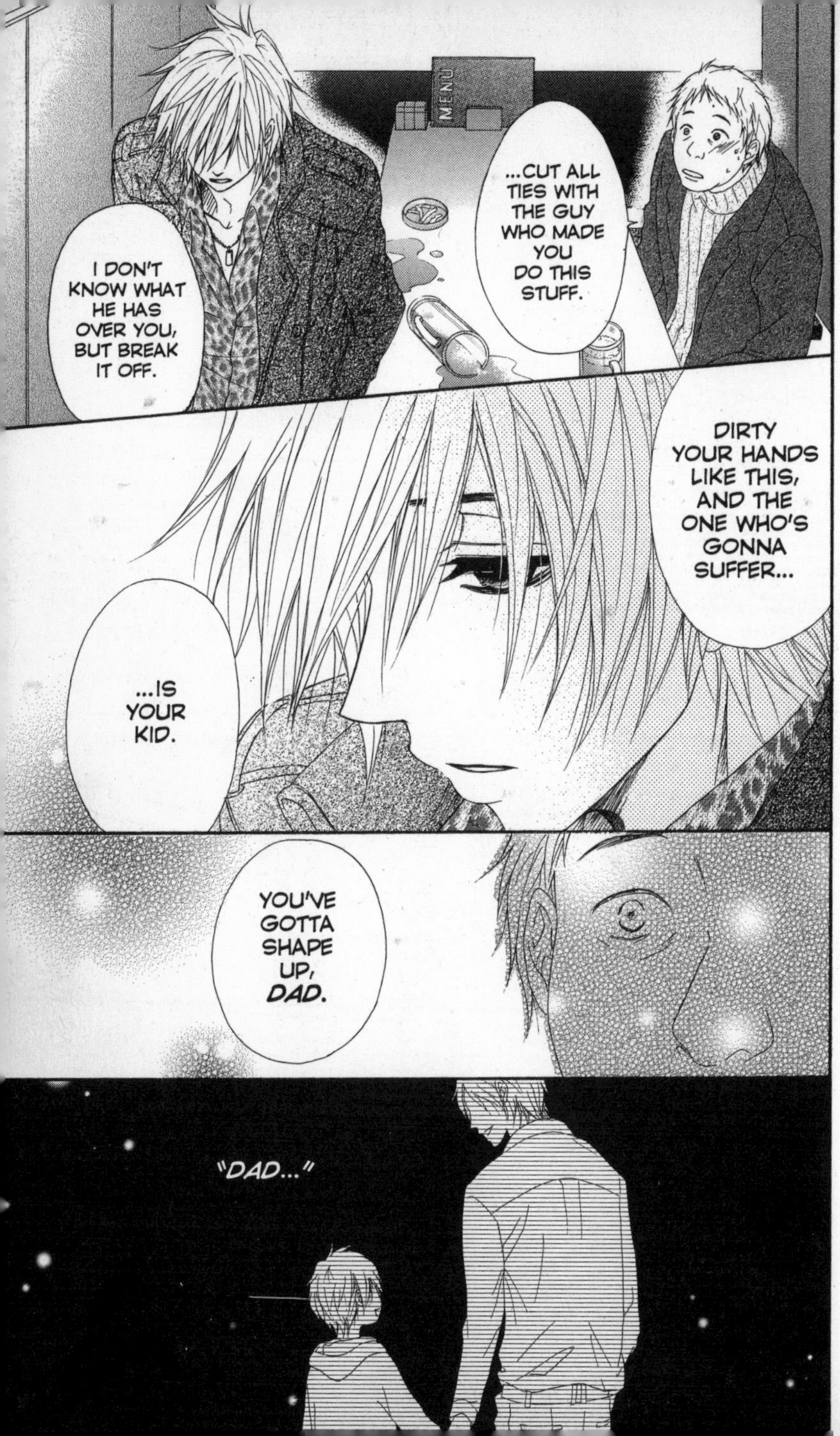
...CUT ALL TIES WITH THE GUY WHO MADE YOU DO THIS STUFF.
I DON'T KNOW WHAT HE HAS OVER YOU, BUT BREAK IT OFF.
DIRTY YOUR HANDS LIKE THIS, AND THE ONE WHO'S GONNA SUFFER...
...IS YOUR KID.
YOU'VE GOTTA SHAPE UP, ***DAD***.
"DAD..."

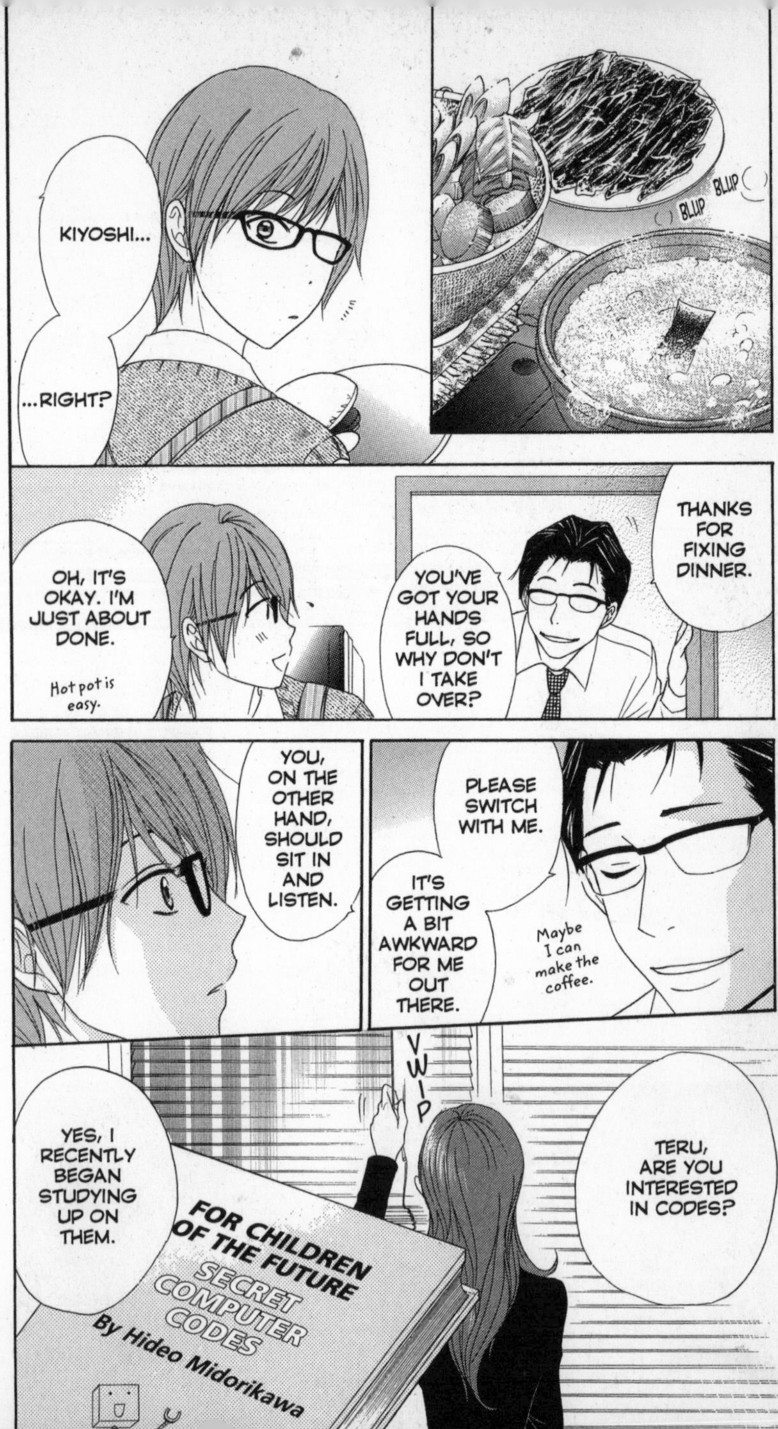
BLUP
BLUP
KIYOSHI...
...RIGHT?
THANKS FOR FIXING DINNER.
YOU'VE GOT YOUR HANDS FULL, SO WHY DON'T I TAKE OVER?
OH, IT'S OKAY. I'M JUST ABOUT DONE.
Hot pot is easy.
PLEASE SWITCH WITH ME.
IT'S GETTING A BIT AWKWARD FOR ME OUT THERE.
Maybe I can make the coffee.
YOU, ON THE OTHER HAND, SHOULD SIT IN AND LISTEN.
VWIP
TERU, ARE YOU INTERESTED IN CODES?
YES, I RECENTLY BEGAN STUDYING UP ON THEM.
FOR CHILDREN OF THE FUTURE
SECRET COMPUTER CODES
By Hideo Midorikawa

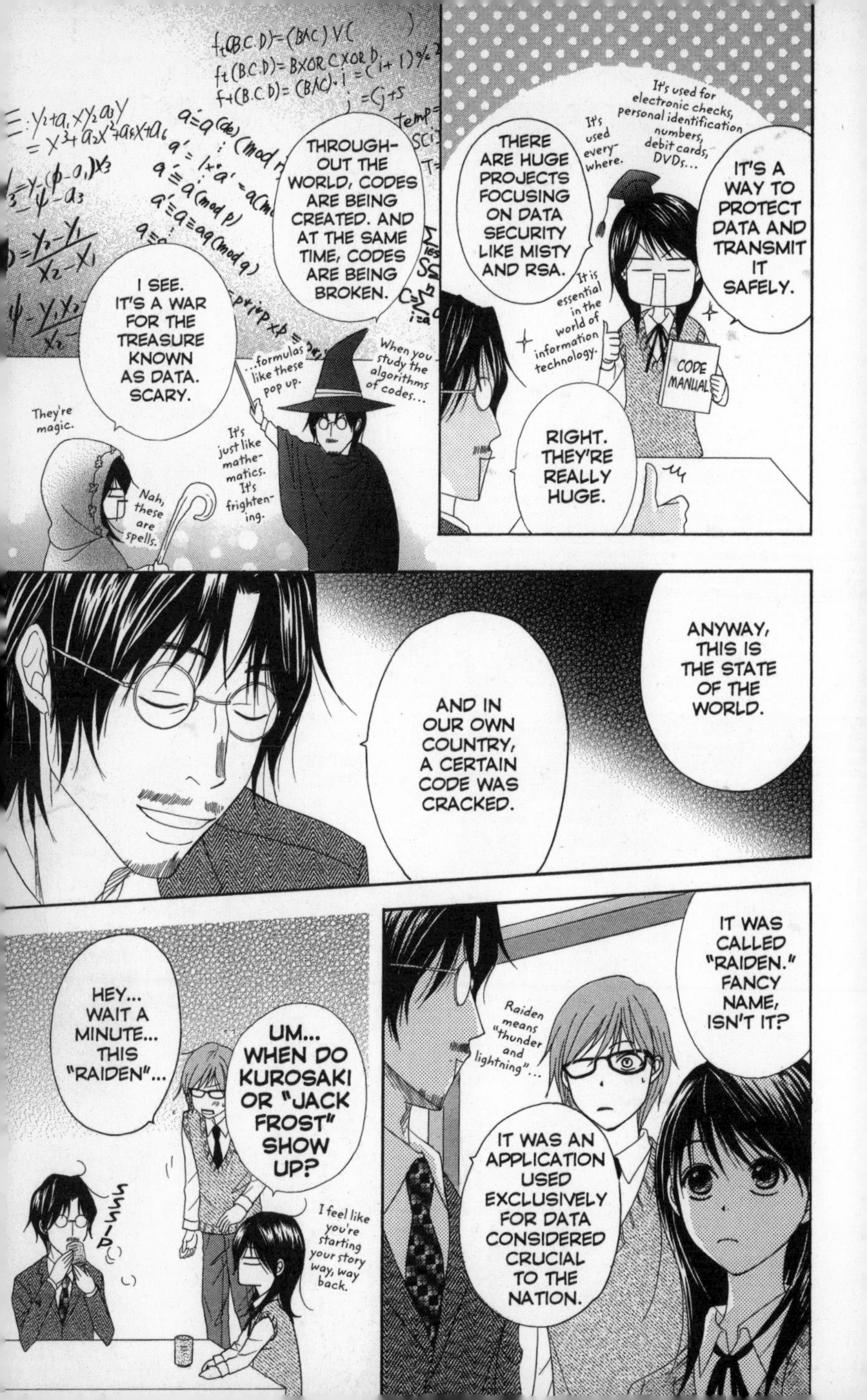
IT'S A WAY TO PROTECT DATA AND TRANSMIT IT SAFELY.
It's used for electronic checks, personal identification numbers, debit cards, DVDs...
It's used every-where.
THERE ARE HUGE PROJECTS FOCUSING ON DATA SECURITY LIKE MISTY AND RSA.
It is essential in the world of information technology.
CODE MANUAL
RIGHT. THEY'RE REALLY HUGE.
THROUGH-OUT THE WORLD, CODES ARE BEING CREATED. AND AT THE SAME TIME, CODES ARE BEING BROKEN.
When you study the algorithms of codes...
...formulas like these pop up.
I SEE. IT'S A WAR FOR THE TREASURE KNOWN AS DATA. SCARY.
It's just like mathe-matics. It's frighten-ing.
They're magic.
Nah, these are spells.
ANYWAY, THIS IS THE STATE OF THE WORLD.
AND IN OUR OWN COUNTRY, A CERTAIN CODE WAS CRACKED.
IT WAS CALLED "RAIDEN." FANCY NAME, ISN'T IT?
Raiden means "thunder and lightning"...
IT WAS AN APPLICATION USED EXCLUSIVELY FOR DATA CONSIDERED CRUCIAL TO THE NATION.
UM... WHEN DO KUROSAKI OR "JACK FROST" SHOW UP?
HEY... WAIT A MINUTE... THIS "RAIDEN"...
I feel like you're starting your story way, way back.

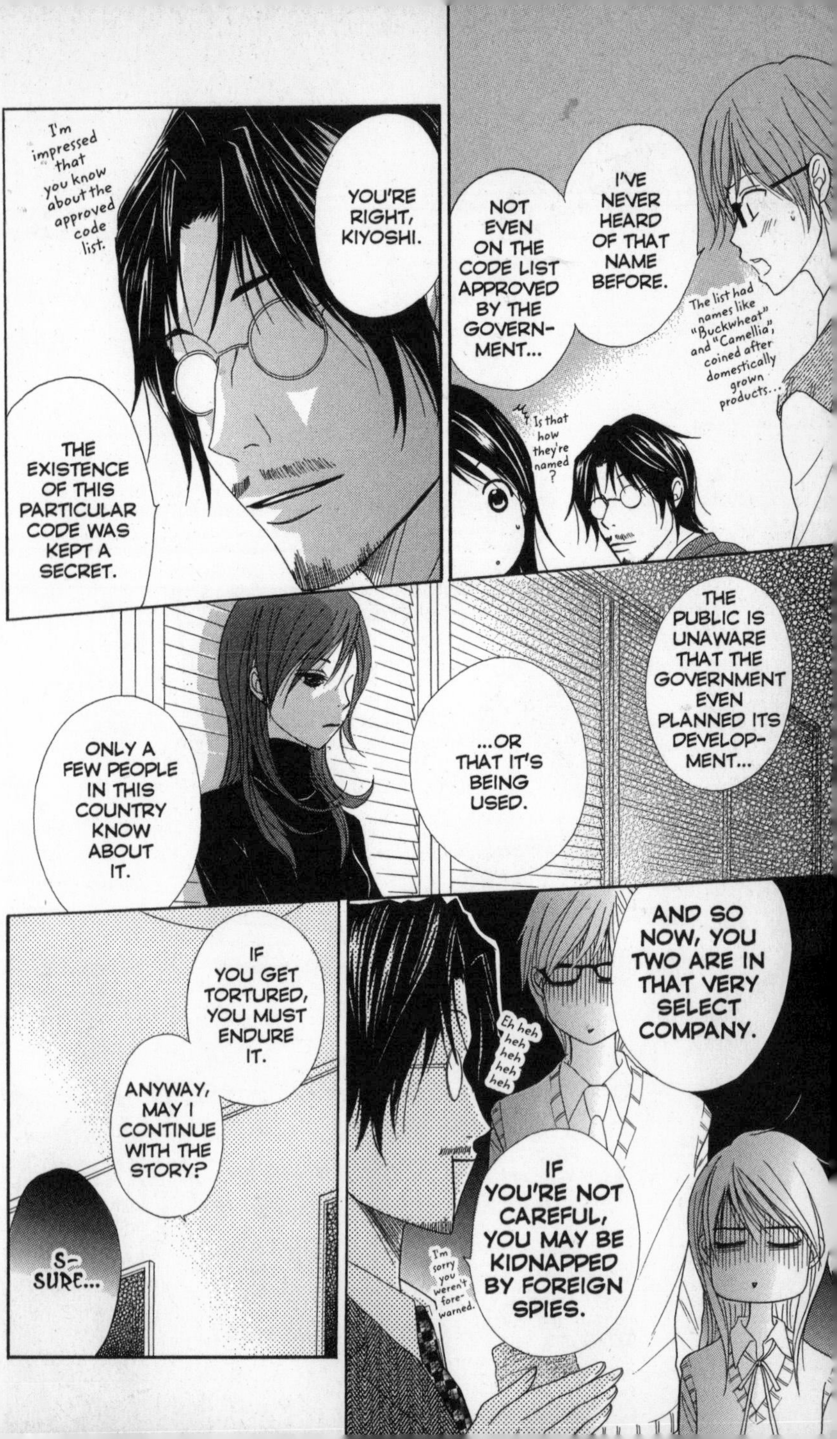
I'VE NEVER HEARD OF THAT NAME BEFORE.
NOT EVEN ON THE CODE LIST APPROVED BY THE GOVERNMENT...
The list had names like "Buckwheat" and "Camellia", coined after domestically grown products...
Is that how they're named?
YOU'RE RIGHT, KIYOSHI.
I'm impressed that you know about the approved code list.
THE EXISTENCE OF THIS PARTICULAR CODE WAS KEPT A SECRET.
THE PUBLIC IS UNAWARE THAT THE GOVERNMENT EVEN PLANNED ITS DEVELOPMENT...
...OR THAT IT'S BEING USED.
ONLY A FEW PEOPLE IN THIS COUNTRY KNOW ABOUT IT.
AND SO NOW, YOU TWO ARE IN THAT VERY SELECT COMPANY.
Eh heh heh heh heh heh
IF YOU'RE NOT CAREFUL, YOU MAY BE KIDNAPPED BY FOREIGN SPIES.
I'm sorry you weren't fore-warned.
IF YOU GET TORTURED, YOU MUST ENDURE IT.
ANYWAY, MAY I CONTINUE WITH THE STORY?
S-SURE...

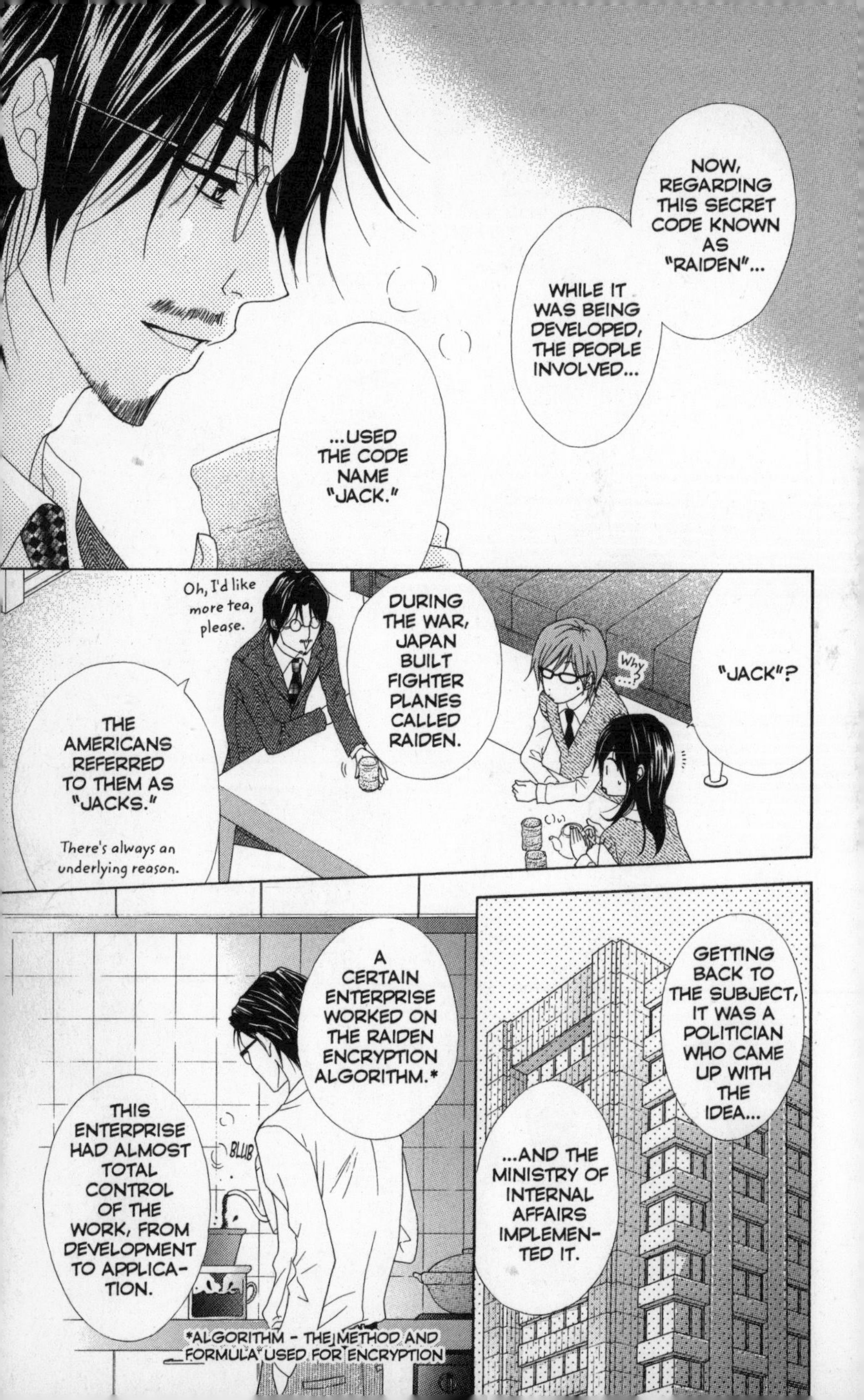
NOW, REGARDING THIS SECRET CODE KNOWN AS "RAIDEN"...
WHILE IT WAS BEING DEVELOPED, THE PEOPLE INVOLVED...
...USED THE CODE NAME "JACK."
"JACK"?
Why...?
DURING THE WAR, JAPAN BUILT FIGHTER PLANES CALLED RAIDEN.
Oh, I'd like more tea, please.
THE AMERICANS REFERRED TO THEM AS "JACKS."
There's always an underlying reason.
GETTING BACK TO THE SUBJECT, IT WAS A POLITICIAN WHO CAME UP WITH THE IDEA...
...AND THE MINISTRY OF INTERNAL AFFAIRS IMPLEMENTED IT.
A CERTAIN ENTERPRISE WORKED ON THE RAIDEN ENCRYPTION ALGORITHM.*
BLUB
THIS ENTERPRISE HAD ALMOST TOTAL CONTROL OF THE WORK, FROM DEVELOPMENT TO APPLICATION.
*ALGORITHM - THE METHOD AND FORMULA USED FOR ENCRYPTION

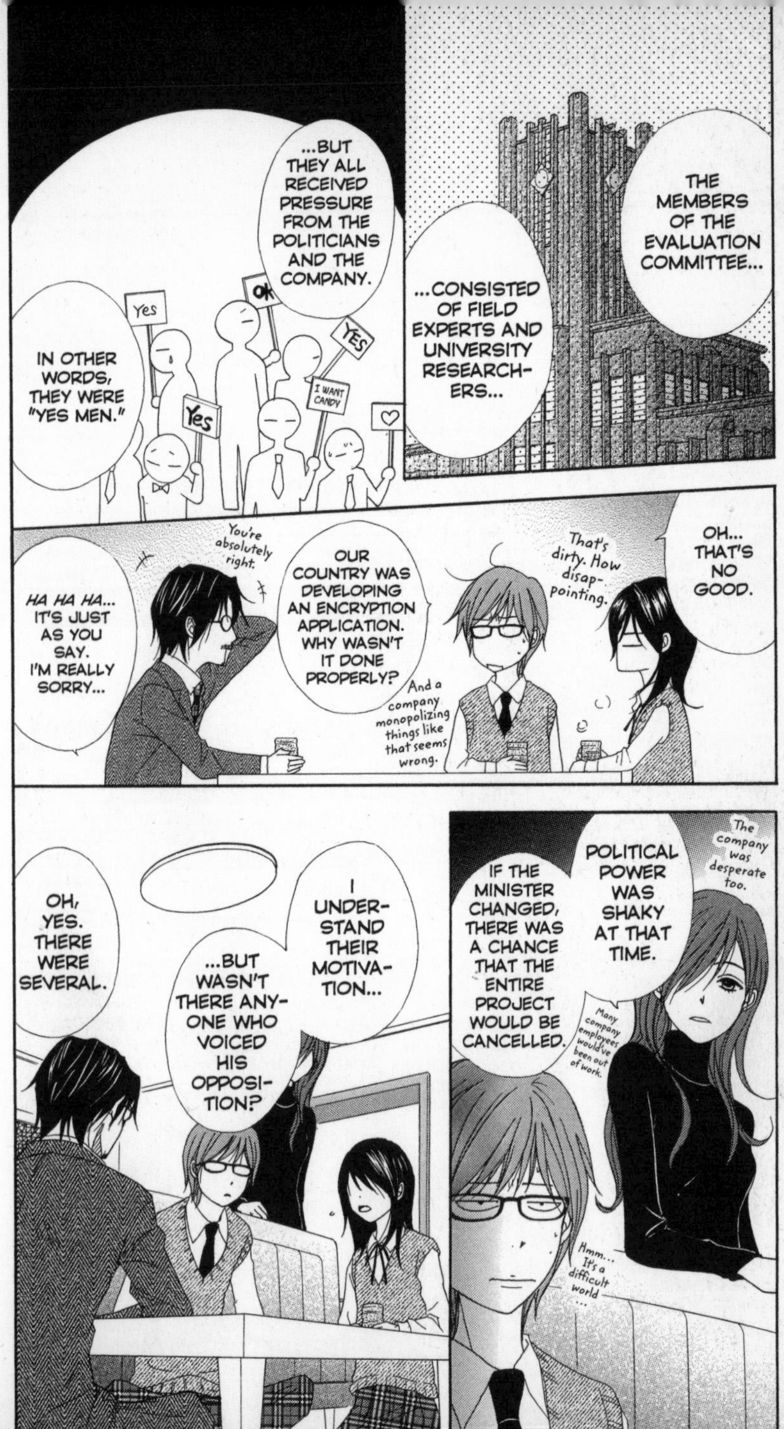
THE MEMBERS OF THE EVALUATION COMMITTEE...
...CONSISTED OF FIELD EXPERTS AND UNIVERSITY RESEARCHERS...
...BUT THEY ALL RECEIVED PRESSURE FROM THE POLITICIANS AND THE COMPANY.
OK
YES
Yes
I WANT CANDY
Yes
IN OTHER WORDS, THEY WERE "YES MEN."
OH... THAT'S NO GOOD.
That's dirty. How disappointing.
OUR COUNTRY WAS DEVELOPING AN ENCRYPTION APPLICATION. WHY WASN'T IT DONE PROPERLY?
And a company monopolizing things like that seems wrong.
You're absolutely right.
HA HA HA... IT'S JUST AS YOU SAY. I'M REALLY SORRY...
POLITICAL POWER WAS SHAKY AT THAT TIME.
The company was desperate too.
IF THE MINISTER CHANGED, THERE WAS A CHANCE THAT THE ENTIRE PROJECT WOULD BE CANCELLED.
Many company employees would've been out of work.
Hmm... It's a difficult world...
I UNDERSTAND THEIR MOTIVATION...
...BUT WASN'T THERE ANYONE WHO VOICED HIS OPPOSITION?
OH, YES. THERE WERE SEVERAL.

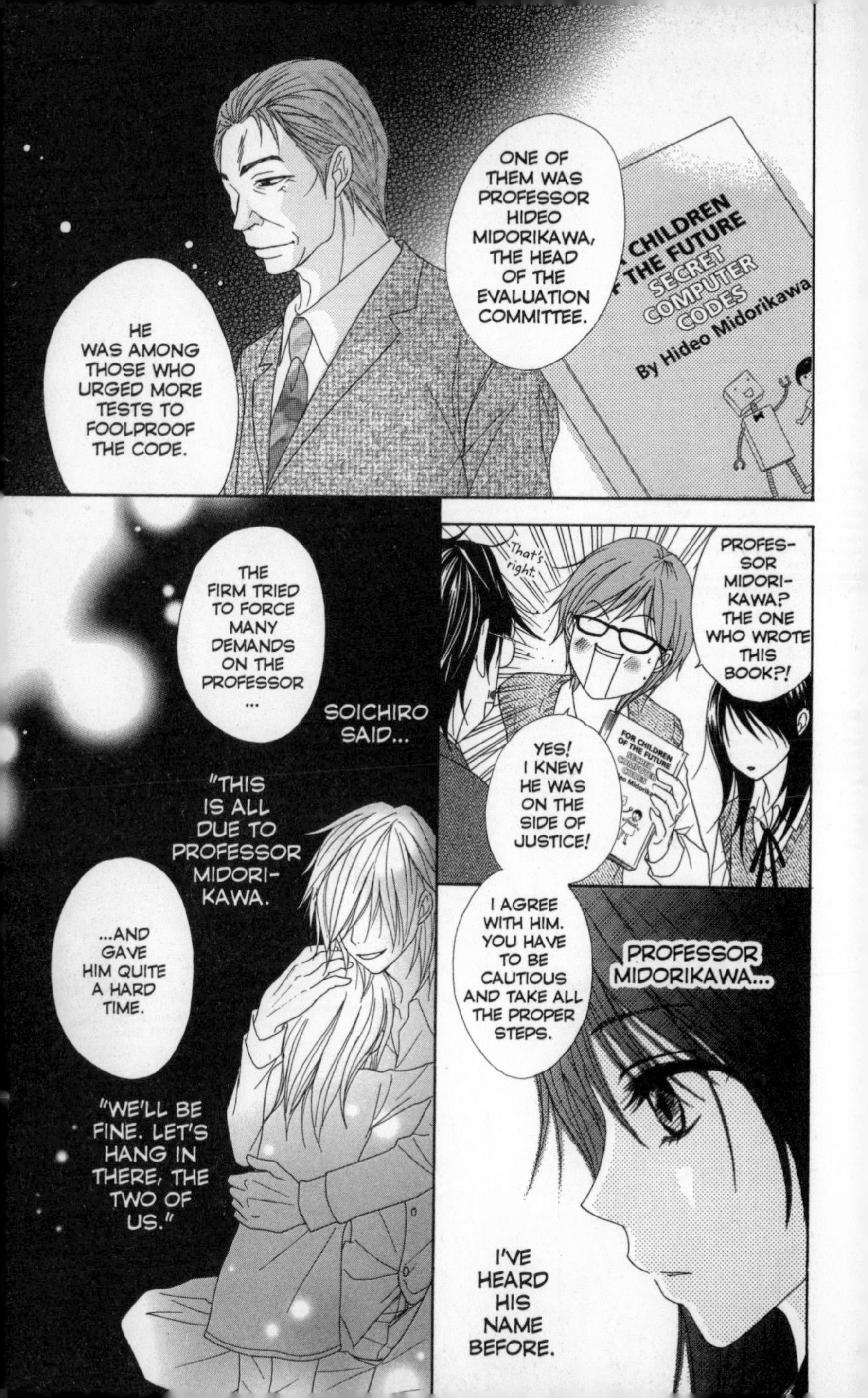
ONE OF THEM WAS PROFESSOR HIDEO MIDORIKAWA, THE HEAD OF THE EVALUATION COMMITTEE.
CHILDREN
THE FUTURE
SECRET COMPUTER CODES
By Hideo Midorikawa
HE WAS AMONG THOSE WHO URGED MORE TESTS TO FOOLPROOF THE CODE.
PROFESSOR MIDORIKAWA? THE ONE WHO WROTE THIS BOOK?!
That's right.
YES! I KNEW HE WAS ON THE SIDE OF JUSTICE!
FOR CHILDREN OF THE FUTURE
I AGREE WITH HIM. YOU HAVE TO BE CAUTIOUS AND TAKE ALL THE PROPER STEPS.
PROFESSOR MIDORIKAWA...
I'VE HEARD HIS NAME BEFORE.
THE FIRM TRIED TO FORCE MANY DEMANDS ON THE PROFESSOR ...
SOICHIRO SAID...
"THIS IS ALL DUE TO PROFESSOR MIDORIKAWA.
...AND GAVE HIM QUITE A HARD TIME.
"WE'LL BE FINE. LET'S HANG IN THERE, THE TWO OF US."

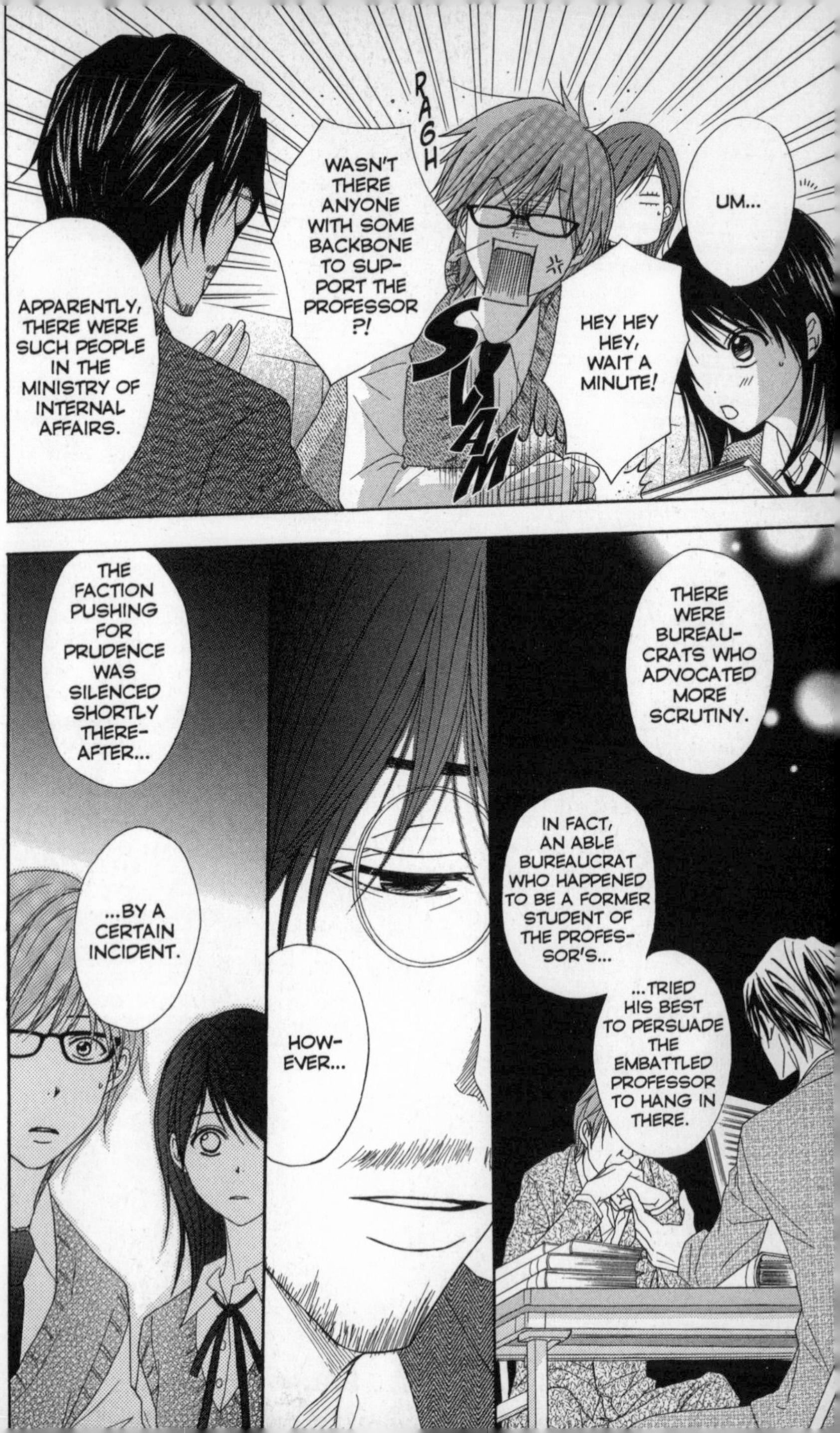
UM...
HEY HEY HEY, WAIT A MINUTE!
RAGH
WASN'T THERE ANYONE WITH SOME BACKBONE TO SUPPORT THE PROFESSOR?!
SLAM
APPARENTLY, THERE WERE SUCH PEOPLE IN THE MINISTRY OF INTERNAL AFFAIRS.
THERE WERE BUREAUCRATS WHO ADVOCATED MORE SCRUTINY.
IN FACT, AN ABLE BUREAUCRAT WHO HAPPENED TO BE A FORMER STUDENT OF THE PROFESSOR'S...
...TRIED HIS BEST TO PERSUADE THE EMBATTLED PROFESSOR TO HANG IN THERE.
HOWEVER...
THE FACTION PUSHING FOR PRUDENCE WAS SILENCED SHORTLY THEREAFTER...
...BY A CERTAIN INCIDENT.

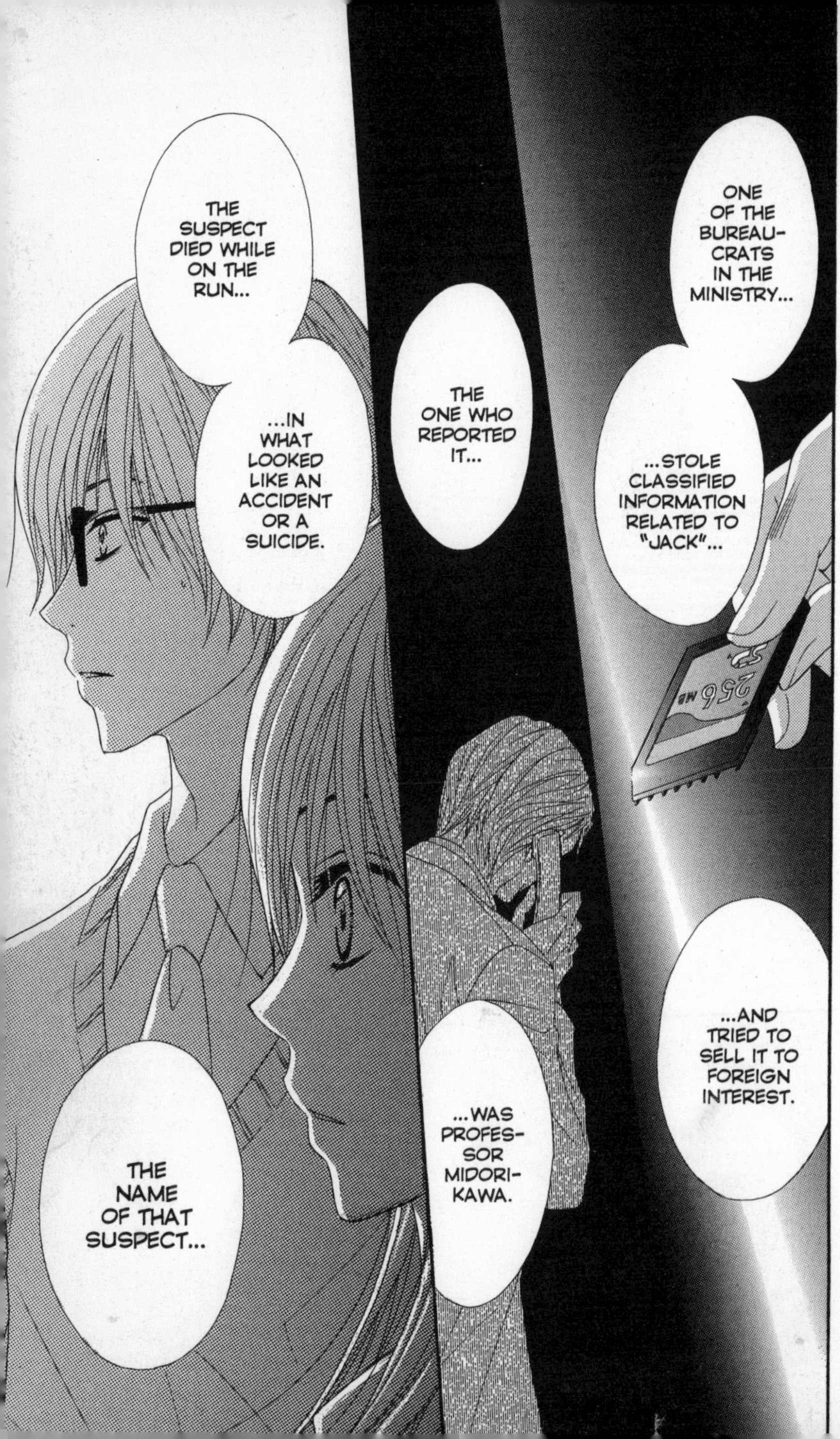
ONE OF THE BUREAUCRATS IN THE MINISTRY...
...STOLE CLASSIFIED INFORMATION RELATED TO "JACK"...
...AND TRIED TO SELL IT TO FOREIGN INTEREST.
THE ONE WHO REPORTED IT...
...WAS PROFESSOR MIDORIKAWA.
THE SUSPECT DIED WHILE ON THE RUN...
...IN WHAT LOOKED LIKE AN ACCIDENT OR A SUICIDE.
THE NAME OF THAT SUSPECT...

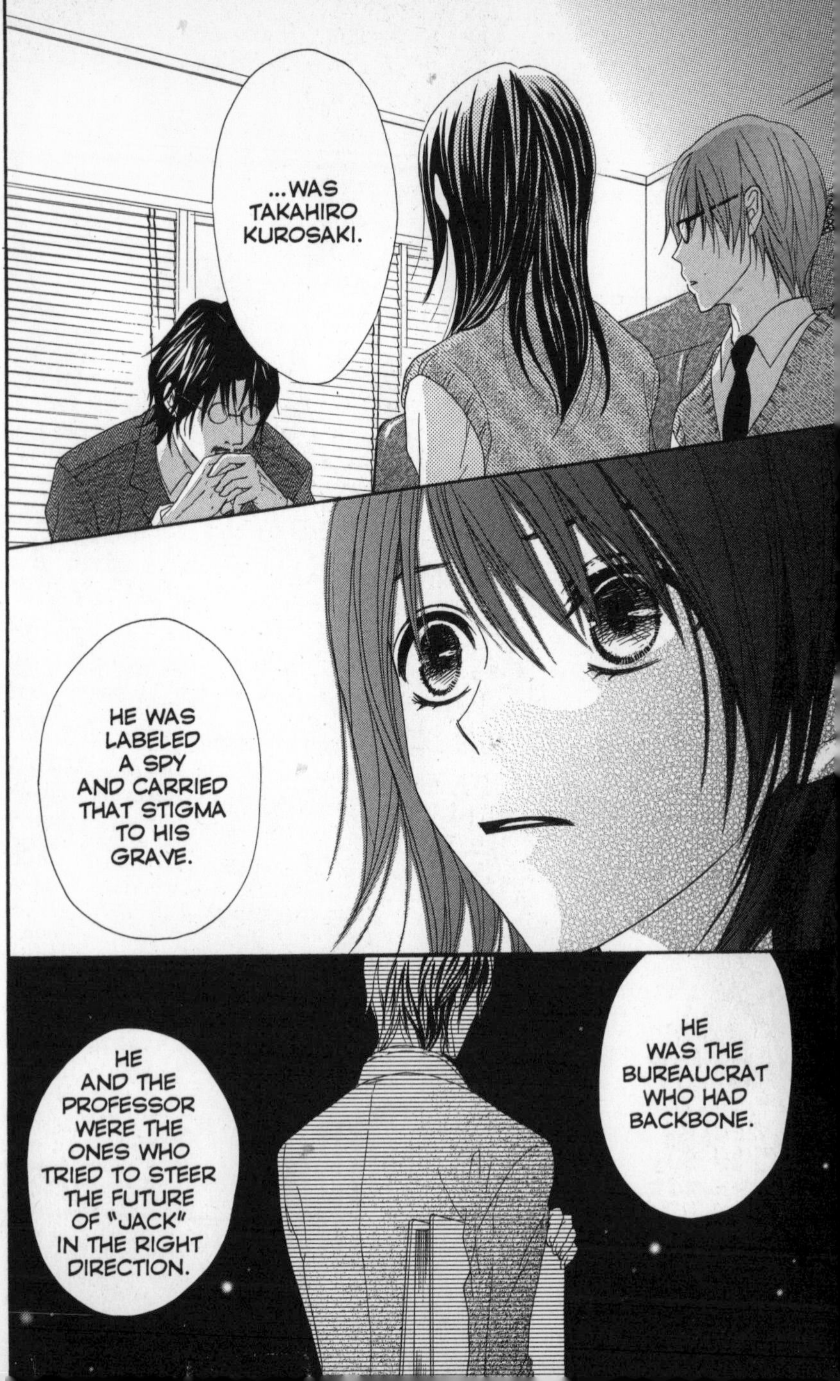
...WAS TAKAHIRO KUROSAKI.
HE WAS LABELED A SPY AND CARRIED THAT STIGMA TO HIS GRAVE.
HE WAS THE BUREAUCRAT WHO HAD BACKBONE.
HE AND THE PROFESSOR WERE THE ONES WHO TRIED TO STEER THE FUTURE OF "JACK" IN THE RIGHT DIRECTION.

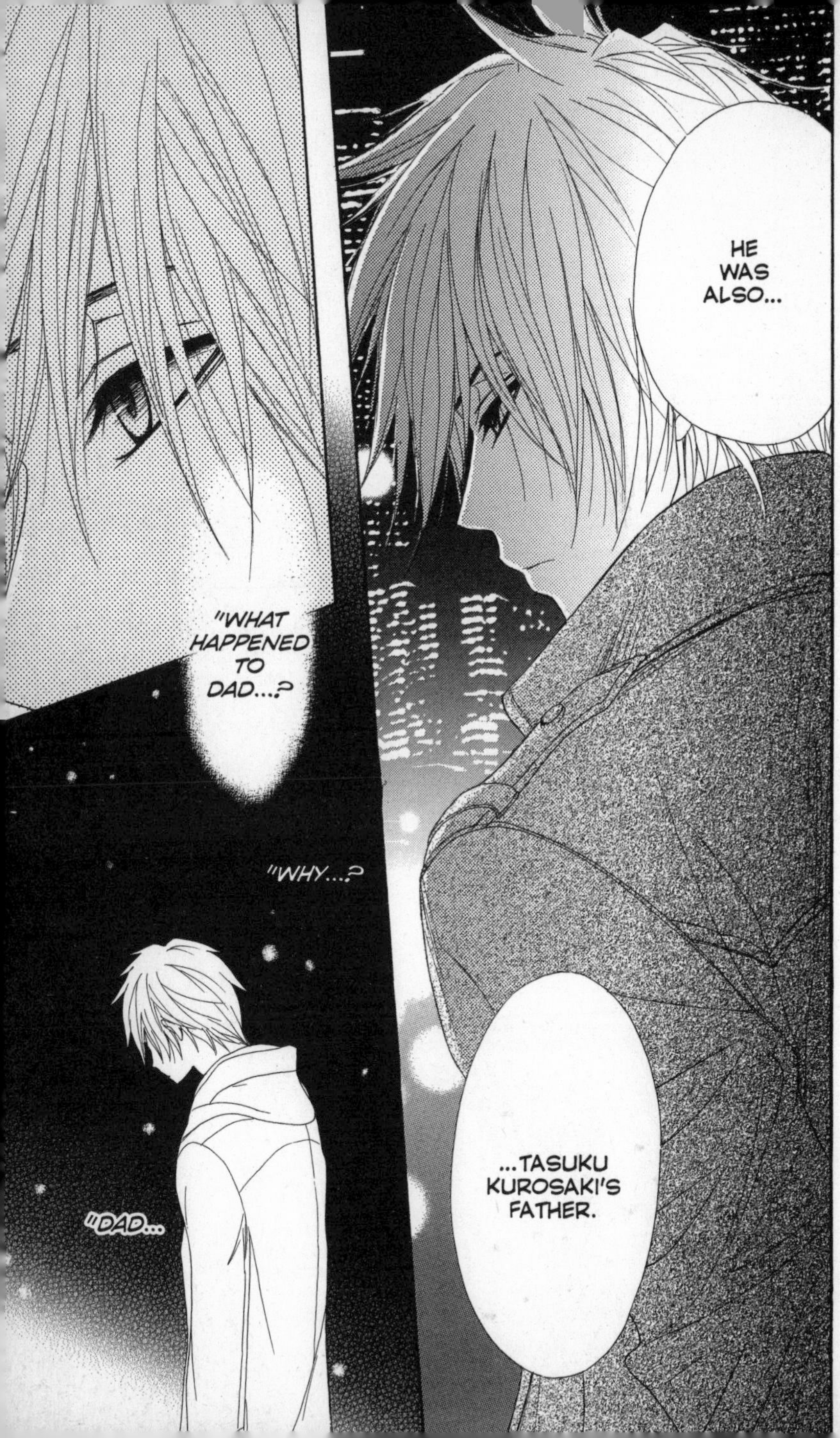
HE WAS ALSO...
...TASUKU KUROSAKI'S FATHER.
"WHAT HAPPENED TO DAD...?
"WHY...?
"DAD...

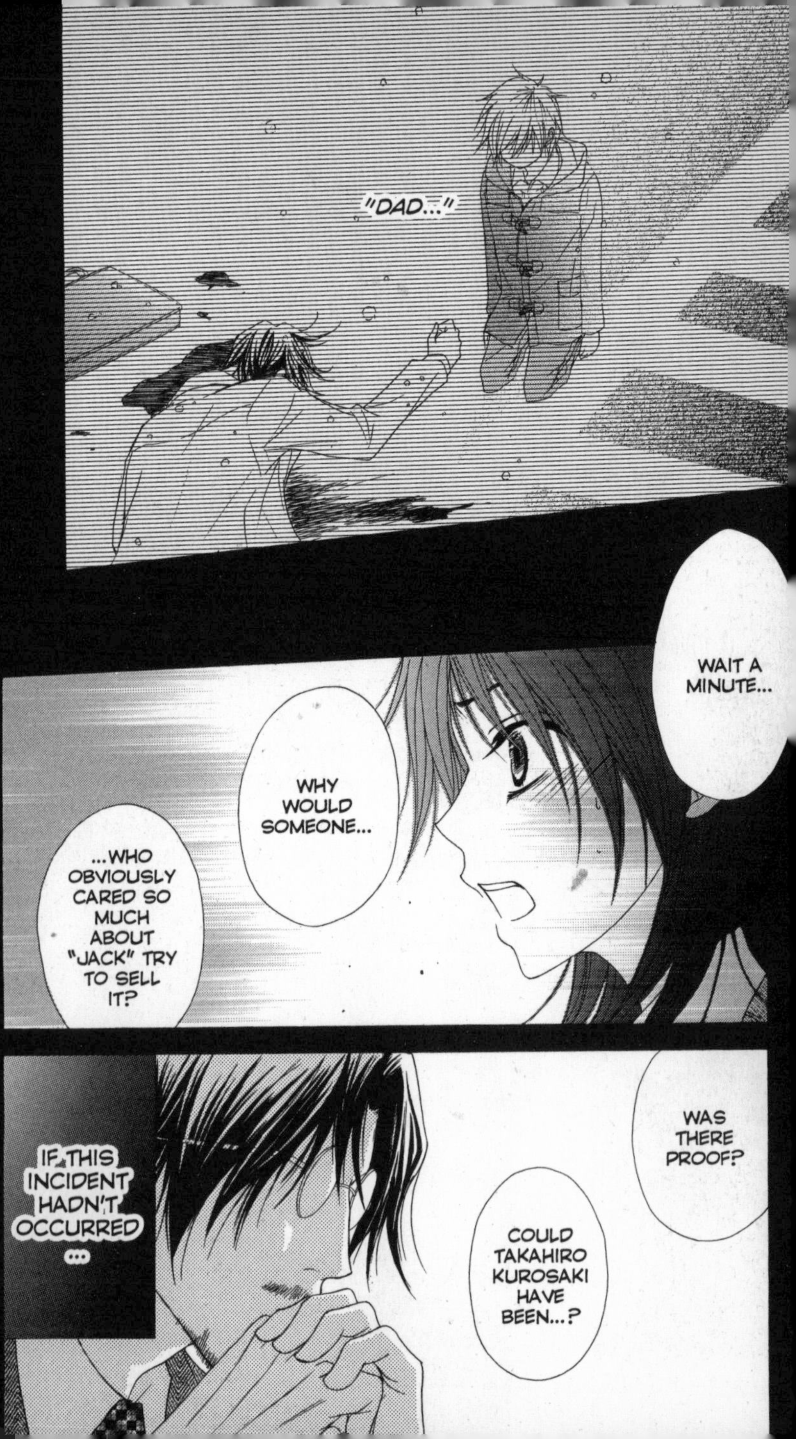
"DAD..."
WAIT A MINUTE...
WHY WOULD SOMEONE...
...WHO OBVIOUSLY CARED SO MUCH ABOUT "JACK" TRY TO SELL IT?
WAS THERE PROOF?
COULD TAKAHIRO KUROSAKI HAVE BEEN...?
IF THIS INCIDENT HADN'T OCCURRED...

YOU'RE RIGHT. SEVERAL YEARS AFTER THAT, STARTING WITH THE MINISTRY OF INTERNAL AFFAIRS...
...THOSE CONNECTED TO "JACK" CAME UNDER A CRACKER'S ATTACK.
...KUROSAKI WOULD HAVE REMAINED JUST THE WAY HE WAS.
AND THIS UNFORGIVABLE SIN...
IN ORDER TO INVESTIGATE THE CIRCUMSTANCES OF HIS FATHER'S DEATH...
...HE BECAME THE HACKER KNOWN AS "DAISY."
...WOULD NEVER HAVE BEEN COMMITTED.

<SOME BAD LOVEY-DOVEY SKETCHES NO. ②>

I HAVE NO IDEA WHY ALL THE SKETCHES I DID ON THIS DAY TOOK ON THE THEME OF "IF TERU AND KUROSAKI WENT TO THE BEACH, HOW LOVEY-DOVEY WOULD THEY GET?" IT'S A MYSTERY TO ME. PERHAPS IT'S BECAUSE I DREW THEM WHEN SUMMER WAS JUST AROUND THE CORNER.

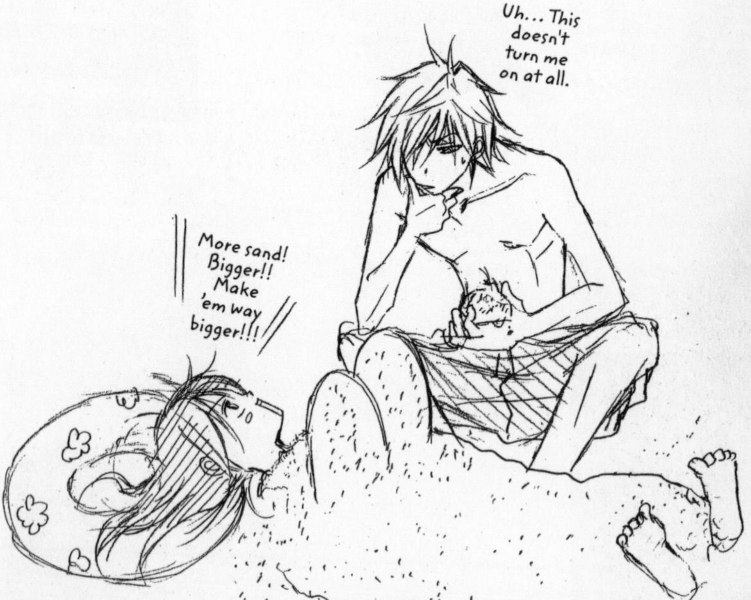
Uh... This doesn't turn me on at all.
More sand! Bigger!! Make 'em way bigger!!!

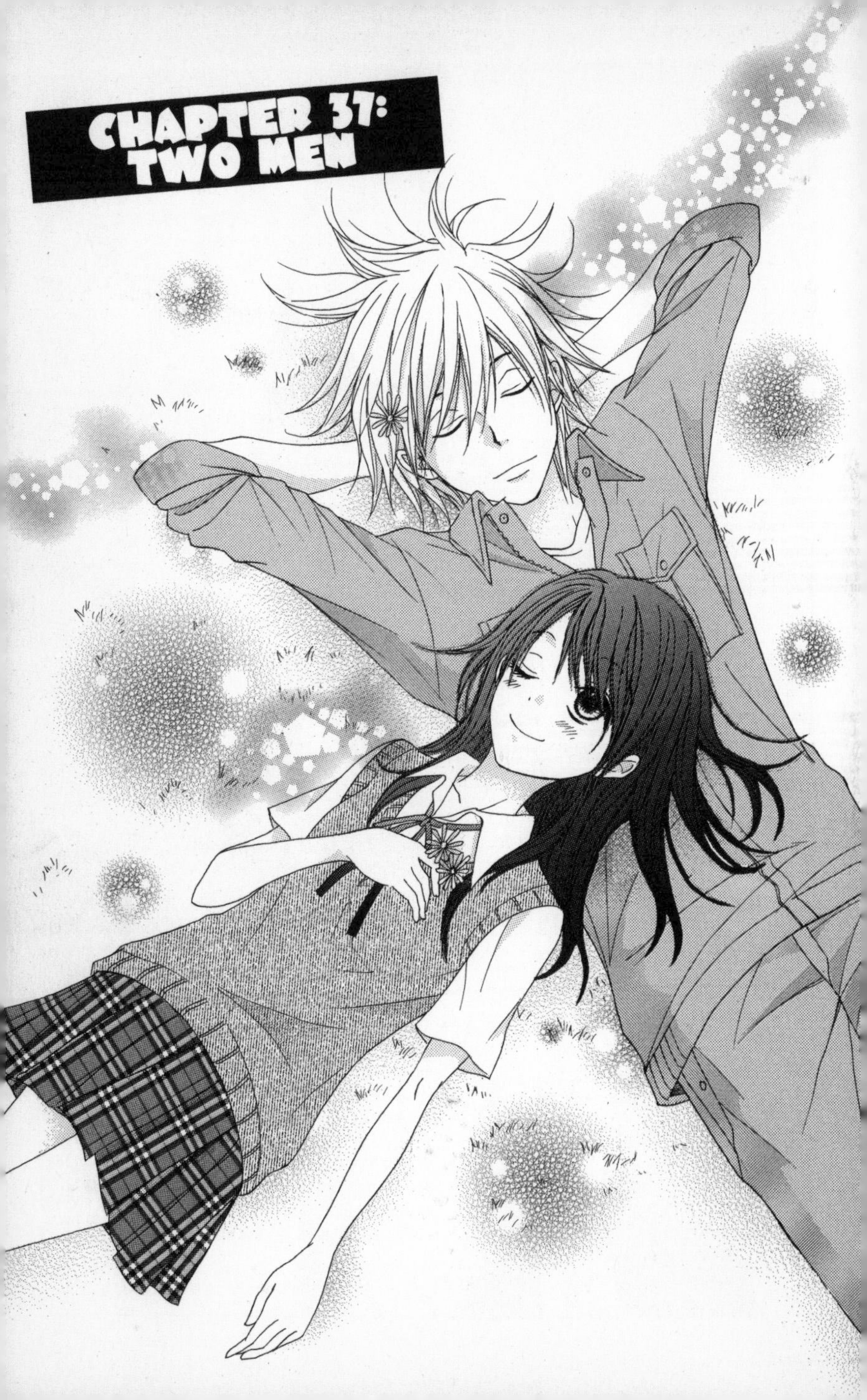
CHAPTER 37:
TWO MEN

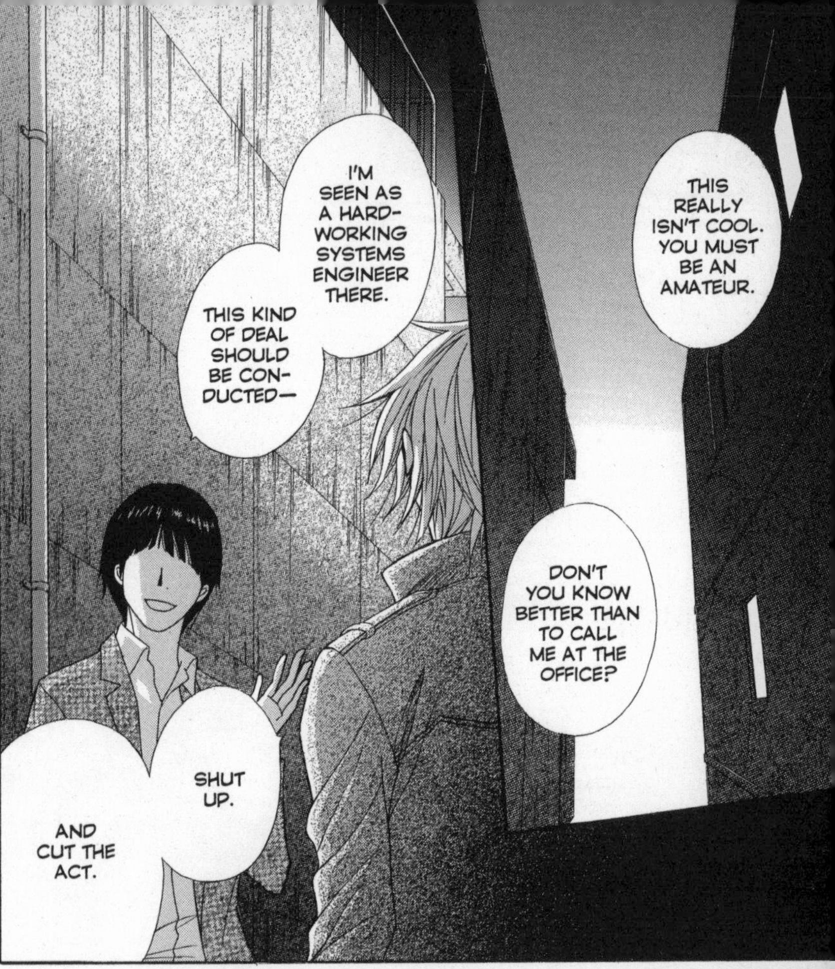
THIS REALLY ISN'T COOL. YOU MUST BE AN AMATEUR.
DON'T YOU KNOW BETTER THAN TO CALL ME AT THE OFFICE?
I'M SEEN AS A HARD-WORKING SYSTEMS ENGINEER THERE.
THIS KIND OF DEAL SHOULD BE CON-DUCTED—
SHUT UP.
AND CUT THE ACT.

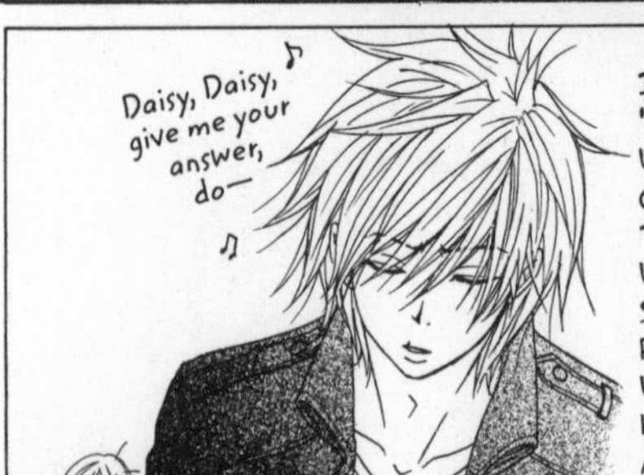
Daisy, Daisy, give me your answer, do—

IN CHAPTER 36, KUROSAKI SINGS "DAISY BELL," AN OLD BRITISH SONG. IT WAS USED IN THE MOVIE, *2001: A SPACE ODYSSEY*.
THAT ASIDE, I HAVE NO IDEA WHY KUROSAKI SUDDENLY STARTED SINGING THIS SONG ALL BY HIMSELF. HE'S A REALLY FUNNY GUY.
WHEN I THINK ABOUT IT, HE STARTED HUMMING THE THEME FROM A●PA●MA● A WHILE BACK. MAYBE IT'S A WEIRD HABIT HE PICKED UP FROM HIS DAD.

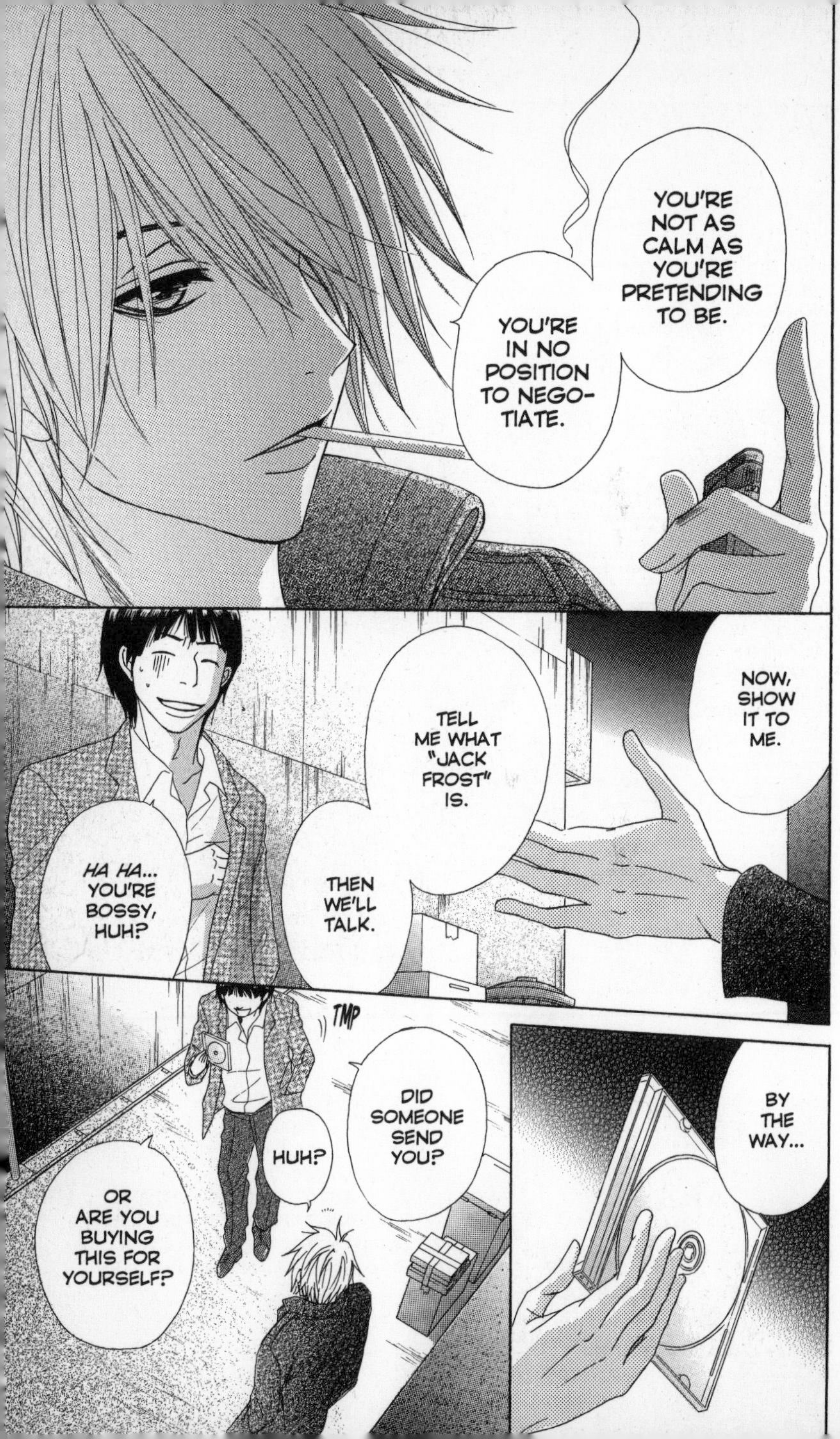
YOU'RE NOT AS CALM AS YOU'RE PRETENDING TO BE.
YOU'RE IN NO POSITION TO NEGO-TIATE.
NOW, SHOW IT TO ME.
TELL ME WHAT "JACK FROST" IS.
THEN WE'LL TALK.
HA HA... YOU'RE BOSSY, HUH?
BY THE WAY...
TMP
DID SOMEONE SEND YOU?
HUH?
OR ARE YOU BUYING THIS FOR YOURSELF?

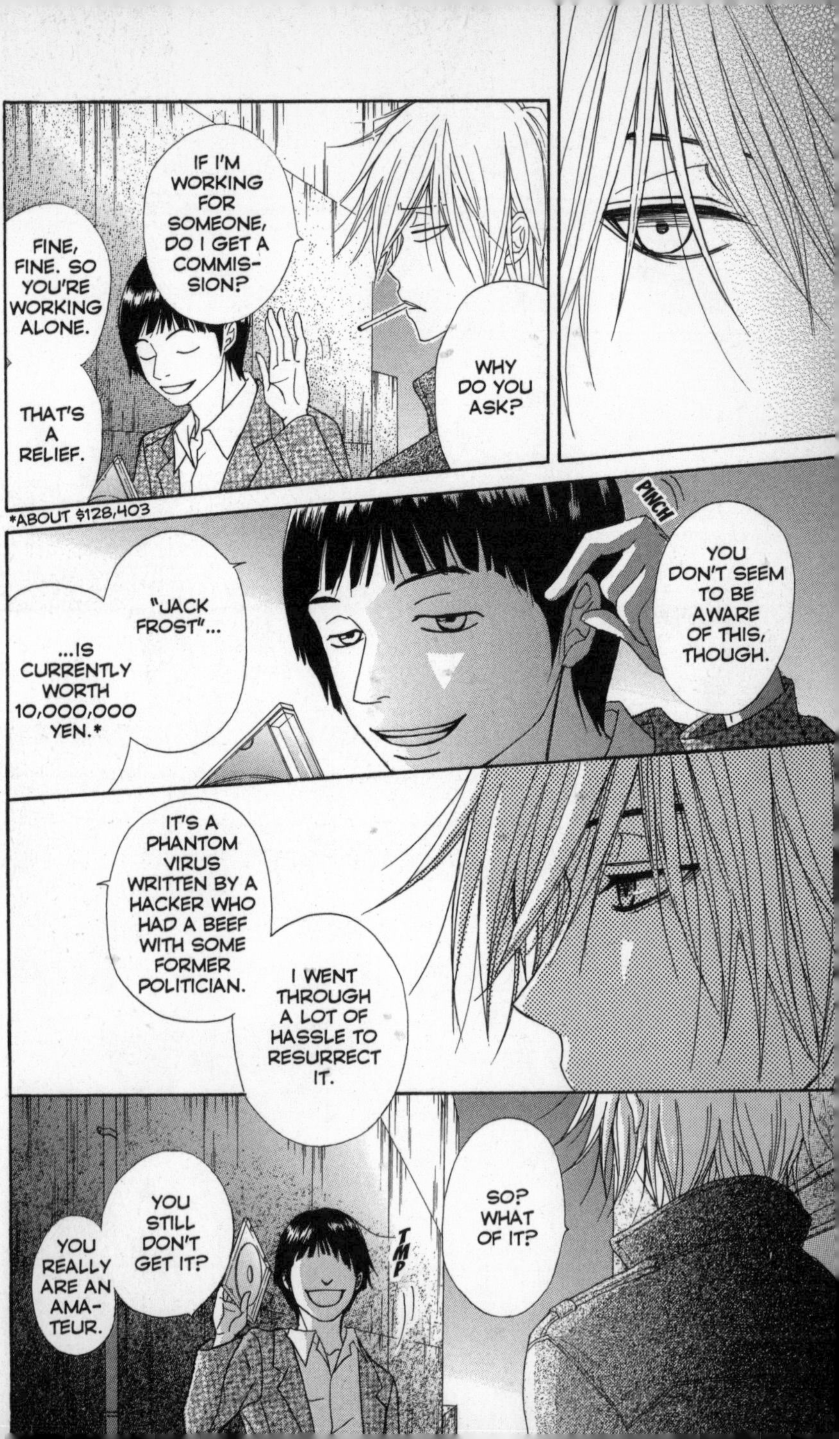
IF I'M WORKING FOR SOMEONE, DO I GET A COMMISSION?
WHY DO YOU ASK?
FINE, FINE. SO YOU'RE WORKING ALONE.
THAT'S A RELIEF.
PINCH
YOU DON'T SEEM TO BE AWARE OF THIS, THOUGH.
"JACK FROST"...
...IS CURRENTLY WORTH 10,000,000 YEN.*
IT'S A PHANTOM VIRUS WRITTEN BY A HACKER WHO HAD A BEEF WITH SOME FORMER POLITICIAN.
I WENT THROUGH A LOT OF HASSLE TO RESURRECT IT.
SO? WHAT OF IT?
TMP
YOU STILL DON'T GET IT?
YOU REALLY ARE AN AMATEUR.
*ABOUT $128,403

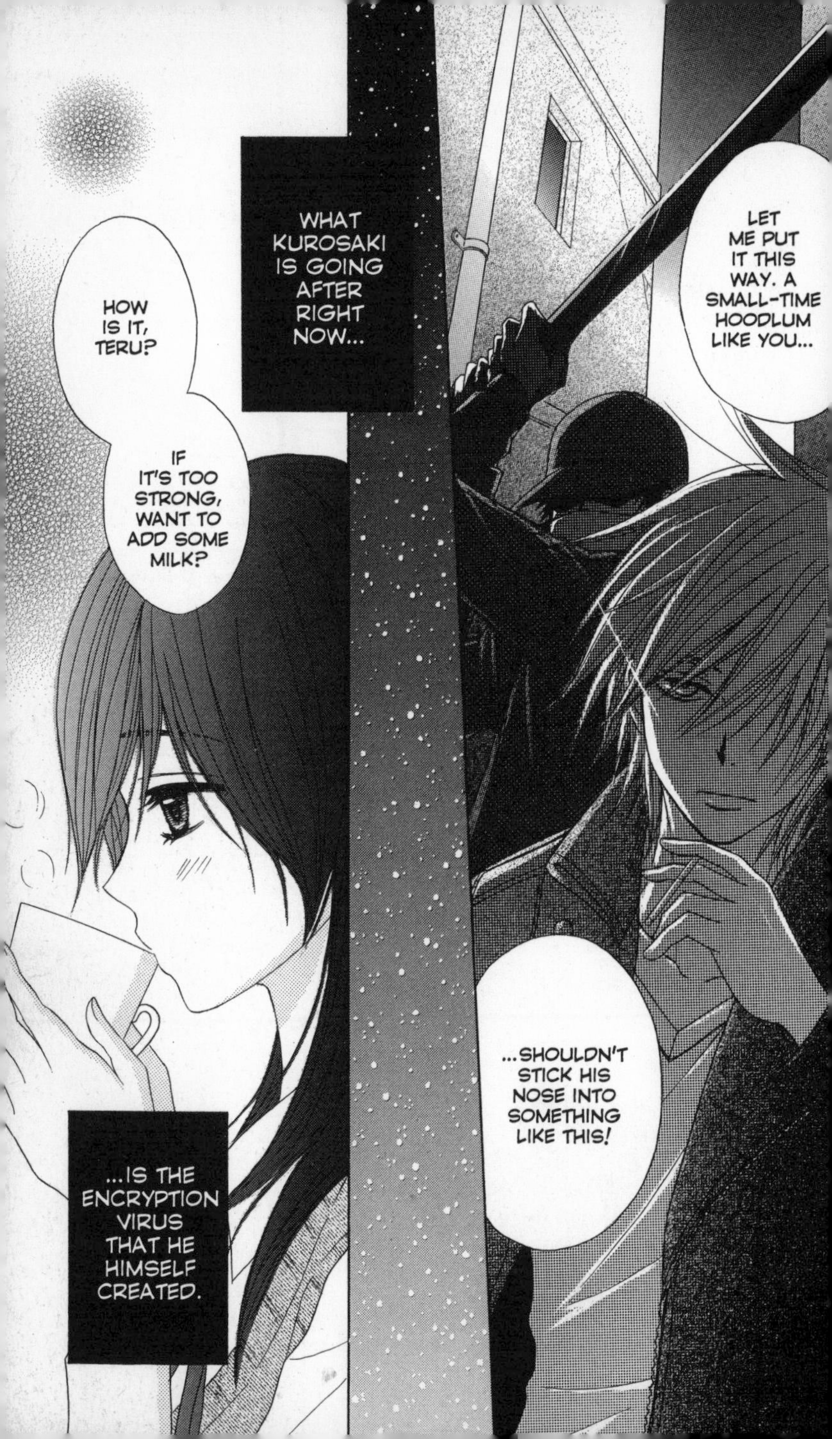
LET ME PUT IT THIS WAY. A SMALL-TIME HOODLUM LIKE YOU...
...SHOULDN'T STICK HIS NOSE INTO SOMETHING LIKE THIS!
WHAT KUROSAKI IS GOING AFTER RIGHT NOW...
HOW IS IT, TERU?
IF IT'S TOO STRONG, WANT TO ADD SOME MILK?
...IS THE ENCRYPTION VIRUS THAT HE HIMSELF CREATED.

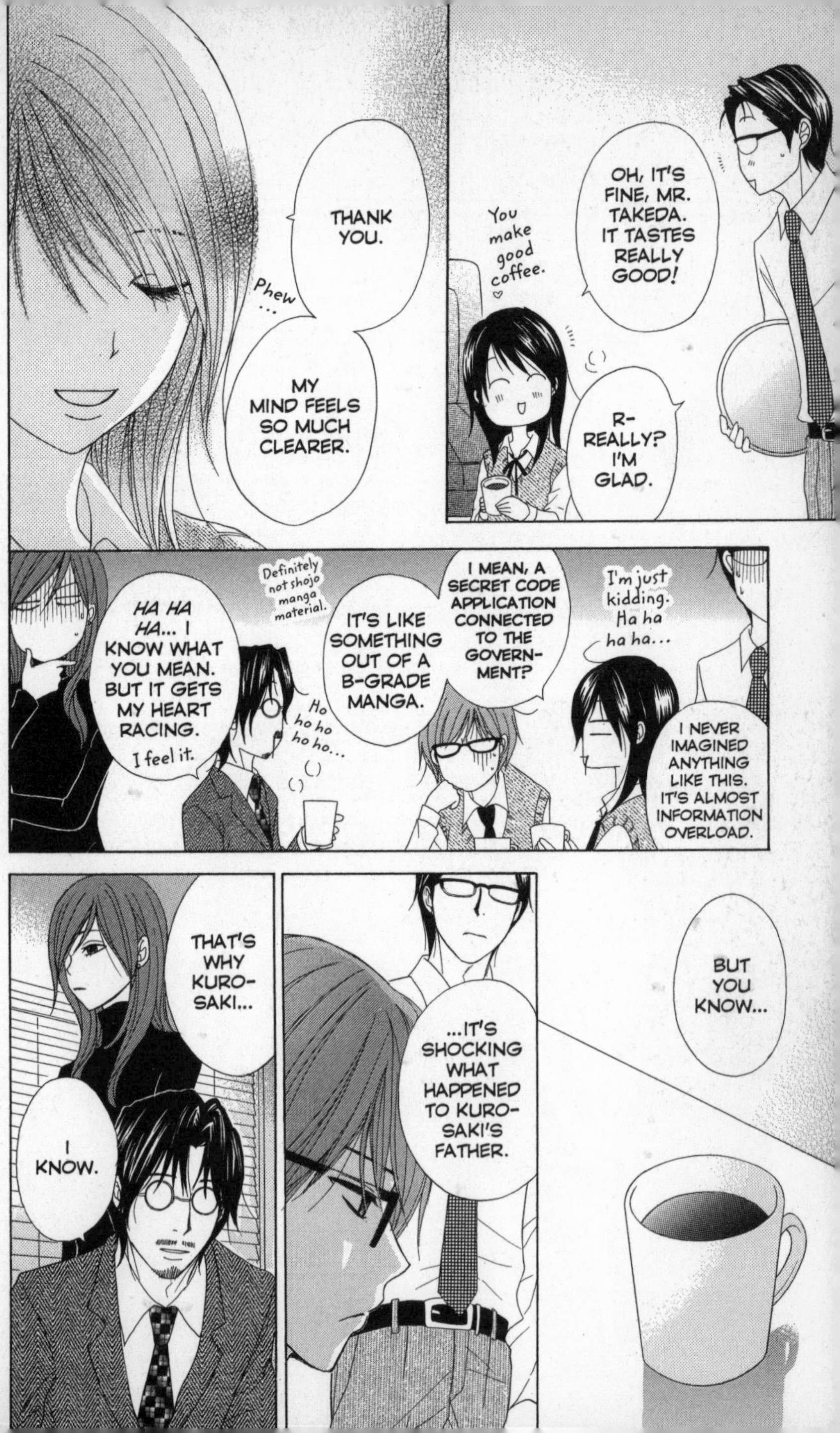
OH, IT'S FINE, MR. TAKEDA. IT TASTES REALLY GOOD!
You make good coffee. ♡
R-REALLY? I'M GLAD.
THANK YOU.
Phew...
MY MIND FEELS SO MUCH CLEARER.
I NEVER IMAGINED ANYTHING LIKE THIS. IT'S ALMOST INFORMATION OVERLOAD.
I MEAN, A SECRET CODE APPLICATION CONNECTED TO THE GOVERNMENT?
I'm just kidding. Ha ha ha ha...
IT'S LIKE SOMETHING OUT OF A B-GRADE MANGA.
Definitely not shojo manga material.
Ho ho ho ho ho...
HA HA HA... I KNOW WHAT YOU MEAN. BUT IT GETS MY HEART RACING.
I feel it.
BUT YOU KNOW...
...IT'S SHOCKING WHAT HAPPENED TO KURO-SAKI'S FATHER.
THAT'S WHY KURO-SAKI...
I KNOW.

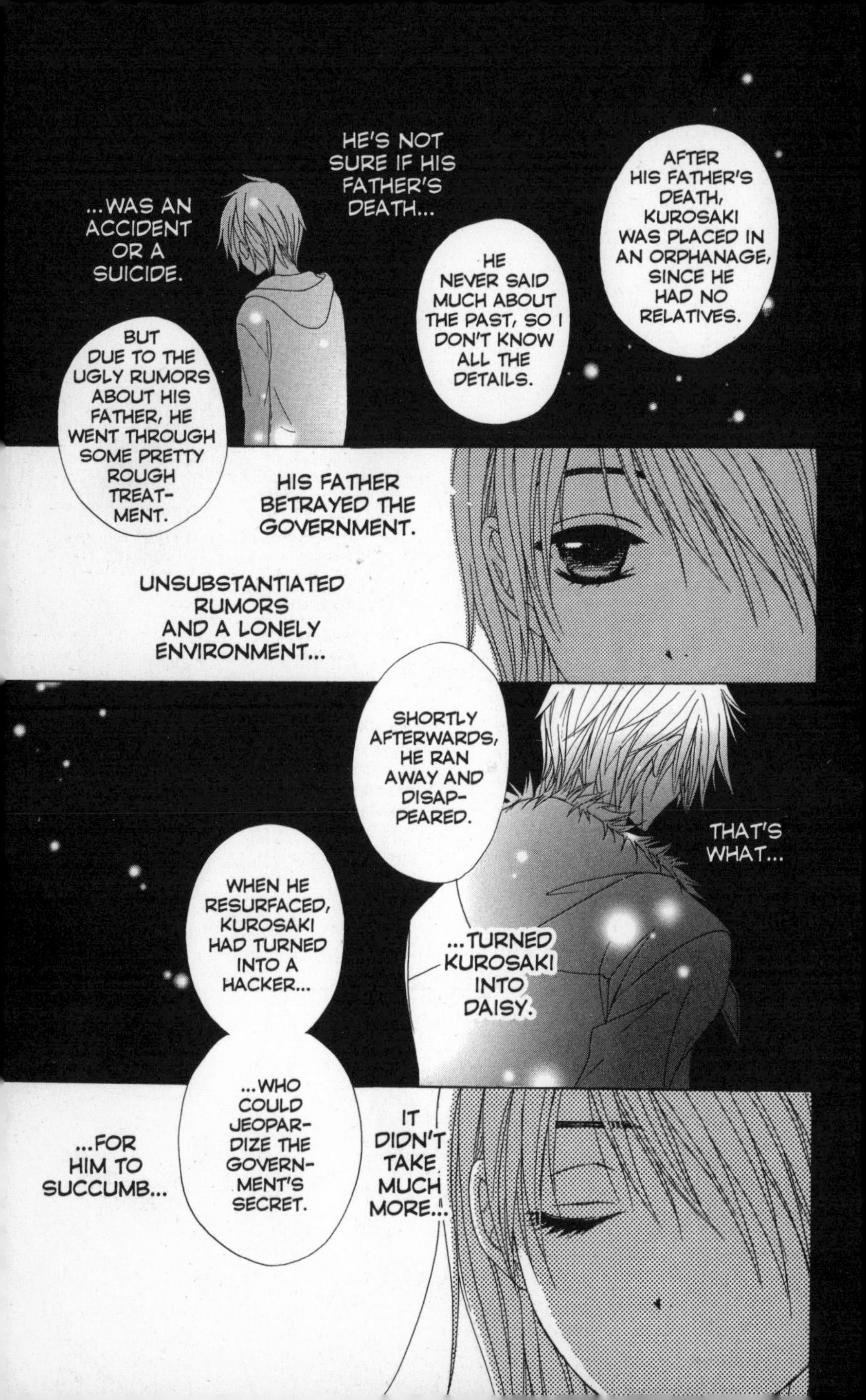

AFTER HIS FATHER'S DEATH, KUROSAKI WAS PLACED IN AN ORPHANAGE, SINCE HE HAD NO RELATIVES.
HE NEVER SAID MUCH ABOUT THE PAST, SO I DON'T KNOW ALL THE DETAILS.
HE'S NOT SURE IF HIS FATHER'S DEATH...
...WAS AN ACCIDENT OR A SUICIDE.
BUT DUE TO THE UGLY RUMORS ABOUT HIS FATHER, HE WENT THROUGH SOME PRETTY ROUGH TREAT-MENT.
HIS FATHER BETRAYED THE GOVERNMENT.
UNSUBSTANTIATED RUMORS AND A LONELY ENVIRONMENT...
SHORTLY AFTERWARDS, HE RAN AWAY AND DISAP-PEARED.
WHEN HE RESURFACED, KUROSAKI HAD TURNED INTO A HACKER...
...WHO COULD JEOPAR-DIZE THE GOVERN-MENT'S SECRET.
THAT'S WHAT...
...TURNED KUROSAKI INTO DAISY.
IT DIDN'T TAKE MUCH MORE...
...FOR HIM TO SUCCUMB...

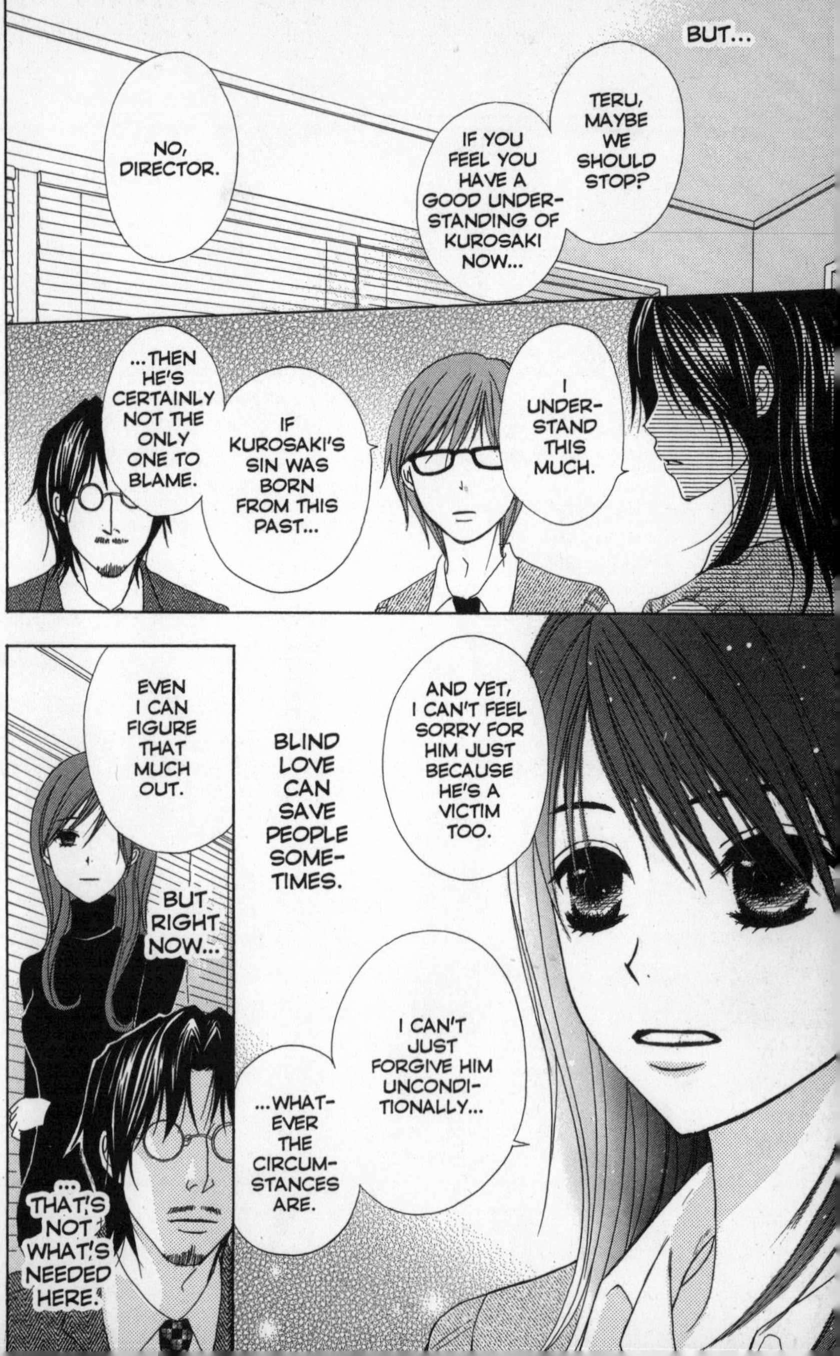
BUT...
TERU, MAYBE WE SHOULD STOP?
IF YOU FEEL YOU HAVE A GOOD UNDER-STANDING OF KUROSAKI NOW...
NO, DIRECTOR.
I UNDER-STAND THIS MUCH.
IF KUROSAKI'S SIN WAS BORN FROM THIS PAST...
...THEN HE'S CERTAINLY NOT THE ONLY ONE TO BLAME.
AND YET, I CAN'T FEEL SORRY FOR HIM JUST BECAUSE HE'S A VICTIM TOO.
BLIND LOVE CAN SAVE PEOPLE SOME-TIMES.
EVEN I CAN FIGURE THAT MUCH OUT.
BUT RIGHT NOW...
I CAN'T JUST FORGIVE HIM UNCONDI-TIONALLY...
...WHAT-EVER THE CIRCUM-STANCES ARE.
...THAT'S NOT WHAT'S NEEDED HERE.

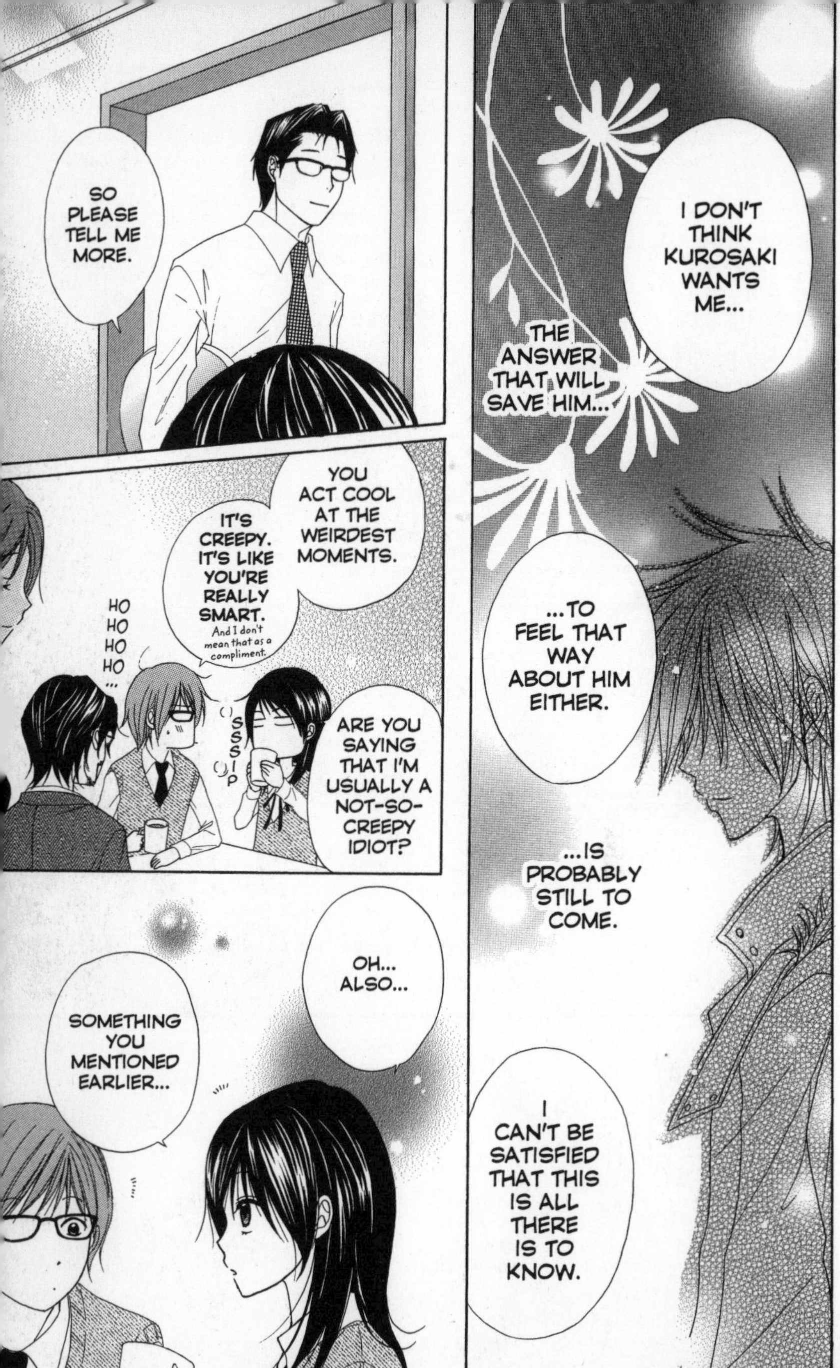
I DON'T THINK KUROSAKI WANTS ME...
THE ANSWER THAT WILL SAVE HIM...
...TO FEEL THAT WAY ABOUT HIM EITHER.
...IS PROBABLY STILL TO COME.
I CAN'T BE SATISFIED THAT THIS IS ALL THERE IS TO KNOW.
SO PLEASE TELL ME MORE.
YOU ACT COOL AT THE WEIRDEST MOMENTS.
IT'S CREEPY. IT'S LIKE YOU'RE REALLY SMART.
And I don't mean that as a compliment.
HO HO HO HO...
SSSIP
ARE YOU SAYING THAT I'M USUALLY A NOT-SO-CREEPY IDIOT?
OH... ALSO...
SOMETHING YOU MENTIONED EARLIER...

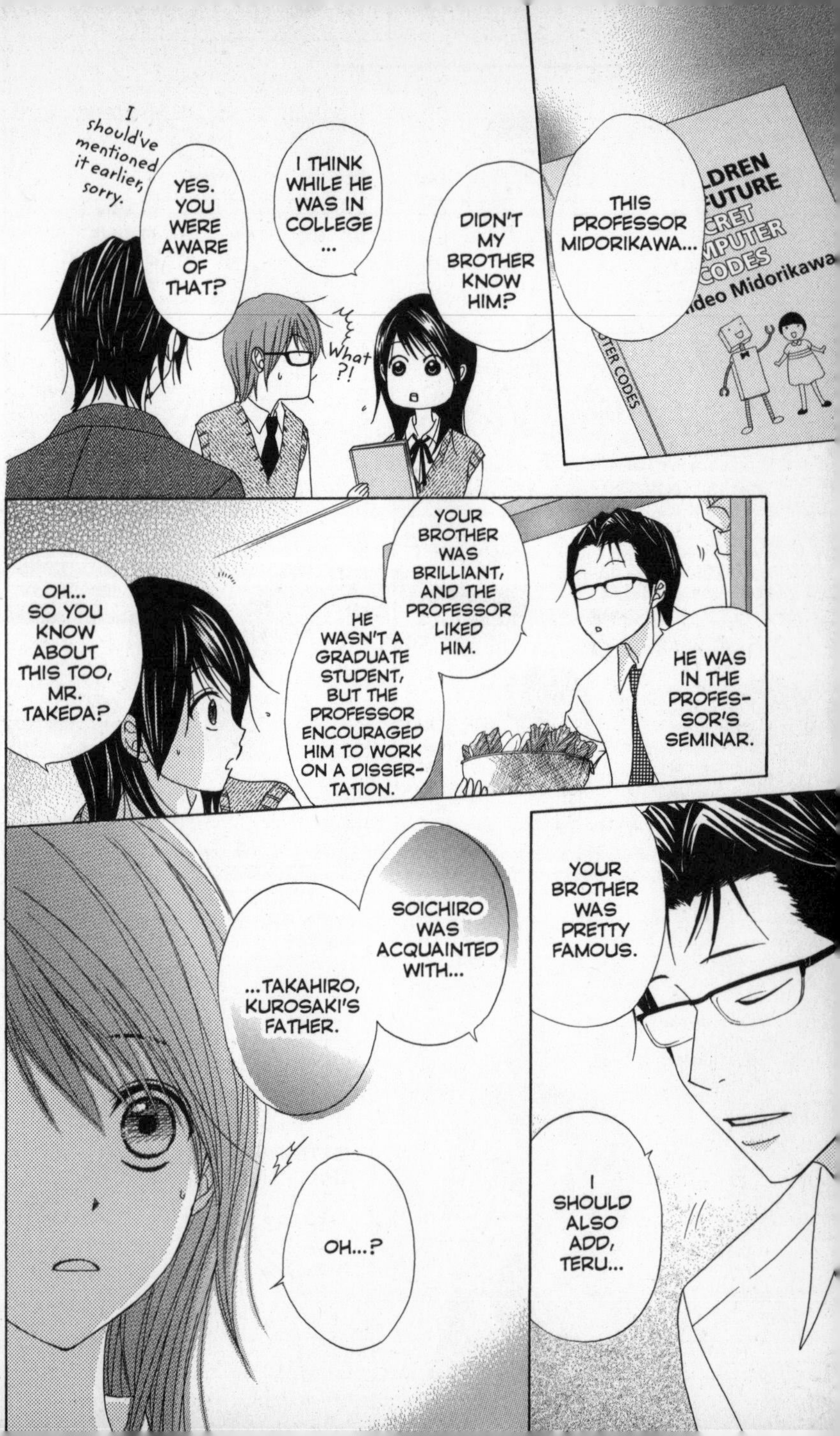
THIS PROFESSOR MIDORIKAWA...
DIDN'T MY BROTHER KNOW HIM?
I THINK WHILE HE WAS IN COLLEGE ...
What ?!
YES. YOU WERE AWARE OF THAT?
I should've mentioned it earlier, sorry.
HE WAS IN THE PROFES-SOR'S SEMINAR.
YOUR BROTHER WAS BRILLIANT, AND THE PROFESSOR LIKED HIM.
HE WASN'T A GRADUATE STUDENT, BUT THE PROFESSOR ENCOURAGED HIM TO WORK ON A DISSER-TATION.
OH... SO YOU KNOW ABOUT THIS TOO, MR. TAKEDA?
YOUR BROTHER WAS PRETTY FAMOUS.
I SHOULD ALSO ADD, TERU...
SOICHIRO WAS ACQUAINTED WITH...
...TAKAHIRO, KUROSAKI'S FATHER.
OH...?

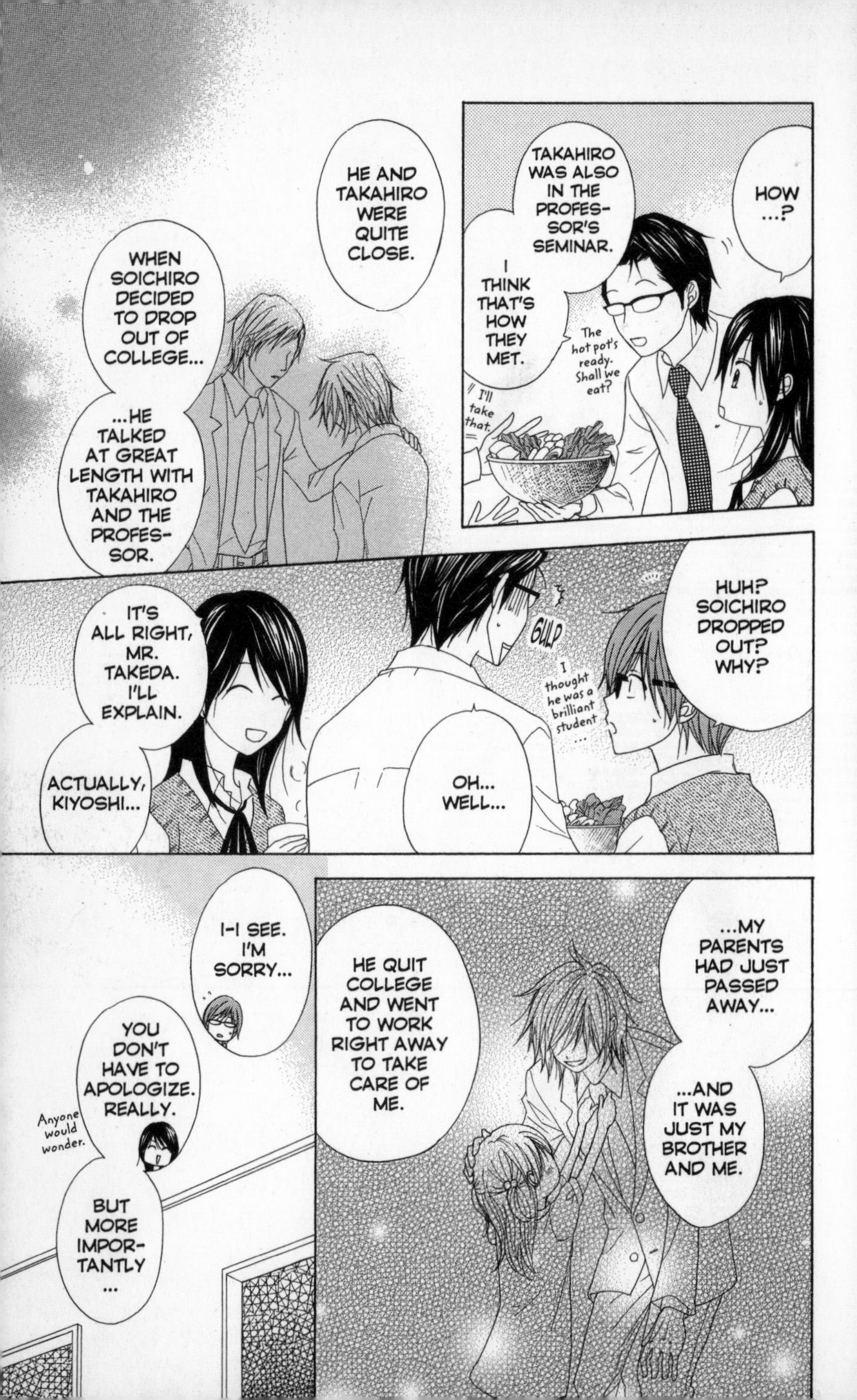
HOW ...?
TAKAHIRO WAS ALSO IN THE PROFESSOR'S SEMINAR.
I THINK THAT'S HOW THEY MET.
The hot pot's ready. Shall we eat?
I'll take that.
HE AND TAKAHIRO WERE QUITE CLOSE.
WHEN SOICHIRO DECIDED TO DROP OUT OF COLLEGE...
...HE TALKED AT GREAT LENGTH WITH TAKAHIRO AND THE PROFESSOR.
HUH? SOICHIRO DROPPED OUT? WHY?
I thought he was a brilliant student...
GULP
OH... WELL...
IT'S ALL RIGHT, MR. TAKEDA. I'LL EXPLAIN.
ACTUALLY, KIYOSHI...
...MY PARENTS HAD JUST PASSED AWAY...
...AND IT WAS JUST MY BROTHER AND ME.
HE QUIT COLLEGE AND WENT TO WORK RIGHT AWAY TO TAKE CARE OF ME.
I-I SEE. I'M SORRY...
YOU DON'T HAVE TO APOLOGIZE. REALLY.
Anyone would wonder.
BUT MORE IMPORTANTLY ...

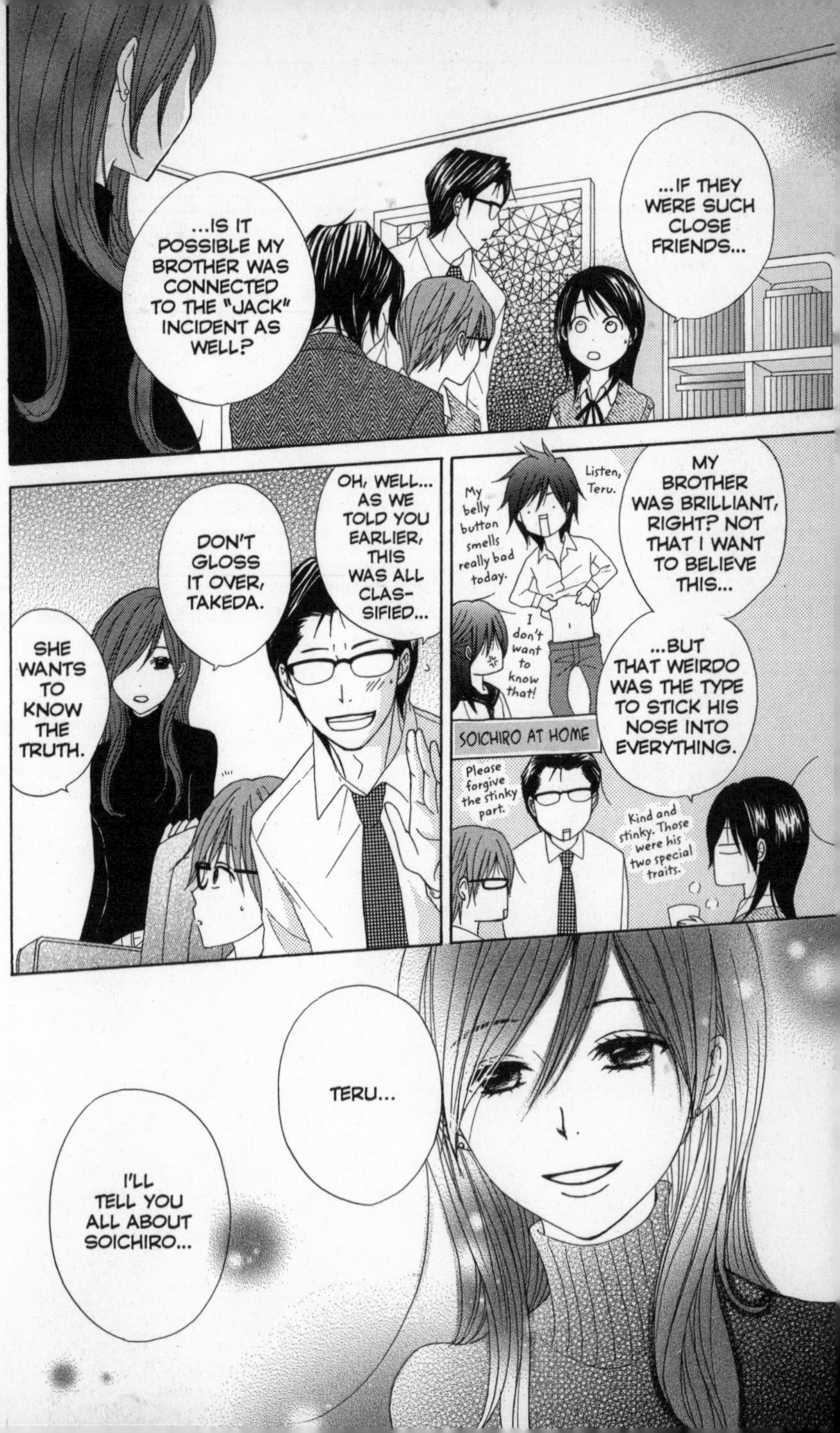
...IF THEY WERE SUCH CLOSE FRIENDS...
...IS IT POSSIBLE MY BROTHER WAS CONNECTED TO THE "JACK" INCIDENT AS WELL?
MY BROTHER WAS BRILLIANT, RIGHT? NOT THAT I WANT TO BELIEVE THIS...
Listen, Teru.
My belly button smells really bad today.
I don't want to know that!
...BUT THAT WEIRDO WAS THE TYPE TO STICK HIS NOSE INTO EVERYTHING.
SOICHIRO AT HOME
Kind and stinky. Those were his two special traits.
Please forgive the stinky part.
OH, WELL... AS WE TOLD YOU EARLIER, THIS WAS ALL CLAS-SIFIED...
DON'T GLOSS IT OVER, TAKEDA.
SHE WANTS TO KNOW THE TRUTH.
TERU...
I'LL TELL YOU ALL ABOUT SOICHIRO...

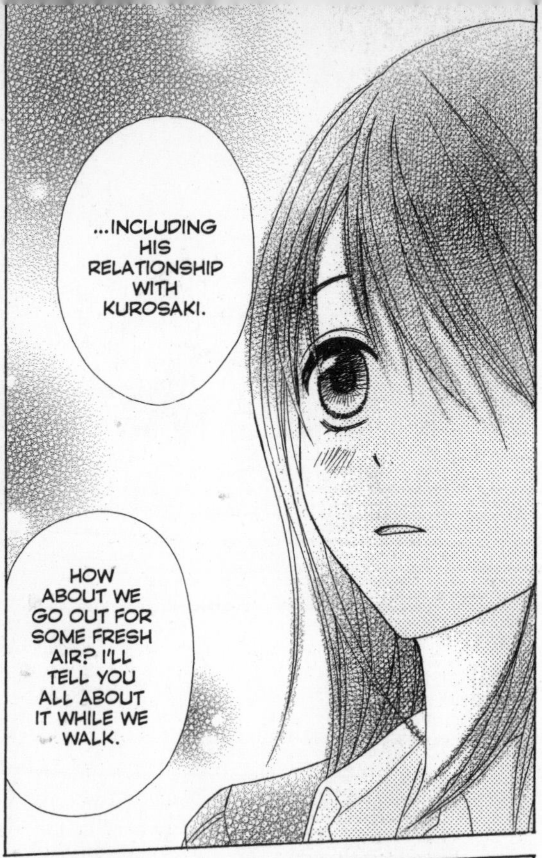
...INCLUDING HIS RELATIONSHIP WITH KUROSAKI.
HOW ABOUT WE GO OUT FOR SOME FRESH AIR? I'LL TELL YOU ALL ABOUT IT WHILE WE WALK.

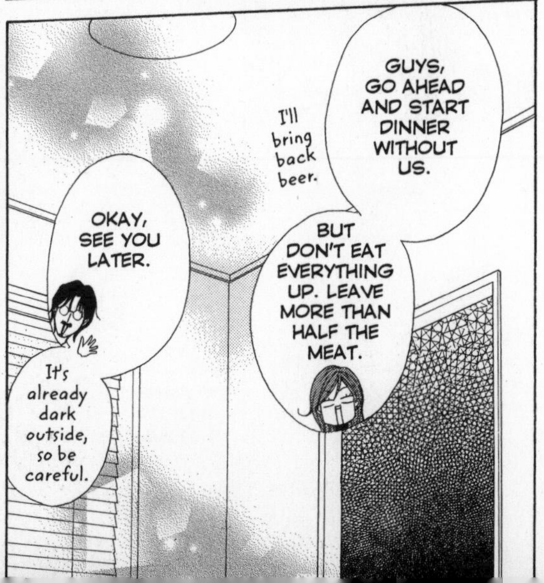
GUYS, GO AHEAD AND START DINNER WITHOUT US.
I'll bring back beer.
BUT DON'T EAT EVERYTHING UP. LEAVE MORE THAN HALF THE MEAT.
OKAY, SEE YOU LATER.
It's already dark outside, so be careful.

DENGEKI DAISY QUESTION CORNER

BALDLY ASK!! ③

Q.

WHEN KUROSAKI LOSES ALL HIS HAIR AND GOES TOTALLY BALD, WILL THE HAIR THAT GROWS OUT AFTERWARD BE BLACK?

(M.M., KANAGAWA PREFECTURE)

A.

WE HAVEN'T HAD A BALD HAIR QUESTION IN A WHILE. ANYWAY, THIS ISN'T SOME BIG SECRET OR ANYTHING. REGARDING THE QUESTION OF "WHAT'S KUROSAKI'S REAL HAIR COLOR?", THE HINT VAGUELY CAME UP IN THE MAIN STORY IN VOLUME 7, SO PLEASE CHECK IT OUT. ALSO, IF KUROSAKI WERE TO GO TOTALLY BALD, HIS HAIR WON'T GROW BACK. (THE AUTHOR WON'T LET IT.) NOT BLACK OR BLOND HAIR. SO KUROSAKI, TAKE CARE OF THE HAIR YOU HAVE NOW.

Q.

(IN CHAPTER 32 OF VOLUME 7) TERU AND KUROSAKI WERE HEADING TO A RAMEN SHOP. DID THEY EVER REACH THEIR DESTINATION? CONSIDERING THE STORYLINE, I HOPE THEY DID.

(MANGETSU, AICHI PREFECTURE)

A.

YOU'RE ABSOLUTELY RIGHT. OTHERWISE, WHAT WAS THE POINT OF BRINGING UP THAT NICE STORY ABOUT SOICHIRO? THEY GOT ROMANTIC AND HUGGED, BUT ROMANCE AND FOOD ARE SEPARATE THINGS. THEY FOUND THE RAMEN SHOP AND ATE RAMEN. TERU LIKES MISO RAMEN WHILE KUROSAKI LIKES SALT-BASED ONES.

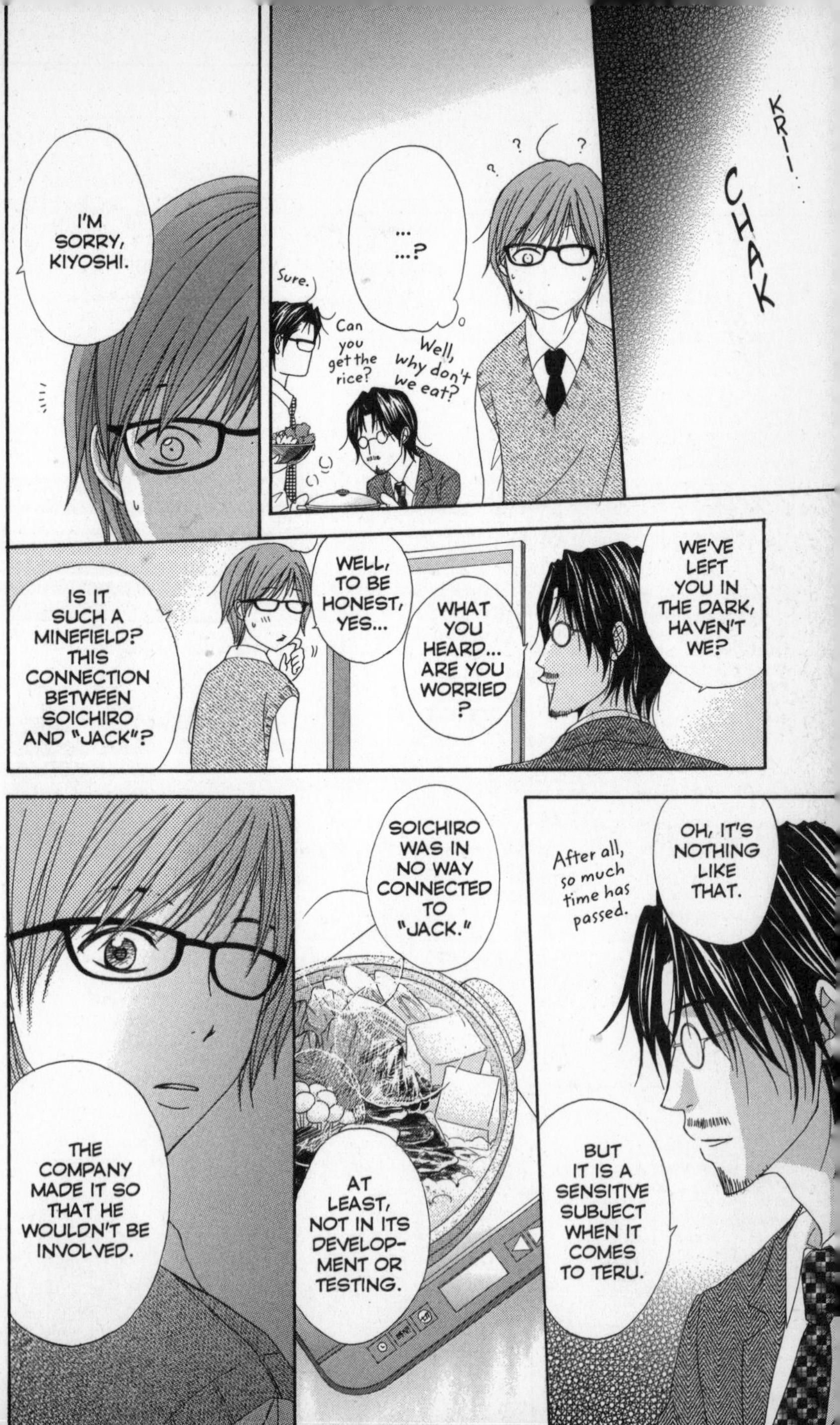
KRII...
CHAK
...
...?
Well, why don't we eat?
Can you get the rice?
Sure.
I'M SORRY, KIYOSHI.
WE'VE LEFT YOU IN THE DARK, HAVEN'T WE?
WHAT YOU HEARD... ARE YOU WORRIED?
WELL, TO BE HONEST, YES...
IS IT SUCH A MINEFIELD? THIS CONNECTION BETWEEN SOICHIRO AND "JACK"?
OH, IT'S NOTHING LIKE THAT.
After all, so much time has passed.
BUT IT IS A SENSITIVE SUBJECT WHEN IT COMES TO TERU.
SOICHIRO WAS IN NO WAY CONNECTED TO "JACK."
AT LEAST, NOT IN ITS DEVELOPMENT OR TESTING.
THE COMPANY MADE IT SO THAT HE WOULDN'T BE INVOLVED.

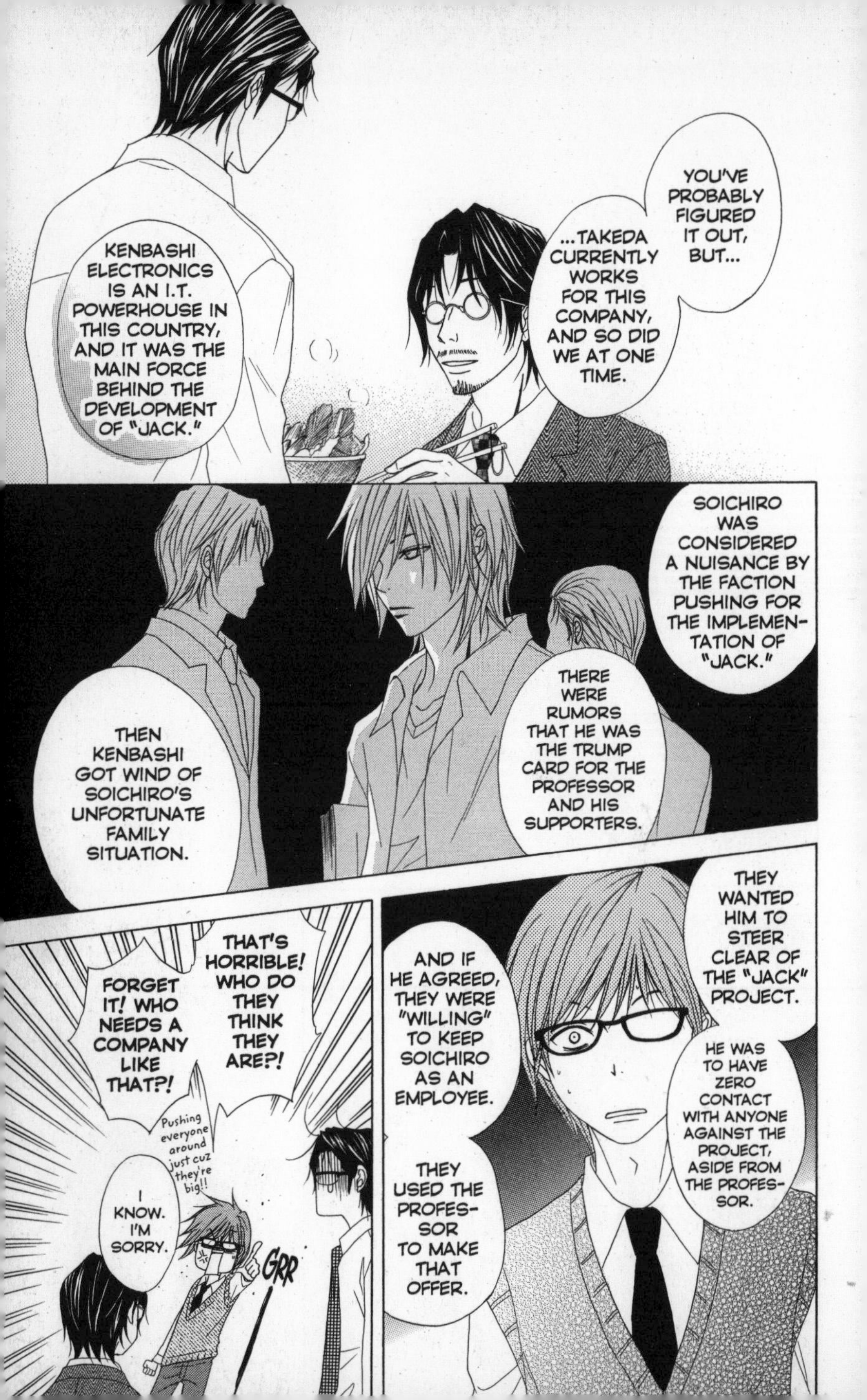
YOU'VE PROBABLY FIGURED IT OUT, BUT...
...TAKEDA CURRENTLY WORKS FOR THIS COMPANY, AND SO DID WE AT ONE TIME.
KENBASHI ELECTRONICS IS AN I.T. POWERHOUSE IN THIS COUNTRY, AND IT WAS THE MAIN FORCE BEHIND THE DEVELOPMENT OF "JACK."
SOICHIRO WAS CONSIDERED A NUISANCE BY THE FACTION PUSHING FOR THE IMPLEMENTATION OF "JACK."
THERE WERE RUMORS THAT HE WAS THE TRUMP CARD FOR THE PROFESSOR AND HIS SUPPORTERS.
THEN KENBASHI GOT WIND OF SOICHIRO'S UNFORTUNATE FAMILY SITUATION.
THEY WANTED HIM TO STEER CLEAR OF THE "JACK" PROJECT.
HE WAS TO HAVE ZERO CONTACT WITH ANYONE AGAINST THE PROJECT, ASIDE FROM THE PROFESSOR.
AND IF HE AGREED, THEY WERE "WILLING" TO KEEP SOICHIRO AS AN EMPLOYEE.
THEY USED THE PROFESSOR TO MAKE THAT OFFER.
THAT'S HORRIBLE! WHO DO THEY THINK THEY ARE?!
FORGET IT! WHO NEEDS A COMPANY LIKE THAT?!
Pushing everyone around just cuz they're big!!
I KNOW. I'M SORRY.
GRR

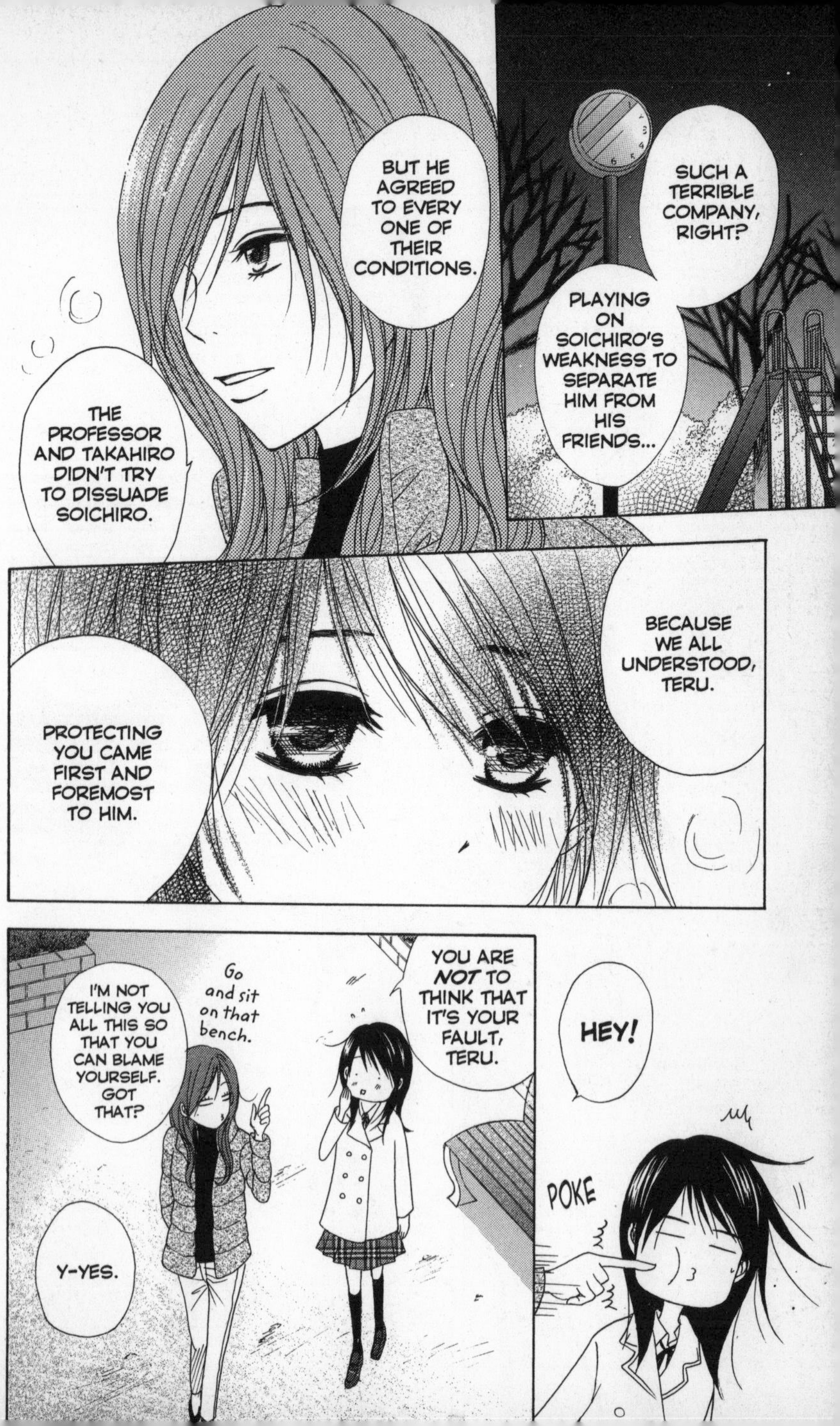
SUCH A TERRIBLE COMPANY, RIGHT?
PLAYING ON SOICHIRO'S WEAKNESS TO SEPARATE HIM FROM HIS FRIENDS...
BUT HE AGREED TO EVERY ONE OF THEIR CONDITIONS.
THE PROFESSOR AND TAKAHIRO DIDN'T TRY TO DISSUADE SOICHIRO.
BECAUSE WE ALL UNDERSTOOD, TERU.
PROTECTING YOU CAME FIRST AND FOREMOST TO HIM.
HEY!
POKE
YOU ARE *NOT* TO THINK THAT IT'S YOUR FAULT, TERU.
I'M NOT TELLING YOU ALL THIS SO THAT YOU CAN BLAME YOURSELF. GOT THAT?
Go and sit on that bench.
Y-YES.

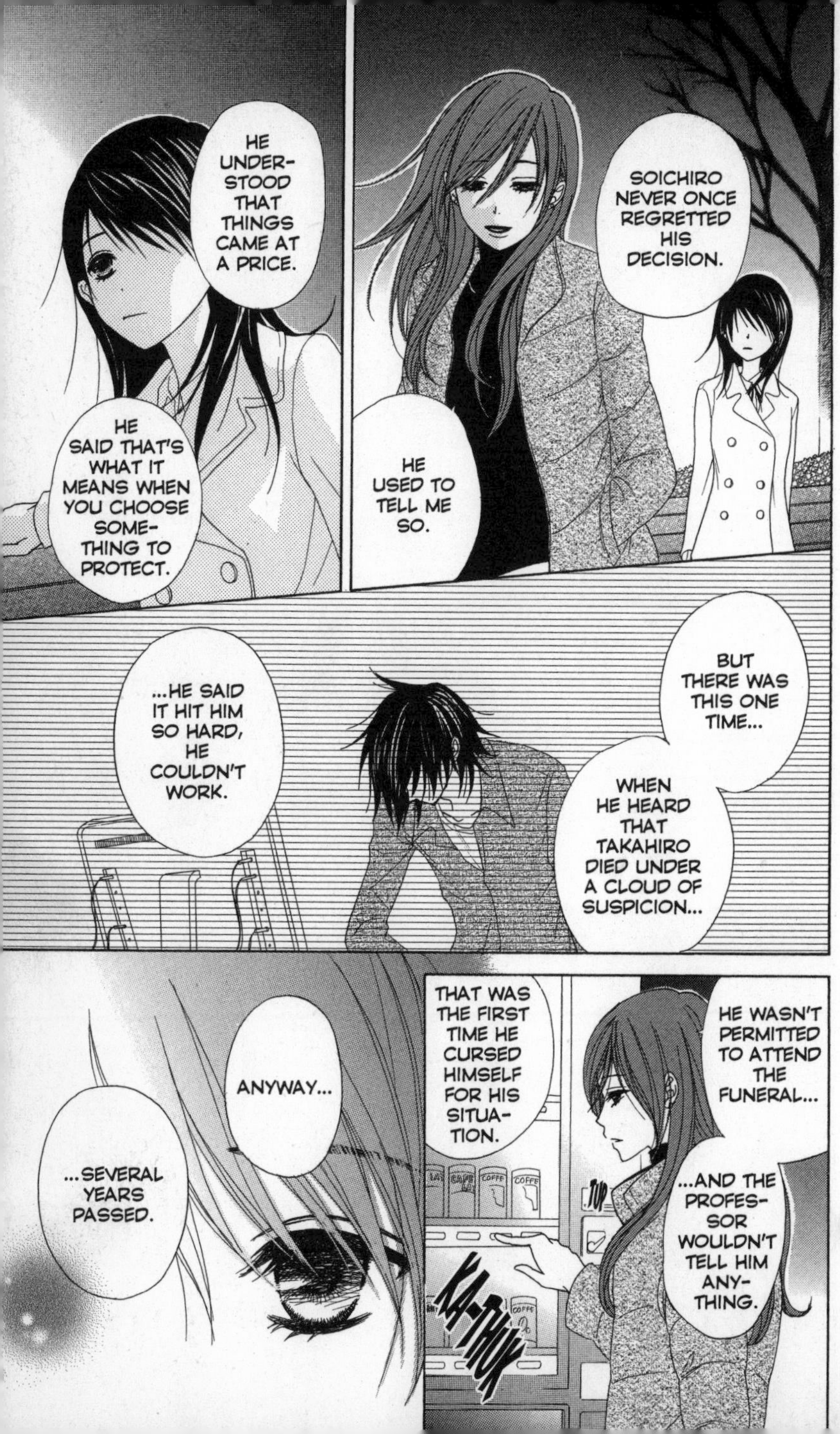
SOICHIRO NEVER ONCE REGRETTED HIS DECISION.
HE USED TO TELL ME SO.
HE UNDERSTOOD THAT THINGS CAME AT A PRICE.
HE SAID THAT'S WHAT IT MEANS WHEN YOU CHOOSE SOMETHING TO PROTECT.
BUT THERE WAS THIS ONE TIME...
WHEN HE HEARD THAT TAKAHIRO DIED UNDER A CLOUD OF SUSPICION...
...HE SAID IT HIT HIM SO HARD, HE COULDN'T WORK.
HE WASN'T PERMITTED TO ATTEND THE FUNERAL...
...AND THE PROFESSOR WOULDN'T TELL HIM ANYTHING.
THAT WAS THE FIRST TIME HE CURSED HIMSELF FOR HIS SITUATION.
KA-THUK
ANYWAY...
...SEVERAL YEARS PASSED.

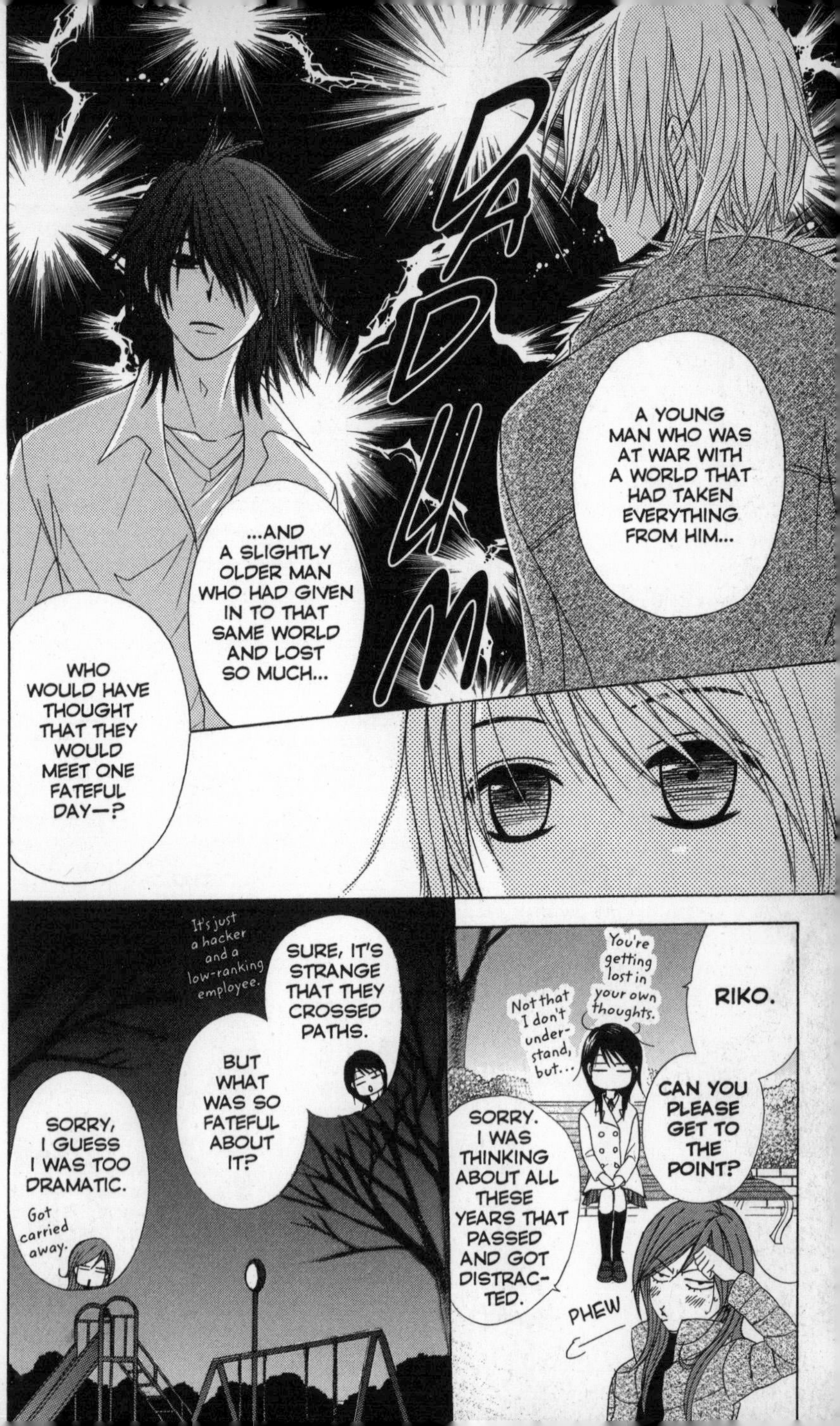
A YOUNG MAN WHO WAS AT WAR WITH A WORLD THAT HAD TAKEN EVERYTHING FROM HIM...
DADUM
...AND A SLIGHTLY OLDER MAN WHO HAD GIVEN IN TO THAT SAME WORLD AND LOST SO MUCH...
WHO WOULD HAVE THOUGHT THAT THEY WOULD MEET ONE FATEFUL DAY—?
RIKO.
You're getting lost in your own thoughts.
Not that I don't under-stand, but...
CAN YOU PLEASE GET TO THE POINT?
SORRY. I WAS THINKING ABOUT ALL THESE YEARS THAT PASSED AND GOT DISTRAC-TED.
PHEW
SURE, IT'S STRANGE THAT THEY CROSSED PATHS.
It's just a hacker and a low-ranking employee.
BUT WHAT WAS SO FATEFUL ABOUT IT?
SORRY, I GUESS I WAS TOO DRAMATIC.
Got carried away.

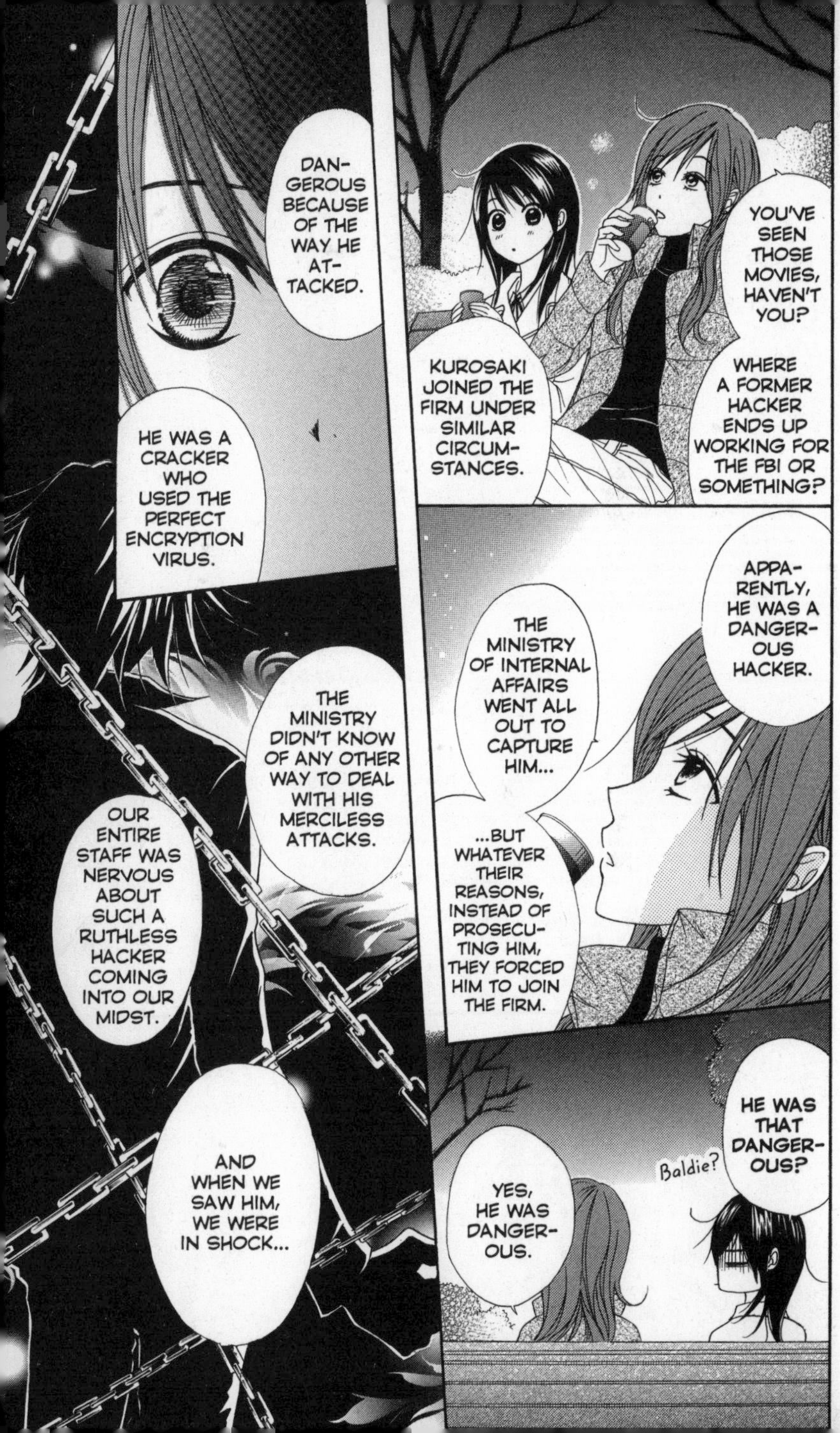
YOU'VE SEEN THOSE MOVIES, HAVEN'T YOU?
WHERE A FORMER HACKER ENDS UP WORKING FOR THE FBI OR SOMETHING?
KUROSAKI JOINED THE FIRM UNDER SIMILAR CIRCUM-STANCES.
APPA-RENTLY, HE WAS A DANGER-OUS HACKER.
THE MINISTRY OF INTERNAL AFFAIRS WENT ALL OUT TO CAPTURE HIM...
...BUT WHATEVER THEIR REASONS, INSTEAD OF PROSECU-TING HIM, THEY FORCED HIM TO JOIN THE FIRM.
HE WAS THAT DANGER-OUS?
Baldie?
YES, HE WAS DANGER-OUS.
DAN-GEROUS BECAUSE OF THE WAY HE AT-TACKED.
HE WAS A CRACKER WHO USED THE PERFECT ENCRYPTION VIRUS.
THE MINISTRY DIDN'T KNOW OF ANY OTHER WAY TO DEAL WITH HIS MERCILESS ATTACKS.
OUR ENTIRE STAFF WAS NERVOUS ABOUT SUCH A RUTHLESS HACKER COMING INTO OUR MIDST.
AND WHEN WE SAW HIM, WE WERE IN SHOCK...

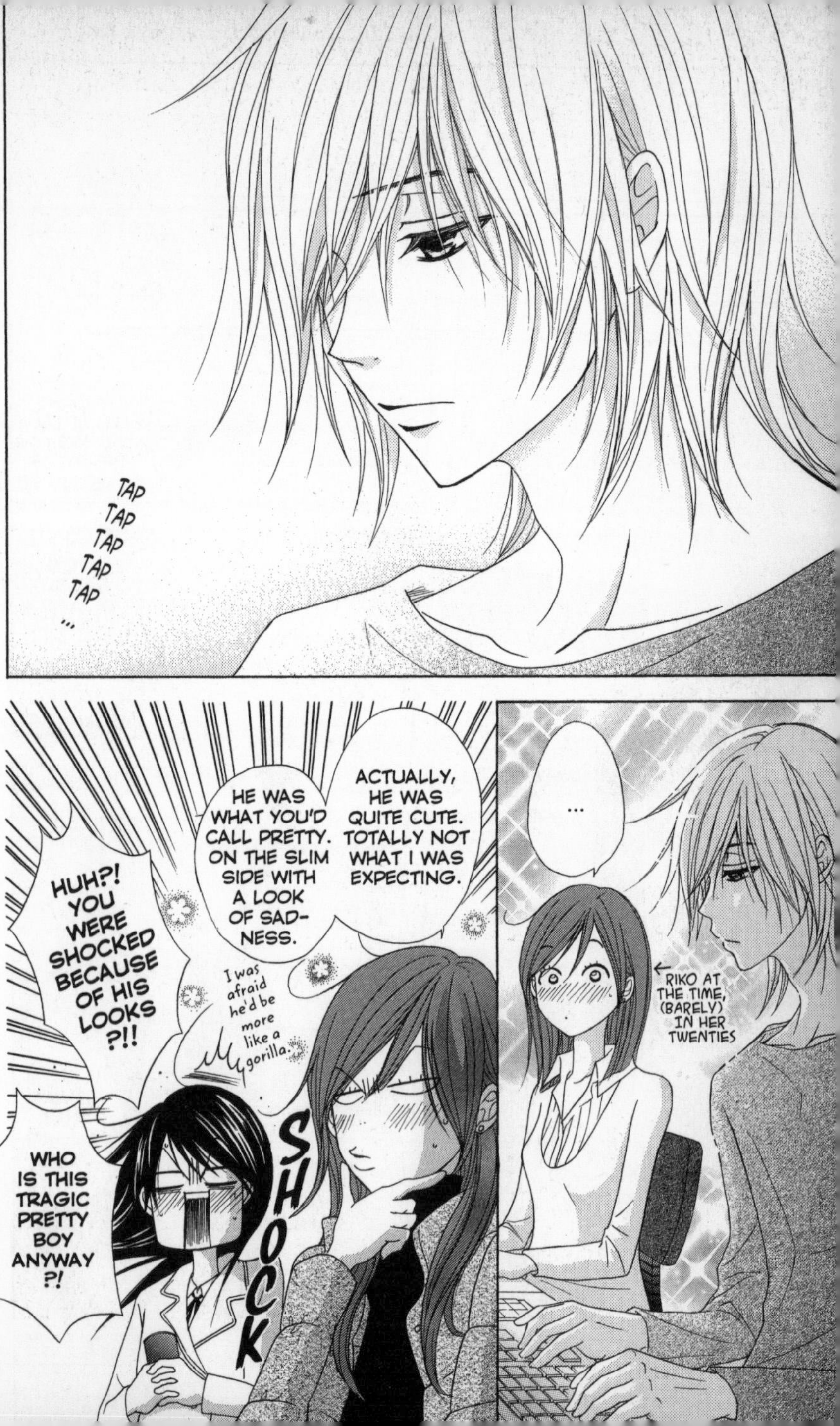

TAP TAP TAP TAP TAP ...
...
← RIKO AT THE TIME, (BARELY) IN HER TWENTIES
ACTUALLY, HE WAS QUITE CUTE. TOTALLY NOT WHAT I WAS EXPECTING.
HE WAS WHAT YOU'D CALL PRETTY. ON THE SLIM SIDE WITH A LOOK OF SAD-NESS.
I was afraid he'd be more like a gorilla.
HUH?! YOU WERE SHOCKED BECAUSE OF HIS LOOKS ?!!
SHOCK
WHO IS THIS TRAGIC PRETTY BOY ANYWAY ?!

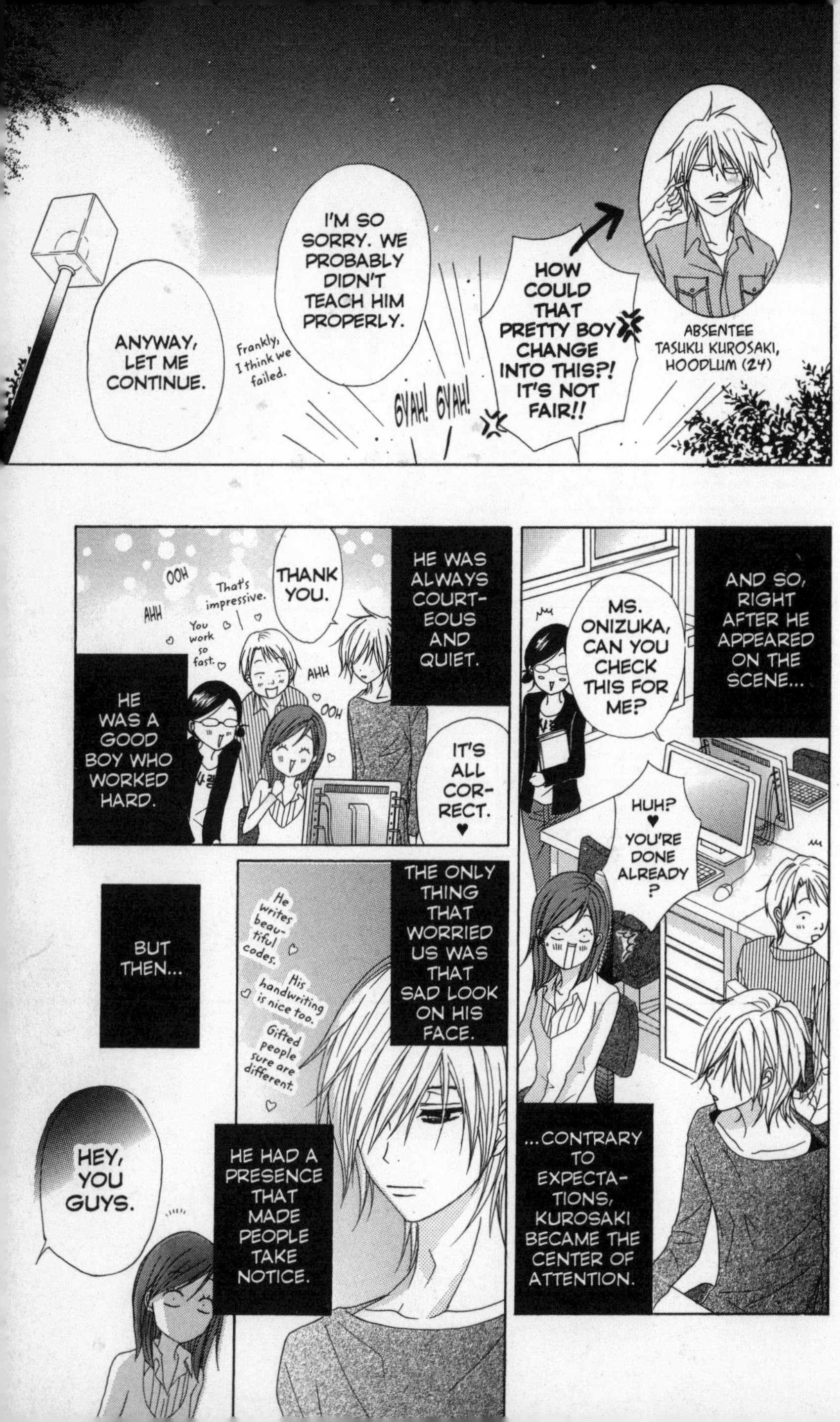

ABSENTEE TASUKU KUROSAKI, HOODLUM (24)
HOW COULD THAT PRETTY BOY CHANGE INTO THIS?! IT'S NOT FAIR!!
GYAH! GYAH!
I'M SO SORRY. WE PROBABLY DIDN'T TEACH HIM PROPERLY.
Frankly, I think we failed.
ANYWAY, LET ME CONTINUE.
AND SO, RIGHT AFTER HE APPEARED ON THE SCENE...
MS. ONIZUKA, CAN YOU CHECK THIS FOR ME?
HUH? ♥ YOU'RE DONE ALREADY?
...CONTRARY TO EXPECTATIONS, KUROSAKI BECAME THE CENTER OF ATTENTION.
HE WAS ALWAYS COURTEOUS AND QUIET.
THANK YOU.
OOH
That's impressive.
AHH
You work so fast.
AHH
OOH
IT'S ALL CORRECT. ♥
HE WAS A GOOD BOY WHO WORKED HARD.
THE ONLY THING THAT WORRIED US WAS THAT SAD LOOK ON HIS FACE.
He writes beautiful codes.
His handwriting is nice too.
Gifted people sure are different.
HE HAD A PRESENCE THAT MADE PEOPLE TAKE NOTICE.
BUT THEN...
HEY, YOU GUYS.

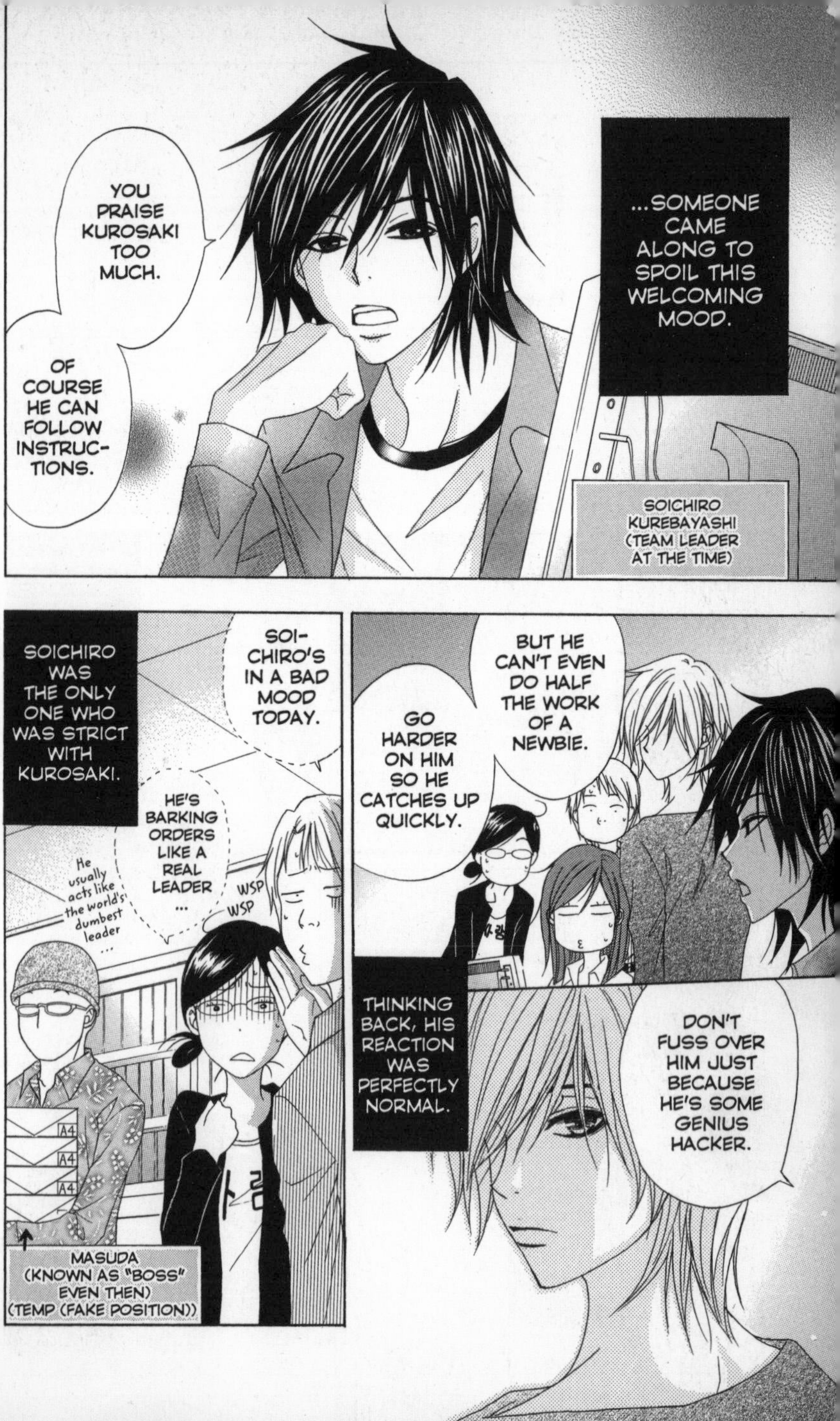
...SOMEONE CAME ALONG TO SPOIL THIS WELCOMING MOOD.
SOICHIRO KUREBAYASHI (TEAM LEADER AT THE TIME)
YOU PRAISE KUROSAKI TOO MUCH.
OF COURSE HE CAN FOLLOW INSTRUC-TIONS.
BUT HE CAN'T EVEN DO HALF THE WORK OF A NEWBIE.
GO HARDER ON HIM SO HE CATCHES UP QUICKLY.
DON'T FUSS OVER HIM JUST BECAUSE HE'S SOME GENIUS HACKER.
THINKING BACK, HIS REACTION WAS PERFECTLY NORMAL.
SOI-CHIRO'S IN A BAD MOOD TODAY.
SOICHIRO WAS THE ONLY ONE WHO WAS STRICT WITH KUROSAKI.
HE'S BARKING ORDERS LIKE A REAL LEADER...
WSP WSP
He usually acts like the world's dumbest leader...
A4
A4
A4
MASUDA (KNOWN AS "BOSS" EVEN THEN) (TEMP (FAKE POSITION))

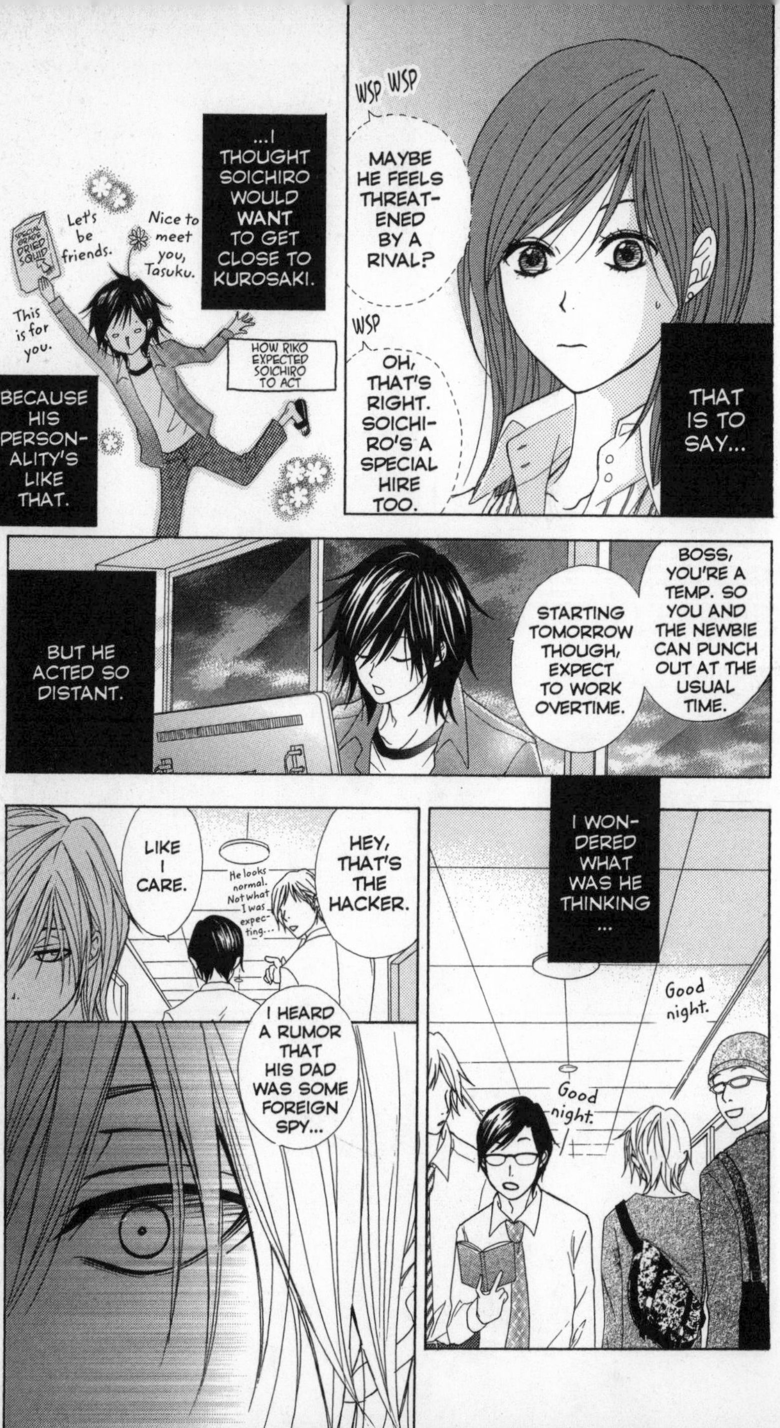
WSP WSP
MAYBE HE FEELS THREAT-ENED BY A RIVAL?
WSP
OH, THAT'S RIGHT. SOICHI-RO'S A SPECIAL HIRE TOO.
THAT IS TO SAY...
...I THOUGHT SOICHIRO WOULD WANT TO GET CLOSE TO KUROSAKI.
Nice to meet you, Tasuku.
Let's be friends.
SPECIAL GRADE DRIED SQUID
This is for you.
HOW RIKO EXPECTED SOICHIRO TO ACT
BECAUSE HIS PERSON-ALITY'S LIKE THAT.
BOSS, YOU'RE A TEMP. SO YOU AND THE NEWBIE CAN PUNCH OUT AT THE USUAL TIME.
STARTING TOMORROW THOUGH, EXPECT TO WORK OVERTIME.
BUT HE ACTED SO DISTANT.
I WON-DERED WHAT WAS HE THINKING ...
Good night.
Good night.
HEY, THAT'S THE HACKER.
He looks normal. Not what I was expec-ting...
LIKE I CARE.
I HEARD A RUMOR THAT HIS DAD WAS SOME FOREIGN SPY...

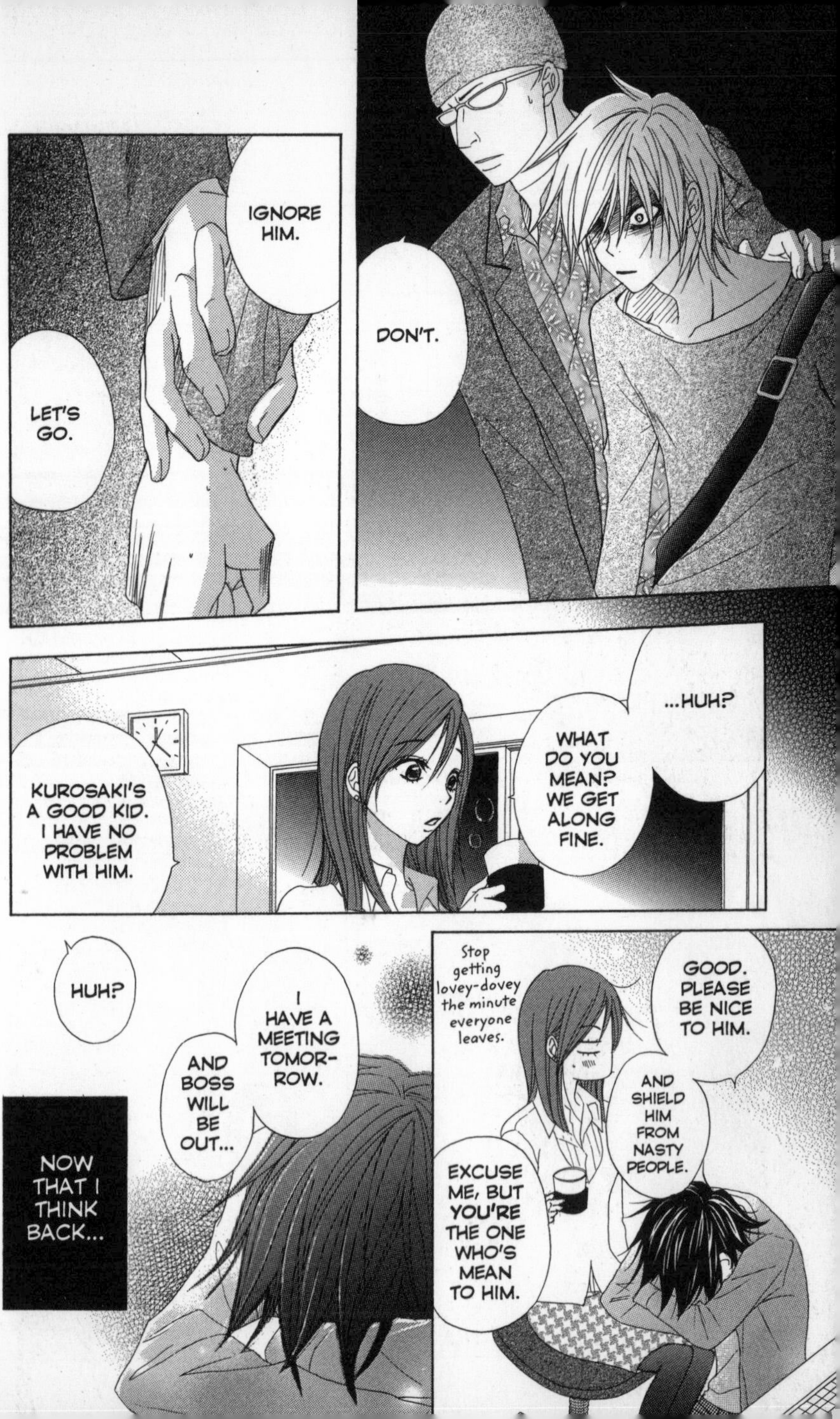
DON'T.
IGNORE HIM.
LET'S GO.
...HUH?
WHAT DO YOU MEAN? WE GET ALONG FINE.
KUROSAKI'S A GOOD KID. I HAVE NO PROBLEM WITH HIM.
GOOD. PLEASE BE NICE TO HIM.
AND SHIELD HIM FROM NASTY PEOPLE.
Stop getting lovey-dovey the minute everyone leaves.
EXCUSE ME, BUT YOU'RE THE ONE WHO'S MEAN TO HIM.
I HAVE A MEETING TOMOR-ROW.
AND BOSS WILL BE OUT...
HUH?
NOW THAT I THINK BACK...

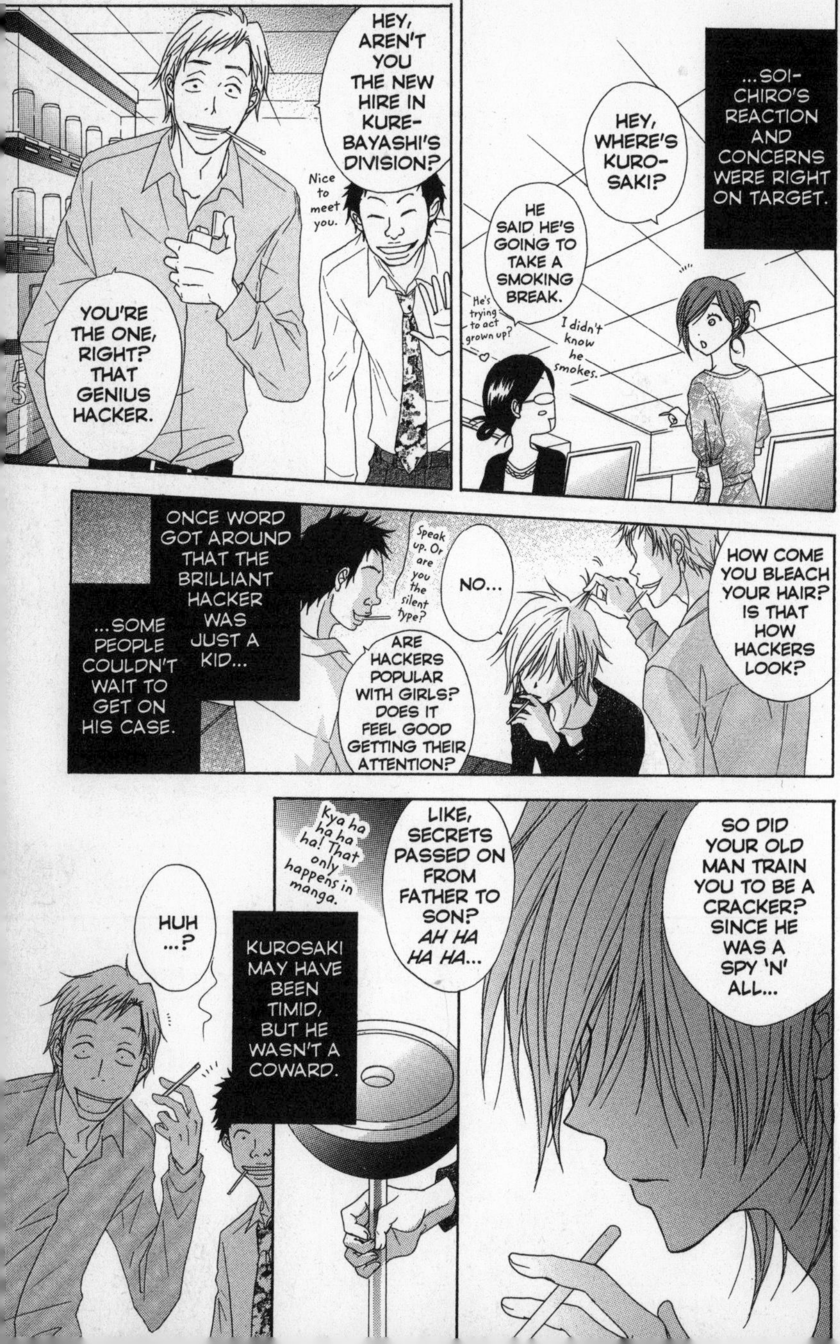
...SOICHIRO'S REACTION AND CONCERNS WERE RIGHT ON TARGET.
HEY, WHERE'S KUROSAKI?
HE SAID HE'S GOING TO TAKE A SMOKING BREAK.
I didn't know he smokes.
He's trying to act grown up?
HEY, AREN'T YOU THE NEW HIRE IN KUREBAYASHI'S DIVISION?
Nice to meet you.
YOU'RE THE ONE, RIGHT? THAT GENIUS HACKER.
HOW COME YOU BLEACH YOUR HAIR? IS THAT HOW HACKERS LOOK?
NO...
Speak up. Or are you the silent type?
ARE HACKERS POPULAR WITH GIRLS? DOES IT FEEL GOOD GETTING THEIR ATTENTION?
ONCE WORD GOT AROUND THAT THE BRILLIANT HACKER WAS JUST A KID...
...SOME PEOPLE COULDN'T WAIT TO GET ON HIS CASE.
SO DID YOUR OLD MAN TRAIN YOU TO BE A CRACKER? SINCE HE WAS A SPY 'N' ALL...
LIKE, SECRETS PASSED ON FROM FATHER TO SON? *AH HA HA HA...*
Kya ha ha ha ha! That only happens in manga.
KUROSAKI MAY HAVE BEEN TIMID, BUT HE WASN'T A COWARD.
HUH ...?

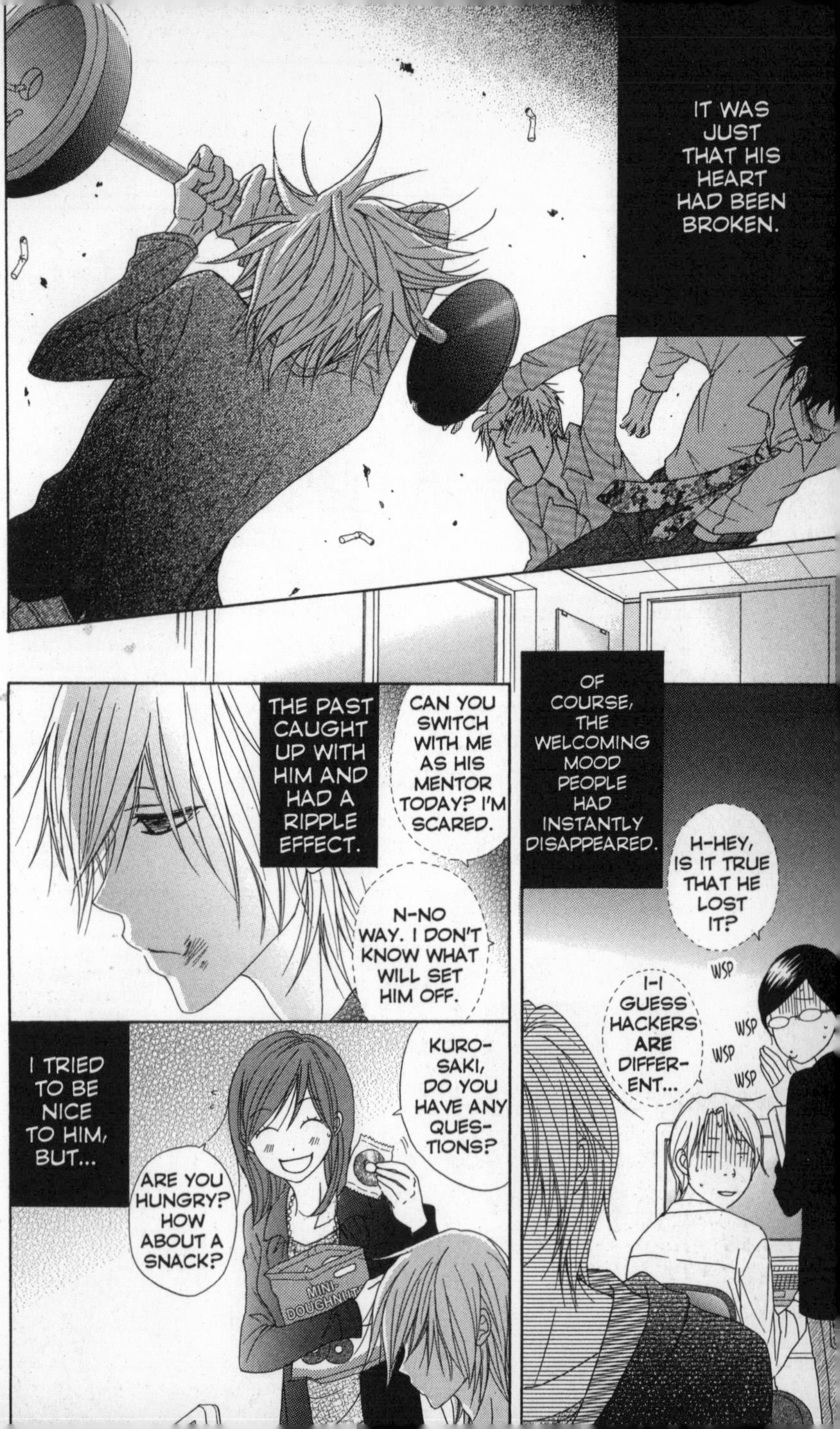
IT WAS JUST THAT HIS HEART HAD BEEN BROKEN.
OF COURSE, THE WELCOMING MOOD PEOPLE HAD INSTANTLY DISAPPEARED.
H-HEY, IS IT TRUE THAT HE LOST IT?
WSP
I-I GUESS HACKERS ARE DIFFER-ENT...
WSP
WSP
WSP
CAN YOU SWITCH WITH ME AS HIS MENTOR TODAY? I'M SCARED.
THE PAST CAUGHT UP WITH HIM AND HAD A RIPPLE EFFECT.
N-NO WAY. I DON'T KNOW WHAT WILL SET HIM OFF.
KURO-SAKI, DO YOU HAVE ANY QUES-TIONS?
I TRIED TO BE NICE TO HIM, BUT...
ARE YOU HUNGRY? HOW ABOUT A SNACK?
MINI-DOUGHNUT

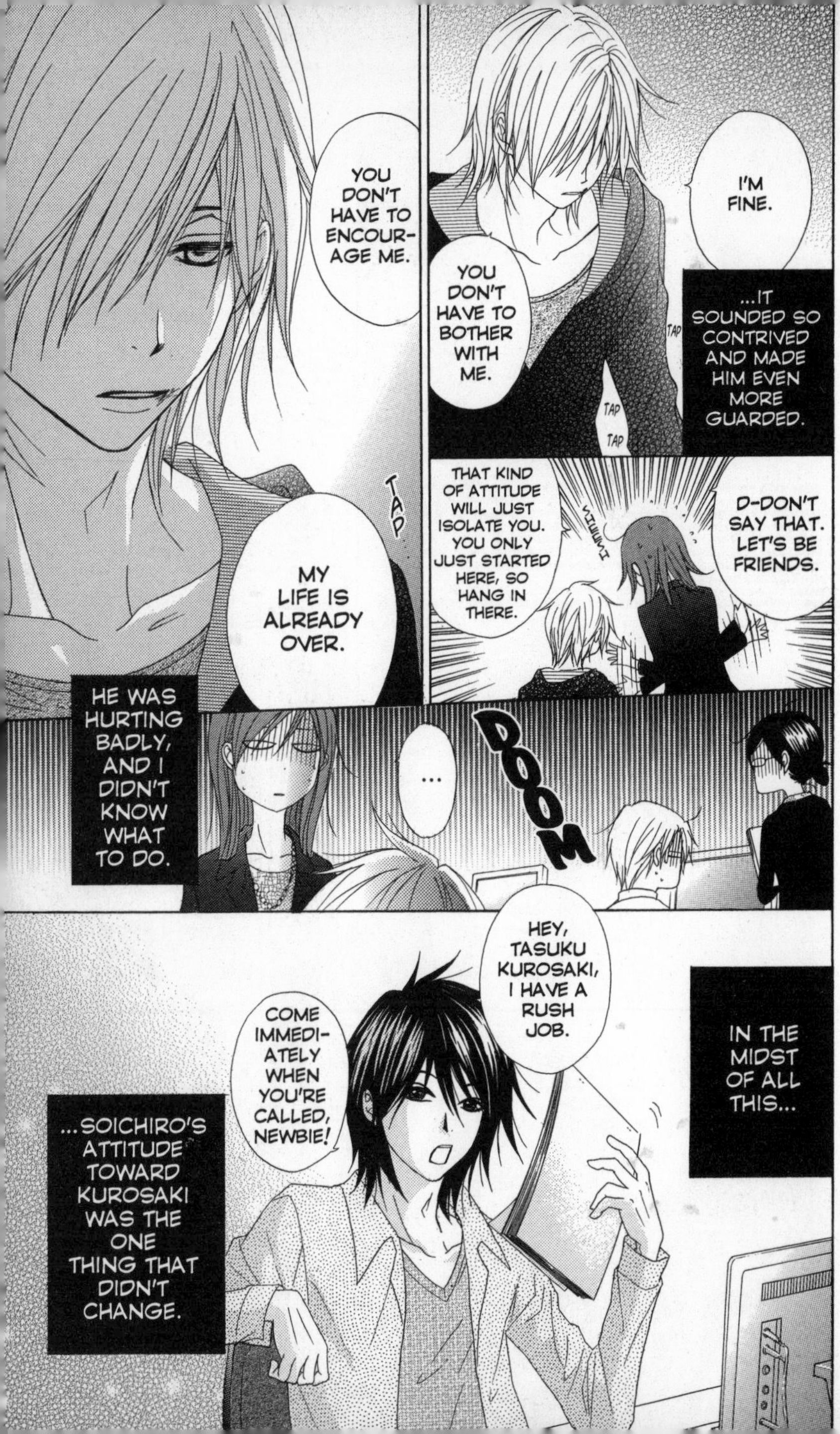
I'M FINE.
YOU DON'T HAVE TO BOTHER WITH ME.
...IT SOUNDED SO CONTRIVED AND MADE HIM EVEN MORE GUARDED.
TAP
TAP
TAP
D-DON'T SAY THAT. LET'S BE FRIENDS.
THAT KIND OF ATTITUDE WILL JUST ISOLATE YOU. YOU ONLY JUST STARTED HERE, SO HANG IN THERE.
YOU DON'T HAVE TO ENCOURAGE ME.
TAP
MY LIFE IS ALREADY OVER.
DOOM
...
HE WAS HURTING BADLY, AND I DIDN'T KNOW WHAT TO DO.
IN THE MIDST OF ALL THIS...
HEY, TASUKU KUROSAKI, I HAVE A RUSH JOB.
COME IMMEDIATELY WHEN YOU'RE CALLED, NEWBIE!
...SOICHIRO'S ATTITUDE TOWARD KUROSAKI WAS THE ONE THING THAT DIDN'T CHANGE.

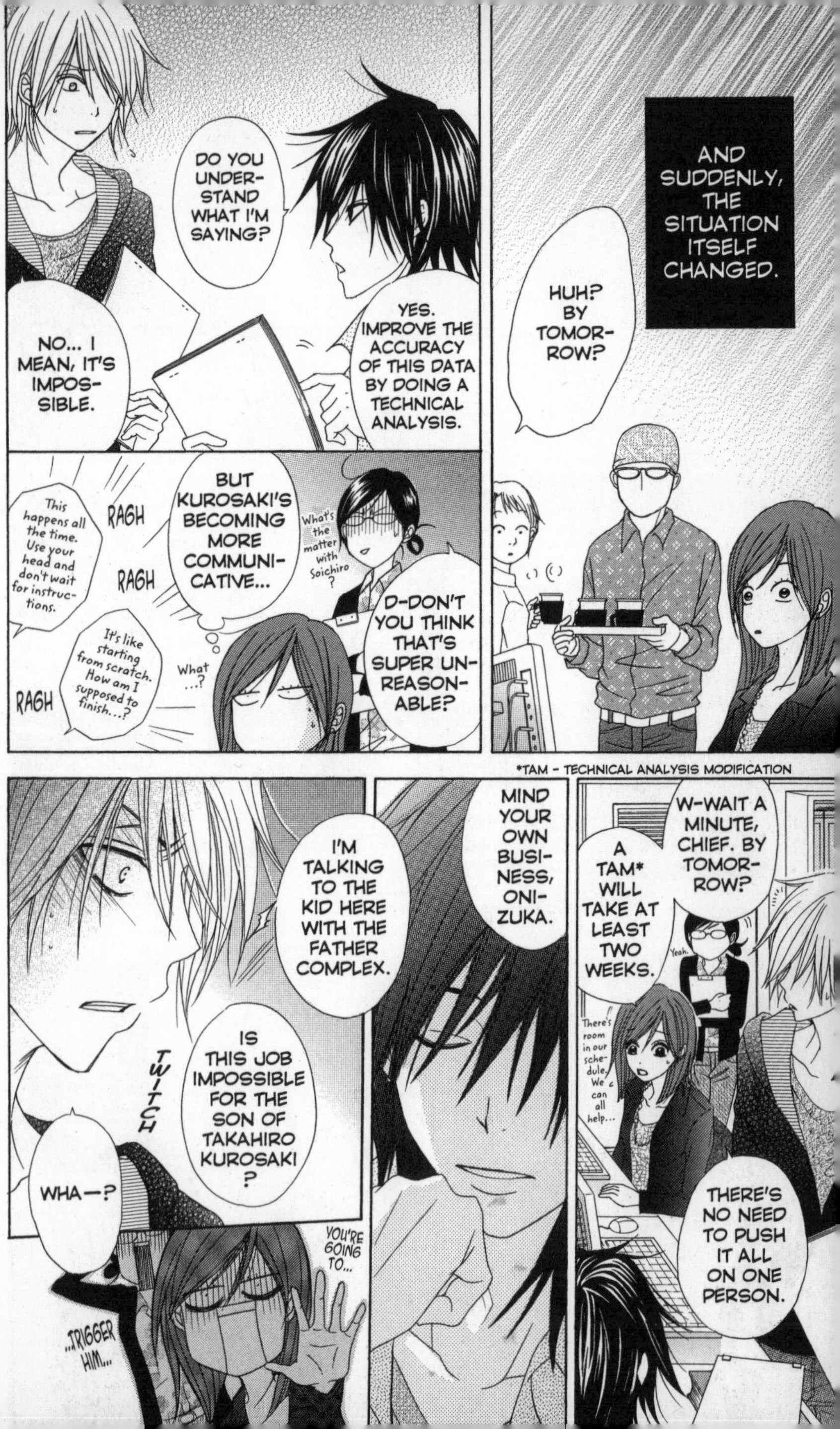
AND SUDDENLY, THE SITUATION ITSELF CHANGED.
HUH? BY TOMORROW?
YES. IMPROVE THE ACCURACY OF THIS DATA BY DOING A TECHNICAL ANALYSIS.
DO YOU UNDERSTAND WHAT I'M SAYING?
NO... I MEAN, IT'S IMPOSSIBLE.
BUT KUROSAKI'S BECOMING MORE COMMUNICATIVE...
What's the matter with Soichiro?
D-DON'T YOU THINK THAT'S SUPER UNREASONABLE?
What...?
RAGH
This happens all the time. Use your head and don't wait for instructions.
RAGH
It's like starting from scratch. How am I supposed to finish...?
RAGH
W-WAIT A MINUTE, CHIEF. BY TOMORROW?
A TAM* WILL TAKE AT LEAST TWO WEEKS.
Yeah.
There's room in our schedule. We can all help...
THERE'S NO NEED TO PUSH IT ALL ON ONE PERSON.
MIND YOUR OWN BUSINESS, ONIZUKA.
I'M TALKING TO THE KID HERE WITH THE FATHER COMPLEX.
IS THIS JOB IMPOSSIBLE FOR THE SON OF TAKAHIRO KUROSAKI?
TWITCH
WHA—?
YOU'RE GOING TO...
...TRIGGER HIM...

*TAM - TECHNICAL ANALYSIS MODIFICATION

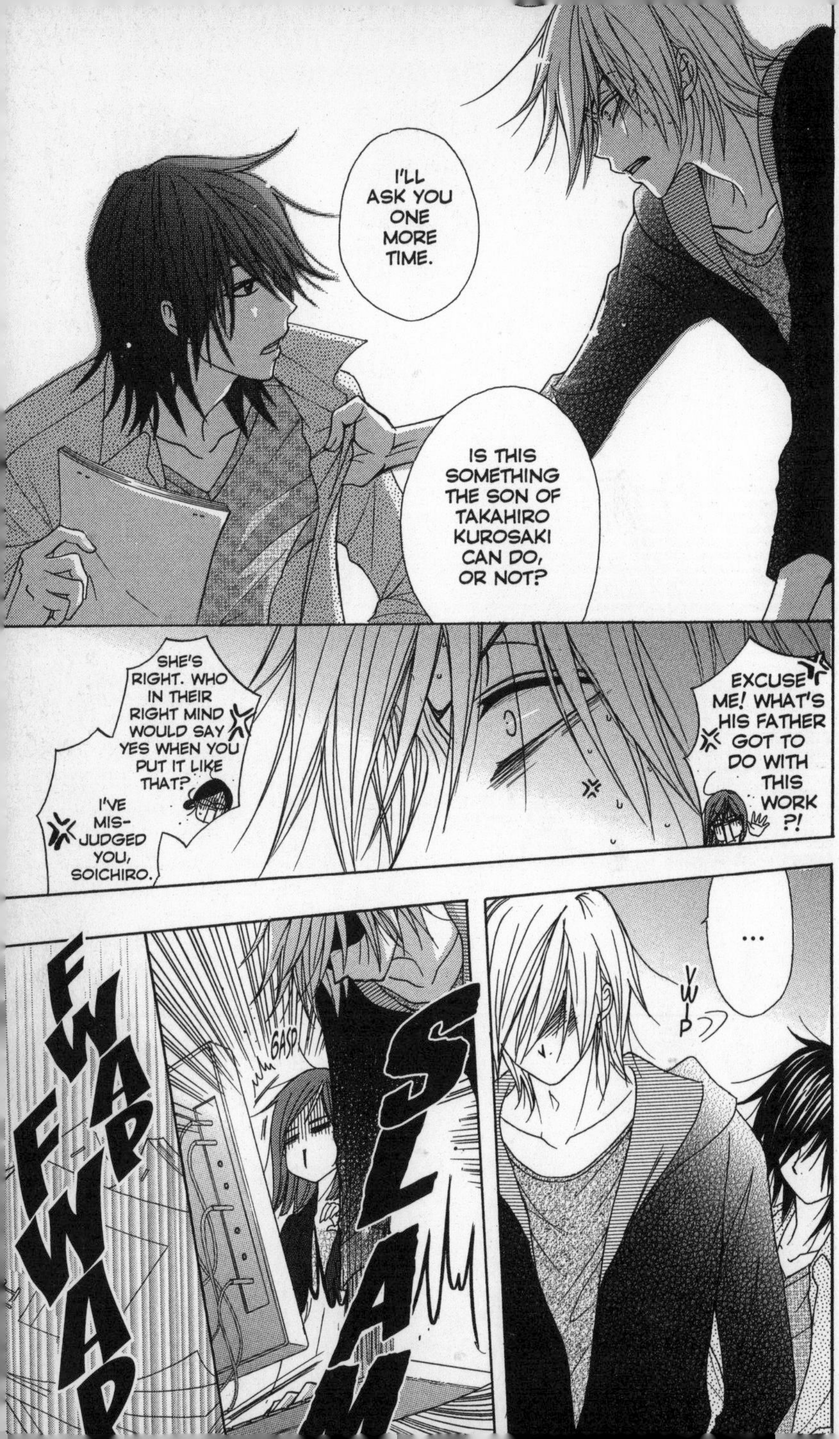
I'LL ASK YOU ONE MORE TIME.
IS THIS SOMETHING THE SON OF TAKAHIRO KUROSAKI CAN DO, OR NOT?
EXCUSE ME! WHAT'S HIS FATHER GOT TO DO WITH THIS WORK ?!
SHE'S RIGHT. WHO IN THEIR RIGHT MIND WOULD SAY YES WHEN YOU PUT IT LIKE THAT?
I'VE MIS-JUDGED YOU, SOICHIRO.
...
VWIP
SLAM
GASP
FWAP FWAP

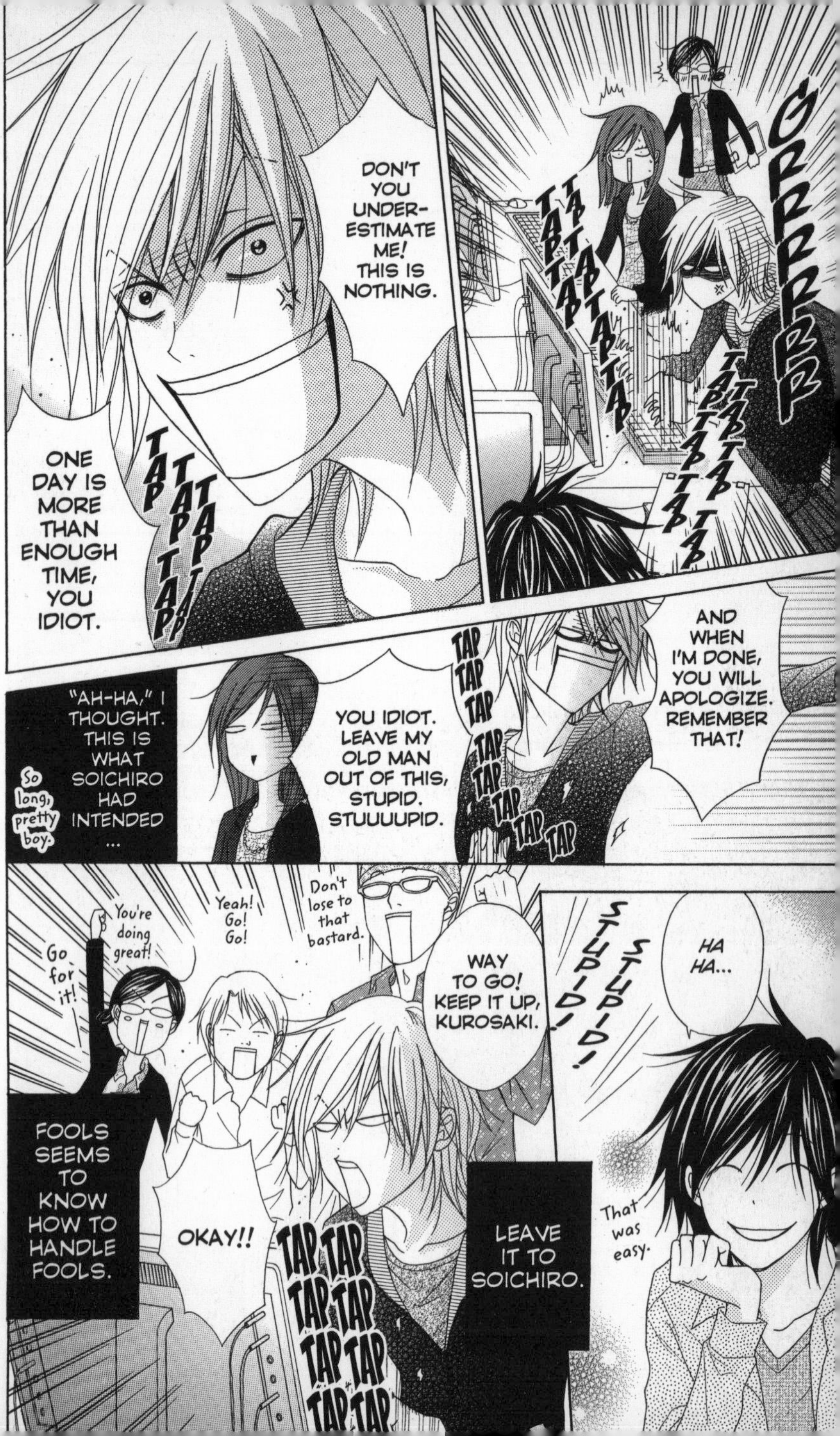
GRRRRRR
TAP TAP TAP TAP TAP TAP TAP
TAP TAP TAP TAP TAP TAP TAP
DON'T YOU UNDER-ESTIMATE ME! THIS IS NOTHING.
ONE DAY IS MORE THAN ENOUGH TIME, YOU IDIOT.
TAP TAP TAP
AND WHEN I'M DONE, YOU WILL APOLOGIZE. REMEMBER THAT!
TAP TAP TAP TAP TAP TAP TAP TAP
YOU IDIOT. LEAVE MY OLD MAN OUT OF THIS, STUPID. STUUUUPID.
"AH-HA," I THOUGHT. THIS IS WHAT SOICHIRO HAD INTENDED ...
So long, pretty boy.
HA HA...
STUPID! STUPID!
That was easy.
LEAVE IT TO SOICHIRO.
WAY TO GO! KEEP IT UP, KUROSAKI.
Don't lose to that bastard.
Yeah! Go! Go!
You're doing great!
Go for it!
OKAY!!
TAP TAP TAP TAP TAP TAP TAP TAP TAP TAP
FOOLS SEEMS TO KNOW HOW TO HANDLE FOOLS.

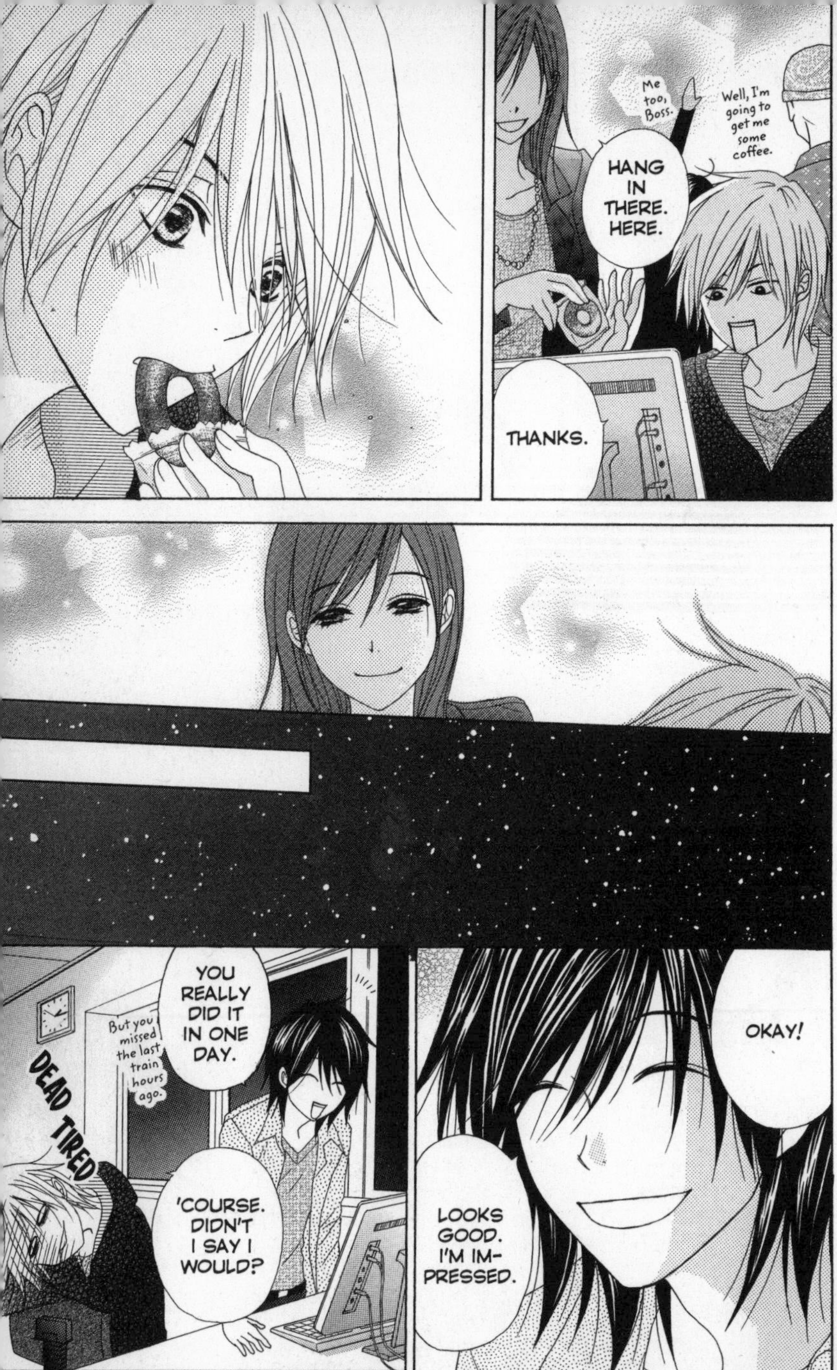
Well, I'm going to get me some coffee.
Me too, Boss.
HANG IN THERE. HERE.
THANKS.
OKAY!
LOOKS GOOD. I'M IM-PRESSED.
YOU REALLY DID IT IN ONE DAY.
But you missed the last train hours ago.
DEAD TIRED
'COURSE. DIDN'T I SAY I WOULD?

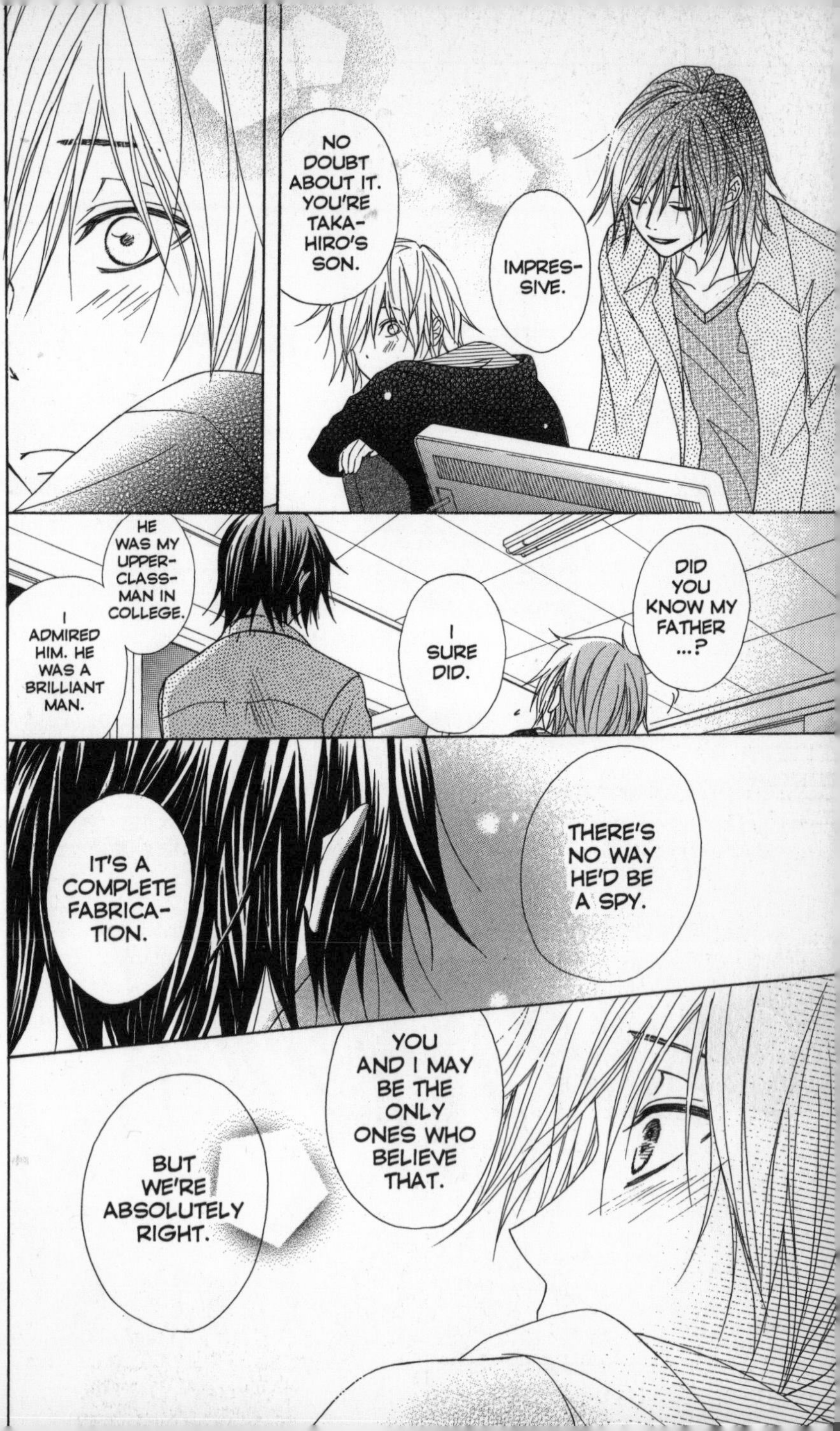
IMPRES-SIVE.
NO DOUBT ABOUT IT. YOU'RE TAKA-HIRO'S SON.
DID YOU KNOW MY FATHER ...?
I SURE DID.
HE WAS MY UPPER-CLASS-MAN IN COLLEGE.
I ADMIRED HIM. HE WAS A BRILLIANT MAN.
THERE'S NO WAY HE'D BE A SPY.
IT'S A COMPLETE FABRICA-TION.
YOU AND I MAY BE THE ONLY ONES WHO BELIEVE THAT.
BUT WE'RE ABSOLUTELY RIGHT.

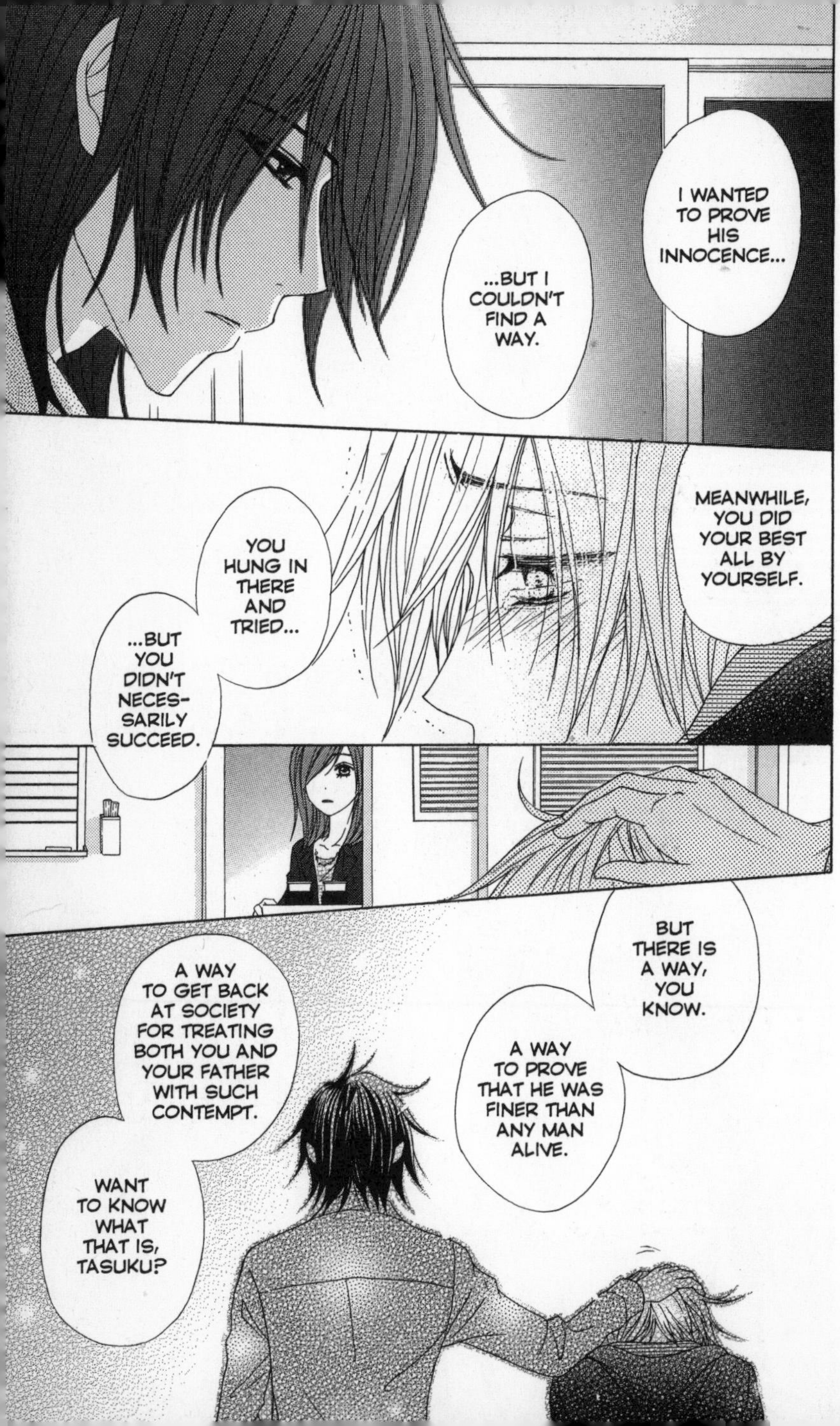
I WANTED TO PROVE HIS INNOCENCE...
...BUT I COULDN'T FIND A WAY.
MEANWHILE, YOU DID YOUR BEST ALL BY YOURSELF.
YOU HUNG IN THERE AND TRIED...
...BUT YOU DIDN'T NECES-SARILY SUCCEED.
BUT THERE IS A WAY, YOU KNOW.
A WAY TO PROVE THAT HE WAS FINER THAN ANY MAN ALIVE.
A WAY TO GET BACK AT SOCIETY FOR TREATING BOTH YOU AND YOUR FATHER WITH SUCH CONTEMPT.
WANT TO KNOW WHAT THAT IS, TASUKU?

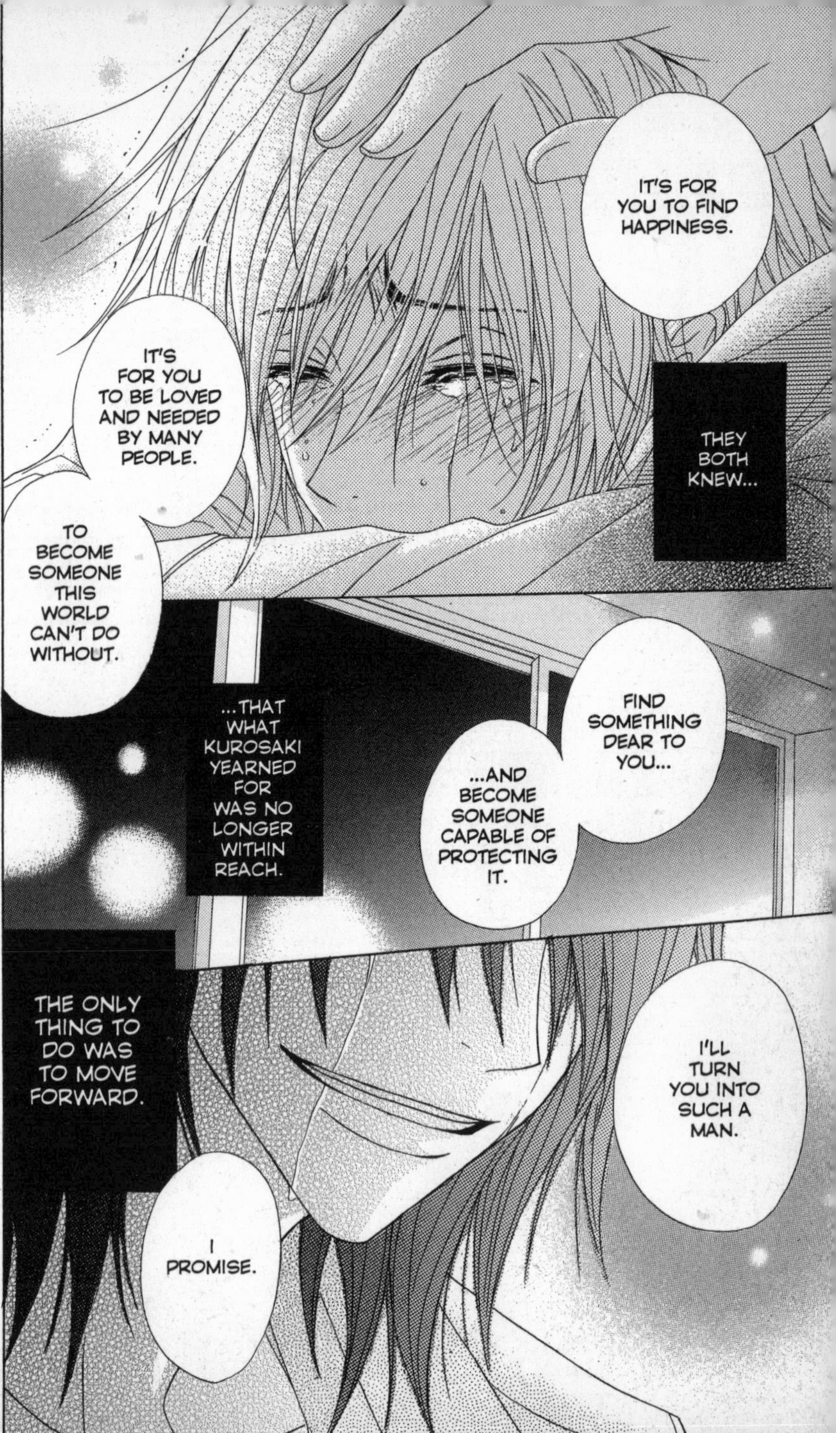
IT'S FOR YOU TO FIND HAPPINESS.
IT'S FOR YOU TO BE LOVED AND NEEDED BY MANY PEOPLE.
TO BECOME SOMEONE THIS WORLD CAN'T DO WITHOUT.
THEY BOTH KNEW...
FIND SOMETHING DEAR TO YOU...
...AND BECOME SOMEONE CAPABLE OF PROTECTING IT.
...THAT WHAT KUROSAKI YEARNED FOR WAS NO LONGER WITHIN REACH.
I'LL TURN YOU INTO SUCH A MAN.
THE ONLY THING TO DO WAS TO MOVE FORWARD.
I PROMISE.

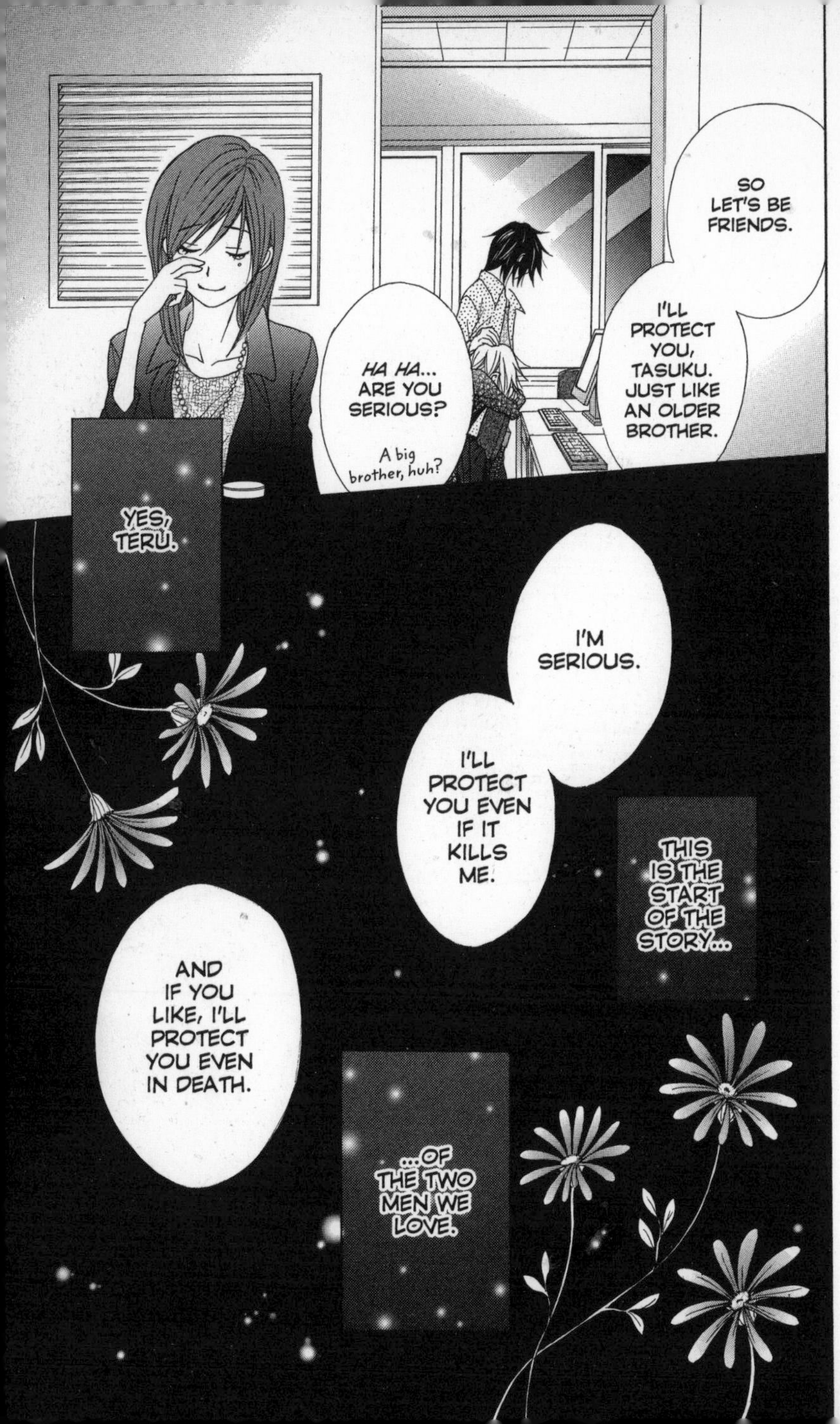
SO LET'S BE FRIENDS.
I'LL PROTECT YOU, TASUKU. JUST LIKE AN OLDER BROTHER.
HA HA... ARE YOU SERIOUS?
A big brother, huh?
YES, TERU.
I'M SERIOUS.
I'LL PROTECT YOU EVEN IF IT KILLS ME.
THIS IS THE START OF THE STORY...
AND IF YOU LIKE, I'LL PROTECT YOU EVEN IN DEATH.
...OF THE TWO MEN WE LOVE.

<SOME BAD LOVEY-DOVEY SKETCHES NO.③>

I DON'T KNOW IF IT'S BECAUSE OF THESE
SKETCHES OR JUST THAT THE DAY WAS GOING
BADLY, BUT I'VE BEEN CHOSEN TO DRAW
SOMETHING FOR THE *BETSUCOMI* JULY-AUGUST
SUPPLEMENTAL CALENDAR. SO I'LL BE DOING MORE
(RAUNCHY, HALF-NAKED) TERU AND KUROSAKI
SWIMMING-SUIT COLOR ILLUSTRATIONS... DAMN...
(THE CALENDAR IMAGE WILL PROBABLY BE IN
SOME SMALL CORNER IN THE NEXT VOLUME.)

I THOUGHT PUBLISHING THIS
DRAWING WOULD BE PROBLEMATIC
(IN A MORAL SENSE), BUT THE
EDITOR OKAYED IT, SO...

↓

I got
sand
inside.

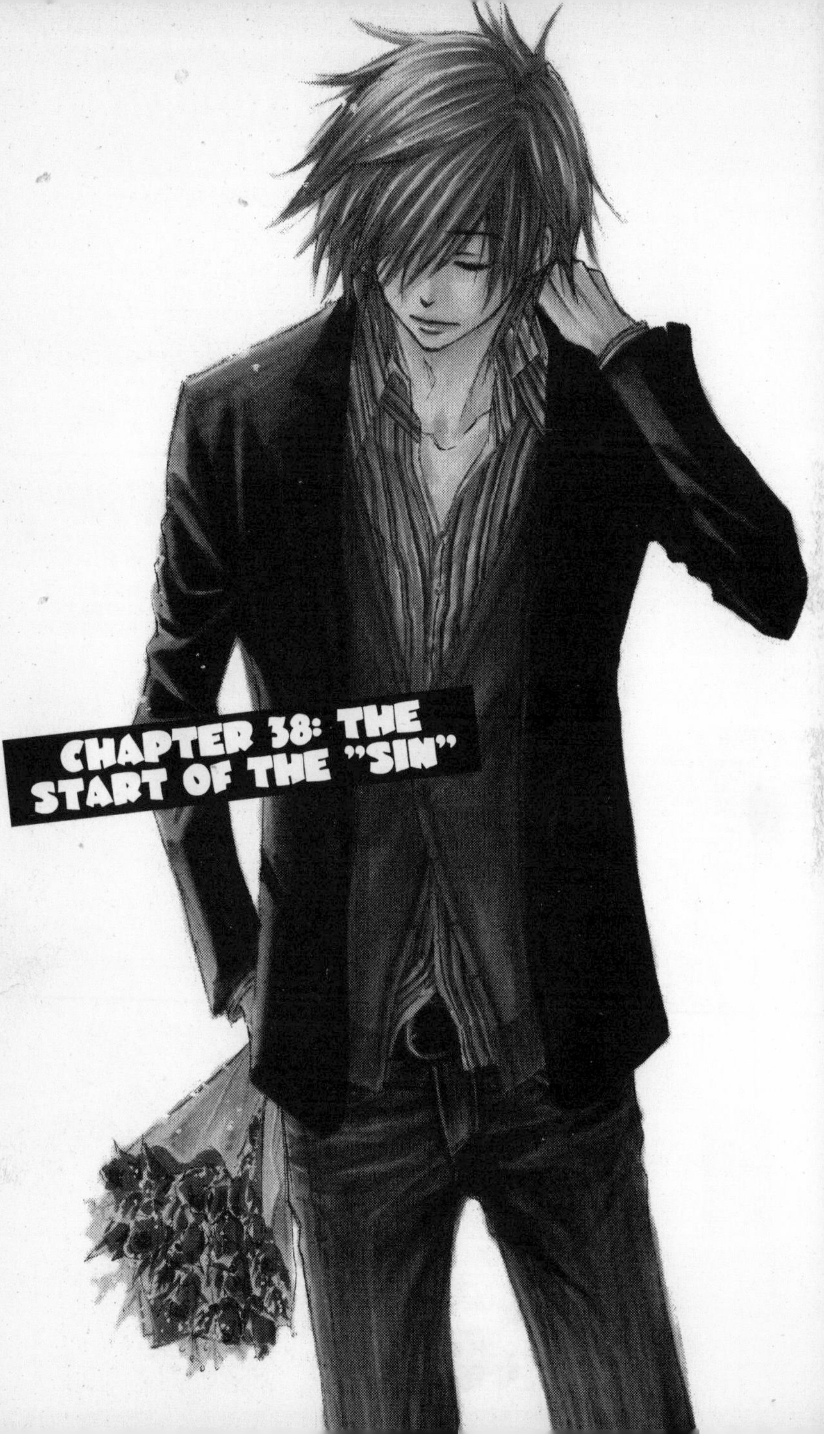
CHAPTER 38: THE START OF THE "SIN"

THE BEST ☆ OF ☆ THE SECRET STILL UP AND RUNNING! THE THIRD ONE! SCHOOL CUSTODIAN OFFICE ♥

THERE IS A *DENGEKI DAISY* FAN SEGMENT BOLDLY FEATURED IN *BETSUCOMI* THAT IS APTLY TITLED "THE SECRET SCHOOL CUSTODIAN OFFICE ♥"!
WITH DISCRIMINATING EYES, WE EXAMINED ALL THE GREAT WORK FEATURED THERE AND PICKED THE "BEST" AMONG THEM THAT WE WANTED TO LEAVE FOR POSTERITY!

THE "BEST OF" FOR VOLUME 8...IS A "KUROSAKI FESTIVAL"!

WE WANT TO GIVE A CHEER TO KUROSAKI IN THIS SECTION. ONE OPINION WAS THAT WE WERE JUST MESSING WITH HIM. IN ANY CASE, DO YOUR BEST TO KEEP YOUR HAIR, KUROSAKI!

KUROSAKI FESTIVAL (AKA "KUROSAKI MATSURI")!!

ITEMS 1-2 ARE WHAT JAPANESE READERS SUBMITTED DURING THE MAY THROUGH JULY ISSUES OF *BETSUCOMI*! ITEM 3 IS FROM FANS INSIDE THE VIZ MEDIA OFFICE!

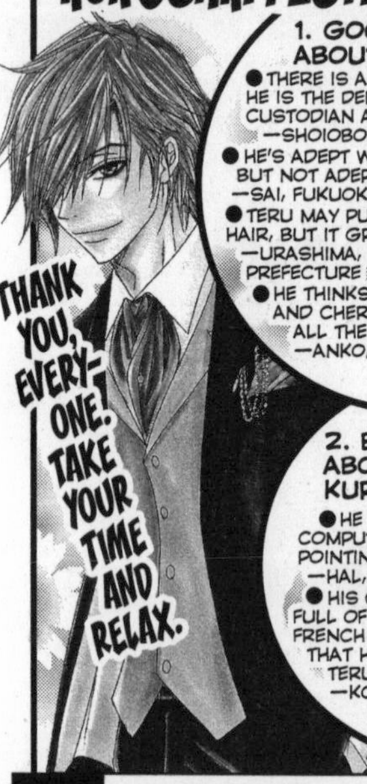

THANK YOU, EVERYONE. TAKE YOUR TIME AND RELAX.

1. GOOD THINGS ABOUT KUROSAKI!

- THERE IS A DIFFERENCE WHEN HE IS THE DELINQUENT SCHOOL CUSTODIAN AND WHEN HE IS DAISY. —SHOIOBON, MIE PREFECTURE
- HE'S ADEPT WITH HIS FINGERS BUT NOT ADEPT AT LOVE. —SAI, FUKUOKA PREFECTURE
- TERU MAY PULL OUT HIS HAIR, BUT IT GROWS BACK. —URASHIMA, KUMAMOTO PREFECTURE
- HE THINKS OF TERU AND CHERISHES HER ALL THE TIME. —ANKO, TOKYO

TERU...

2. BAD THINGS ABOUT KUROSAKI!

- HE TYPES ON THE COMPUTER WITH HIS POINTING FINGER. —HAL, CHIBA PREFECTURE
- HIS CLOSET IS PACKED FULL OF LINGERIE AND A FRENCH MAID'S COSTUME THAT HE'D LIKE TO SEE TERU IN. —KOGEICHIGO, NIIGATA PREFECTURE

NO, IT ISN'T.

3. GREAT ILLUSTRATIONS OF KUROSAKI!

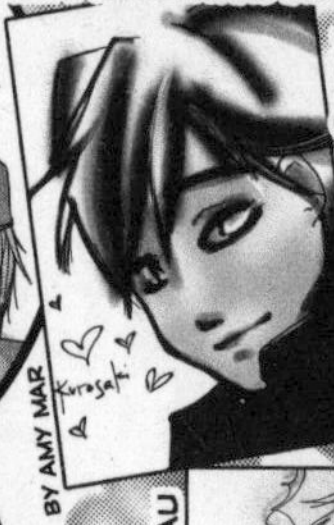

Kurosaki

BY AMY MAR

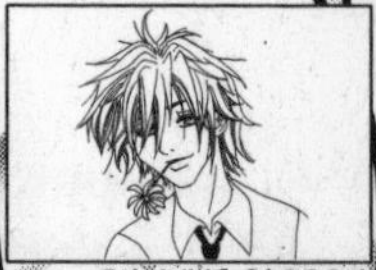
BY JULIE CASSON

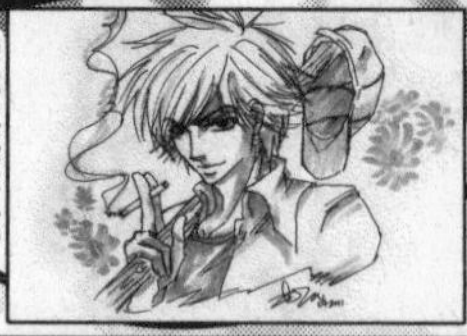
BY FAWN LAU

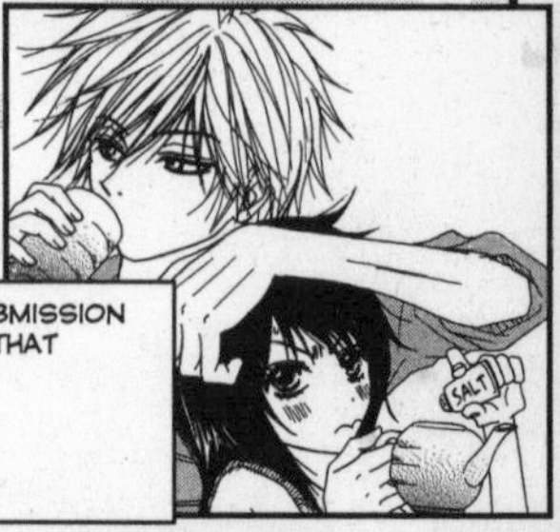

SALT

JUDGES' COMMENTS

HONESTLY, "HIS PERVERTED SIDE" WAS THE NUMBER-ONE SUBMISSION ON THE TOPIC "GOOD THINGS ABOUT KUROSAKI." I FIGURED THAT WOULD BE THE CASE.
(HEAD JUDGE: KYOUSUKE MOTOMI)
OH, COME ON, SENSEI. AS IF THAT ↑ WOULD BE THE CASE. "PERVERTED"? NO WAY.
(JUDGE: EDITOR FOR *DENGEKI DAISY*)

BETSUCOMI, THE MAGAZINE THAT SERIALIZES *DAISY*, GOES ON SALE EVERY MONTH AROUND THE 13TH!
PLEASE LOOK FOR IT IF YOU WANT TO READ "THE SECRET SCHOOL CUSTODIAN OFFICE"! ♥

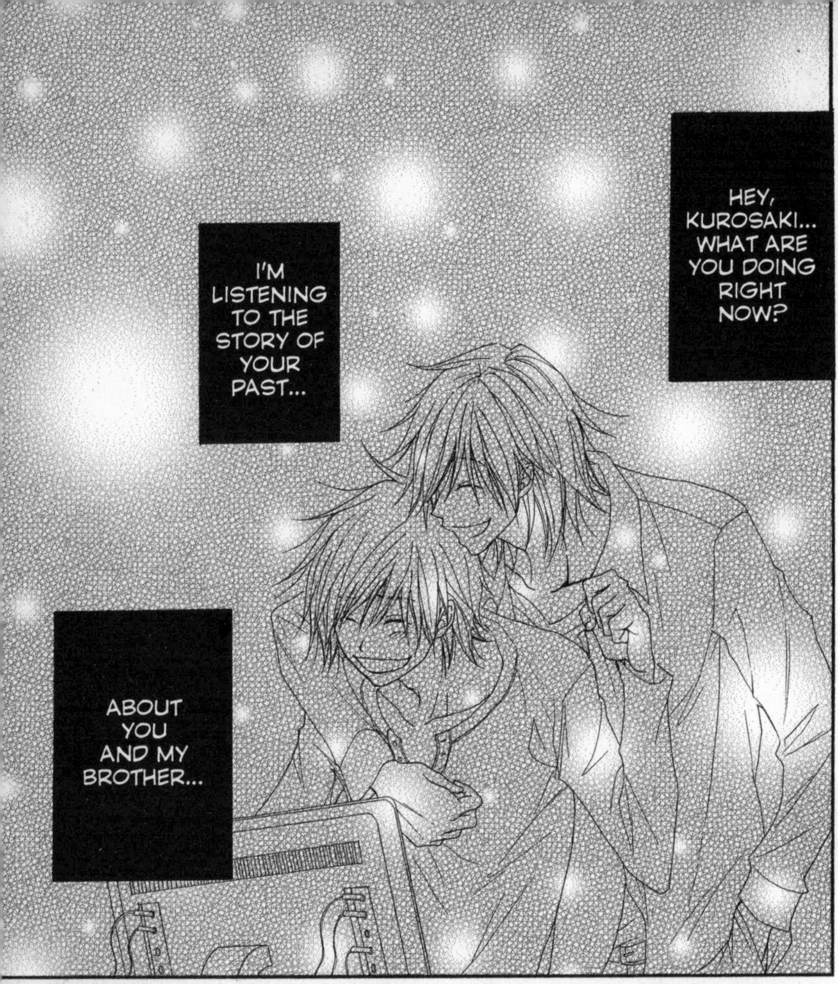
HEY, KUROSAKI... WHAT ARE YOU DOING RIGHT NOW?
I'M LISTENING TO THE STORY OF YOUR PAST...
ABOUT YOU AND MY BROTHER...

ABOUT THE FLASHBACKS IN CHAPTER 37... THIS DIDN'T APPEAR IN THE MAIN STORY, BUT IT'S BELIEVED THAT KUROSAKI LIVED WITH BOSS AT THAT TIME.

AFTER ALL, KUROSAKI WAS SO DEVOID OF FEELING AND HAD TO BE WATCHED CONSTANTLY. BOSS'S NURTURING CARE INSTILLED IN KUROSAKI THE MINIMUM ABILITY TO FIT IN WITH SOCIETY AFTER SPENDING YEARS LIVING A HARD LIFE ALONE. SO KUROSAKI HAS A SPECIAL GRATEFUL FEELING FOR BOSS, BUT IT'S SLIGHTLY DIFFERENT FROM WHAT HE FEELS TOWARD SOICHIRO. IF SOICHIRO IS AN OLDER BROTHER, BOSS IS LIKE A FOSTER MOM. MAYBE.

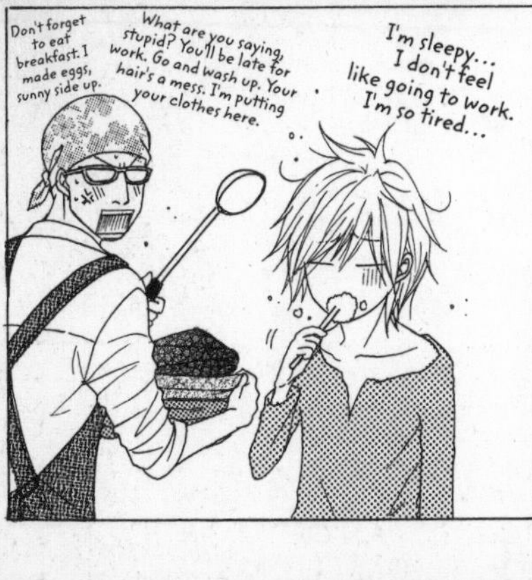
I'm sleepy... I don't feel like going to work. I'm so tired...
What are you saying, stupid? You'll be late for work. Go and wash up. Your hair's a mess. I'm putting your clothes here.
Don't forget to eat breakfast. I made eggs, sunny side up.

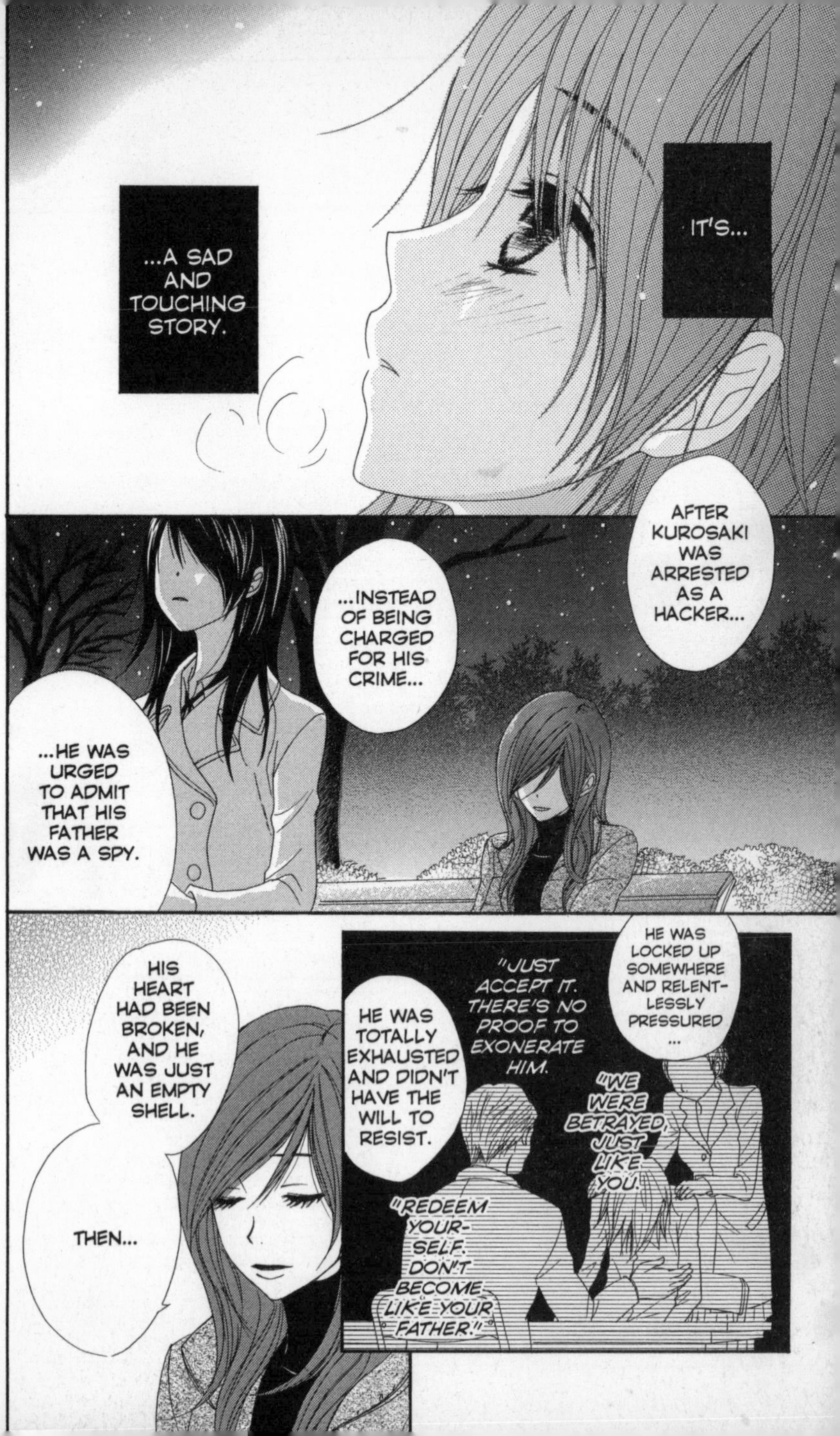
IT'S...
...A SAD AND TOUCHING STORY.
AFTER KUROSAKI WAS ARRESTED AS A HACKER...
...INSTEAD OF BEING CHARGED FOR HIS CRIME...
...HE WAS URGED TO ADMIT THAT HIS FATHER WAS A SPY.
HE WAS LOCKED UP SOMEWHERE AND RELENTLESSLY PRESSURED...
"WE WERE BETRAYED, JUST LIKE YOU."
"JUST ACCEPT IT. THERE'S NO PROOF TO EXONERATE HIM.
"REDEEM YOURSELF. DON'T BECOME LIKE YOUR FATHER."
HE WAS TOTALLY EXHAUSTED AND DIDN'T HAVE THE WILL TO RESIST.
HIS HEART HAD BEEN BROKEN, AND HE WAS JUST AN EMPTY SHELL.
THEN...

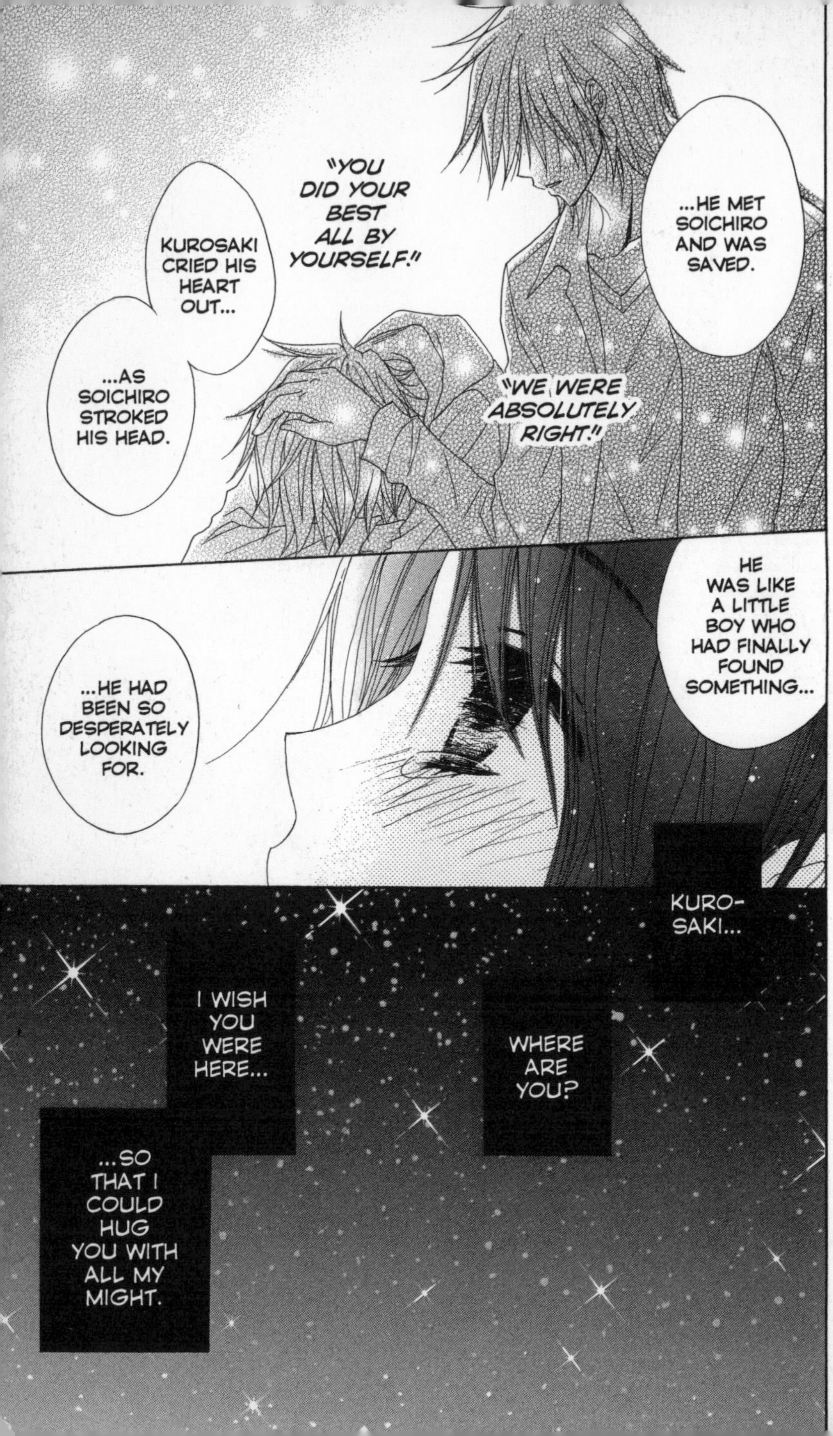
...HE MET SOICHIRO AND WAS SAVED.
"YOU DID YOUR BEST ALL BY YOURSELF!"
"WE WERE ABSOLUTELY RIGHT!"
KUROSAKI CRIED HIS HEART OUT...
...AS SOICHIRO STROKED HIS HEAD.
HE WAS LIKE A LITTLE BOY WHO HAD FINALLY FOUND SOMETHING...
...HE HAD BEEN SO DESPERATELY LOOKING FOR.
KURO-SAKI...
WHERE ARE YOU?
I WISH YOU WERE HERE...
...SO THAT I COULD HUG YOU WITH ALL MY MIGHT.

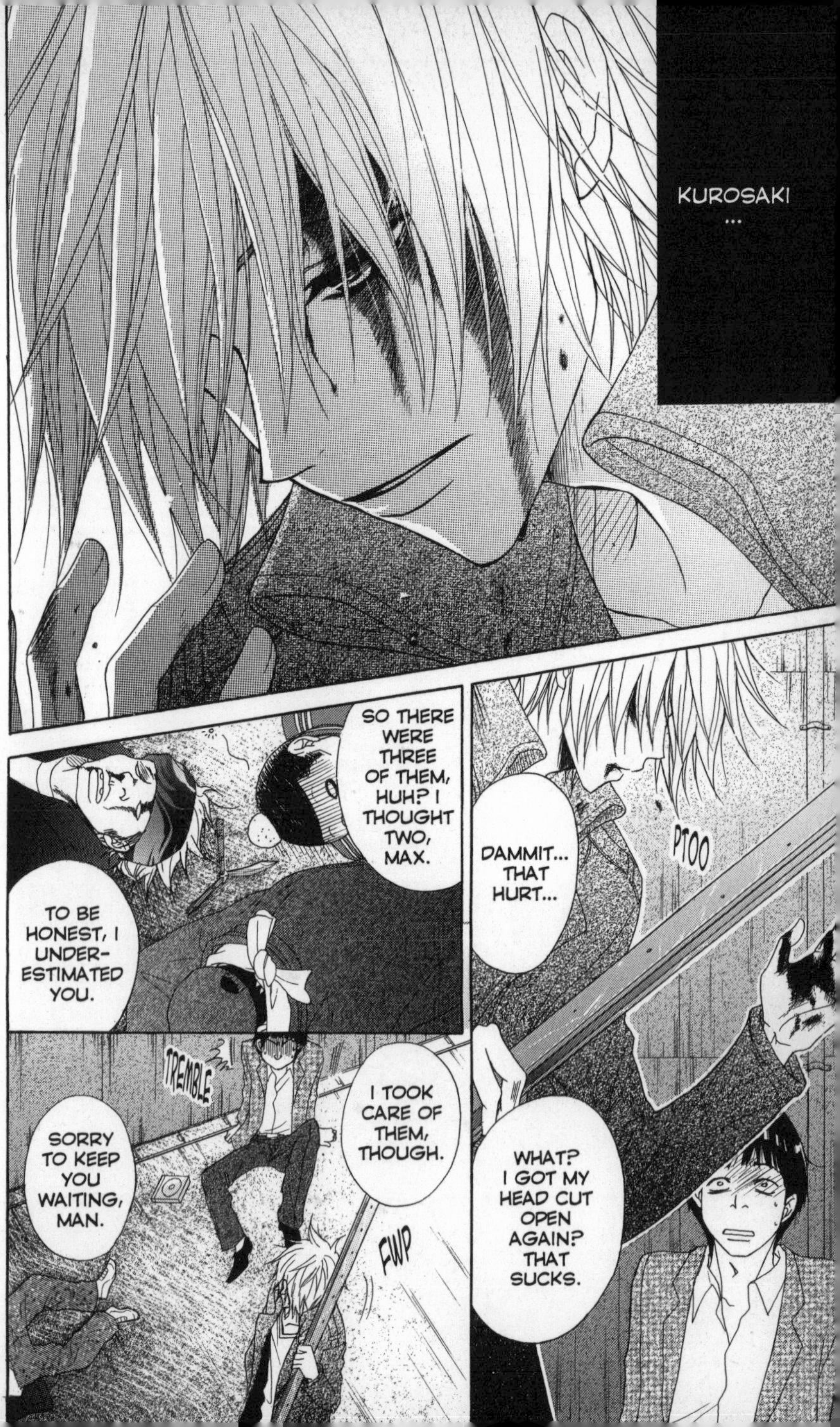
KUROSAKI ...
DAMMIT... THAT HURT...
PTOO
WHAT? I GOT MY HEAD CUT OPEN AGAIN? THAT SUCKS.
SO THERE WERE THREE OF THEM, HUH? I THOUGHT TWO, MAX.
TO BE HONEST, I UNDER-ESTIMATED YOU.
TREMBLE
I TOOK CARE OF THEM, THOUGH.
SORRY TO KEEP YOU WAITING, MAN.
FWP

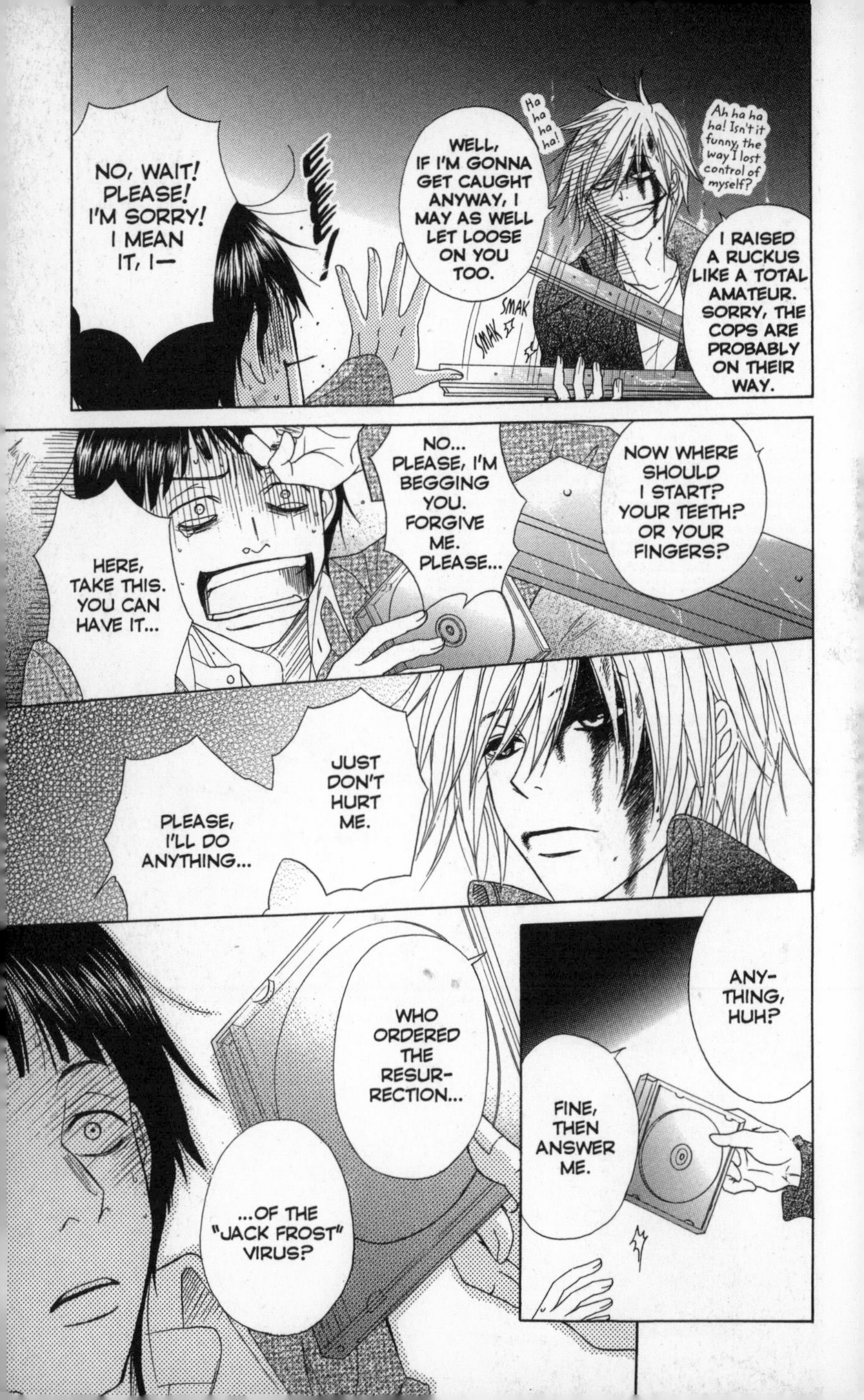
Ah ha ha ha! Isn't it funny, the way I lost control of myself?
I RAISED A RUCKUS LIKE A TOTAL AMATEUR. SORRY, THE COPS ARE PROBABLY ON THEIR WAY.
Ha ha ha ha!
WELL, IF I'M GONNA GET CAUGHT ANYWAY, I MAY AS WELL LET LOOSE ON YOU TOO.
SMAK
SMAK
NO, WAIT! PLEASE! I'M SORRY! I MEAN IT, I—
NOW WHERE SHOULD I START? YOUR TEETH? OR YOUR FINGERS?
NO... PLEASE, I'M BEGGING YOU. FORGIVE ME. PLEASE...
HERE, TAKE THIS. YOU CAN HAVE IT...
JUST DON'T HURT ME.
PLEASE, I'LL DO ANYTHING...
ANY-THING, HUH?
FINE, THEN ANSWER ME.
WHO ORDERED THE RESUR-RECTION...
...OF THE "JACK FROST" VIRUS?

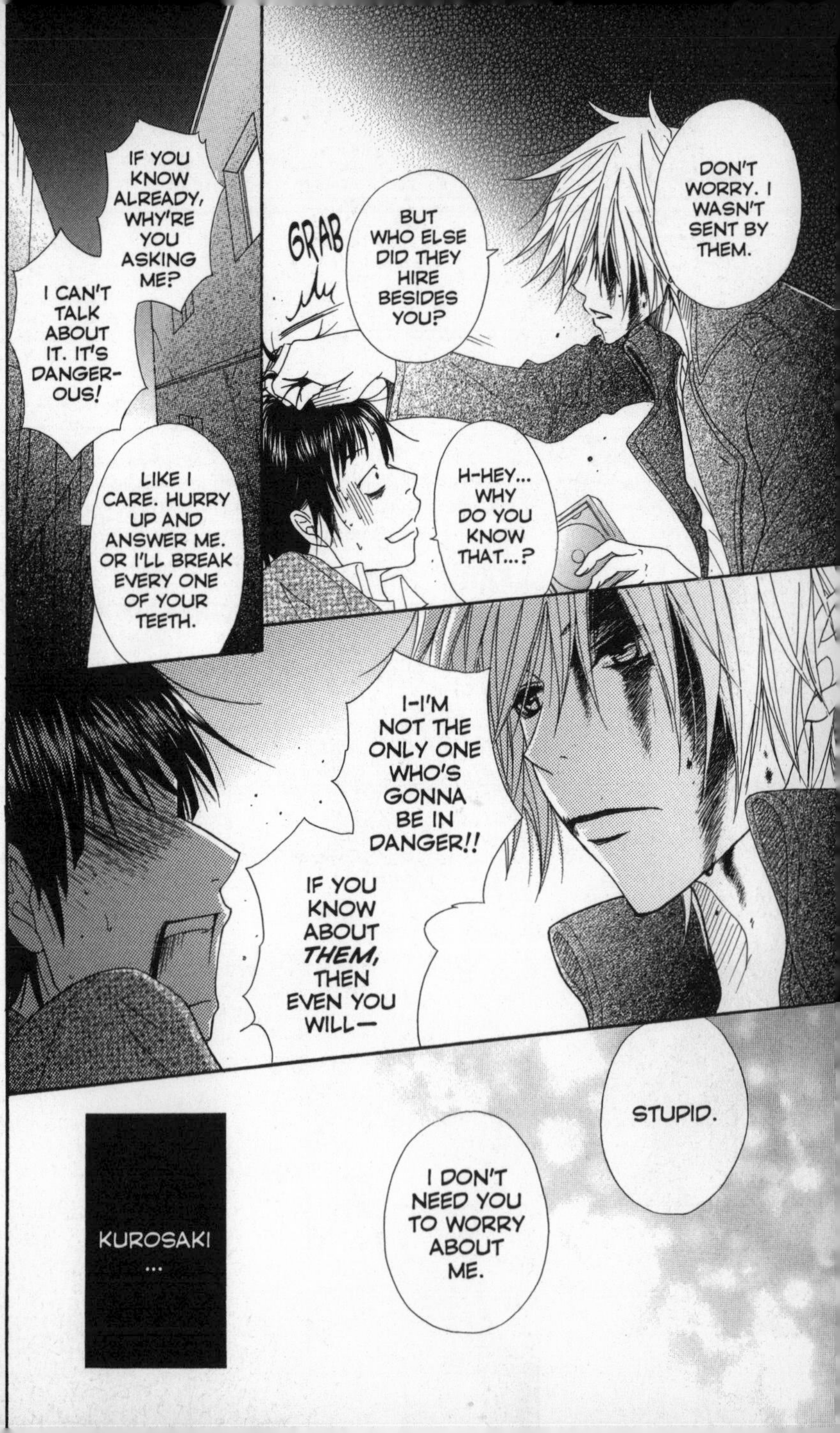
DON'T WORRY. I WASN'T SENT BY THEM.
BUT WHO ELSE DID THEY HIRE BESIDES YOU?
GRAB
H-HEY... WHY DO YOU KNOW THAT...?
IF YOU KNOW ALREADY, WHY'RE YOU ASKING ME?
I CAN'T TALK ABOUT IT. IT'S DANGER-OUS!
LIKE I CARE. HURRY UP AND ANSWER ME. OR I'LL BREAK EVERY ONE OF YOUR TEETH.
I-I'M NOT THE ONLY ONE WHO'S GONNA BE IN DANGER!!
IF YOU KNOW ABOUT *THEM,* THEN EVEN YOU WILL—
STUPID.
I DON'T NEED YOU TO WORRY ABOUT ME.
KUROSAKI ...

WHATEVER HAPPENS, IT'S JUST ME.
SO IT DOESN'T MATTER.
PLEASE TAKE CARE OF YOUR-SELF...
...UNTIL I CAN CATCH UP TO YOU.
PLEASE...
DON'T END UP LIKE MY BROTHER...
...AND GO WHERE I CAN'T REACH YOU...

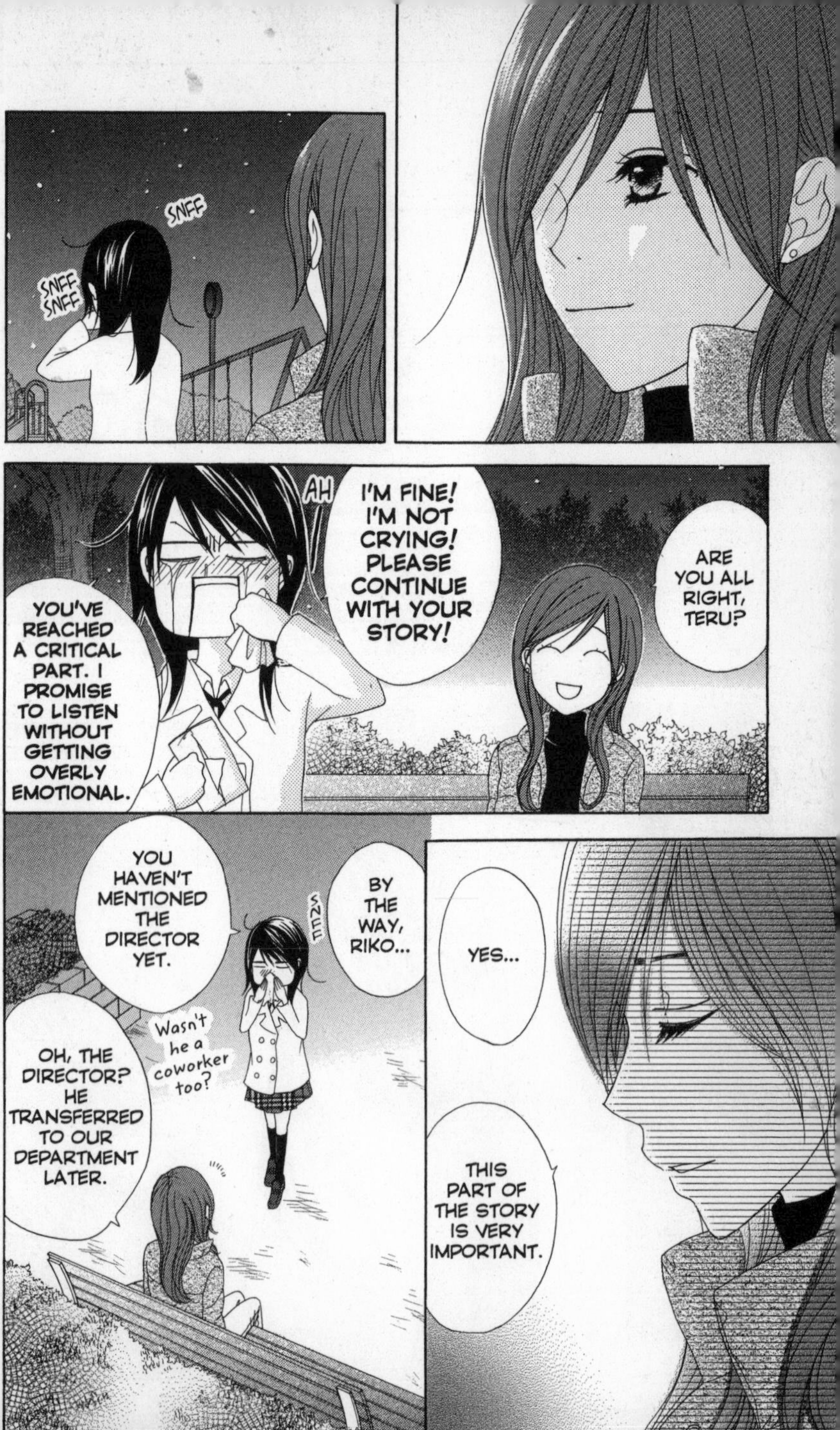
SNFF
SNFF SNFF
ARE YOU ALL RIGHT, TERU?
AH
I'M FINE! I'M NOT CRYING! PLEASE CONTINUE WITH YOUR STORY!
YOU'VE REACHED A CRITICAL PART. I PROMISE TO LISTEN WITHOUT GETTING OVERLY EMOTIONAL.
YES...
THIS PART OF THE STORY IS VERY IMPORTANT.
BY THE WAY, RIKO...
SNFF
YOU HAVEN'T MENTIONED THE DIRECTOR YET.
Wasn't he a coworker too?
OH, THE DIRECTOR? HE TRANSFERRED TO OUR DEPARTMENT LATER.

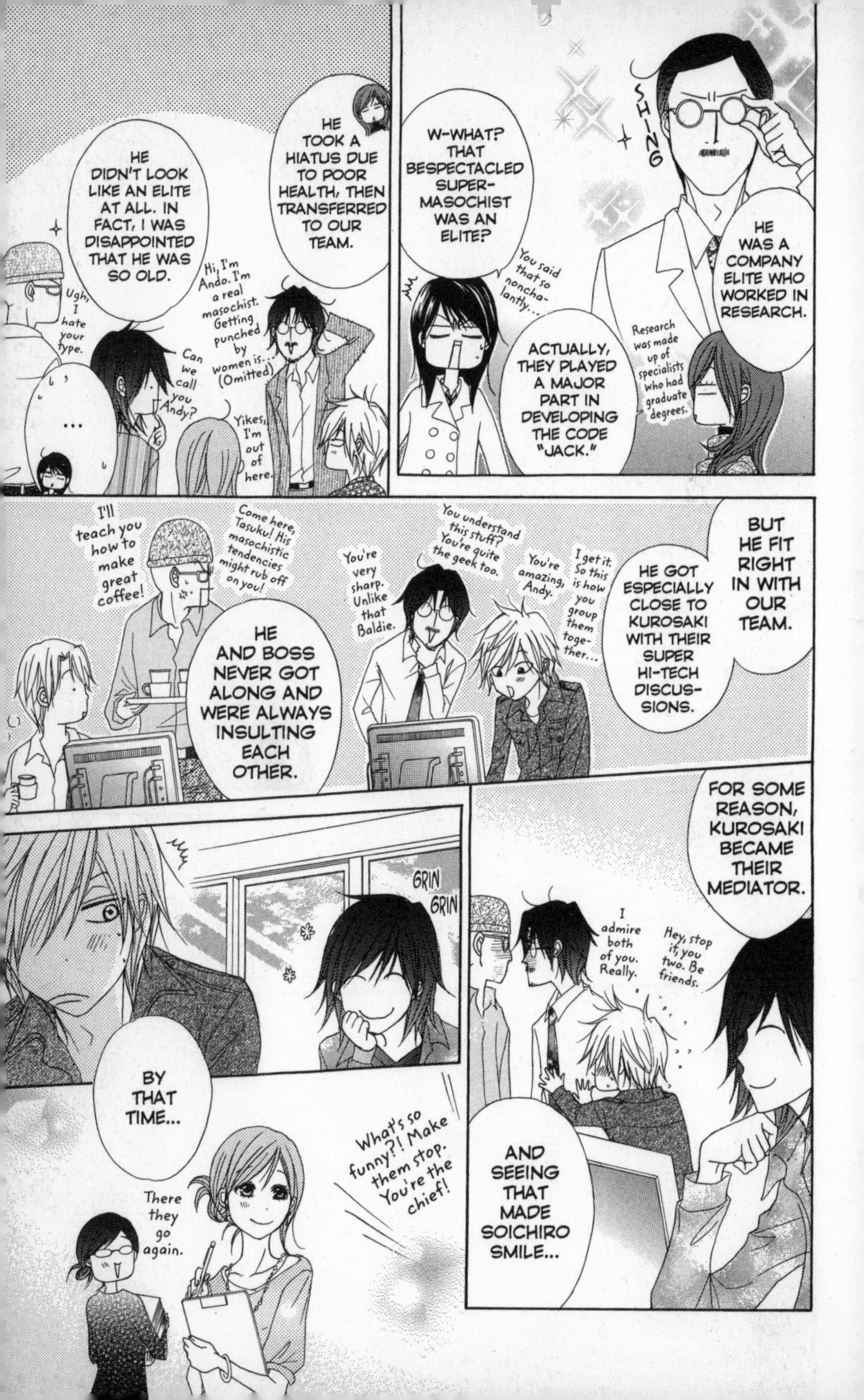
SHING
HE WAS A COMPANY ELITE WHO WORKED IN RESEARCH.
Research was made up of specialists who had graduate degrees.
W-WHAT? THAT BESPECTACLED SUPER-MASOCHIST WAS AN ELITE?
You said that so noncha-lantly...
ACTUALLY, THEY PLAYED A MAJOR PART IN DEVELOPING THE CODE "JACK."
HE TOOK A HIATUS DUE TO POOR HEALTH, THEN TRANSFERRED TO OUR TEAM.
HE DIDN'T LOOK LIKE AN ELITE AT ALL. IN FACT, I WAS DISAPPOINTED THAT HE WAS SO OLD.
Hi, I'm Ando. I'm a real masochist. Getting punched by women is... (Omitted)
Yikes, I'm out of here.
Can we call you Andy?
Ugh, I hate your type.
...
BUT HE FIT RIGHT IN WITH OUR TEAM.
HE GOT ESPECIALLY CLOSE TO KUROSAKI WITH THEIR SUPER HI-TECH DISCUS-SIONS.
I get it. So this is how you group them toge-ther...
You're amazing, Andy.
You understand this stuff? You're quite the geek too.
You're very sharp. Unlike that Baldie.
HE AND BOSS NEVER GOT ALONG AND WERE ALWAYS INSULTING EACH OTHER.
Come here, Tasuku! His masochistic tendencies might rub off on you!
I'll teach you how to make great coffee!
FOR SOME REASON, KUROSAKI BECAME THEIR MEDIATOR.
Hey, stop it, you two. Be friends.
I admire both of you. Really.
AND SEEING THAT MADE SOICHIRO SMILE...
GRIN
GRIN
BY THAT TIME...
What's so funny?! Make them stop. You're the chief!
There they go again.

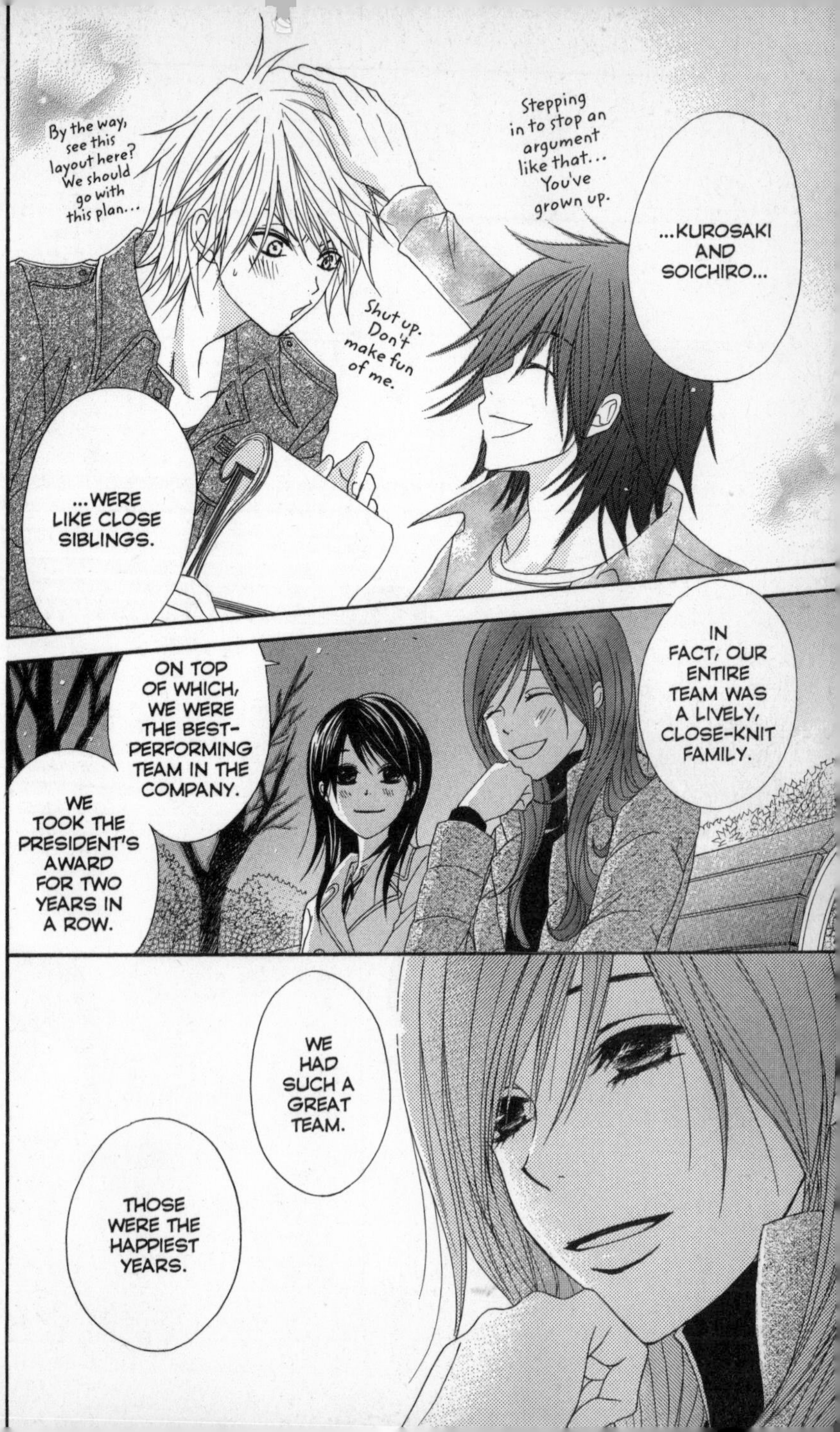
...KUROSAKI AND SOICHIRO...
Stepping in to stop an argument like that... You've grown up.
By the way, see this layout here? We should go with this plan...
Shut up. Don't make fun of me.
...WERE LIKE CLOSE SIBLINGS.
IN FACT, OUR ENTIRE TEAM WAS A LIVELY, CLOSE-KNIT FAMILY.
ON TOP OF WHICH, WE WERE THE BEST-PERFORMING TEAM IN THE COMPANY.
WE TOOK THE PRESIDENT'S AWARD FOR TWO YEARS IN A ROW.
WE HAD SUCH A GREAT TEAM.
THOSE WERE THE HAPPIEST YEARS.

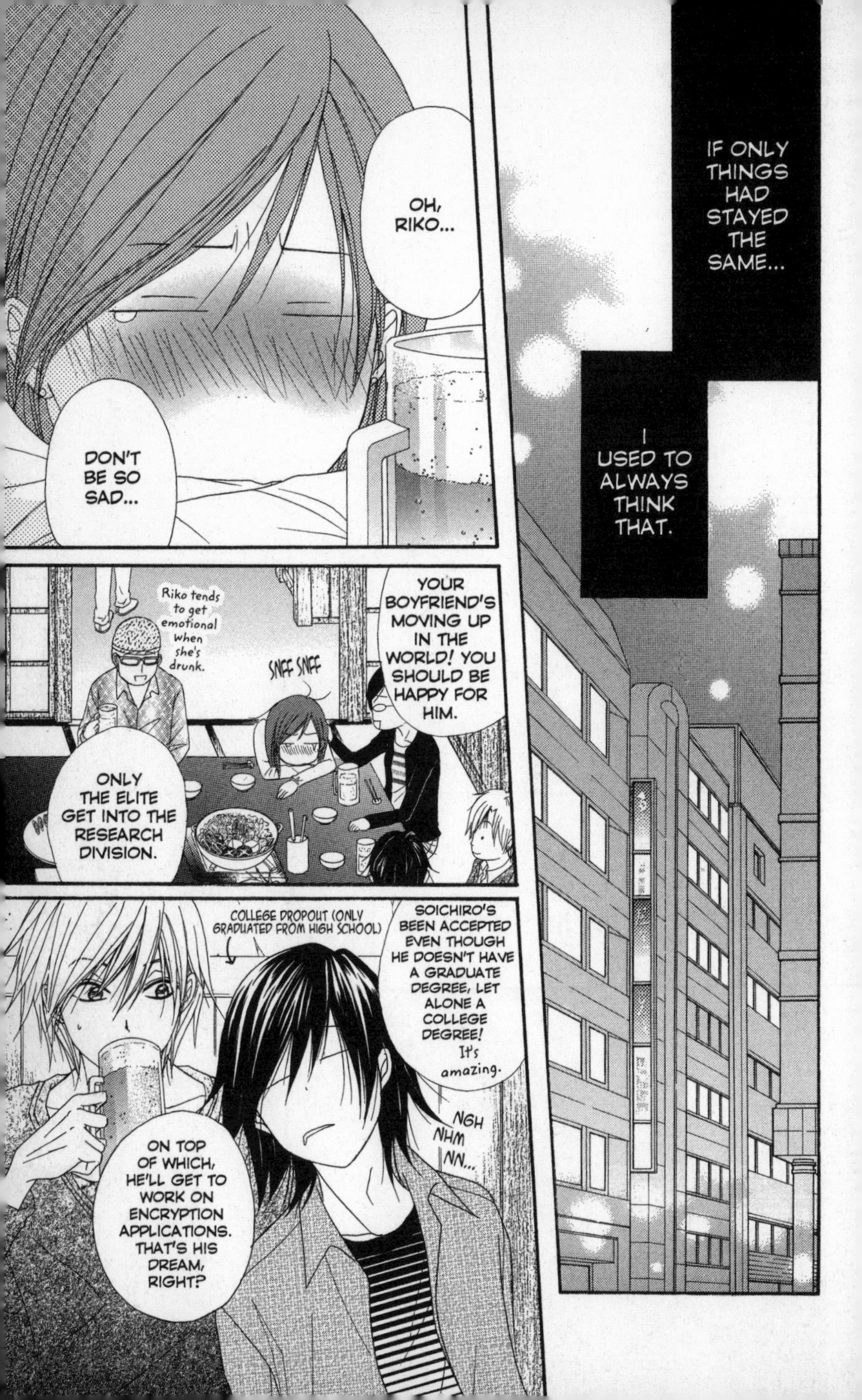
IF ONLY THINGS HAD STAYED THE SAME...
I USED TO ALWAYS THINK THAT.
OH, RIKO...
DON'T BE SO SAD...
YOUR BOYFRIEND'S MOVING UP IN THE WORLD! YOU SHOULD BE HAPPY FOR HIM.
SNIFF SNIFF
Riko tends to get emotional when she's drunk.
ONLY THE ELITE GET INTO THE RESEARCH DIVISION.
SOICHIRO'S BEEN ACCEPTED EVEN THOUGH HE DOESN'T HAVE A GRADUATE DEGREE, LET ALONE A COLLEGE DEGREE!
It's amazing.
COLLEGE DROPOUT (ONLY GRADUATED FROM HIGH SCHOOL)
NGH NHM NN...
ON TOP OF WHICH, HE'LL GET TO WORK ON ENCRYPTION APPLICATIONS. THAT'S HIS DREAM, RIGHT?

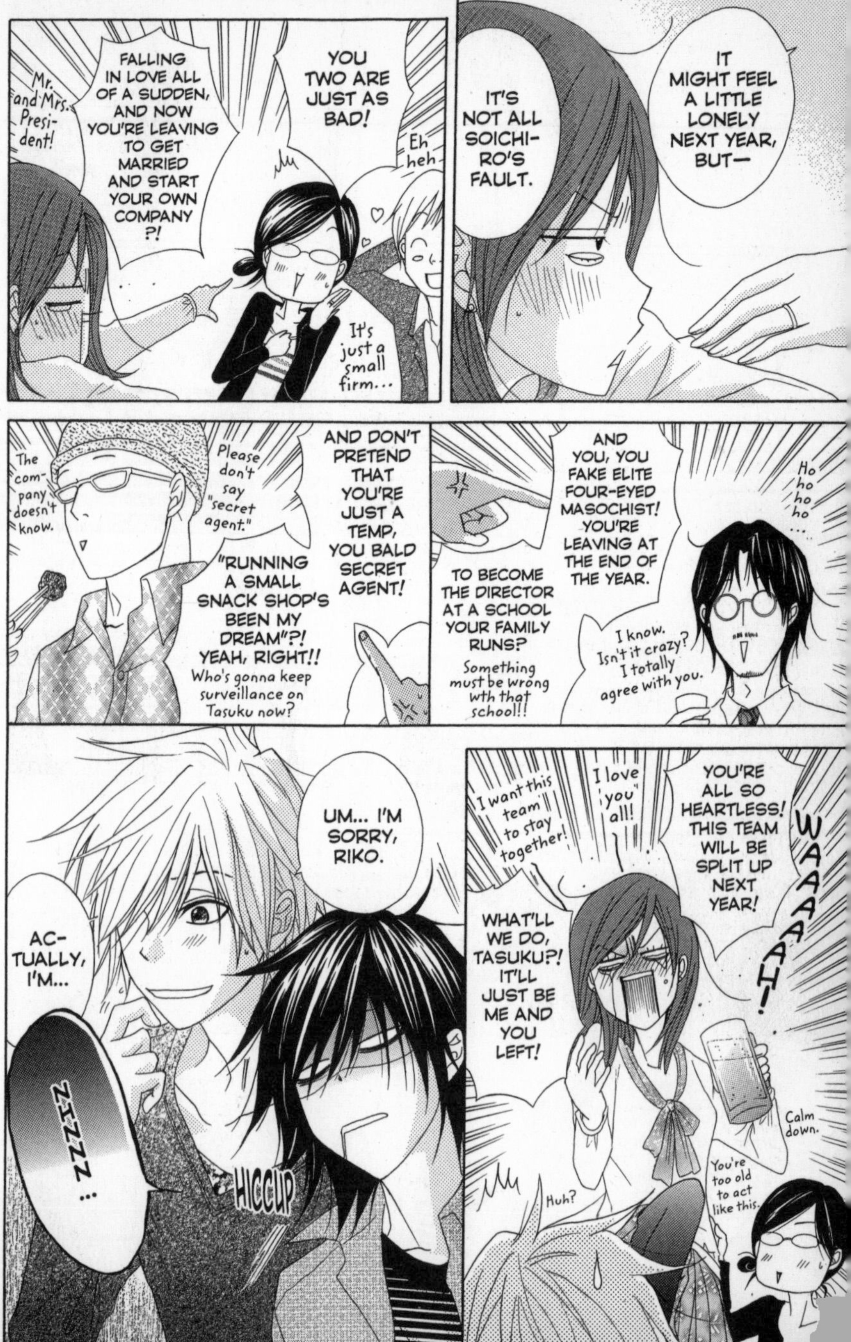
IT MIGHT FEEL A LITTLE LONELY NEXT YEAR, BUT—
IT'S NOT ALL SOICHIRO'S FAULT.
YOU TWO ARE JUST AS BAD!
Eh heh
FALLING IN LOVE ALL OF A SUDDEN, AND NOW YOU'RE LEAVING TO GET MARRIED AND START YOUR OWN COMPANY?!
Mr. and Mrs. President!
It's just a small firm...
Ho ho ho ho...
AND YOU, YOU FAKE ELITE FOUR-EYED MASOCHIST! YOU'RE LEAVING AT THE END OF THE YEAR.
TO BECOME THE DIRECTOR AT A SCHOOL YOUR FAMILY RUNS?
I know. Isn't it crazy? I totally agree with you.
Something must be wrong wth that school!!
AND DON'T PRETEND THAT YOU'RE JUST A TEMP, YOU BALD SECRET AGENT!
Please don't say "secret agent."
The company doesn't know.
"RUNNING A SMALL SNACK SHOP'S BEEN MY DREAM"?! YEAH, RIGHT!!
Who's gonna keep surveillance on Tasuku now?
WAAAAAH!
YOU'RE ALL SO HEARTLESS! THIS TEAM WILL BE SPLIT UP NEXT YEAR!
I love you all!
I want this team to stay together!
WHAT'LL WE DO, TASUKU?! IT'LL JUST BE ME AND YOU LEFT!
Calm down.
You're too old to act like this.
Huh?
UM... I'M SORRY, RIKO.
ACTUALLY, I'M...
HICCUP
ZZZZZ...

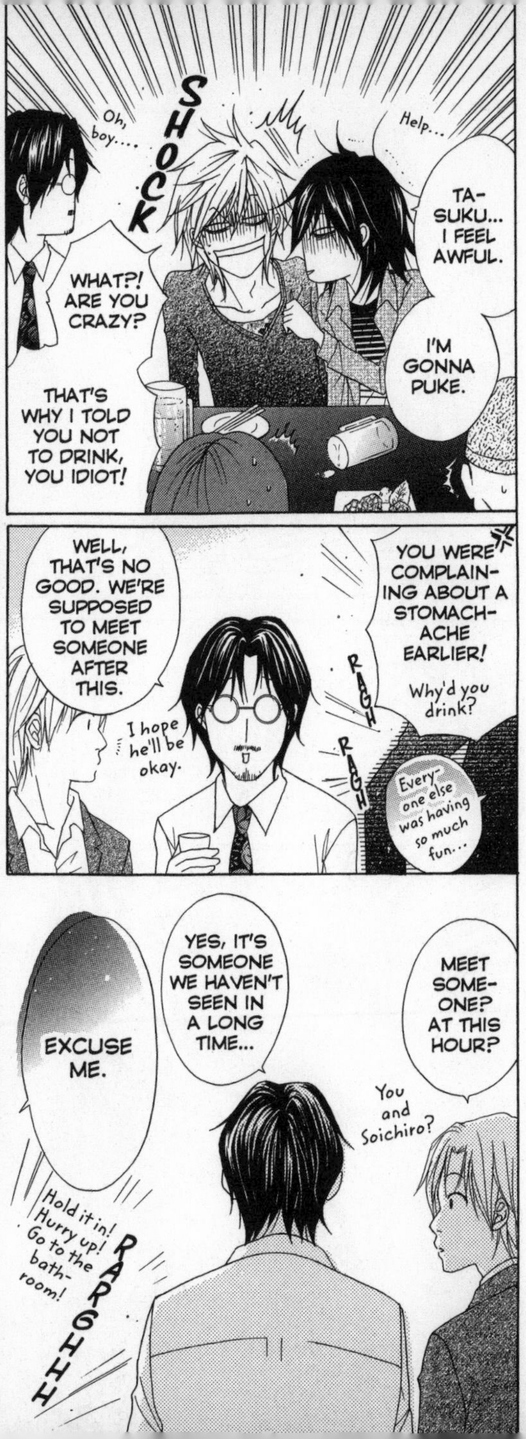
Help...
TA-SUKU... I FEEL AWFUL.
I'M GONNA PUKE.
SHOCK
Oh, boy....
WHAT?! ARE YOU CRAZY?
THAT'S WHY I TOLD YOU NOT TO DRINK, YOU IDIOT!
YOU WERE COMPLAIN-ING ABOUT A STOMACH-ACHE EARLIER!
Why'd you drink?
RAGH
RAGH
Every-one else was having so much fun...
WELL, THAT'S NO GOOD. WE'RE SUPPOSED TO MEET SOMEONE AFTER THIS.
I hope he'll be okay.
MEET SOME-ONE? AT THIS HOUR?
You and Soichiro?
YES, IT'S SOMEONE WE HAVEN'T SEEN IN A LONG TIME...
EXCUSE ME.
RARGHHH
Hold it in! Hurry up! Go to the bath-room!

DENGEKI DAISY QUESTION CORNER

BALDLY ASK!! ④

Q.
BOSS ALWAYS WEARS A BANDANA OR A CAP. WHAT'S UNDER THAT? IS IT A BALD HEAD? OR DOES HE HAVE A SPECIAL HAIRSTYLE...?

(AYUMI, YAMAGATA PREFECTURE)

A.
BOSS IS BALD. THERE'S A REASON FOR ALWAYS COVERING UP HIS HEAD. IT MAY COME UP IN THE SERIES. IN PAST CHAPTERS, I WONDERED IF HIS WEARING A CAP AT WORK MIGHT BE PROBLEMATIC. BUT DRAWING HIM WITH A WIG WOULD BE SO FUNNY THAT I DIDN'T THINK HE'D BE TAKEN SERIOUSLY. SO I STUCK TO THE CAP.

Q.
DOESN'T KUROSAKI PLAY WITH ADULT TOYS? HE SEEMS PERVERTED, SO I THOUGHT SURELY... ANYWAY, I WAS A LITTLE SHOCKED WHEN I HEARD THAT HE'S NOT THE TYPE TO USE THEM... BUT REALLY, DOESN'T HE? DON'T BE SHY. TELL US.

(RIKOPIN, FUKUOKA PREFECTURE)

A.
...HMM... SORRY TO DISAPPOINT YOU. KUROSAKI HAS A PREFERENCE FOR NATURAL MATERIALS. IN FACT, WHEN HE'S DOING HIS MANLY RITUAL, RATHER THAN ADULT VIDEOS, HE LEAVES IT ALL UP TO HIS IMAGINATION. HE'S A LOHAS PERVERT. SORRY.

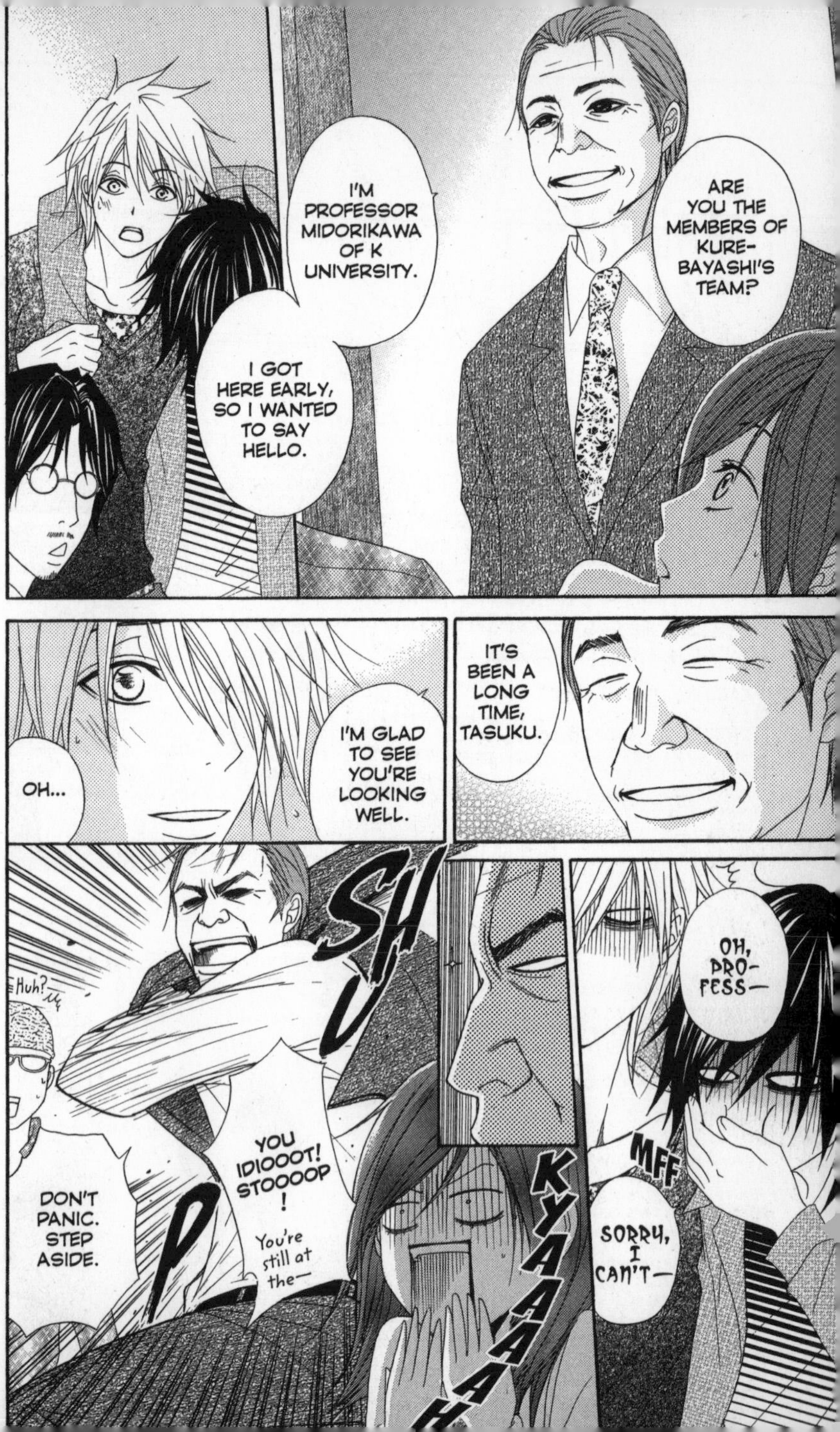
ARE YOU THE MEMBERS OF KURE-BAYASHI'S TEAM?
I'M PROFESSOR MIDORIKAWA OF K UNIVERSITY.
I GOT HERE EARLY, SO I WANTED TO SAY HELLO.
IT'S BEEN A LONG TIME, TASUKU.
I'M GLAD TO SEE YOU'RE LOOKING WELL.
OH...
OH, PRO-FESS—
MFF
SORRY, I CAN'T—
KYAAAAAH
SH
YOU IDIOOOT! STOOOOP!
You're still at the—
P
DON'T PANIC. STEP ASIDE.
Huh?

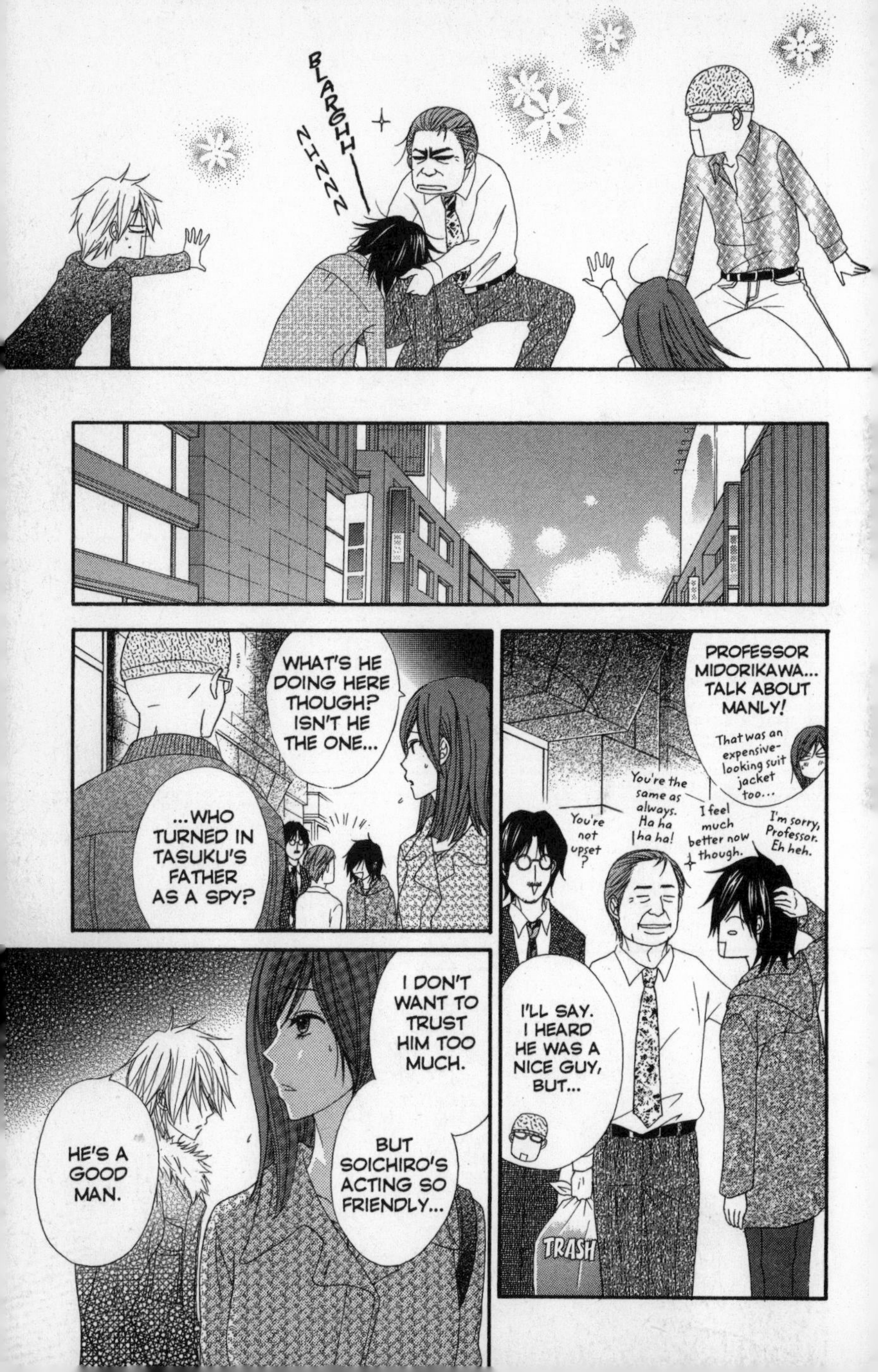
BLARGHH
NHNNN
PROFESSOR MIDORIKAWA... TALK ABOUT MANLY!
That was an expensive-looking suit jacket too...
I'm sorry, Professor. Eh heh.
I feel much better now though.
You're the same as always. Ha ha ha ha!
You're not upset?
I'LL SAY. I HEARD HE WAS A NICE GUY, BUT...
TRASH
WHAT'S HE DOING HERE THOUGH? ISN'T HE THE ONE...
...WHO TURNED IN TASUKU'S FATHER AS A SPY?
I DON'T WANT TO TRUST HIM TOO MUCH.
BUT SOICHIRO'S ACTING SO FRIENDLY...
HE'S A GOOD MAN.

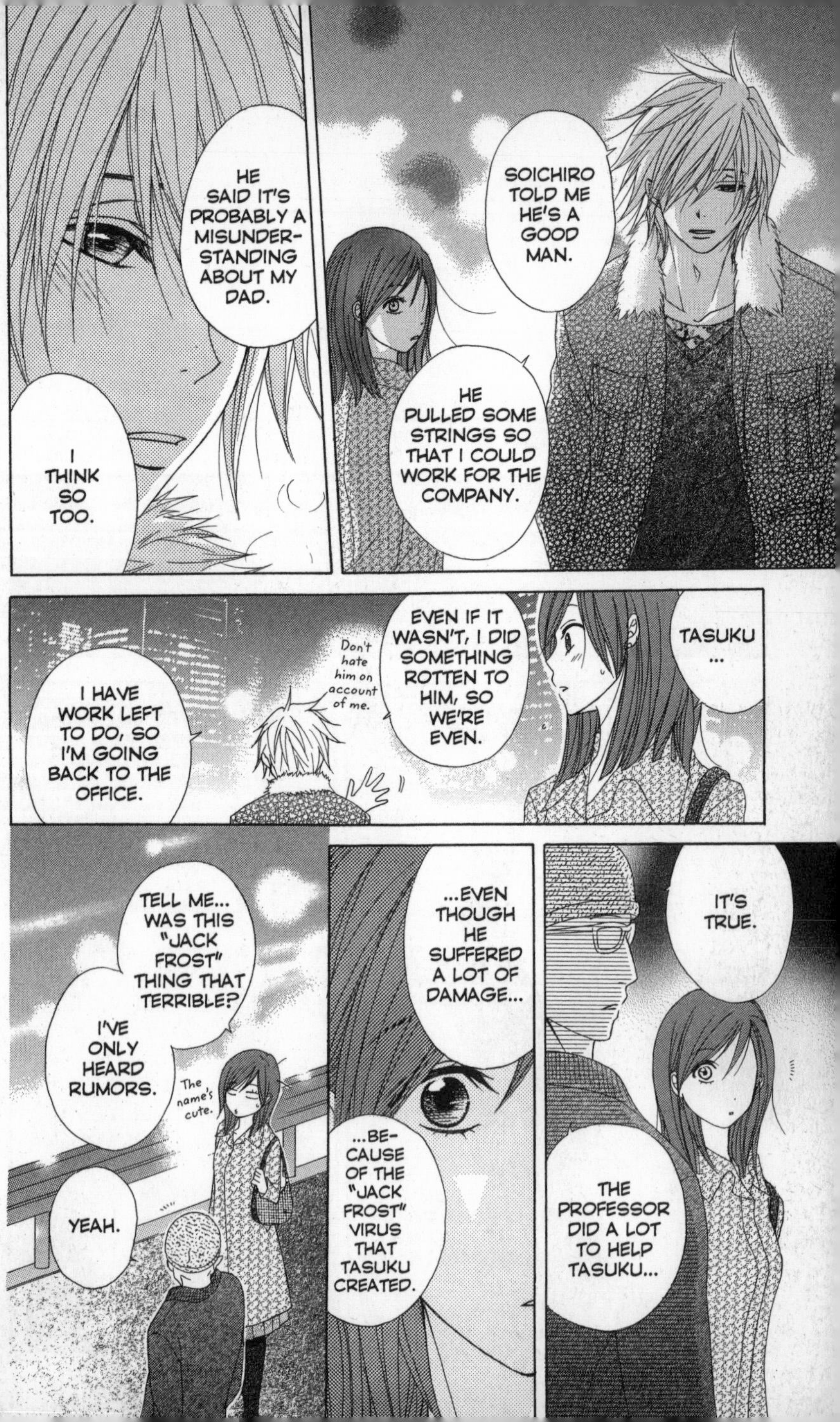
SOICHIRO TOLD ME HE'S A GOOD MAN.
HE PULLED SOME STRINGS SO THAT I COULD WORK FOR THE COMPANY.
HE SAID IT'S PROBABLY A MISUNDERSTANDING ABOUT MY DAD.
I THINK SO TOO.
TASUKU...
EVEN IF IT WASN'T, I DID SOMETHING ROTTEN TO HIM, SO WE'RE EVEN.
Don't hate him on account of me.
I HAVE WORK LEFT TO DO, SO I'M GOING BACK TO THE OFFICE.
IT'S TRUE.
THE PROFESSOR DID A LOT TO HELP TASUKU...
...EVEN THOUGH HE SUFFERED A LOT OF DAMAGE...
...BECAUSE OF THE "JACK FROST" VIRUS THAT TASUKU CREATED.
TELL ME... WAS THIS "JACK FROST" THING THAT TERRIBLE?
I'VE ONLY HEARD RUMORS.
The name's cute.
YEAH.

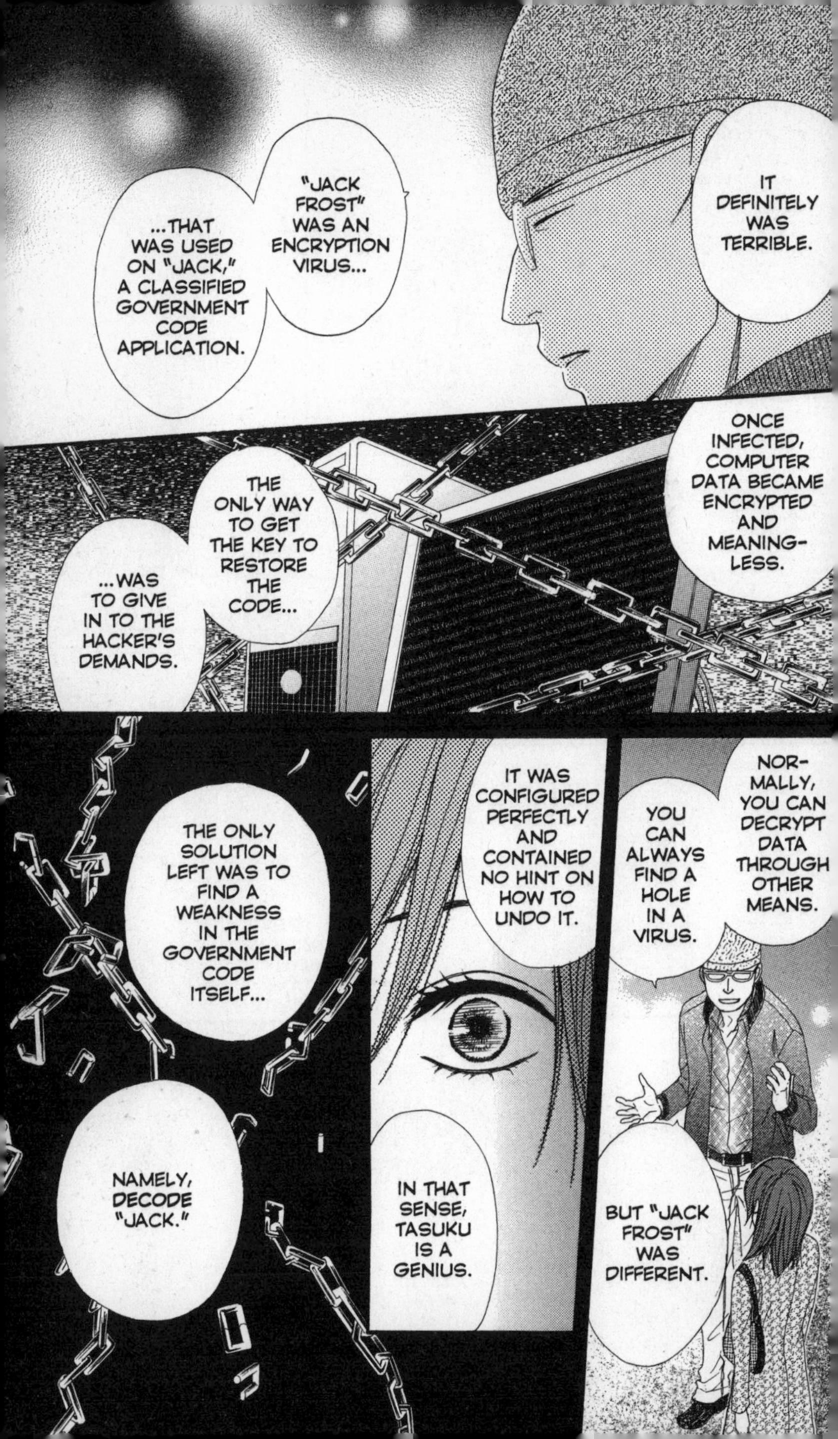
IT DEFINITELY WAS TERRIBLE.
"JACK FROST" WAS AN ENCRYPTION VIRUS...
...THAT WAS USED ON "JACK," A CLASSIFIED GOVERNMENT CODE APPLICATION.
ONCE INFECTED, COMPUTER DATA BECAME ENCRYPTED AND MEANING-LESS.
THE ONLY WAY TO GET THE KEY TO RESTORE THE CODE...
...WAS TO GIVE IN TO THE HACKER'S DEMANDS.
NOR-MALLY, YOU CAN DECRYPT DATA THROUGH OTHER MEANS.
YOU CAN ALWAYS FIND A HOLE IN A VIRUS.
BUT "JACK FROST" WAS DIFFERENT.
IT WAS CONFIGURED PERFECTLY AND CONTAINED NO HINT ON HOW TO UNDO IT.
IN THAT SENSE, TASUKU IS A GENIUS.
THE ONLY SOLUTION LEFT WAS TO FIND A WEAKNESS IN THE GOVERNMENT CODE ITSELF...
NAMELY, DECODE "JACK."

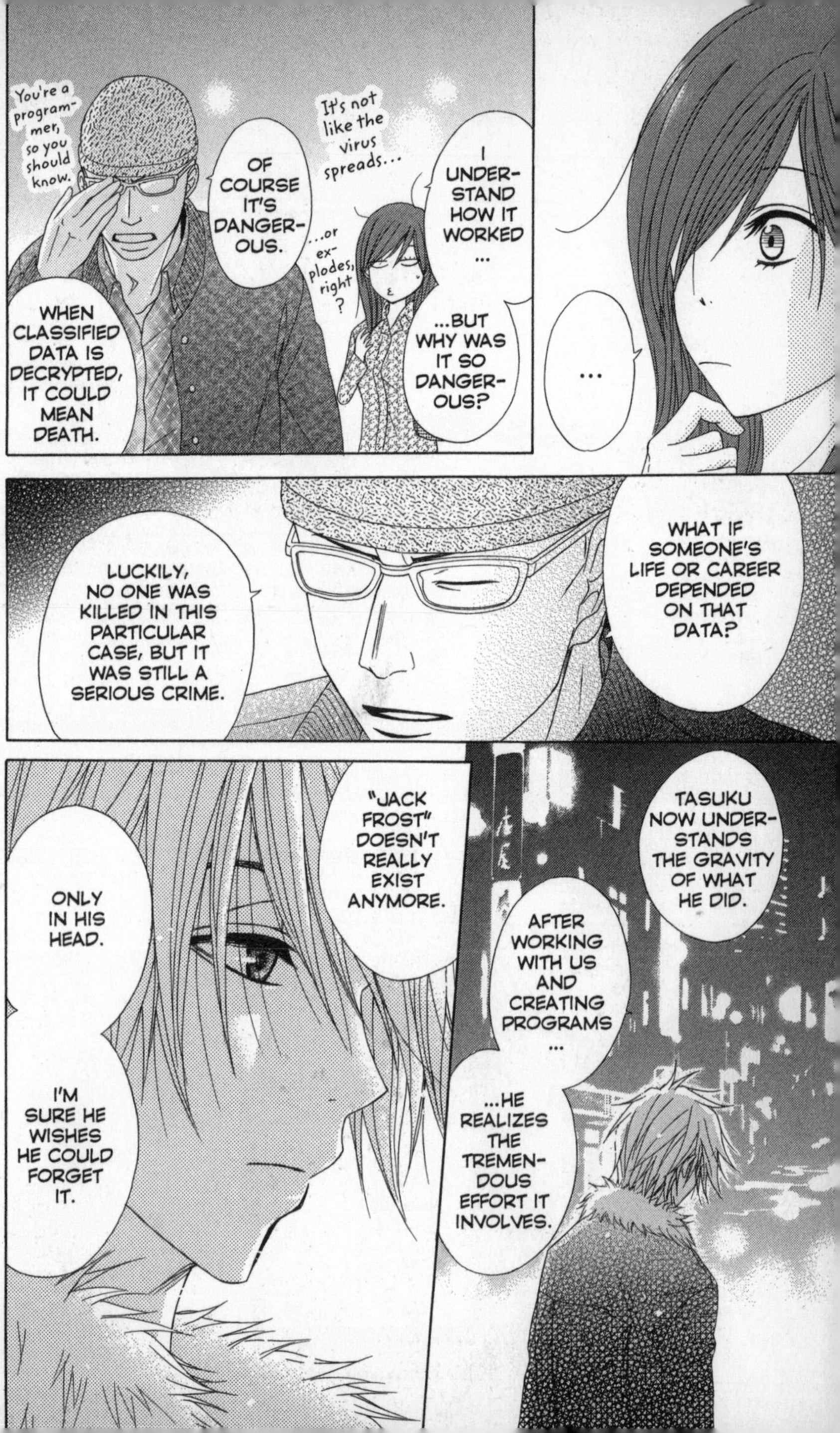
...
I UNDERSTAND HOW IT WORKED ...
...BUT WHY WAS IT SO DANGEROUS?
It's not like the virus spreads...
...or explodes, right?
OF COURSE IT'S DANGEROUS.
You're a programmer, so you should know.
WHEN CLASSIFIED DATA IS DECRYPTED, IT COULD MEAN DEATH.
WHAT IF SOMEONE'S LIFE OR CAREER DEPENDED ON THAT DATA?
LUCKILY, NO ONE WAS KILLED IN THIS PARTICULAR CASE, BUT IT WAS STILL A SERIOUS CRIME.
TASUKU NOW UNDERSTANDS THE GRAVITY OF WHAT HE DID.
AFTER WORKING WITH US AND CREATING PROGRAMS ...
...HE REALIZES THE TREMENDOUS EFFORT IT INVOLVES.
"JACK FROST" DOESN'T REALLY EXIST ANYMORE.
ONLY IN HIS HEAD.
I'M SURE HE WISHES HE COULD FORGET IT.

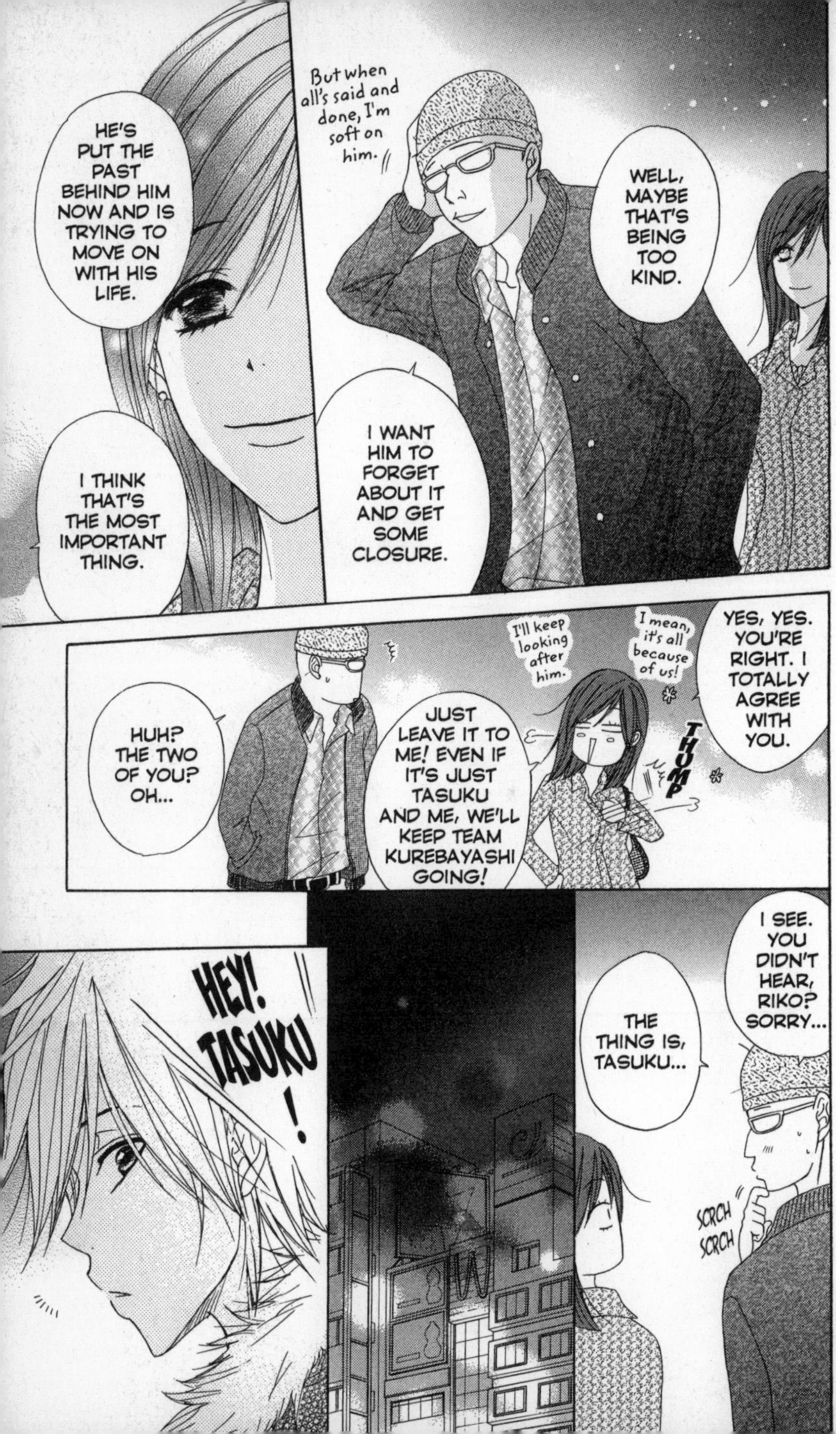
WELL, MAYBE THAT'S BEING TOO KIND.
But when all's said and done, I'm soft on him.
I WANT HIM TO FORGET ABOUT IT AND GET SOME CLOSURE.
HE'S PUT THE PAST BEHIND HIM NOW AND IS TRYING TO MOVE ON WITH HIS LIFE.
I THINK THAT'S THE MOST IMPORTANT THING.
YES, YES. YOU'RE RIGHT. I TOTALLY AGREE WITH YOU.
I mean, it's all because of us!
I'll keep looking after him.
THUMP
JUST LEAVE IT TO ME! EVEN IF IT'S JUST TASUKU AND ME, WE'LL KEEP TEAM KUREBAYASHI GOING!
HUH? THE TWO OF YOU? OH...
I SEE. YOU DIDN'T HEAR, RIKO? SORRY...
THE THING IS, TASUKU...
SCRCH SCRCH
HEY! TASUKU!

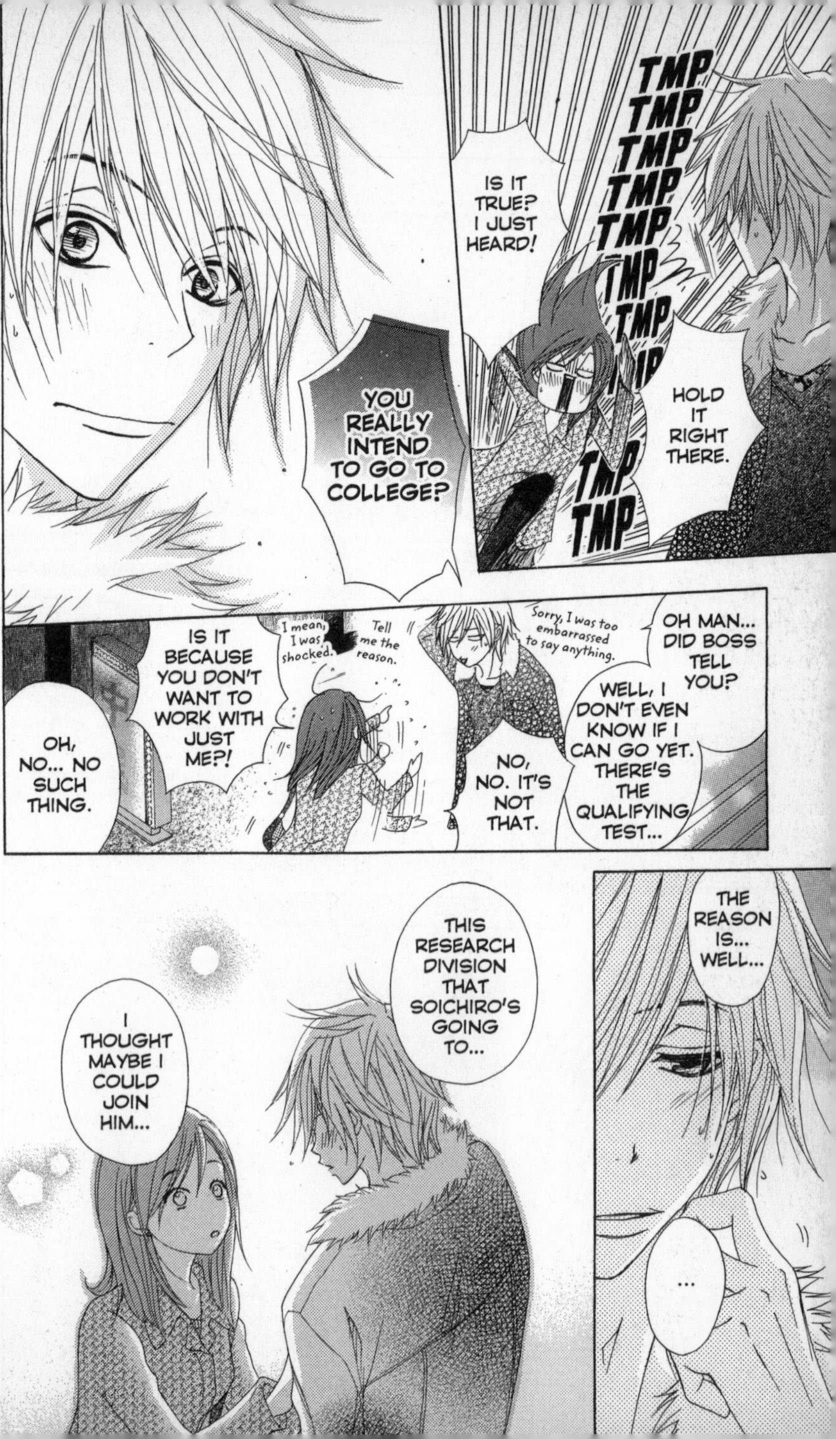
TMP TMP TMP TMP TMP TMP TMP TMP TMP TMP TMP
IS IT TRUE? I JUST HEARD!
HOLD IT RIGHT THERE.
YOU REALLY INTEND TO GO TO COLLEGE?
OH MAN... DID BOSS TELL YOU?
Sorry, I was too embarrassed to say anything.
WELL, I DON'T EVEN KNOW IF I CAN GO YET. THERE'S THE QUALIFYING TEST...
NO, NO. IT'S NOT THAT.
Tell me the reason.
I mean, I was shocked.
IS IT BECAUSE YOU DON'T WANT TO WORK WITH JUST ME?!
OH, NO... NO SUCH THING.
THE REASON IS... WELL...
...
THIS RESEARCH DIVISION THAT SOICHIRO'S GOING TO...
I THOUGHT MAYBE I COULD JOIN HIM...

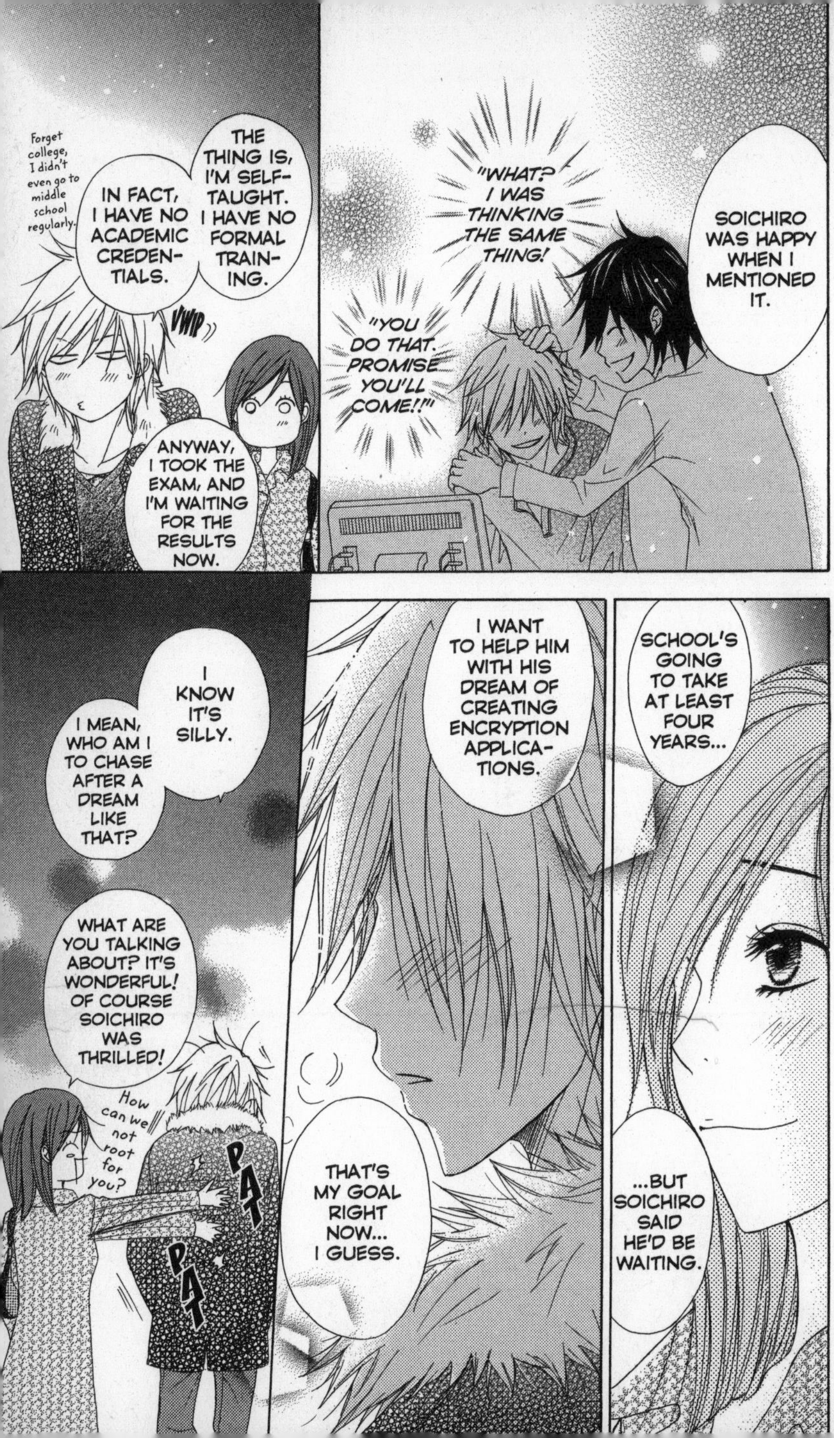
SOICHIRO WAS HAPPY WHEN I MENTIONED IT.
"WHAT? I WAS THINKING THE SAME THING!
"YOU DO THAT. PROMISE YOU'LL COME!!"
THE THING IS, I'M SELF-TAUGHT. I HAVE NO FORMAL TRAINING.
IN FACT, I HAVE NO ACADEMIC CREDENTIALS.
Forget college, I didn't even go to middle school regularly.
VWIP
ANYWAY, I TOOK THE EXAM, AND I'M WAITING FOR THE RESULTS NOW.
SCHOOL'S GOING TO TAKE AT LEAST FOUR YEARS...
...BUT SOICHIRO SAID HE'D BE WAITING.
I WANT TO HELP HIM WITH HIS DREAM OF CREATING ENCRYPTION APPLICA-TIONS.
THAT'S MY GOAL RIGHT NOW... I GUESS.
I KNOW IT'S SILLY.
I MEAN, WHO AM I TO CHASE AFTER A DREAM LIKE THAT?
WHAT ARE YOU TALKING ABOUT? IT'S WONDERFUL! OF COURSE SOICHIRO WAS THRILLED!
How can we not root for you?
PAT
PAT
PAT

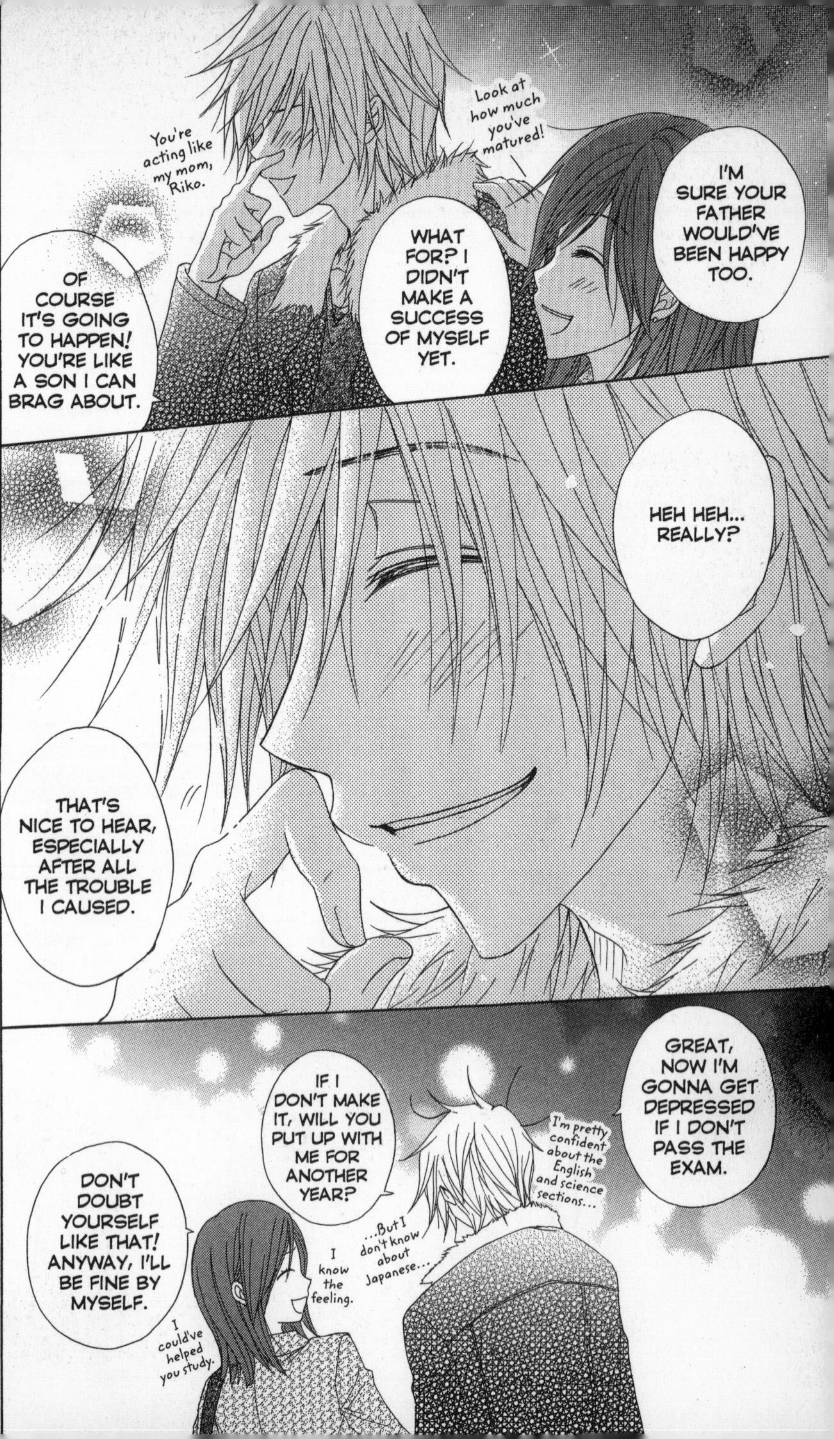
I'M SURE YOUR FATHER WOULD'VE BEEN HAPPY TOO.
Look at how much you've matured!
WHAT FOR? I DIDN'T MAKE A SUCCESS OF MYSELF YET.
You're acting like my mom, Riko.
OF COURSE IT'S GOING TO HAPPEN! YOU'RE LIKE A SON I CAN BRAG ABOUT.
HEH HEH... REALLY?
THAT'S NICE TO HEAR, ESPECIALLY AFTER ALL THE TROUBLE I CAUSED.
GREAT, NOW I'M GONNA GET DEPRESSED IF I DON'T PASS THE EXAM.
I'm pretty confident about the English and science sections...
IF I DON'T MAKE IT, WILL YOU PUT UP WITH ME FOR ANOTHER YEAR?
...But I don't know about Japanese...
DON'T DOUBT YOURSELF LIKE THAT! ANYWAY, I'LL BE FINE BY MYSELF.
I know the feeling.
I could've helped you study.

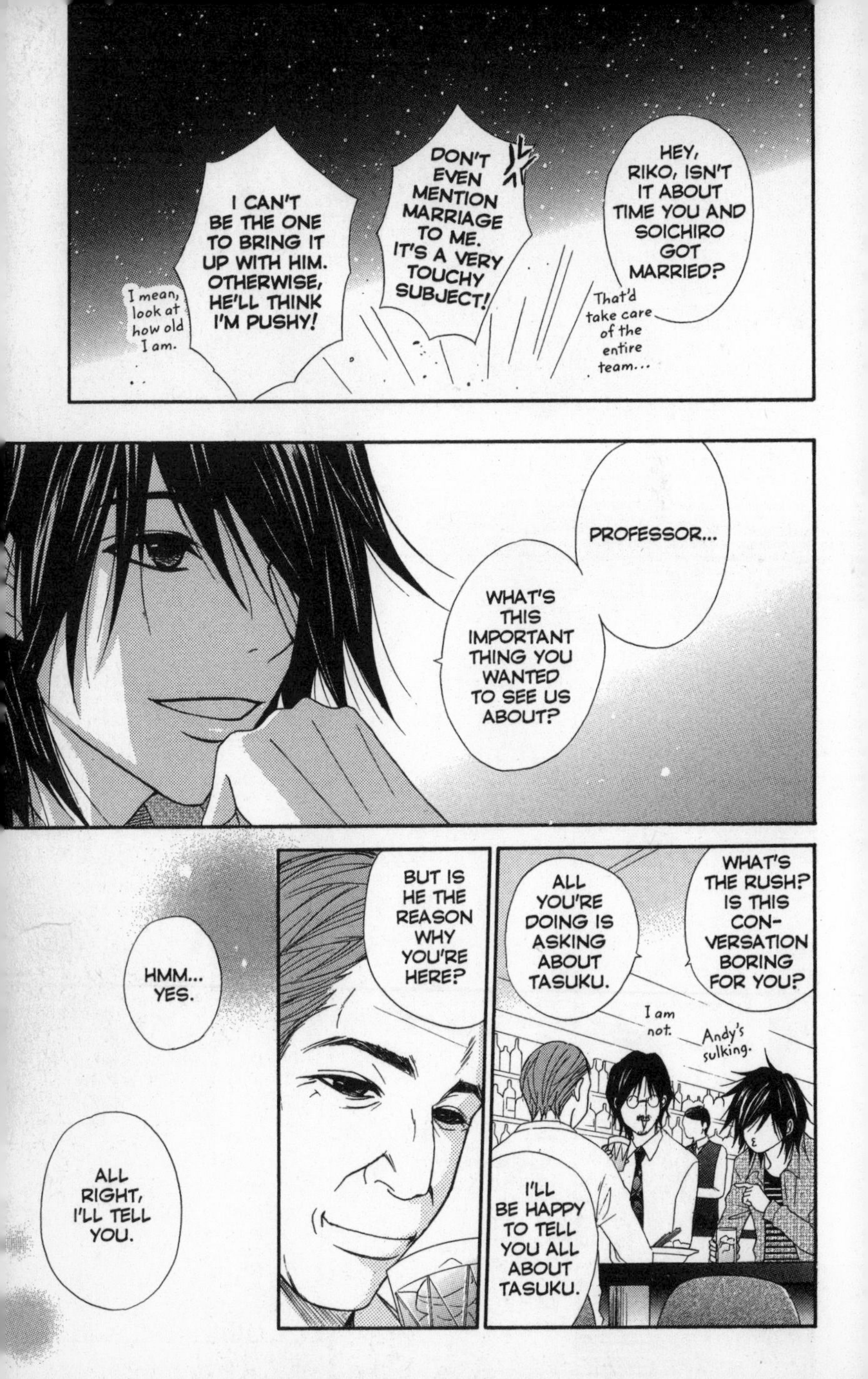
HEY, RIKO, ISN'T IT ABOUT TIME YOU AND SOICHIRO GOT MARRIED?
That'd take care of the entire team...
DON'T EVEN MENTION MARRIAGE TO ME. IT'S A VERY TOUCHY SUBJECT!
I CAN'T BE THE ONE TO BRING IT UP WITH HIM. OTHERWISE, HE'LL THINK I'M PUSHY!
I mean, look at how old I am.
PROFESSOR...
WHAT'S THIS IMPORTANT THING YOU WANTED TO SEE US ABOUT?
WHAT'S THE RUSH? IS THIS CON-VERSATION BORING FOR YOU?
ALL YOU'RE DOING IS ASKING ABOUT TASUKU.
I am not.
Andy's sulking.
I'LL BE HAPPY TO TELL YOU ALL ABOUT TASUKU.
BUT IS HE THE REASON WHY YOU'RE HERE?
HMM... YES.
ALL RIGHT, I'LL TELL YOU.

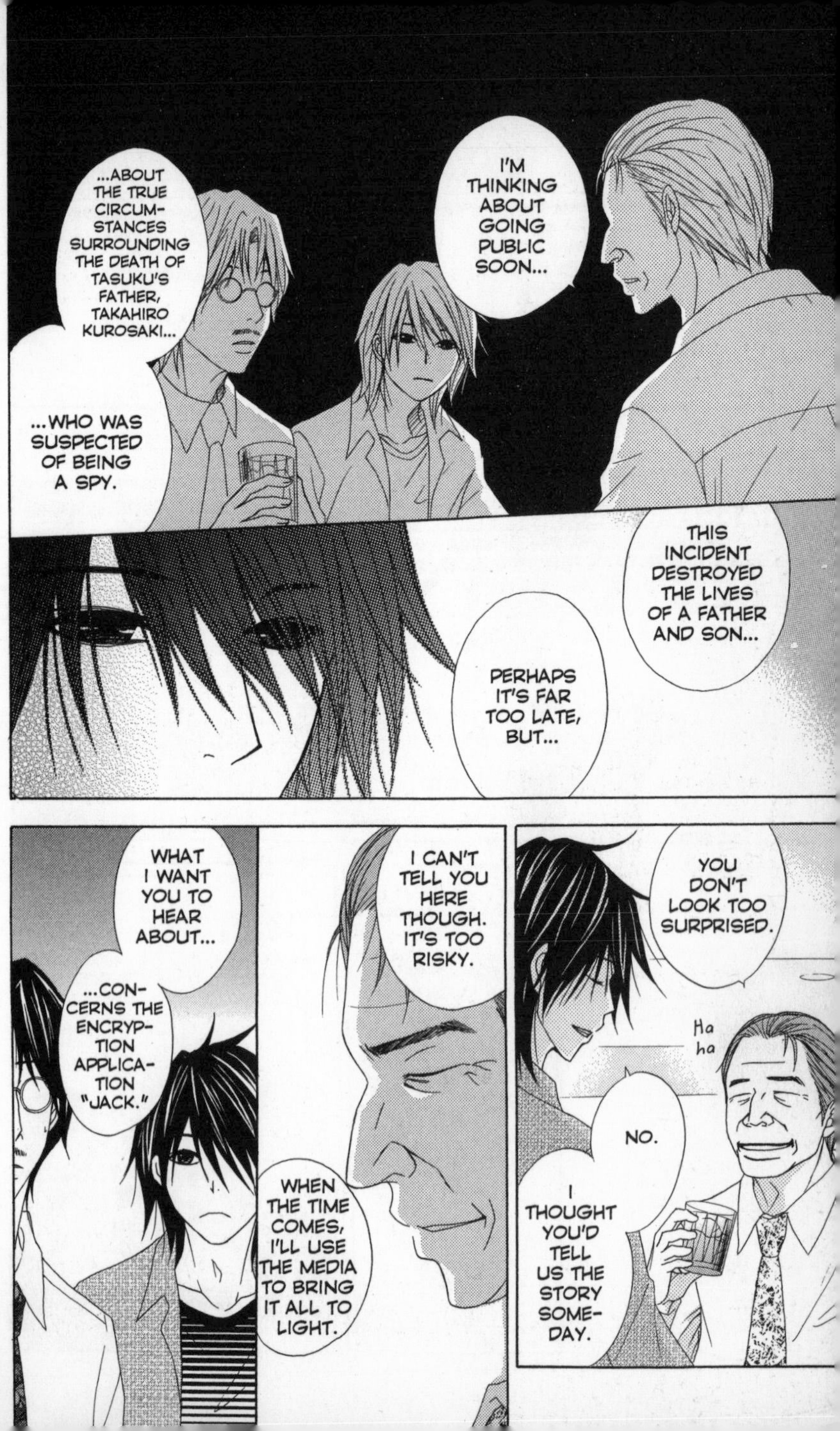
I'M THINKING ABOUT GOING PUBLIC SOON...
...ABOUT THE TRUE CIRCUM-STANCES SURROUNDING THE DEATH OF TASUKU'S FATHER, TAKAHIRO KUROSAKI...
...WHO WAS SUSPECTED OF BEING A SPY.
THIS INCIDENT DESTROYED THE LIVES OF A FATHER AND SON...
PERHAPS IT'S FAR TOO LATE, BUT...
YOU DON'T LOOK TOO SURPRISED.
Ha ha
NO.
I THOUGHT YOU'D TELL US THE STORY SOME-DAY.
I CAN'T TELL YOU HERE THOUGH. IT'S TOO RISKY.
WHEN THE TIME COMES, I'LL USE THE MEDIA TO BRING IT ALL TO LIGHT.
WHAT I WANT YOU TO HEAR ABOUT...
...CON-CERNS THE ENCRYP-TION APPLICA-TION "JACK."

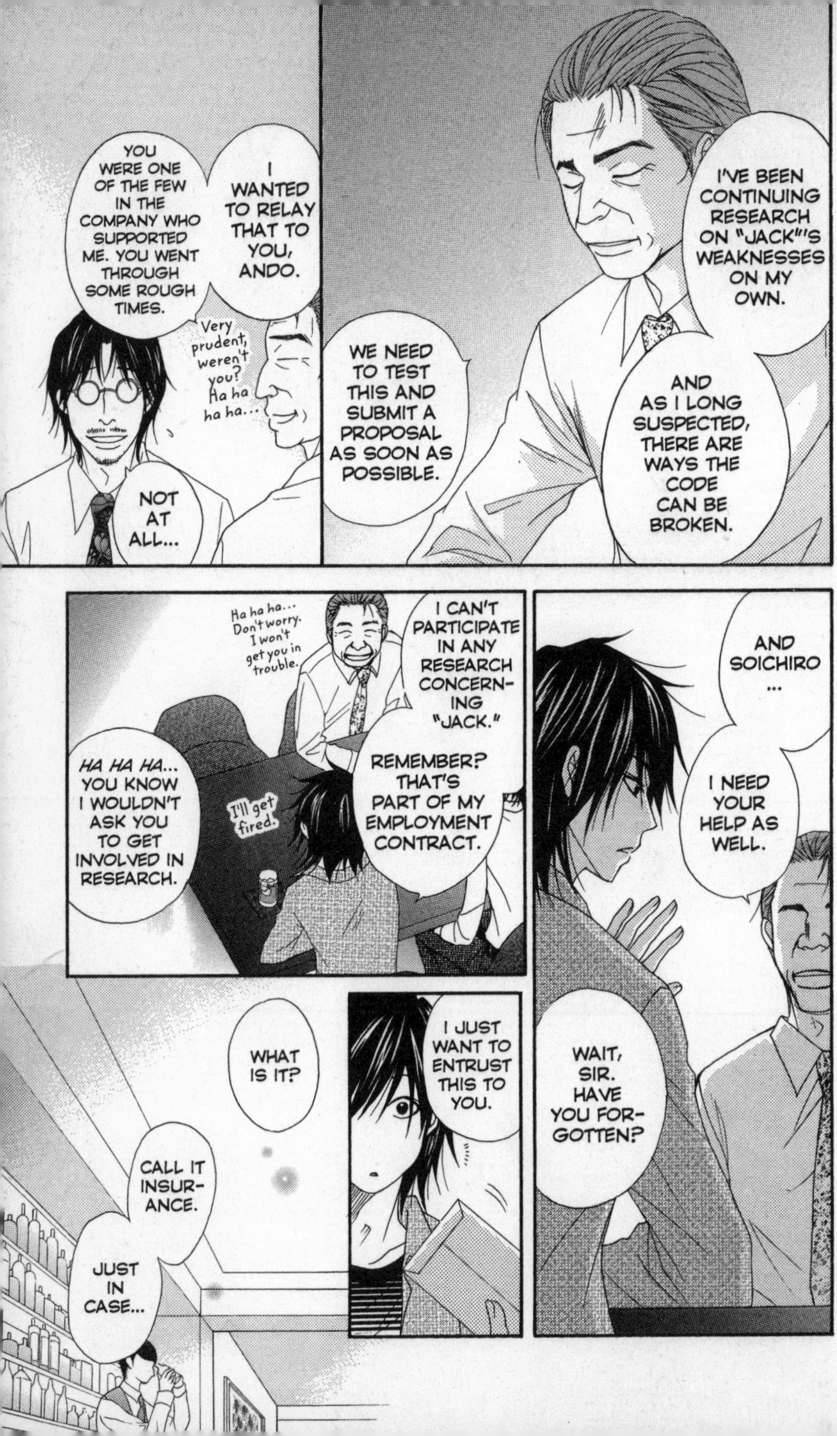
I'VE BEEN CONTINUING RESEARCH ON "JACK"'S WEAKNESSES ON MY OWN.
AND AS I LONG SUSPECTED, THERE ARE WAYS THE CODE CAN BE BROKEN.
WE NEED TO TEST THIS AND SUBMIT A PROPOSAL AS SOON AS POSSIBLE.
I WANTED TO RELAY THAT TO YOU, ANDO.
YOU WERE ONE OF THE FEW IN THE COMPANY WHO SUPPORTED ME. YOU WENT THROUGH SOME ROUGH TIMES.
Very prudent, weren't you? Ha ha ha ha...
NOT AT ALL...
AND SOICHIRO ...
I NEED YOUR HELP AS WELL.
WAIT, SIR. HAVE YOU FORGOTTEN?
I CAN'T PARTICIPATE IN ANY RESEARCH CONCERNING "JACK."
REMEMBER? THAT'S PART OF MY EMPLOYMENT CONTRACT.
I'll get fired.
Ha ha ha... Don't worry. I won't get you in trouble.
HA HA HA... YOU KNOW I WOULDN'T ASK YOU TO GET INVOLVED IN RESEARCH.
I JUST WANT TO ENTRUST THIS TO YOU.
WHAT IS IT?
CALL IT INSURANCE.
JUST IN CASE...

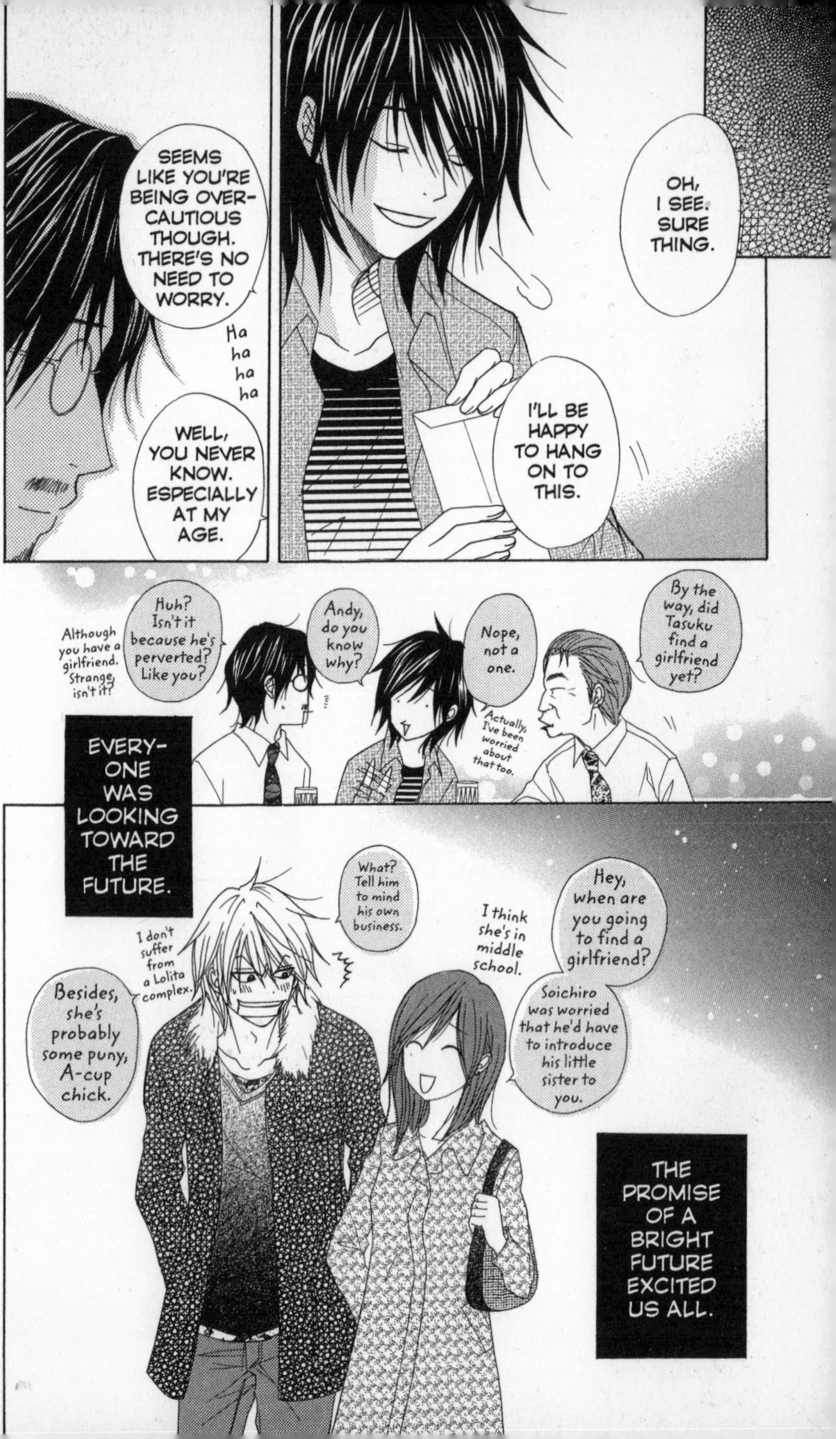

OH, I SEE. SURE THING.
I'LL BE HAPPY TO HANG ON TO THIS.
SEEMS LIKE YOU'RE BEING OVER-CAUTIOUS THOUGH. THERE'S NO NEED TO WORRY.
Ha ha ha ha
WELL, YOU NEVER KNOW. ESPECIALLY AT MY AGE.
By the way, did Tasuku find a girlfriend yet?
Nope, not a one.
Actually, I've been worried about that too.
Andy, do you know why?
Huh? Isn't it because he's perverted? Like you?
Although you have a girlfriend. Strange, isn't it?
EVERY-ONE WAS LOOKING TOWARD THE FUTURE.
Hey, when are you going to find a girlfriend?
Soichiro was worried that he'd have to introduce his little sister to you.
I think she's in middle school.
What? Tell him to mind his own business.
I don't suffer from a Lolita complex.
Besides, she's probably some puny, A-cup chick.
THE PROMISE OF A BRIGHT FUTURE EXCITED US ALL.

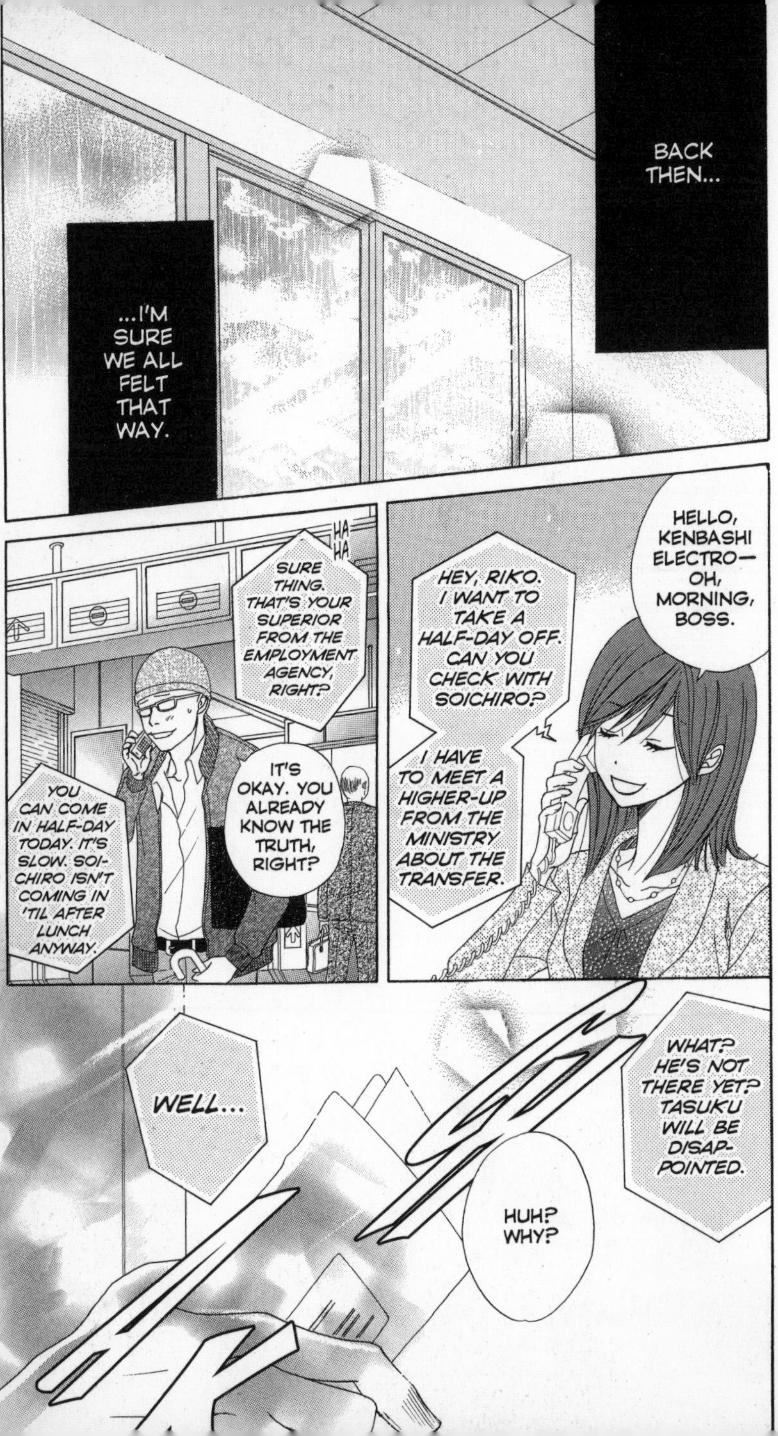
BACK THEN...
...I'M SURE WE ALL FELT THAT WAY.
HELLO, KENBASHI ELECTRO— OH, MORNING, BOSS.
HEY, RIKO. I WANT TO TAKE A HALF-DAY OFF. CAN YOU CHECK WITH SOICHIRO?
I HAVE TO MEET A HIGHER-UP FROM THE MINISTRY ABOUT THE TRANSFER.
HA HA
SURE THING. THAT'S YOUR SUPERIOR FROM THE EMPLOYMENT AGENCY, RIGHT?
IT'S OKAY. YOU ALREADY KNOW THE TRUTH, RIGHT?
YOU CAN COME IN HALF-DAY TODAY. IT'S SLOW. SOICHIRO ISN'T COMING IN 'TIL AFTER LUNCH ANYWAY.
WHAT? HE'S NOT THERE YET? TASUKU WILL BE DISAPPOINTED.
HUH? WHY?
WELL...

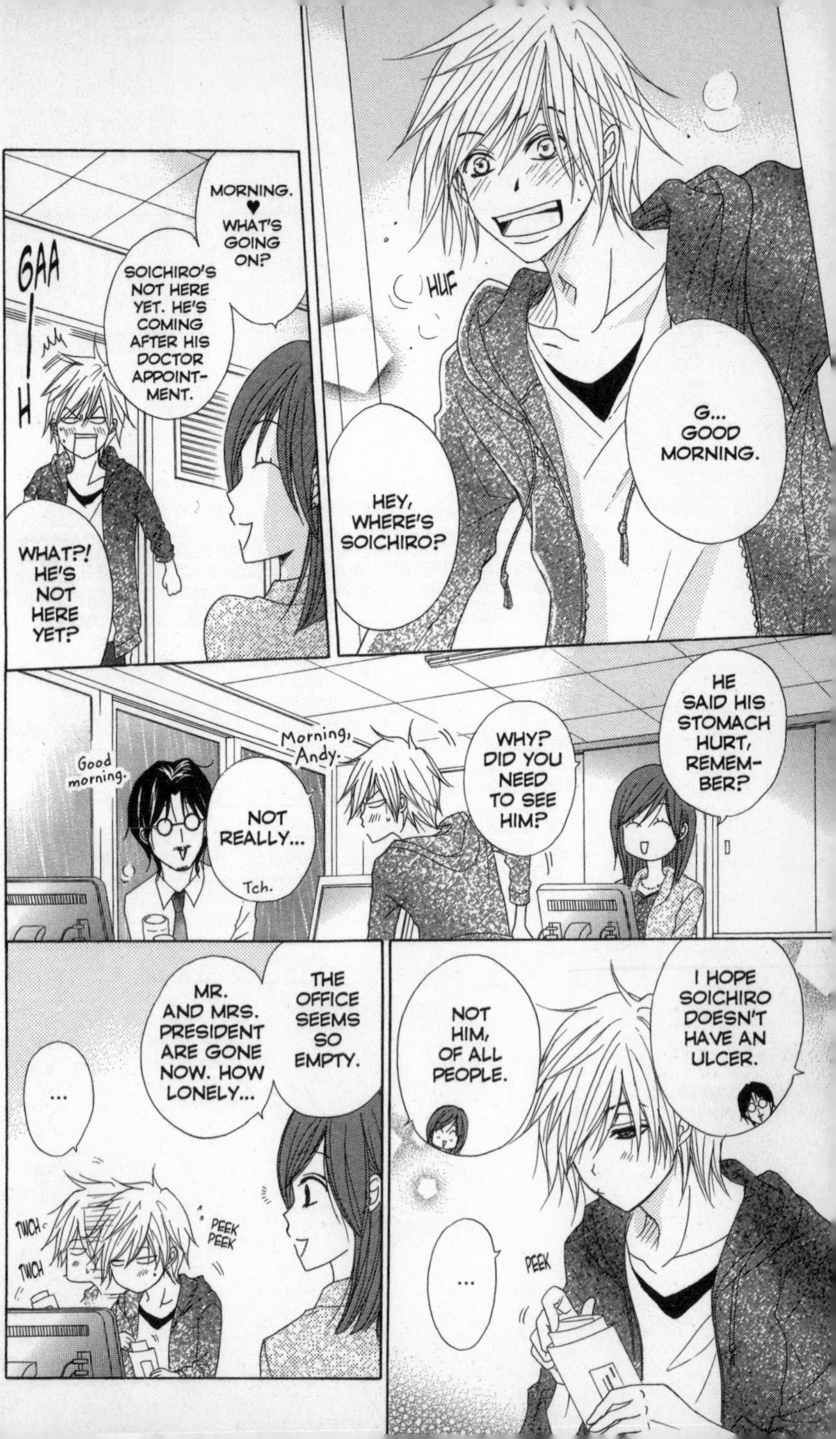
G... GOOD MORNING.
HUF
HEY, WHERE'S SOICHIRO?
MORNING. ♥ WHAT'S GOING ON?
SOICHIRO'S NOT HERE YET. HE'S COMING AFTER HIS DOCTOR APPOINT-MENT.
GAA H
WHAT?! HE'S NOT HERE YET?
HE SAID HIS STOMACH HURT, REMEM-BER?
WHY? DID YOU NEED TO SEE HIM?
Morning, Andy.
NOT REALLY...
Tch.
Good morning.
I HOPE SOICHIRO DOESN'T HAVE AN ULCER.
NOT HIM, OF ALL PEOPLE.
PEEK
...
THE OFFICE SEEMS SO EMPTY.
MR. AND MRS. PRESIDENT ARE GONE NOW. HOW LONELY...
...
PEEK PEEK
TWCH
TWCH

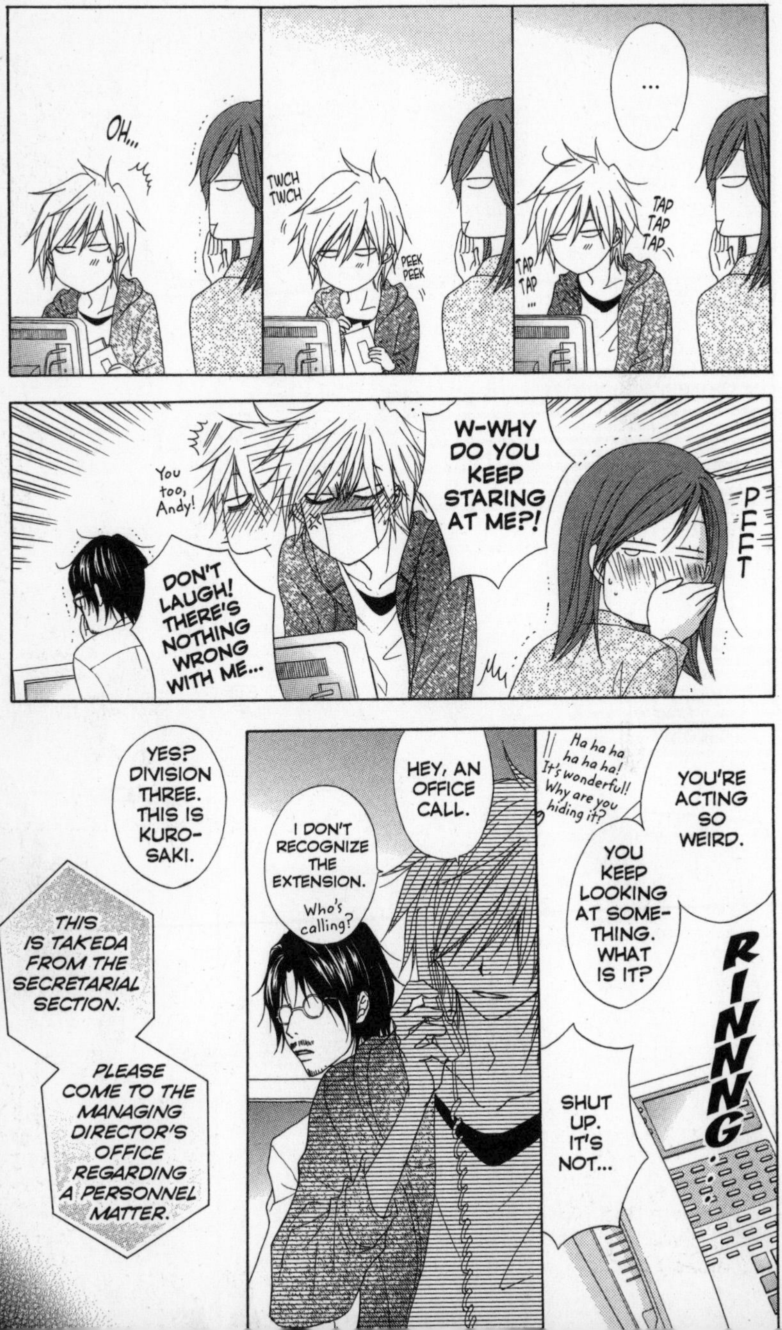
...
TAP TAP TAP
TAP TAP ...
TWCH TWCH
PEEK PEEK
OH...
PFFT
W-WHY DO YOU KEEP STARING AT ME?!
You too, Andy!
DON'T LAUGH! THERE'S NOTHING WRONG WITH ME...
YOU'RE ACTING SO WEIRD.
Ha ha ha ha ha ha! It's wonderful! Why are you hiding it?
YOU KEEP LOOKING AT SOME-THING. WHAT IS IT?
RINNNG
SHUT UP. IT'S NOT...
HEY, AN OFFICE CALL.
I DON'T RECOGNIZE THE EXTENSION.
Who's calling?
YES? DIVISION THREE. THIS IS KURO-SAKI.
THIS IS TAKEDA FROM THE SECRETARIAL SECTION.
PLEASE COME TO THE MANAGING DIRECTOR'S OFFICE REGARDING A PERSONNEL MATTER.

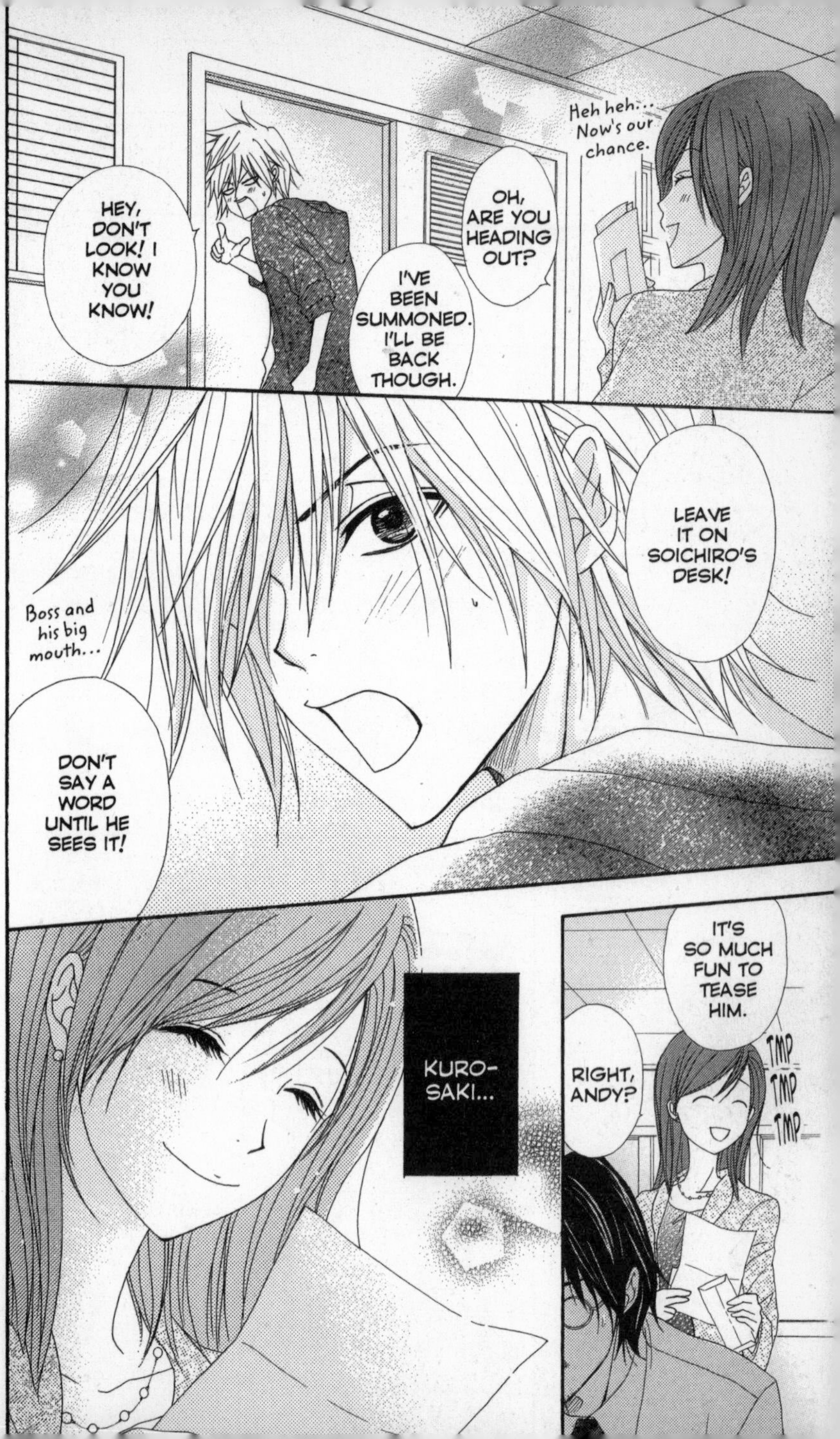
Heh heh... Now's our chance.
OH, ARE YOU HEADING OUT?
I'VE BEEN SUMMONED. I'LL BE BACK THOUGH.
HEY, DON'T LOOK! I KNOW YOU KNOW!
LEAVE IT ON SOICHIRO'S DESK!
Boss and his big mouth...
DON'T SAY A WORD UNTIL HE SEES IT!
IT'S SO MUCH FUN TO TEASE HIM.
TMP TMP TMP
RIGHT, ANDY?
KURO-SAKI...

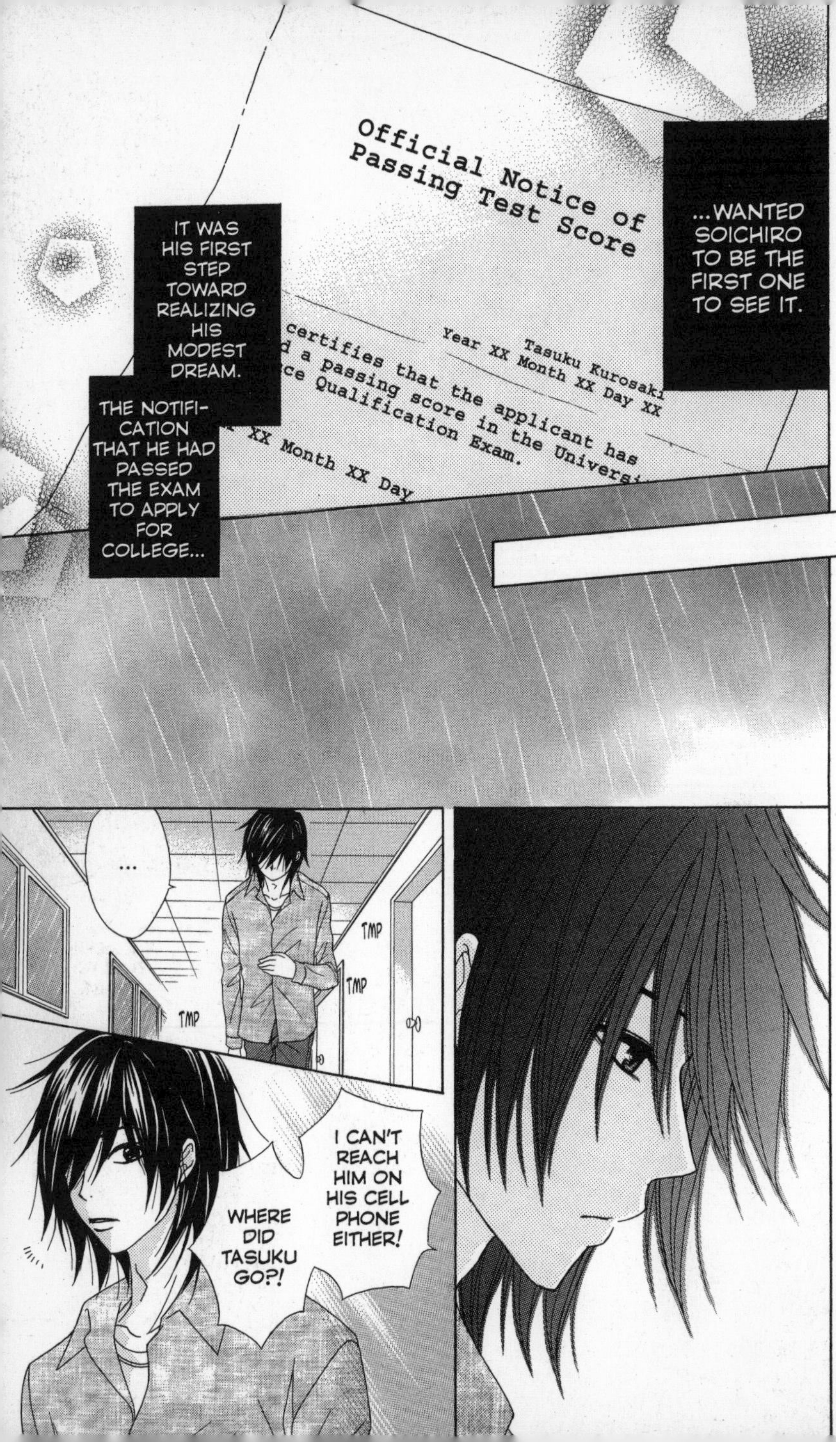
...WANTED SOICHIRO TO BE THE FIRST ONE TO SEE IT.
Official Notice of Passing Test Score
Tasuku Kurosaki
Year XX Month XX Day XX
certifies that the applicant has
d a passing score in the Universi
ce Qualification Exam.
XX Month XX Day
IT WAS HIS FIRST STEP TOWARD REALIZING HIS MODEST DREAM.
THE NOTIFICATION THAT HE HAD PASSED THE EXAM TO APPLY FOR COLLEGE...
...
TMP
TMP
TMP
I CAN'T REACH HIM ON HIS CELL PHONE EITHER!
WHERE DID TASUKU GO?!

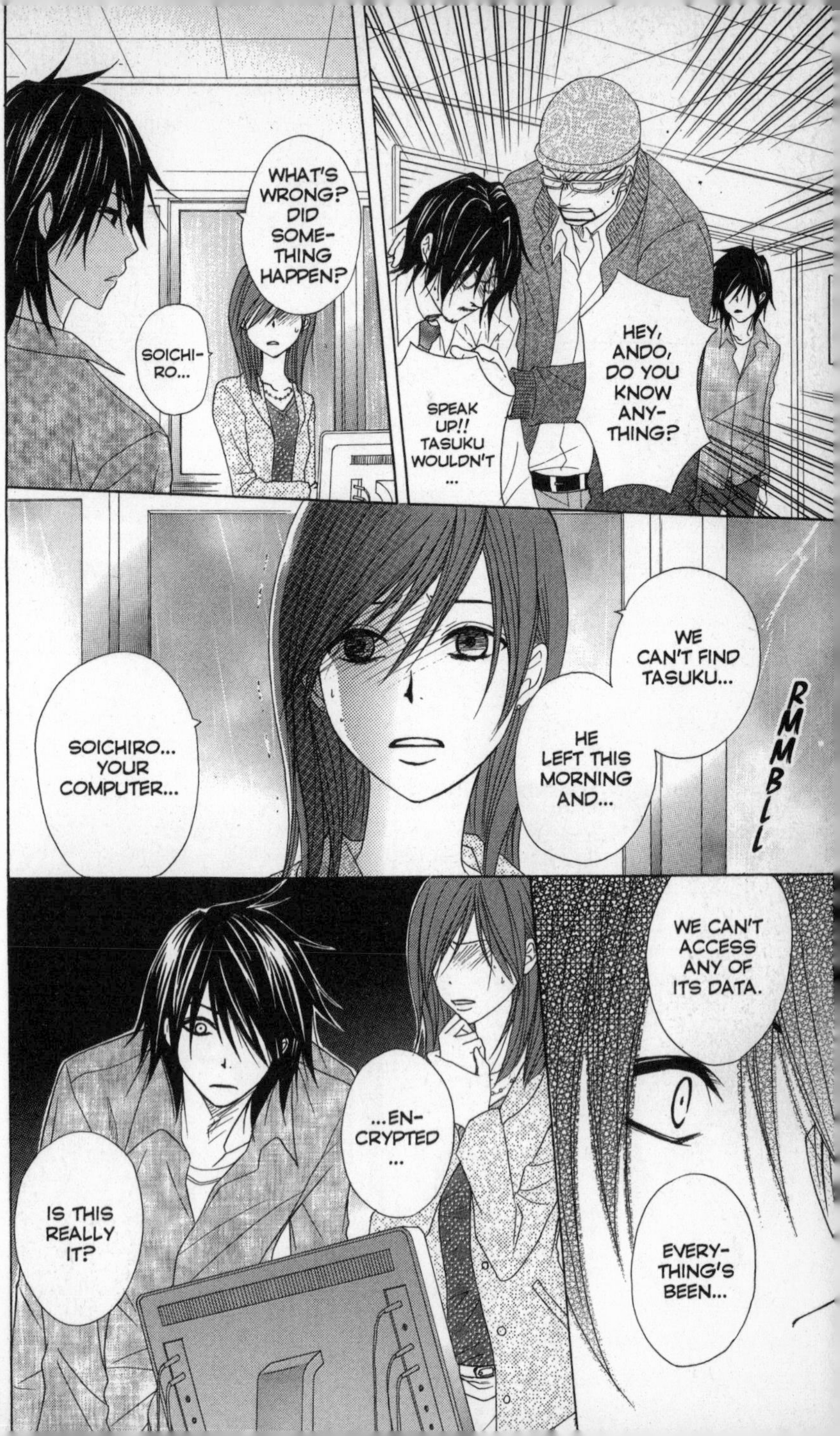
HEY, ANDO, DO YOU KNOW ANY-THING?
SPEAK UP!! TASUKU WOULDN'T ...
WHAT'S WRONG? DID SOME-THING HAPPEN?
SOICHI-RO...
WE CAN'T FIND TASUKU...
HE LEFT THIS MORNING AND...
RMMBLL
SOICHIRO... YOUR COMPUTER...
WE CAN'T ACCESS ANY OF ITS DATA.
EVERY-THING'S BEEN...
...EN-CRYPTED ...
IS THIS REALLY IT?

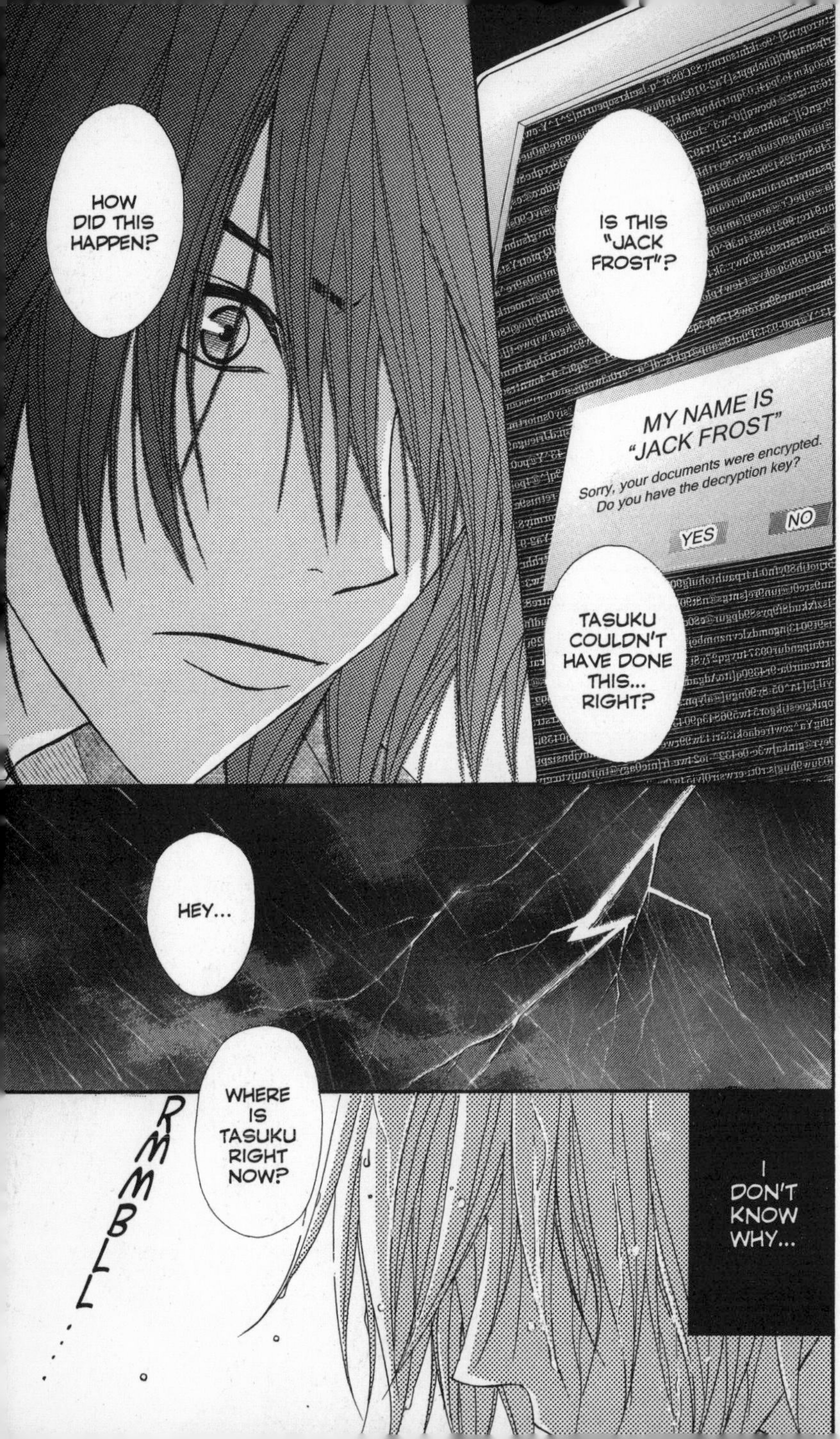
IS THIS "JACK FROST"?
HOW DID THIS HAPPEN?
MY NAME IS "JACK FROST"
Sorry, your documents were encrypted. Do you have the decryption key?
YES
NO
TASUKU COULDN'T HAVE DONE THIS... RIGHT?
HEY...
I DON'T KNOW WHY...
WHERE IS TASUKU RIGHT NOW?
RMMBLL...

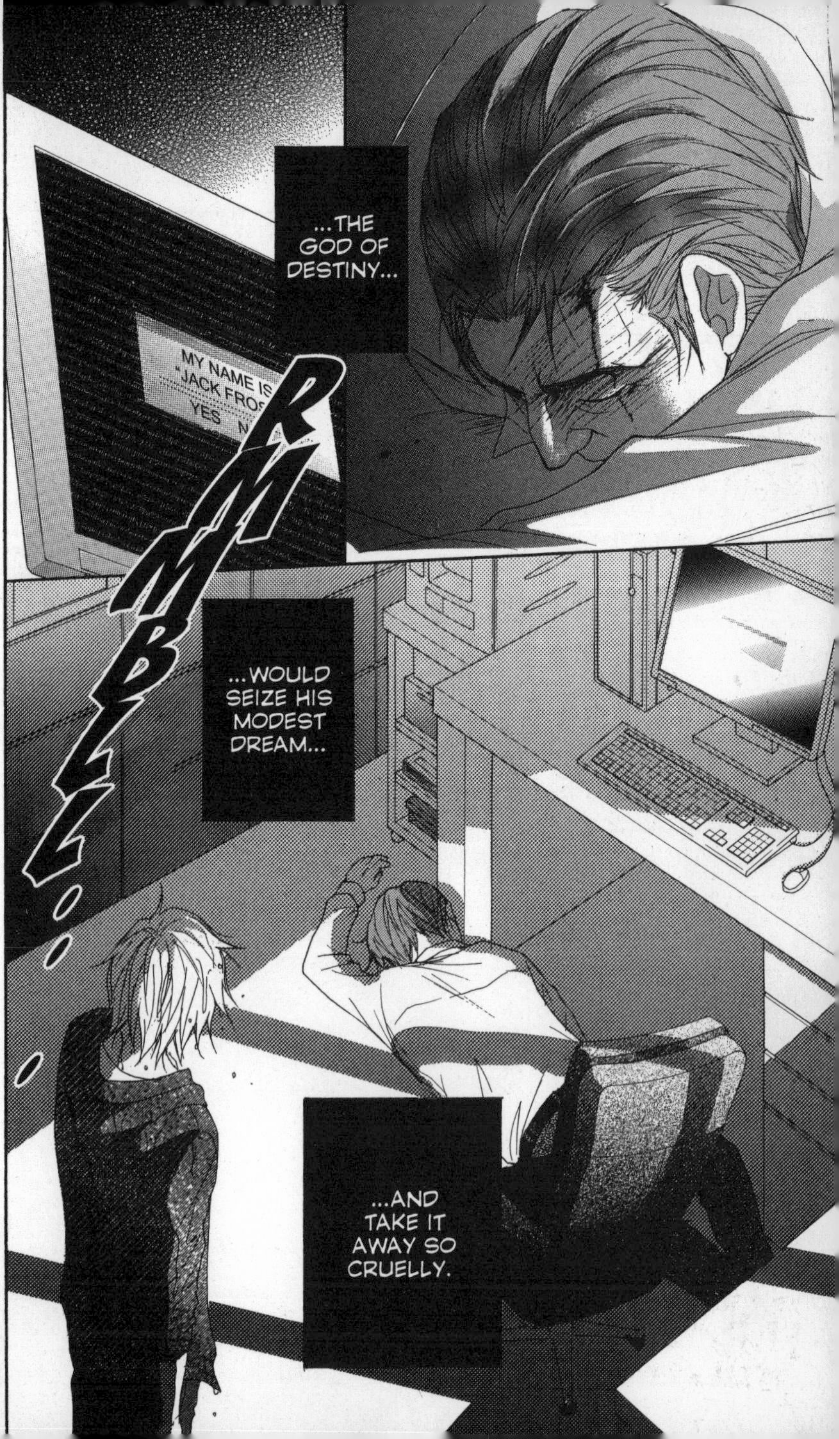
...THE GOD OF DESTINY...
MY NAME IS
"JACK FROS
YES
RMMBLL...
...WOULD SEIZE HIS MODEST DREAM...
...AND TAKE IT AWAY SO CRUELLY.

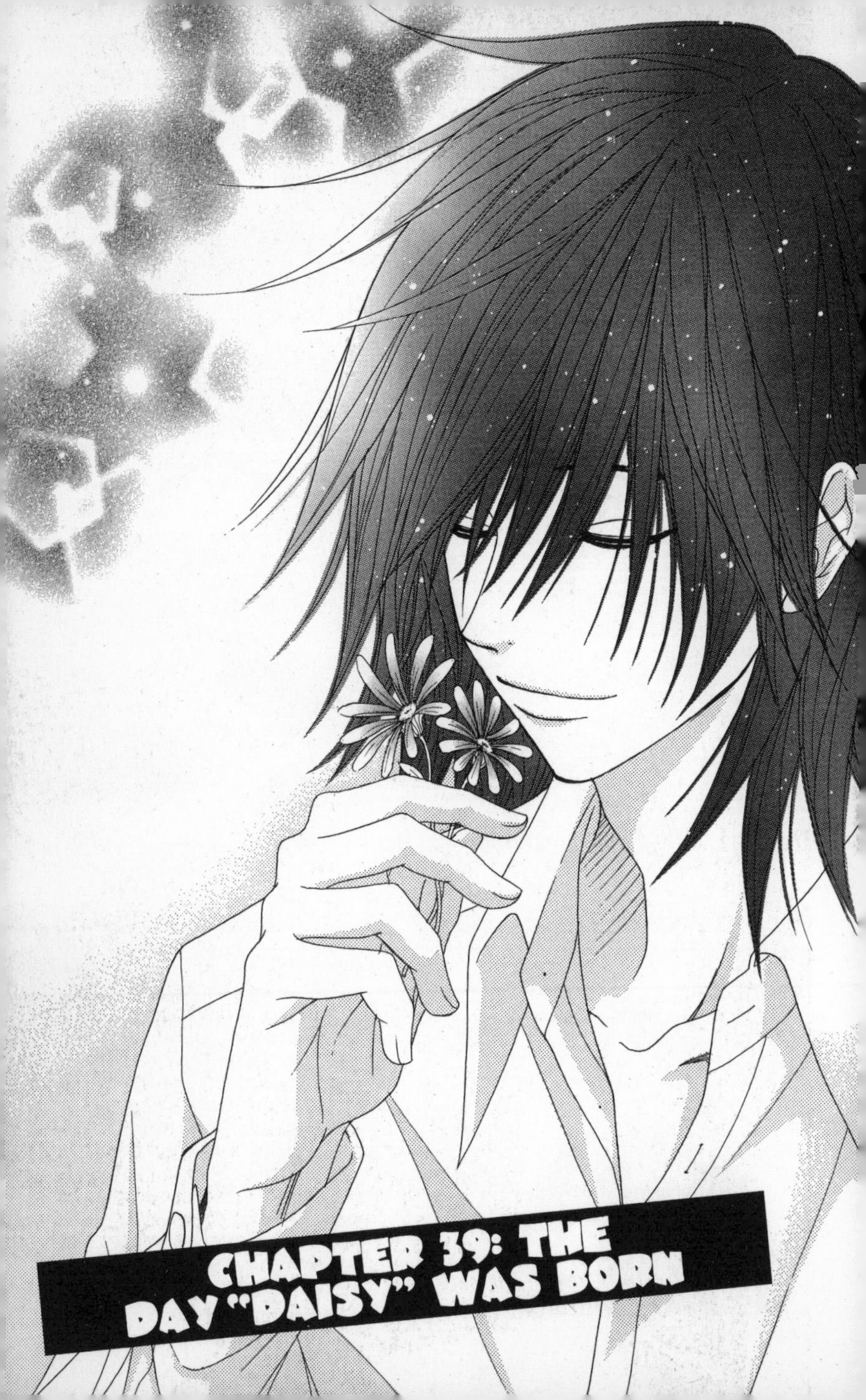
CHAPTER 39: THE
DAY "DAISY" WAS BORN

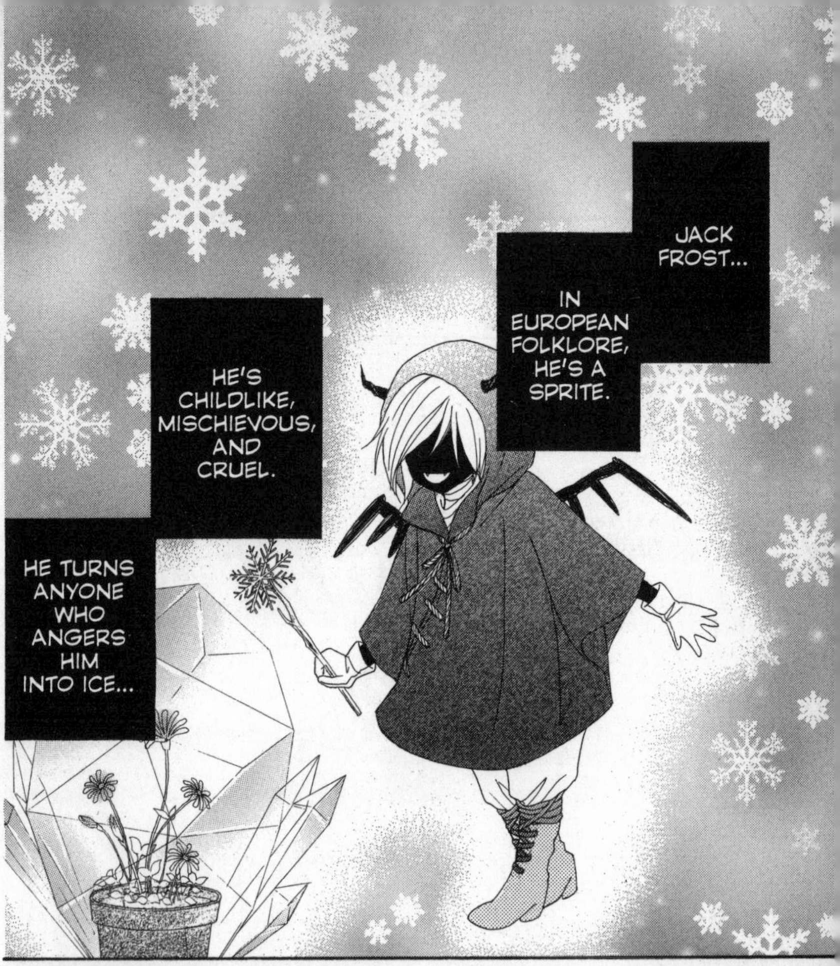
JACK FROST...
IN EUROPEAN FOLKLORE, HE'S A SPRITE.
HE'S CHILDLIKE, MISCHIEVOUS, AND CRUEL.
HE TURNS ANYONE WHO ANGERS HIM INTO ICE...

IN A PAST CHAPTER, THESE TWO APPEARED AS MEMBERS OF SOICHIRO'S TEAM, BUT THEY WEREN'T VERY NOTICEABLE (THEY GOT MARRIED AND LEFT TO START THEIR OWN BUSINESS). ACTUALLY SINCE ABOUT VOLUME 4, WHENEVER SOMEONE TALKED ABOUT "THE PRESIDENT," IT'S THIS COMPANY THEY MEANT. EVEN NOW, KUROSAKI AND RIKO (ESPECIALLY RIKO) KEEP IN TOUCH AND EVEN HELP OUT AT THE FIRM. IT'S A SMALL COMPANY, BUT THEY SEEM TO BE DOING WELL. RIKO AND YUKI ARE THE SAME AGE, SO THEY ARE VERY CLOSE.

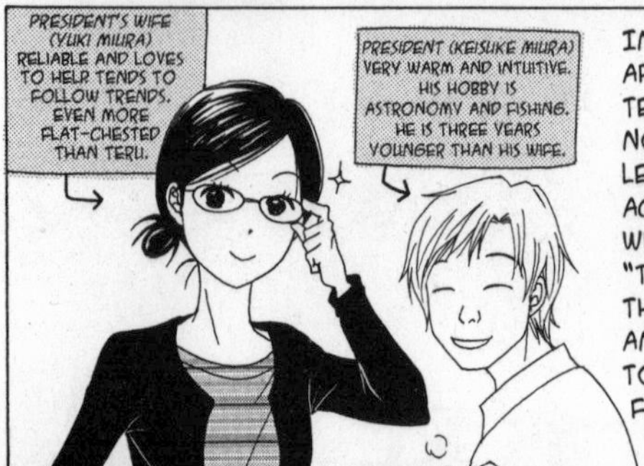
PRESIDENT (KEISUKE MIURA) VERY WARM AND INTUITIVE. HIS HOBBY IS ASTRONOMY AND FISHING. HE IS THREE YEARS YOUNGER THAN HIS WIFE.
PRESIDENT'S WIFE (YUKI MIURA) RELIABLE AND LOVES TO HELP TENDS TO FOLLOW TRENDS. EVEN MORE FLAT-CHESTED THAN TERU.

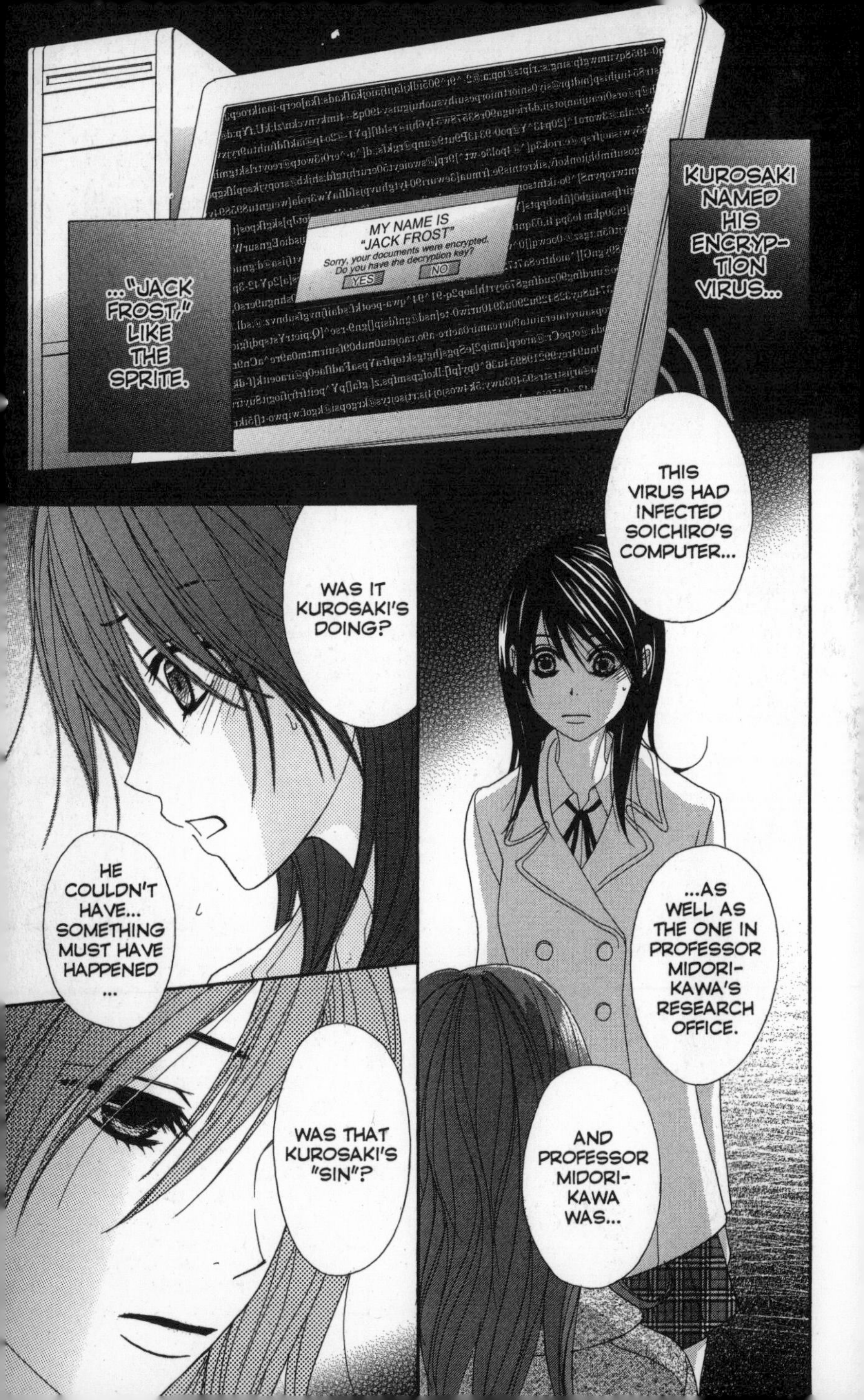

KUROSAKI NAMED HIS ENCRYPTION VIRUS...
MY NAME IS "JACK FROST"
Sorry, your documents were encrypted. Do you have the decryption key?
YES NO
..."JACK FROST," LIKE THE SPRITE.
THIS VIRUS HAD INFECTED SOICHIRO'S COMPUTER...
...AS WELL AS THE ONE IN PROFESSOR MIDORIKAWA'S RESEARCH OFFICE.
AND PROFESSOR MIDORIKAWA WAS...
WAS IT KUROSAKI'S DOING?
HE COULDN'T HAVE... SOMETHING MUST HAVE HAPPENED...
WAS THAT KUROSAKI'S "SIN"?

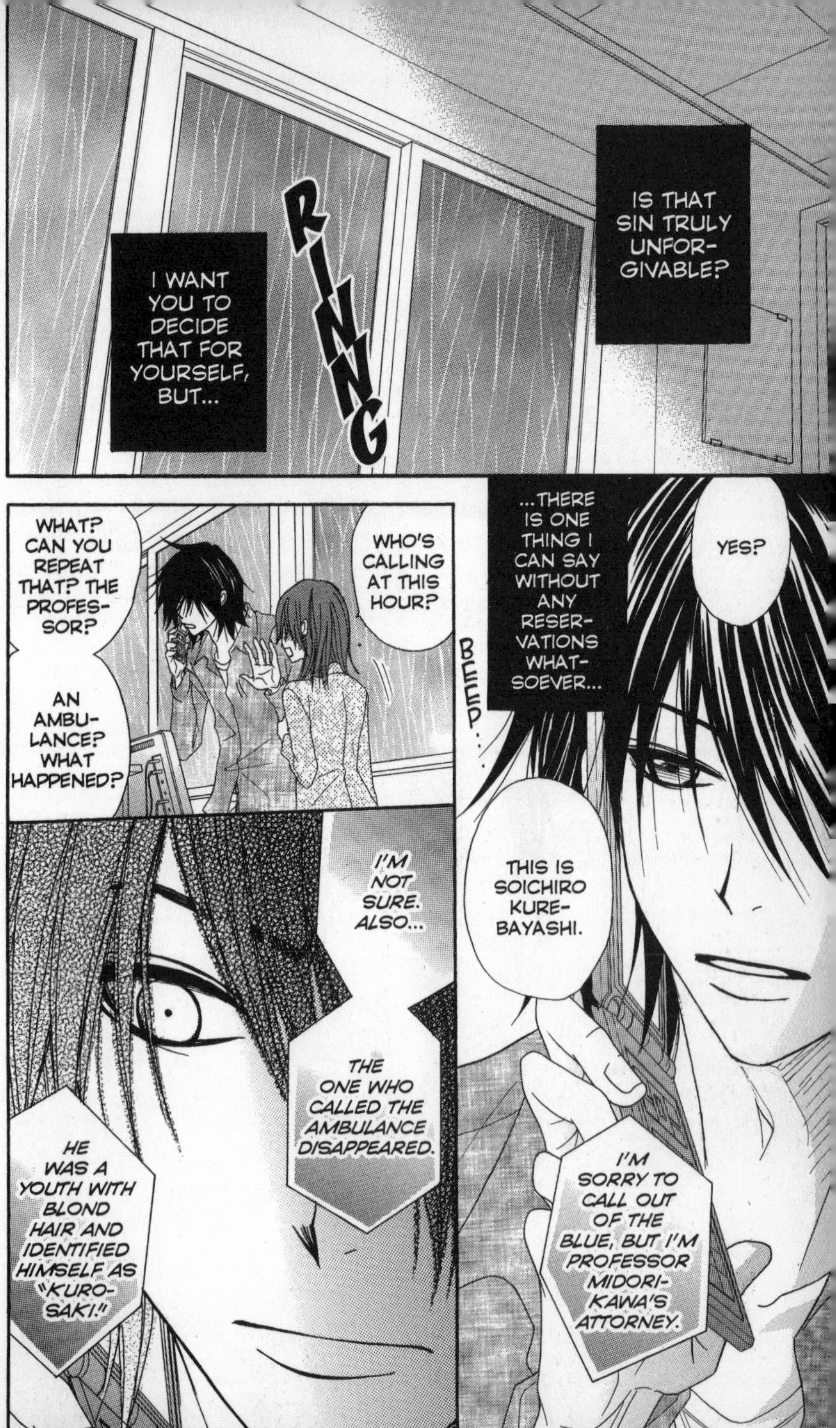

IS THAT SIN TRULY UNFOR-GIVABLE?
RINNG
I WANT YOU TO DECIDE THAT FOR YOURSELF, BUT...
YES?
...THERE IS ONE THING I CAN SAY WITHOUT ANY RESER-VATIONS WHAT-SOEVER...
THIS IS SOICHIRO KURE-BAYASHI.
I'M SORRY TO CALL OUT OF THE BLUE, BUT I'M PROFESSOR MIDORI-KAWA'S ATTORNEY.
BEEP...
WHO'S CALLING AT THIS HOUR?
WHAT? CAN YOU REPEAT THAT? THE PROFES-SOR?
AN AMBU-LANCE? WHAT HAPPENED?
I'M NOT SURE. ALSO...
THE ONE WHO CALLED THE AMBULANCE DISAPPEARED.
HE WAS A YOUTH WITH BLOND HAIR AND IDENTIFIED HIMSELF AS "KURO-SAKI."

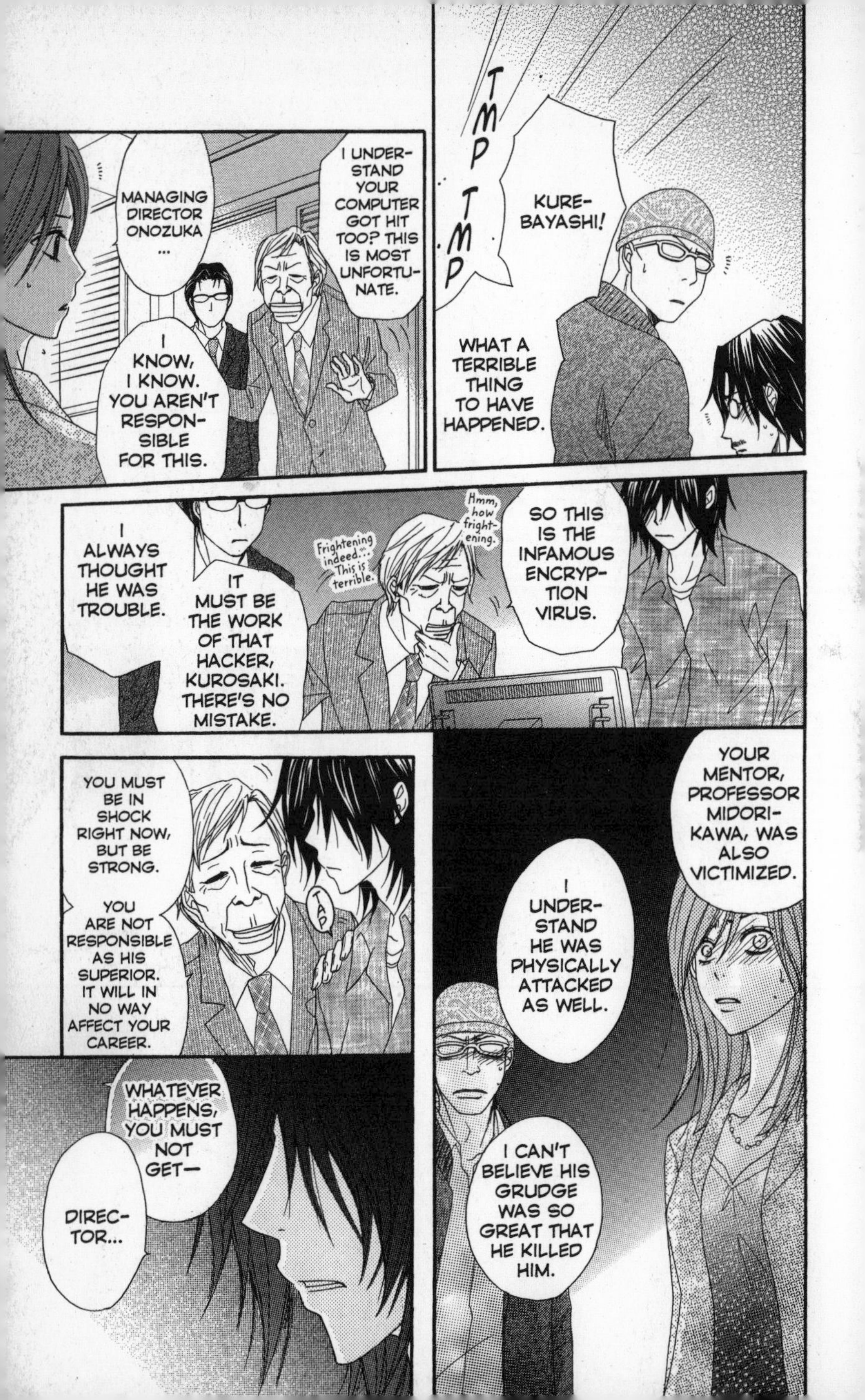
TMP TMP
KURE-BAYASHI!
WHAT A TERRIBLE THING TO HAVE HAPPENED.
I UNDERSTAND YOUR COMPUTER GOT HIT TOO? THIS IS MOST UNFORTUNATE.
MANAGING DIRECTOR ONOZUKA ...
I KNOW, I KNOW. YOU AREN'T RESPONSIBLE FOR THIS.
SO THIS IS THE INFAMOUS ENCRYPTION VIRUS.
Hmm, how frightening.
Frightening indeed... This is terrible.
IT MUST BE THE WORK OF THAT HACKER, KUROSAKI. THERE'S NO MISTAKE.
I ALWAYS THOUGHT HE WAS TROUBLE.
YOUR MENTOR, PROFESSOR MIDORIKAWA, WAS ALSO VICTIMIZED.
I UNDERSTAND HE WAS PHYSICALLY ATTACKED AS WELL.
I CAN'T BELIEVE HIS GRUDGE WAS SO GREAT THAT HE KILLED HIM.
YOU MUST BE IN SHOCK RIGHT NOW, BUT BE STRONG.
TAP
YOU ARE NOT RESPONSIBLE AS HIS SUPERIOR. IT WILL IN NO WAY AFFECT YOUR CAREER.
WHATEVER HAPPENS, YOU MUST NOT GET—
DIRECTOR...

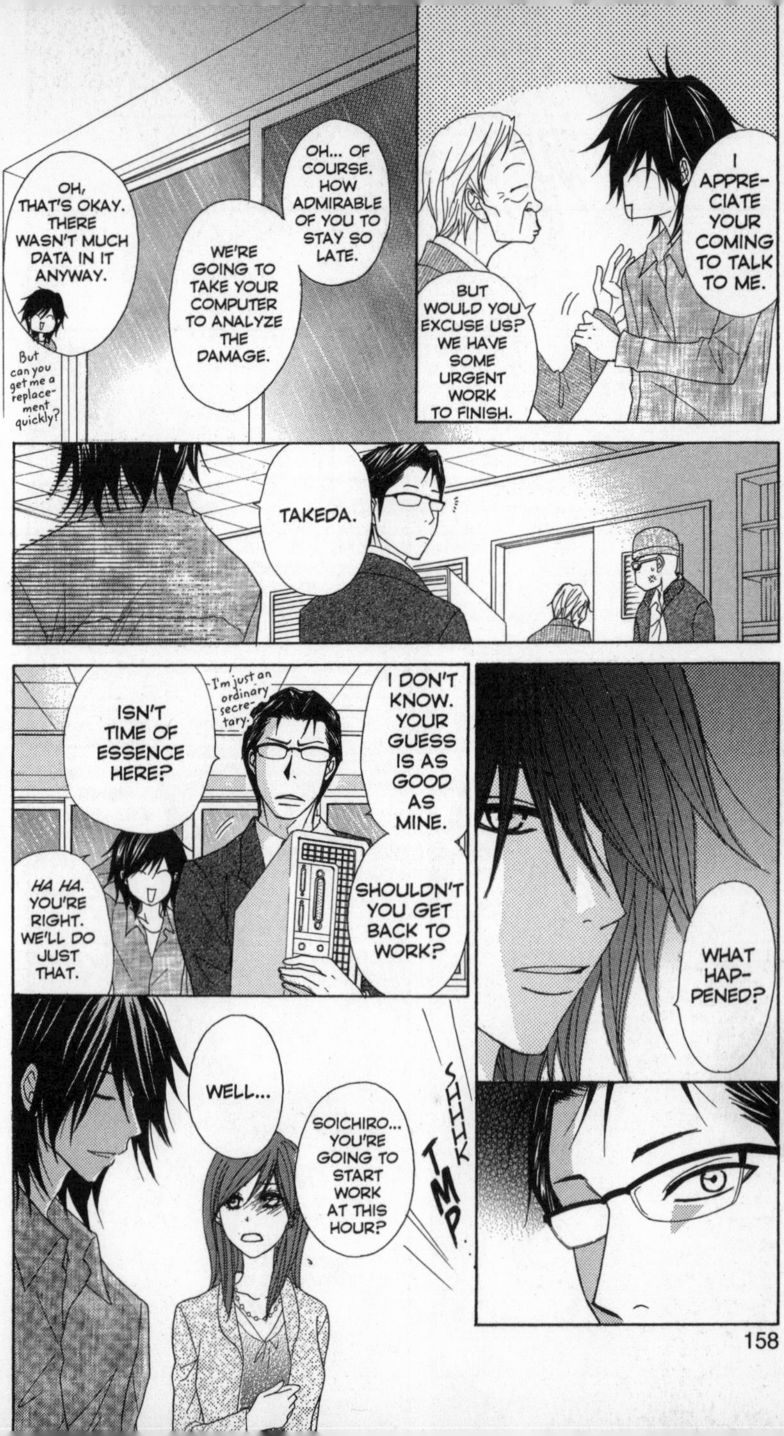
I APPRECIATE YOUR COMING TO TALK TO ME.
BUT WOULD YOU EXCUSE US? WE HAVE SOME URGENT WORK TO FINISH.
OH... OF COURSE. HOW ADMIRABLE OF YOU TO STAY SO LATE.
WE'RE GOING TO TAKE YOUR COMPUTER TO ANALYZE THE DAMAGE.
OH, THAT'S OKAY. THERE WASN'T MUCH DATA IN IT ANYWAY.
But can you get me a replacement quickly?
TAKEDA.
WHAT HAPPENED?
SHHHK
TMP
I DON'T KNOW. YOUR GUESS IS AS GOOD AS MINE.
SHOULDN'T YOU GET BACK TO WORK?
I'm just an ordinary secretary.
ISN'T TIME OF ESSENCE HERE?
HA HA. YOU'RE RIGHT. WE'LL DO JUST THAT.
SOICHIRO... YOU'RE GOING TO START WORK AT THIS HOUR?
WELL...

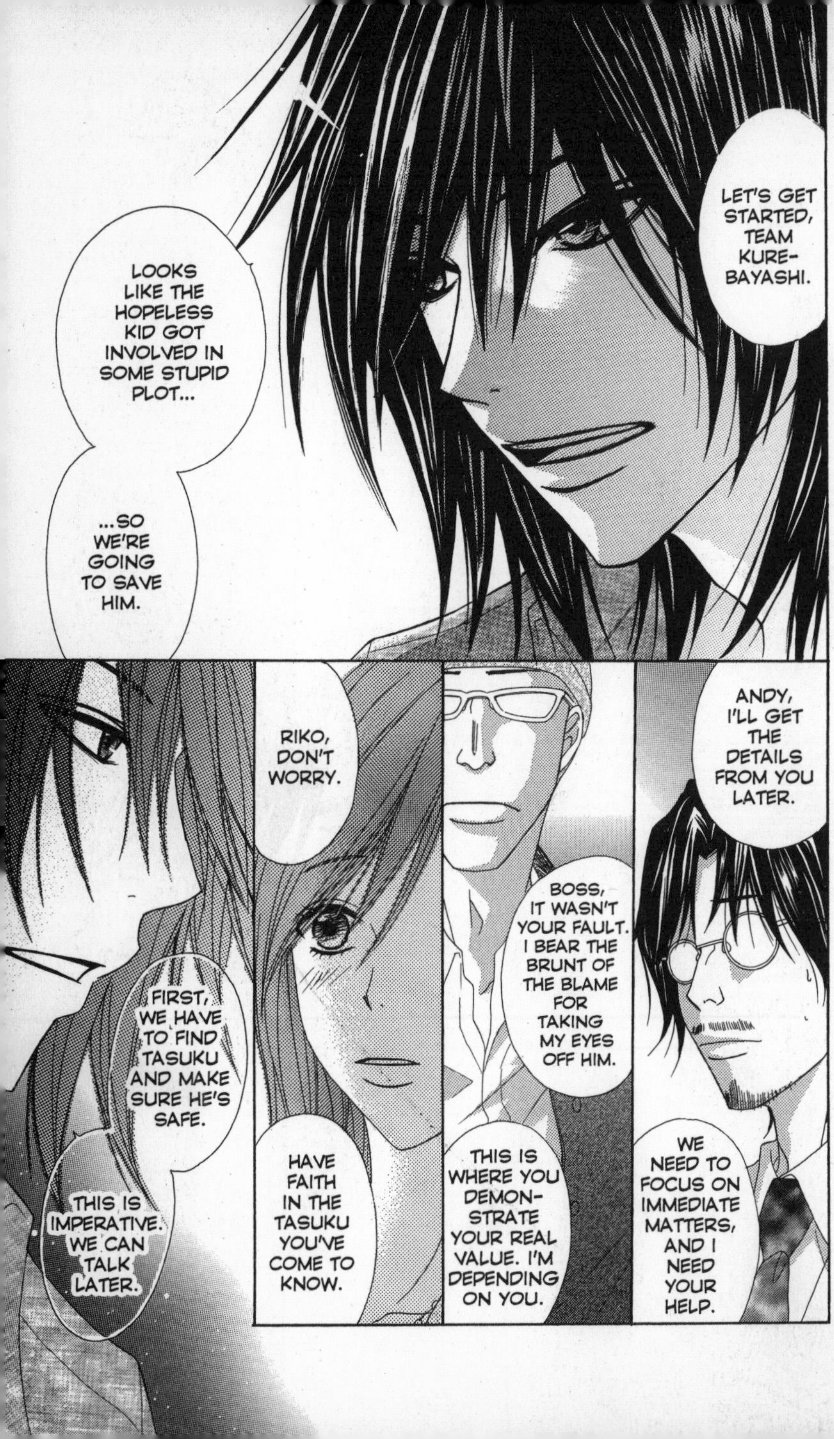
LET'S GET STARTED, TEAM KURE-BAYASHI.
LOOKS LIKE THE HOPELESS KID GOT INVOLVED IN SOME STUPID PLOT...
...SO WE'RE GOING TO SAVE HIM.
ANDY, I'LL GET THE DETAILS FROM YOU LATER.
WE NEED TO FOCUS ON IMMEDIATE MATTERS, AND I NEED YOUR HELP.
BOSS, IT WASN'T YOUR FAULT. I BEAR THE BRUNT OF THE BLAME FOR TAKING MY EYES OFF HIM.
THIS IS WHERE YOU DEMON-STRATE YOUR REAL VALUE. I'M DEPENDING ON YOU.
RIKO, DON'T WORRY.
HAVE FAITH IN THE TASUKU YOU'VE COME TO KNOW.
FIRST, WE HAVE TO FIND TASUKU AND MAKE SURE HE'S SAFE.
THIS IS IMPERATIVE. WE CAN TALK LATER.

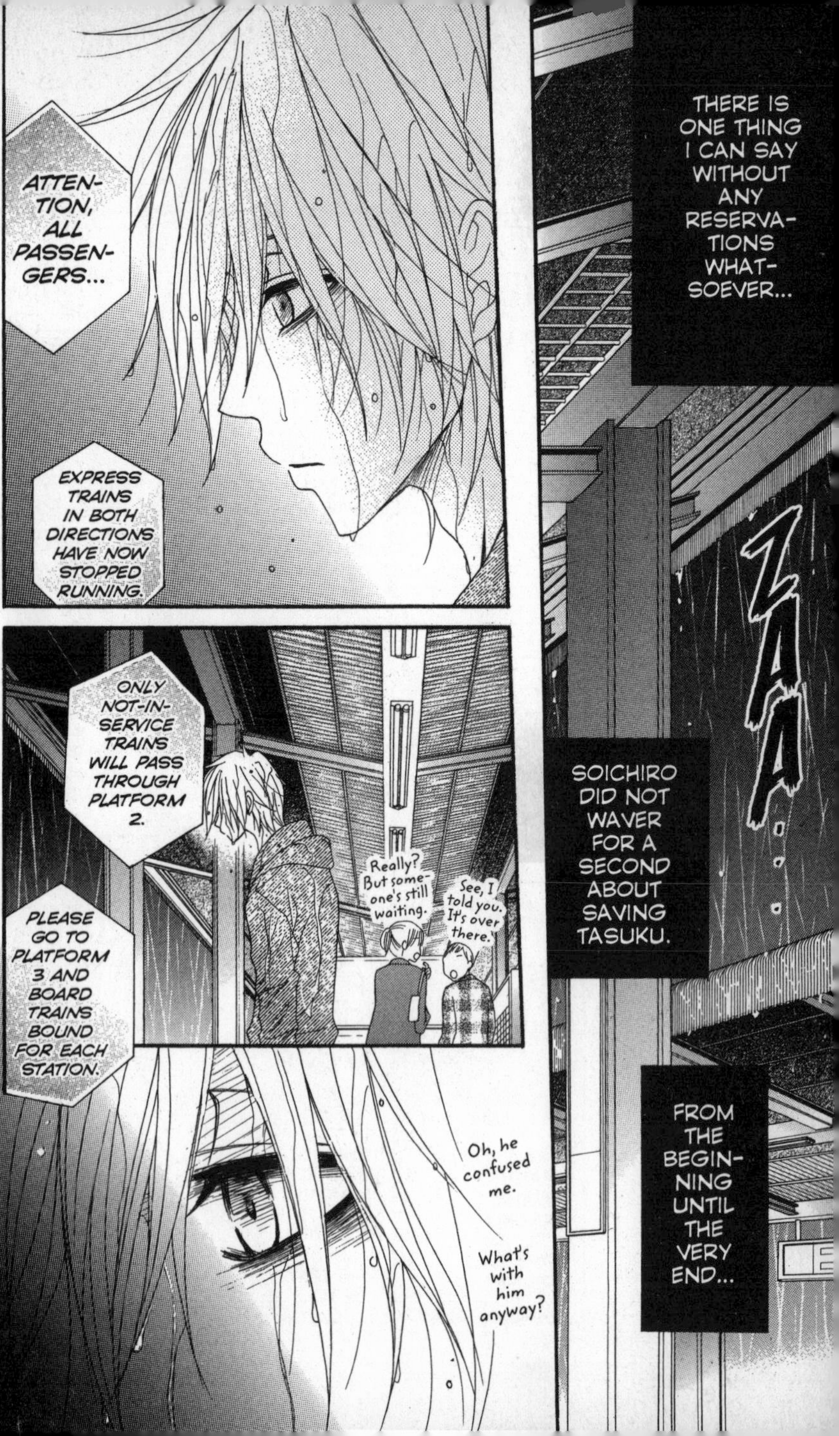
THERE IS ONE THING I CAN SAY WITHOUT ANY RESERVATIONS WHATSOEVER...
ZAAA...
SOICHIRO DID NOT WAVER FOR A SECOND ABOUT SAVING TASUKU.
FROM THE BEGINNING UNTIL THE VERY END...
ATTENTION, ALL PASSENGERS...
EXPRESS TRAINS IN BOTH DIRECTIONS HAVE NOW STOPPED RUNNING.
ONLY NOT-IN-SERVICE TRAINS WILL PASS THROUGH PLATFORM 2.
See, I told you. It's over there.
Really? But someone's still waiting.
PLEASE GO TO PLATFORM 3 AND BOARD TRAINS BOUND FOR EACH STATION.
Oh, he confused me.
What's with him anyway?

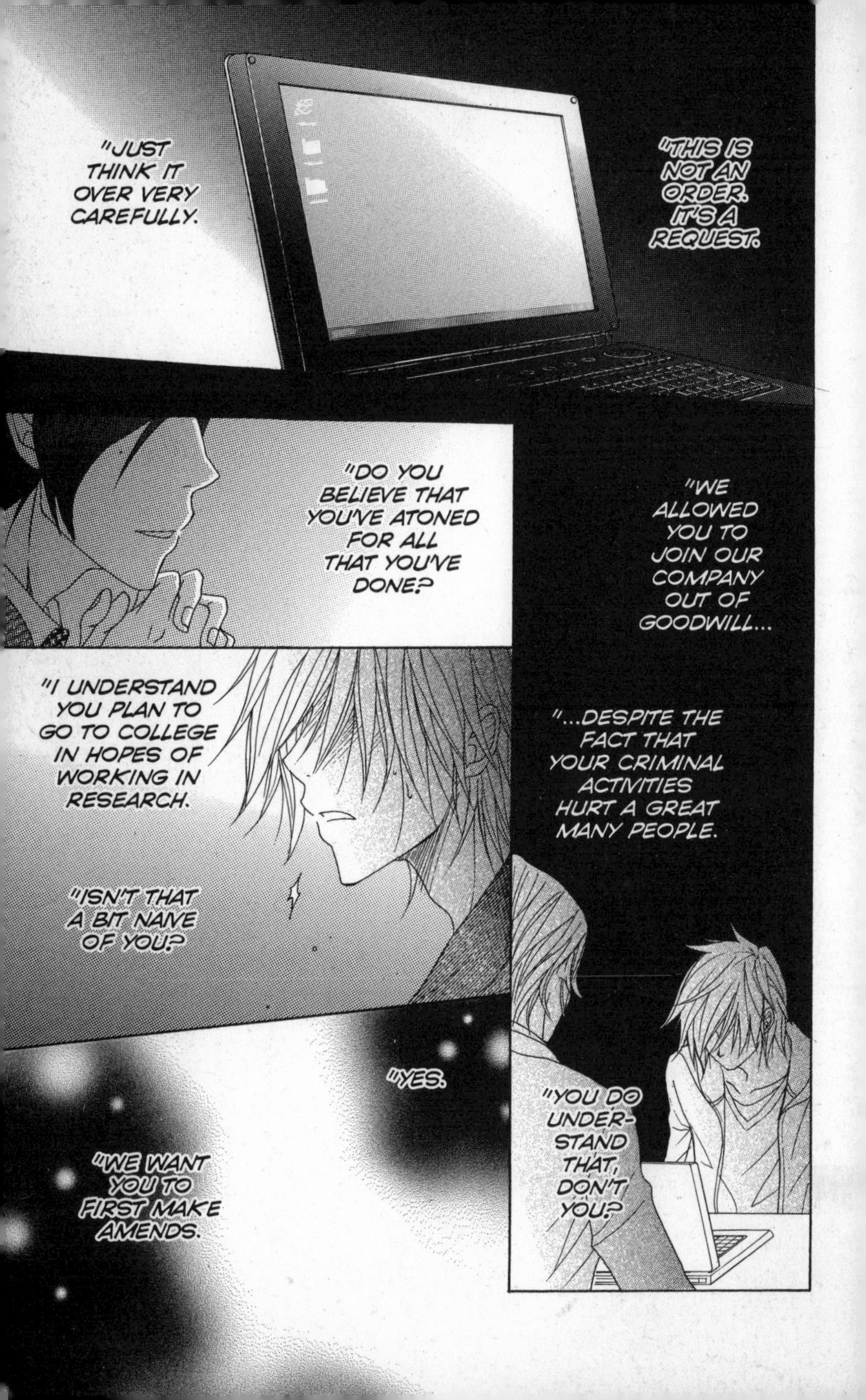
"THIS IS NOT AN ORDER. IT'S A REQUEST.
"JUST THINK IT OVER VERY CAREFULLY.
"WE ALLOWED YOU TO JOIN OUR COMPANY OUT OF GOODWILL...
"...DESPITE THE FACT THAT YOUR CRIMINAL ACTIVITIES HURT A GREAT MANY PEOPLE.
"YOU DO UNDER-STAND THAT, DON'T YOU?
"DO YOU BELIEVE THAT YOU'VE ATONED FOR ALL THAT YOU'VE DONE?
"I UNDERSTAND YOU PLAN TO GO TO COLLEGE IN HOPES OF WORKING IN RESEARCH.
"ISN'T THAT A BIT NAIVE OF YOU?
"YES.
"WE WANT YOU TO FIRST MAKE AMENDS.

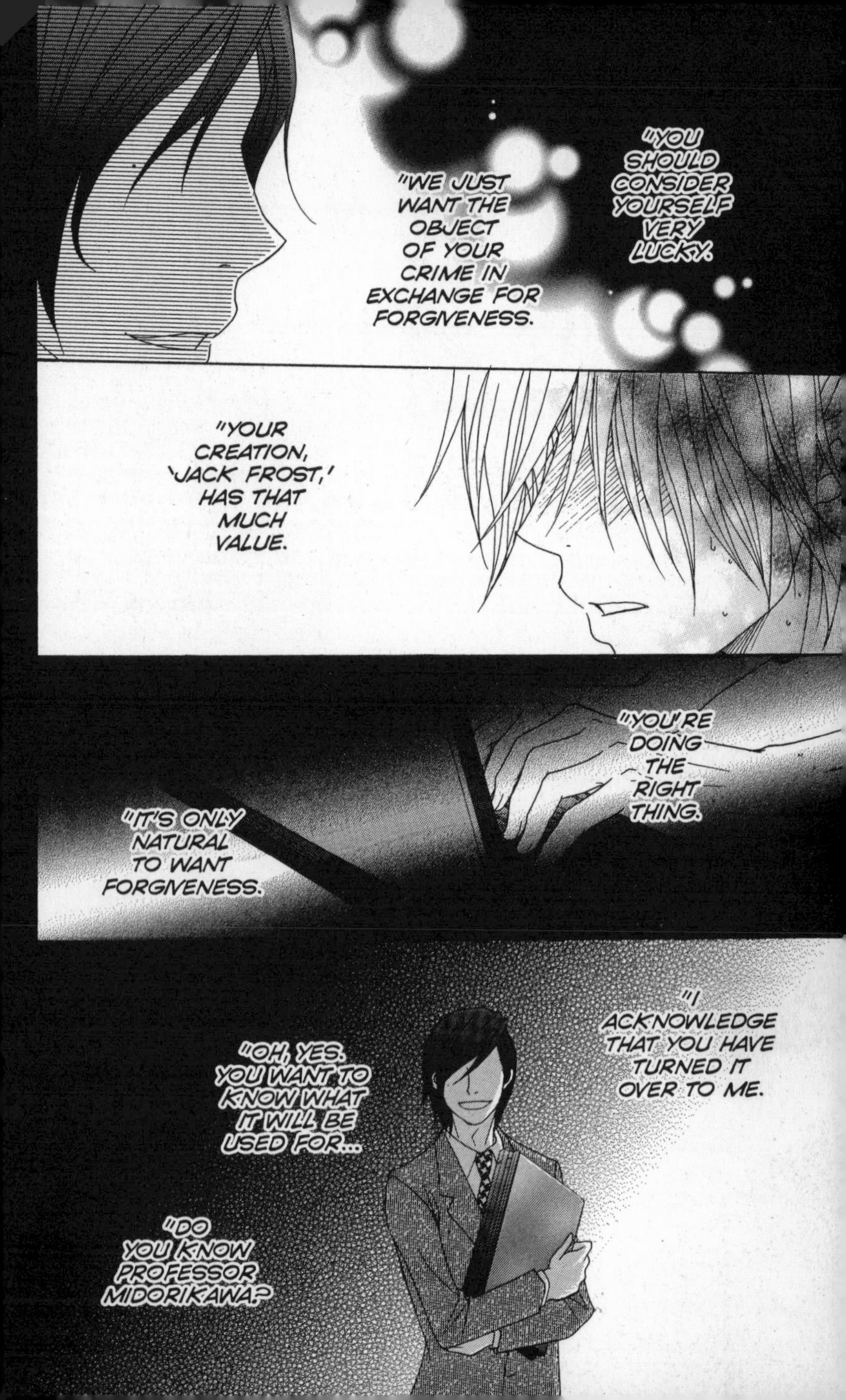
"YOU SHOULD CONSIDER YOURSELF VERY LUCKY.
"WE JUST WANT THE OBJECT OF YOUR CRIME IN EXCHANGE FOR FORGIVENESS.
"YOUR CREATION, 'JACK FROST,' HAS THAT MUCH VALUE.
"YOU'RE DOING THE RIGHT THING.
"IT'S ONLY NATURAL TO WANT FORGIVENESS.
"I ACKNOWLEDGE THAT YOU HAVE TURNED IT OVER TO ME.
"OH, YES. YOU WANT TO KNOW WHAT IT WILL BE USED FOR...
"DO YOU KNOW PROFESSOR MIDORIKAWA?

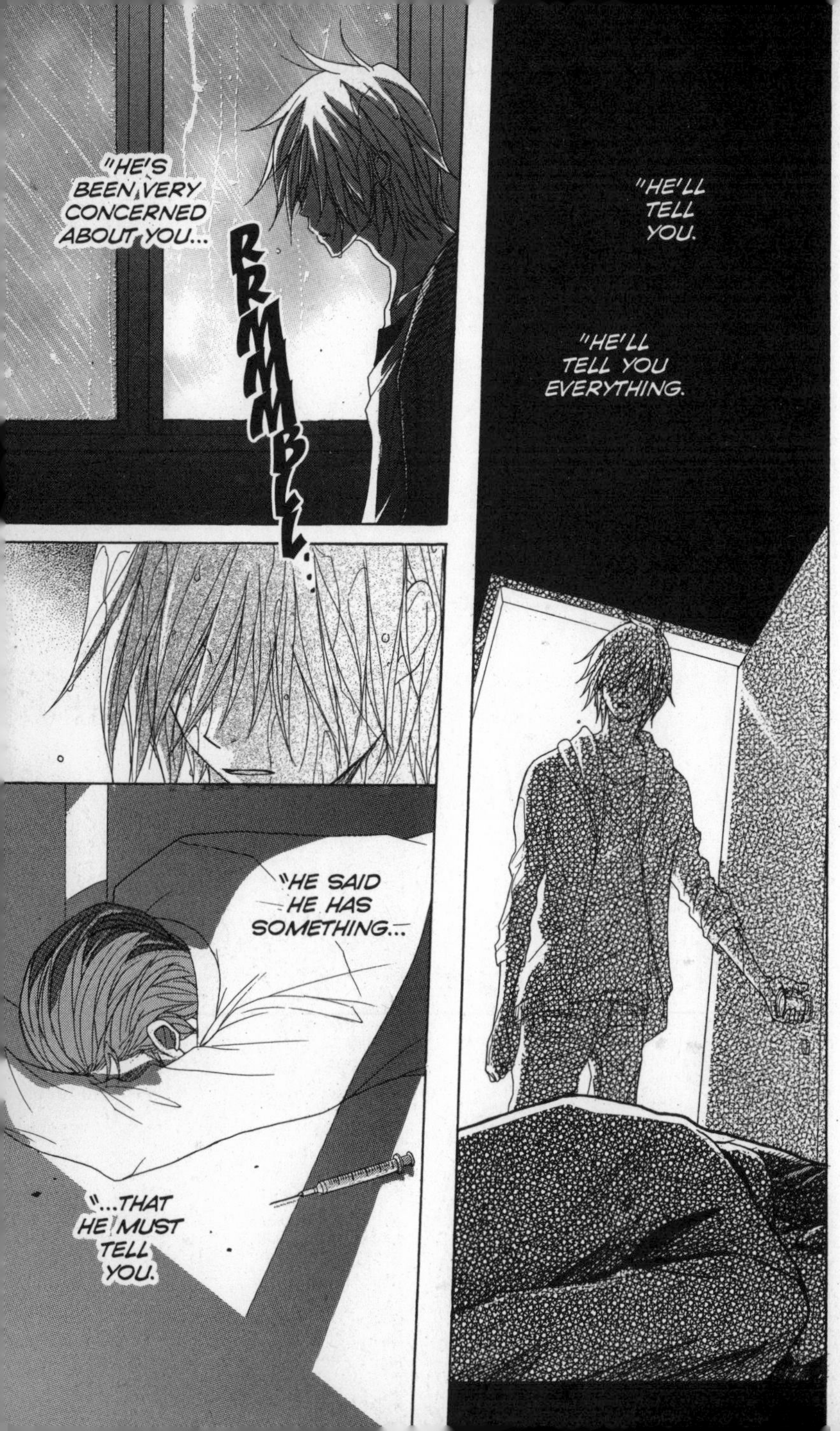
"HE'LL TELL YOU.
"HE'LL TELL YOU EVERYTHING.
"HE'S BEEN VERY CONCERNED ABOUT YOU...
RRMMBLL...
"HE SAID HE HAS SOMETHING...
"...THAT HE MUST TELL YOU.

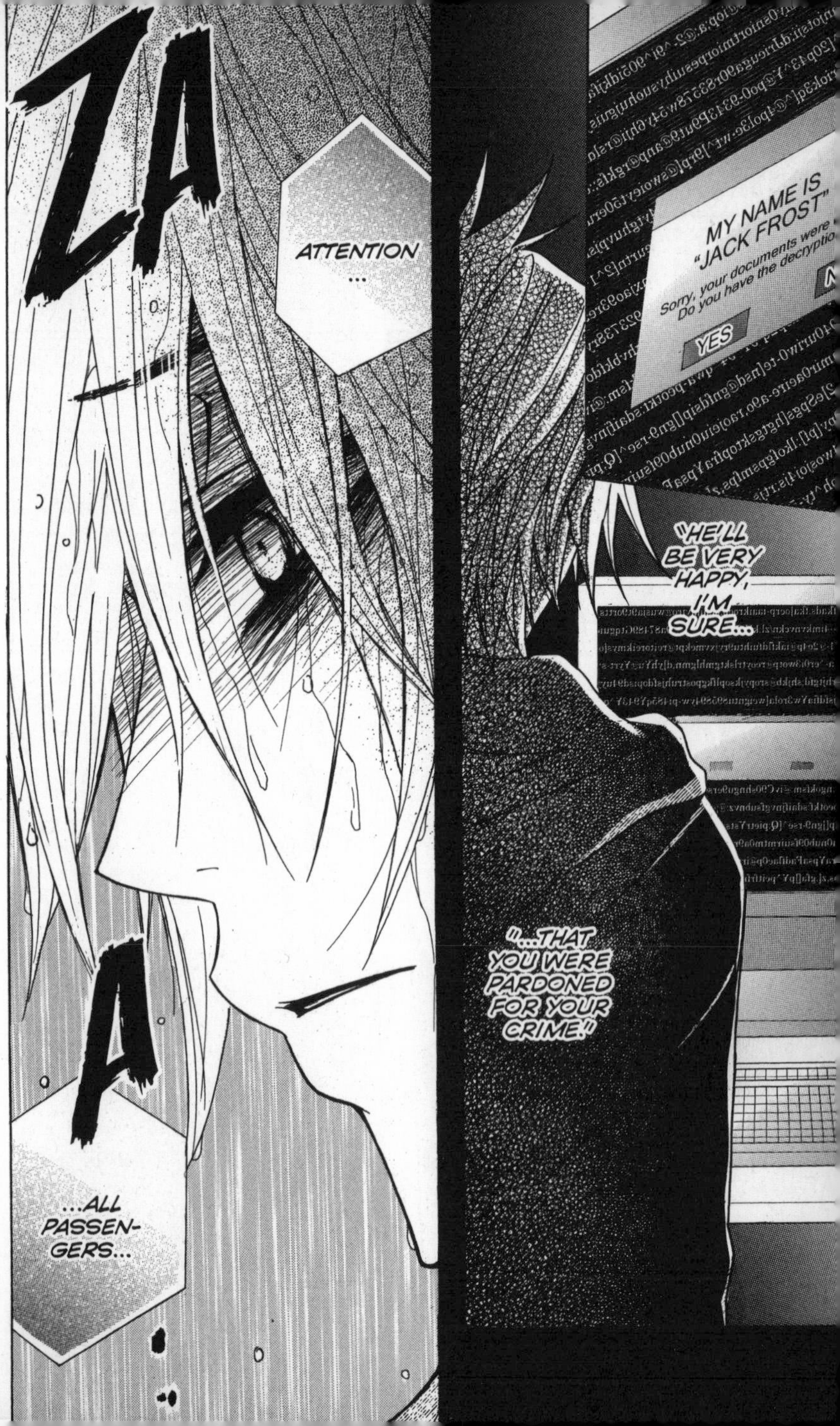
MY NAME IS "JACK FROST"
Sorry, your documents were
Do you have the
YES
"HE'LL BE VERY HAPPY, I'M SURE...
"...THAT YOU WERE PARDONED FOR YOUR CRIME."
ZA
ATTENTION ...
A
...ALL PASSEN-GERS...

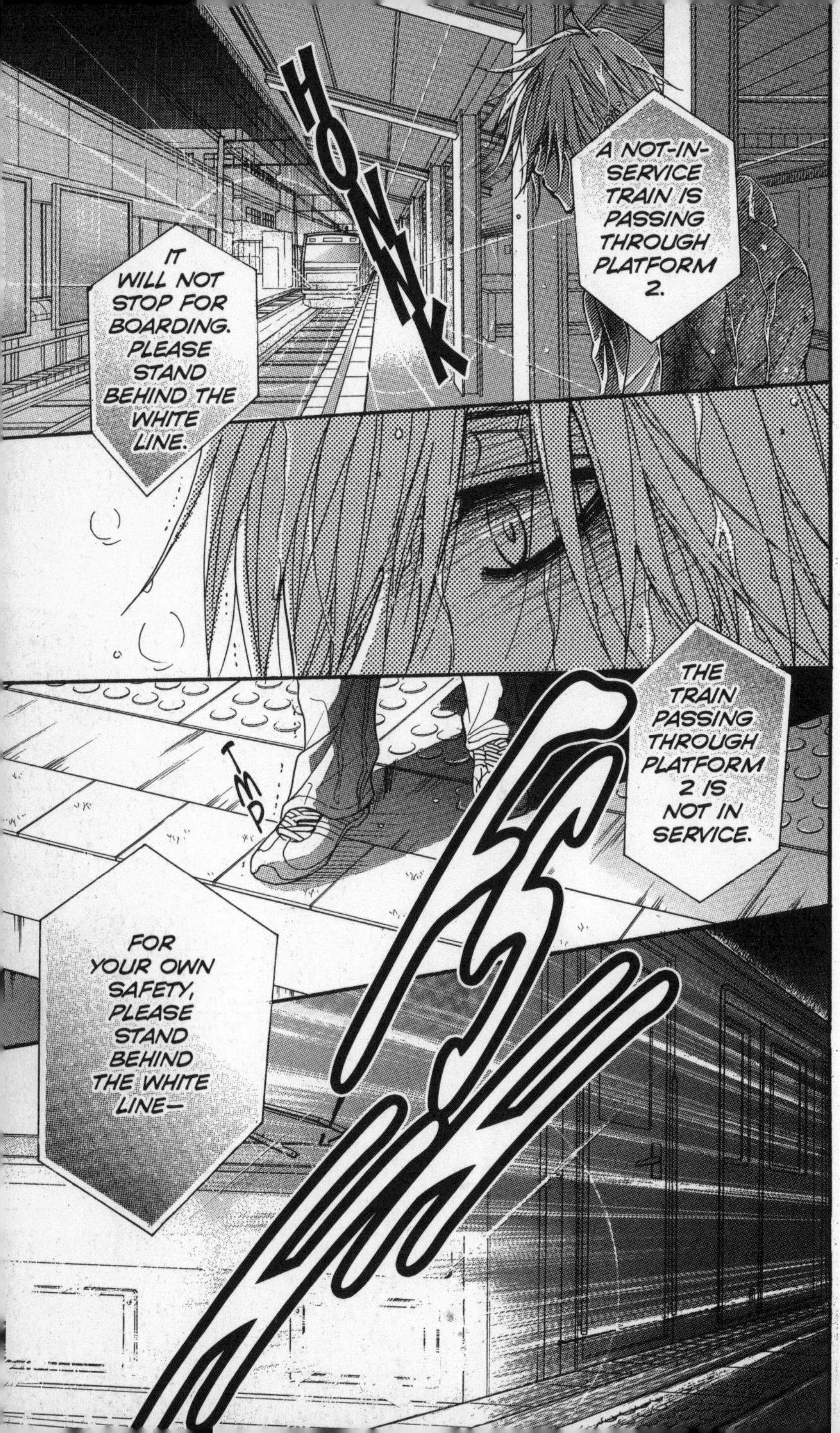
A NOT-IN-SERVICE TRAIN IS PASSING THROUGH PLATFORM 2.
HONNK
IT WILL NOT STOP FOR BOARDING. PLEASE STAND BEHIND THE WHITE LINE.
THE TRAIN PASSING THROUGH PLATFORM 2 IS NOT IN SERVICE.
TMP
FOR YOUR OWN SAFETY, PLEASE STAND BEHIND THE WHITE LINE—

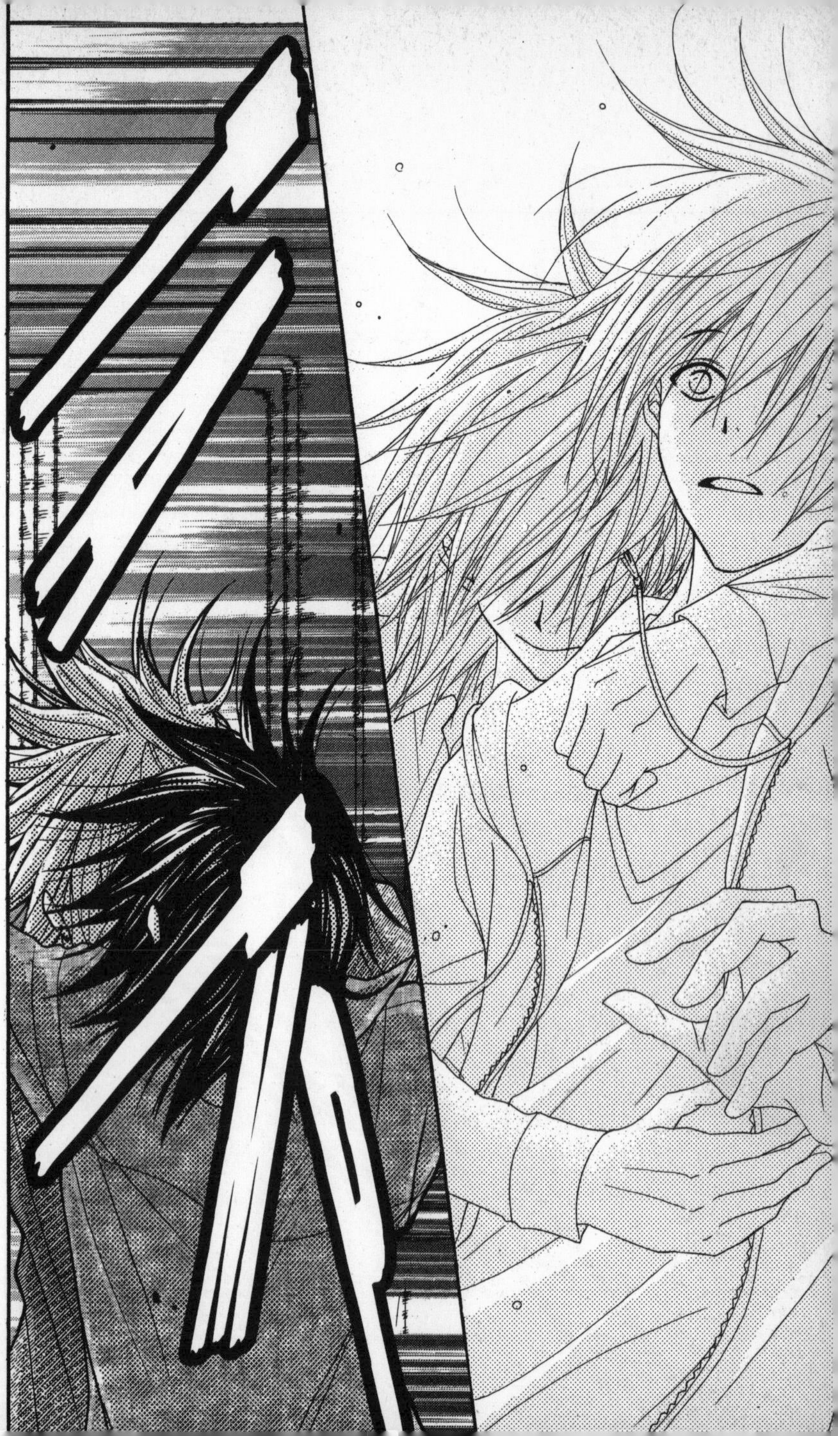

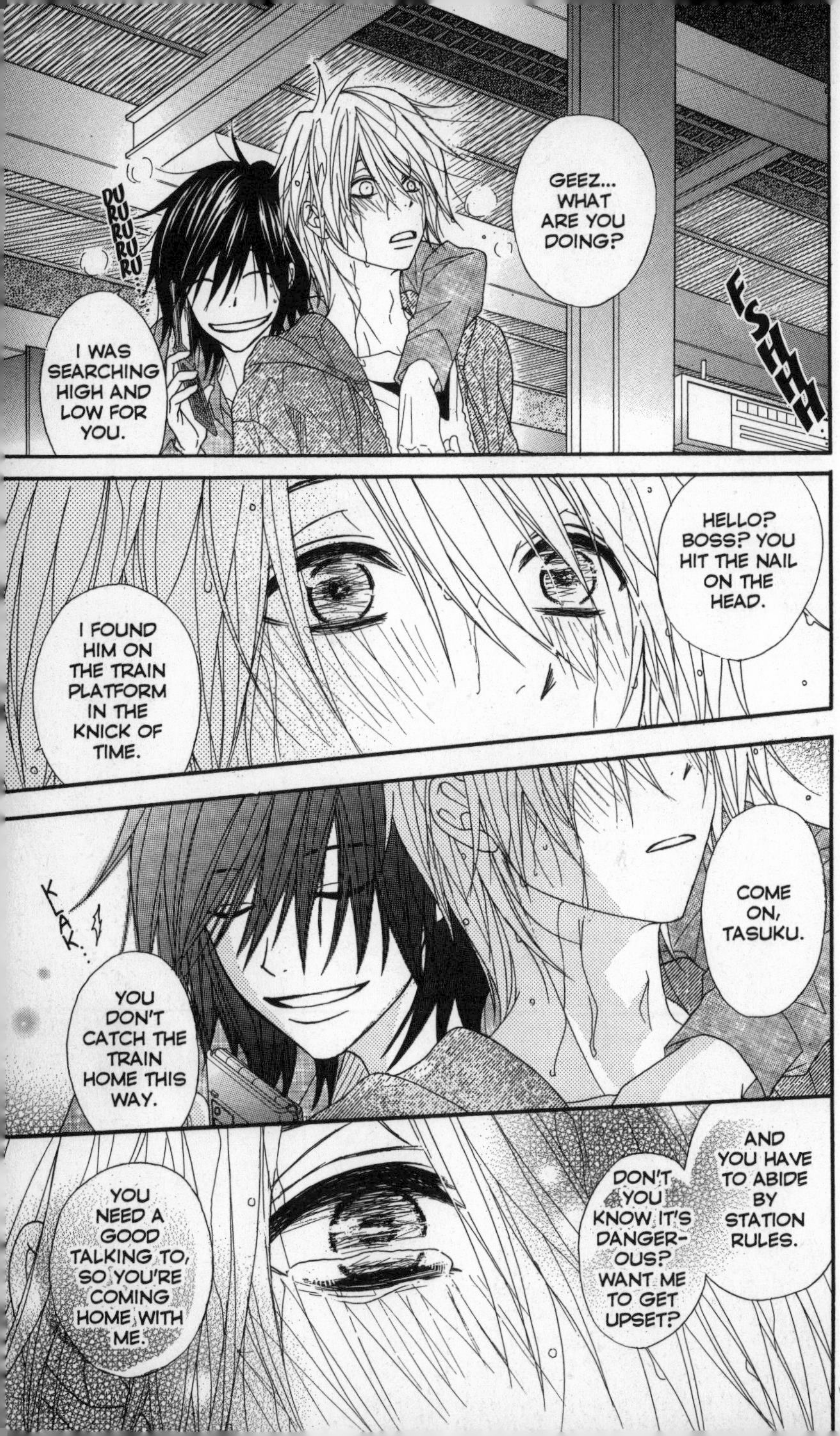
FSHHH
GEEZ... WHAT ARE YOU DOING?
DURURURURU
I WAS SEARCHING HIGH AND LOW FOR YOU.
HELLO? BOSS? YOU HIT THE NAIL ON THE HEAD.
I FOUND HIM ON THE TRAIN PLATFORM IN THE KNICK OF TIME.
COME ON, TASUKU.
KLAK...
YOU DON'T CATCH THE TRAIN HOME THIS WAY.
AND YOU HAVE TO ABIDE BY STATION RULES.
DON'T YOU KNOW IT'S DANGER-OUS? WANT ME TO GET UPSET?
YOU NEED A GOOD TALKING TO, SO YOU'RE COMING HOME WITH ME.

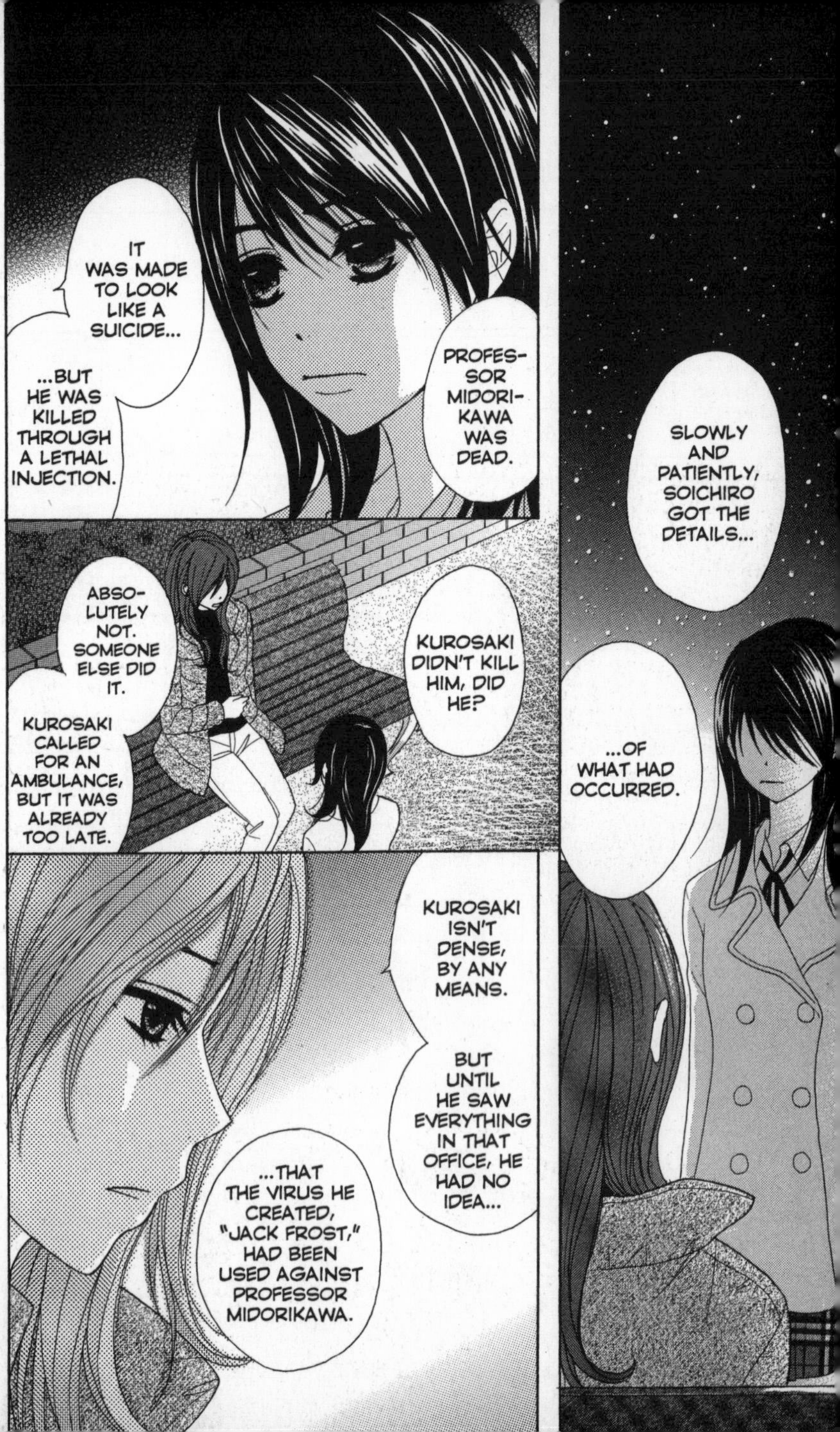
SLOWLY AND PATIENTLY, SOICHIRO GOT THE DETAILS...
...OF WHAT HAD OCCURRED.
PROFES-SOR MIDORI-KAWA WAS DEAD.
IT WAS MADE TO LOOK LIKE A SUICIDE...
...BUT HE WAS KILLED THROUGH A LETHAL INJECTION.
KUROSAKI DIDN'T KILL HIM, DID HE?
ABSO-LUTELY NOT. SOMEONE ELSE DID IT.
KUROSAKI CALLED FOR AN AMBULANCE, BUT IT WAS ALREADY TOO LATE.
KUROSAKI ISN'T DENSE, BY ANY MEANS.
BUT UNTIL HE SAW EVERYTHING IN THAT OFFICE, HE HAD NO IDEA...
...THAT THE VIRUS HE CREATED, "JACK FROST," HAD BEEN USED AGAINST PROFESSOR MIDORIKAWA.

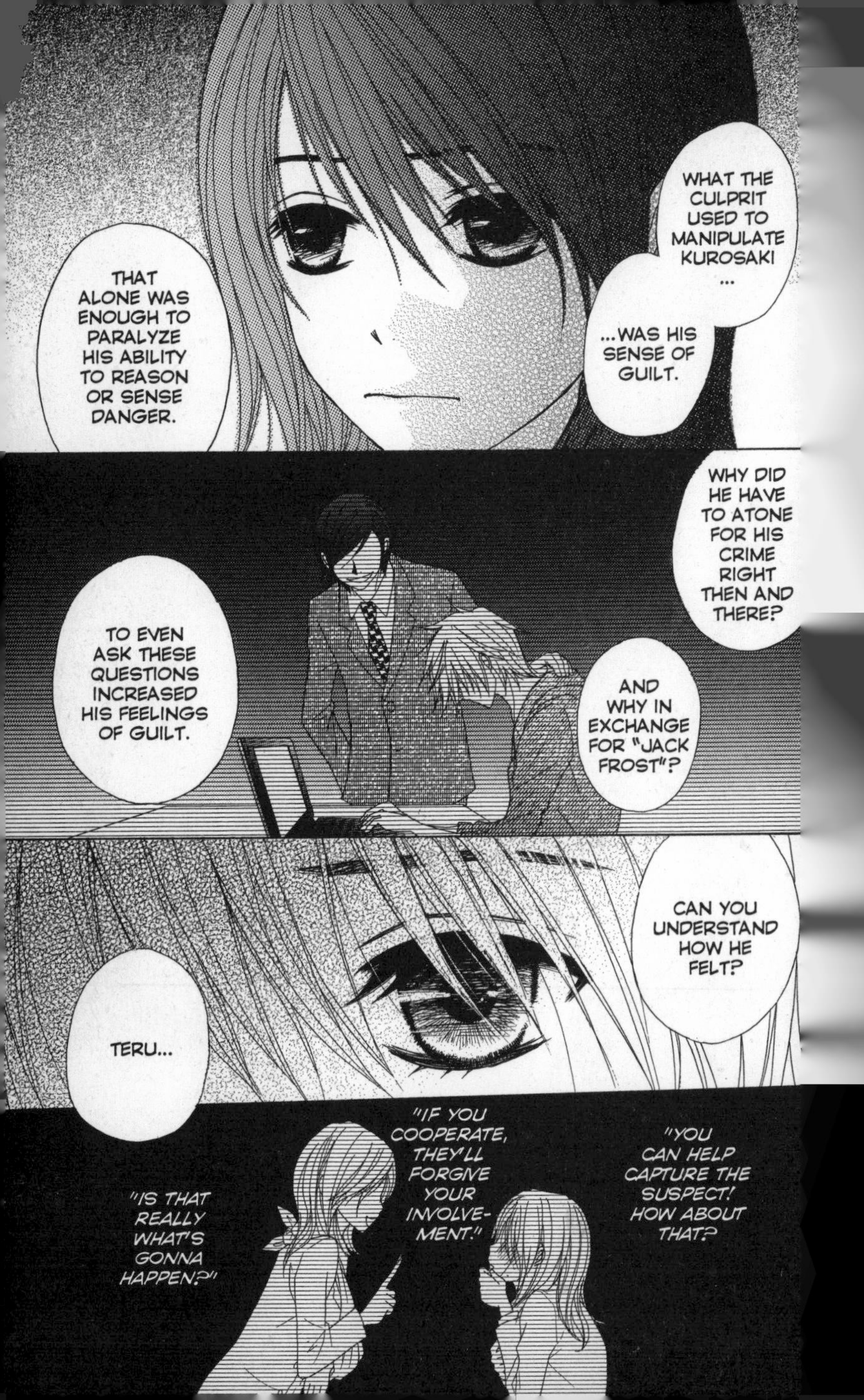
WHAT THE CULPRIT USED TO MANIPULATE KUROSAKI ...
...WAS HIS SENSE OF GUILT.
THAT ALONE WAS ENOUGH TO PARALYZE HIS ABILITY TO REASON OR SENSE DANGER.
WHY DID HE HAVE TO ATONE FOR HIS CRIME RIGHT THEN AND THERE?
AND WHY IN EXCHANGE FOR "JACK FROST"?
TO EVEN ASK THESE QUESTIONS INCREASED HIS FEELINGS OF GUILT.
CAN YOU UNDERSTAND HOW HE FELT?
TERU...
"YOU CAN HELP CAPTURE THE SUSPECT! HOW ABOUT THAT?
"IF YOU COOPERATE, THEY'LL FORGIVE YOUR INVOLVE-MENT."
"IS THAT REALLY WHAT'S GONNA HAPPEN?"

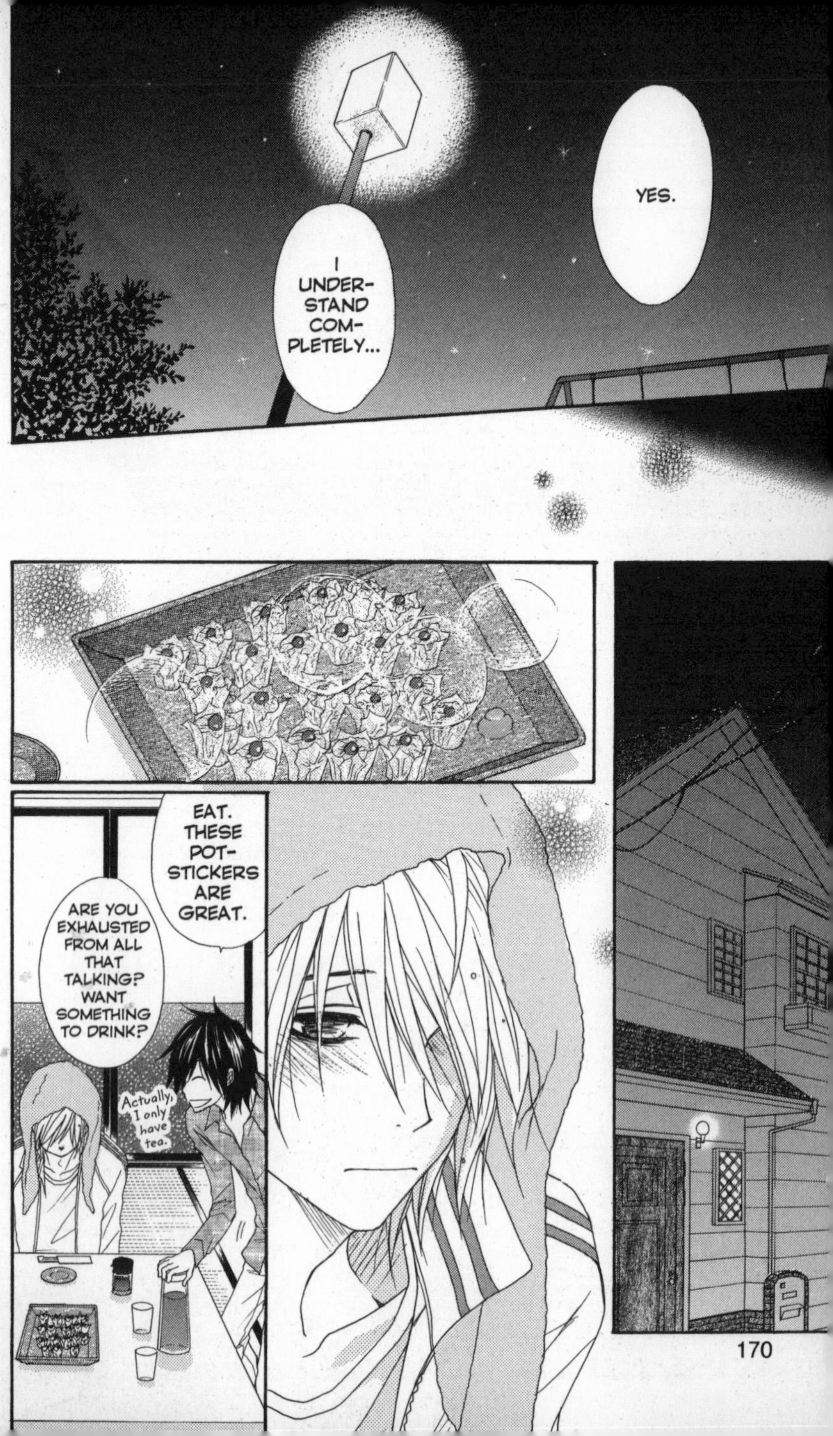
YES.
I UNDER-STAND COM-PLETELY...
EAT. THESE POT-STICKERS ARE GREAT.
ARE YOU EXHAUSTED FROM ALL THAT TALKING? WANT SOMETHING TO DRINK?
Actually, I only have tea.

BALDLY* ASK!!

⑤

Q.
IN CHAPTER 20, TERU SAYS "NUMBER 92, TERU KUREBAYASHI!!" AND GOES ON TO DO HER SPECIALTY, "EIGHT!!!" WHAT WERE NUMBERS 1 THROUGH 91? I CAN'T HELP BUT BE CURIOUS.

(PIYO, TOYAMA PREFECTURE)

A.
I'D LOVE TO ANSWER YOUR QUESTION, BUT IF I DESCRIBED 1 THROUGH 91, THIS CORNER WOULD GO OFF THE PAGE, SO I'LL REFRAIN. BUT NUMBER 36, TERU'S IMPERSONATION OF A *NURIKABE* WHERE SHE USED ALL HER MIGHT, DID SEEM TO BE QUITE APPEALING TO KUROSAKI. (SINCE IT WAS SO MASOCHISTIC.)

Q.
I HAVE A QUESTION FOR TERU AND EVERYONE. ARE YOU M [MASOCHISTIC]? OR S [SADISTIC]? AND IS KUROSAKI "SP" [SUPER PERVERTED]...?

(C.I., SHIZUOKA PREFECTURE)

A.

SS ◄————————————► SM

AKIRA	KIYOSHI	ANDY	SOICHIRO	RIKO	HARUKA	BOSS	TERU	CHIHARU MORI	KUROSAKI	RENA

I'D SAY THIS DIAGRAM PRETTY MUCH COVERS THE RANGE OF CHARACTERS' PREFERENCES. WHILE ANDY IS A MASOCHIST, HE TENDS TO SOUND A BIT SADISTIC... I'M SURE YOU ALL RECOGNIZE KUROSAKI TO BE SUPER MASOCHISTIC AND SUPER PERVERTED. HE CONSIDERS HIMSELF TO BE PRETTY SADISTIC THOUGH. (PLUS, THE EDITORIAL TEAM CALLS HIM SUPER SADISTIC.) NO MATTER WHAT THEY ARE, PLEASE WATCH OVER THEM WITH KIND EYES.

THAT'S IT FOR THIS VOLUME!! TO BE CONTINUED IN THE NEXT VOLUME (AS EXPECTED)!!

I'M NOT GOING TO SAY...

...THAT YOU'RE NOT TO BLAME.

BUT I'M SURE IT WAS TOUGH FOR YOU.

I KNOW.

IT WOULD'VE BEEN HARD FOR ANYONE UNLESS THEY WERE STUBBORN LIKE ME.

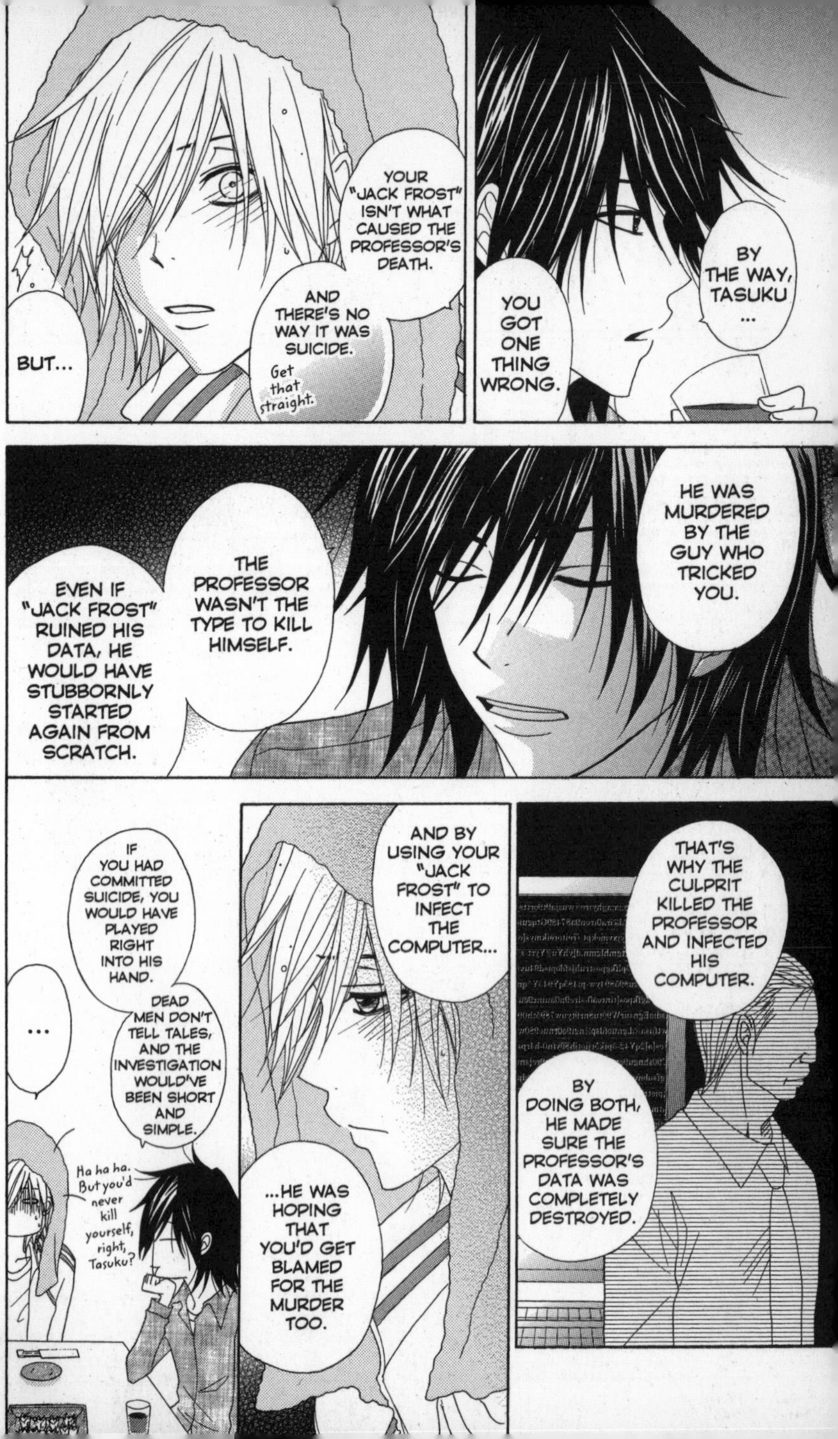
BY THE WAY, TASUKU ...
YOU GOT ONE THING WRONG.
YOUR "JACK FROST" ISN'T WHAT CAUSED THE PROFESSOR'S DEATH.
AND THERE'S NO WAY IT WAS SUICIDE.
Get that straight.
BUT...
HE WAS MURDERED BY THE GUY WHO TRICKED YOU.
THE PROFESSOR WASN'T THE TYPE TO KILL HIMSELF.
EVEN IF "JACK FROST" RUINED HIS DATA, HE WOULD HAVE STUBBORNLY STARTED AGAIN FROM SCRATCH.
THAT'S WHY THE CULPRIT KILLED THE PROFESSOR AND INFECTED HIS COMPUTER.
BY DOING BOTH, HE MADE SURE THE PROFESSOR'S DATA WAS COMPLETELY DESTROYED.
AND BY USING YOUR "JACK FROST" TO INFECT THE COMPUTER...
...HE WAS HOPING THAT YOU'D GET BLAMED FOR THE MURDER TOO.
IF YOU HAD COMMITTED SUICIDE, YOU WOULD HAVE PLAYED RIGHT INTO HIS HAND.
DEAD MEN DON'T TELL TALES, AND THE INVESTIGATION WOULD'VE BEEN SHORT AND SIMPLE.
...
Ha ha ha. But you'd never kill yourself, right, Tasuku?

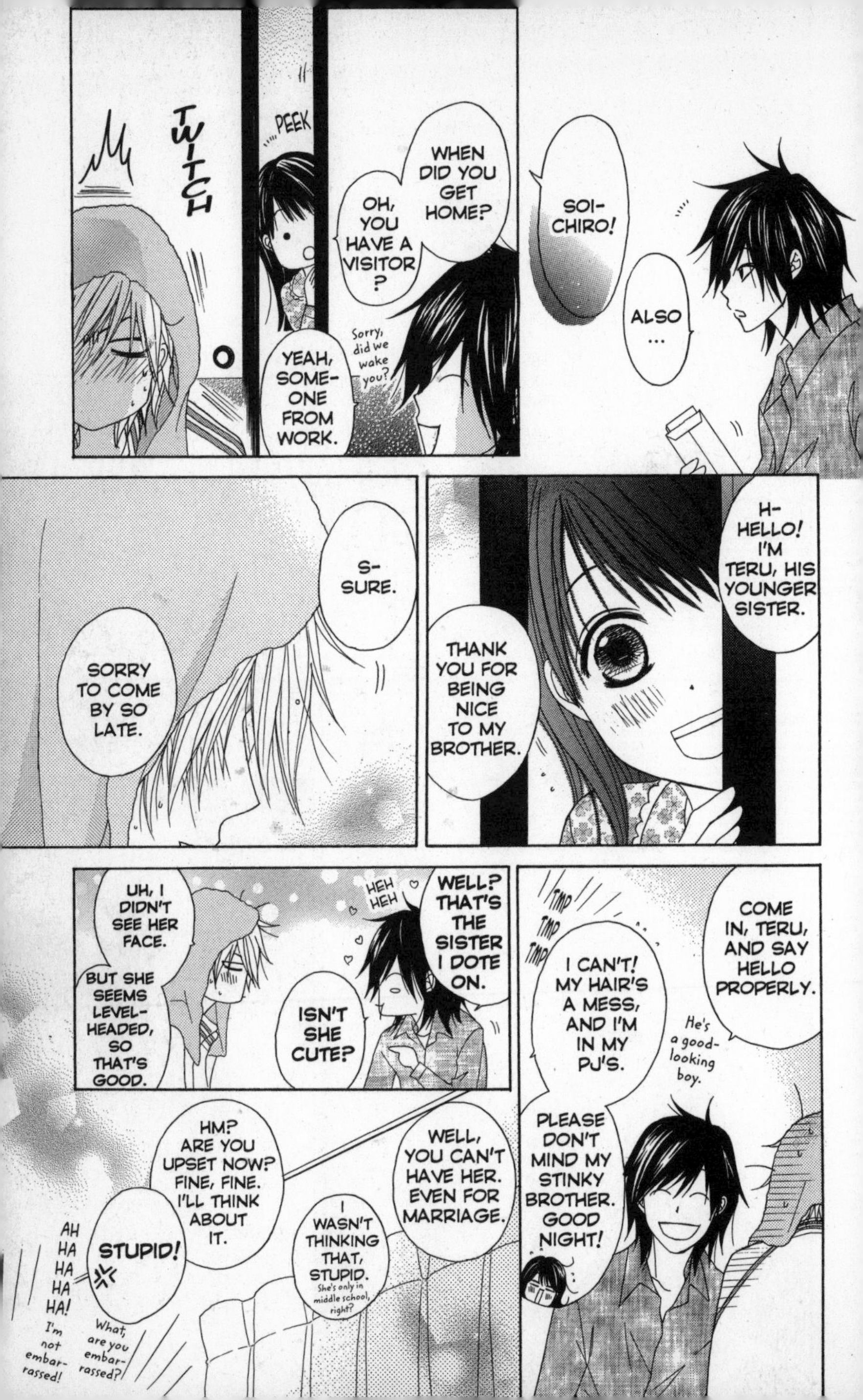
SOI-CHIRO!
ALSO...
WHEN DID YOU GET HOME?
PEEK
OH, YOU HAVE A VISITOR?
Sorry, did we wake you?
YEAH, SOMEONE FROM WORK.
TWITCH
H-HELLO! I'M TERU, HIS YOUNGER SISTER.
THANK YOU FOR BEING NICE TO MY BROTHER.
S-SURE.
SORRY TO COME BY SO LATE.
COME IN, TERU, AND SAY HELLO PROPERLY.
He's a good-looking boy.
TMP TMP TMP
I CAN'T! MY HAIR'S A MESS, AND I'M IN MY PJ'S.
PLEASE DON'T MIND MY STINKY BROTHER. GOOD NIGHT!
WELL? THAT'S THE SISTER I DOTE ON.
HEH HEH
ISN'T SHE CUTE?
UH, I DIDN'T SEE HER FACE.
BUT SHE SEEMS LEVEL-HEADED, SO THAT'S GOOD.
WELL, YOU CAN'T HAVE HER. EVEN FOR MARRIAGE.
I WASN'T THINKING THAT, STUPID.
She's only in middle school, right?
HM? ARE YOU UPSET NOW? FINE, FINE. I'LL THINK ABOUT IT.
STUPID!
What, are you embarrassed?
AH HA HA HA HA!
I'm not embarrassed!

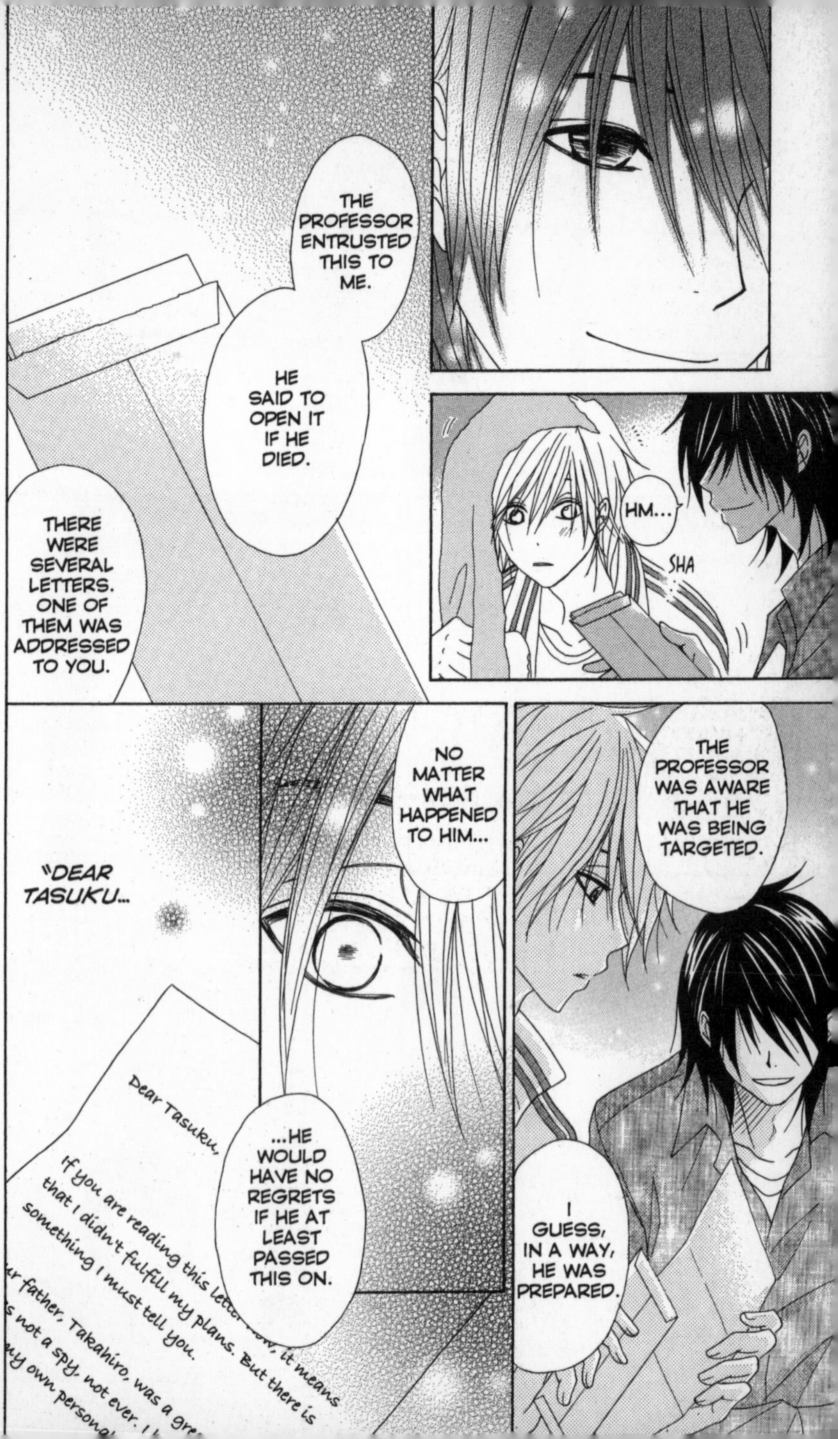
HM...
SHA
THE PROFESSOR ENTRUSTED THIS TO ME.
HE SAID TO OPEN IT IF HE DIED.
THERE WERE SEVERAL LETTERS. ONE OF THEM WAS ADDRESSED TO YOU.
THE PROFESSOR WAS AWARE THAT HE WAS BEING TARGETED.
I GUESS, IN A WAY, HE WAS PREPARED.
NO MATTER WHAT HAPPENED TO HIM...
...HE WOULD HAVE NO REGRETS IF HE AT LEAST PASSED THIS ON.
"DEAR TASUKU...
Dear Tasuku,
If you are reading this lett
ow, it means
that I didn't fulfill my plans. But there is
something I must tell you.
r father, Takahiro, was a gre
s not a spy, not ever.
my own person

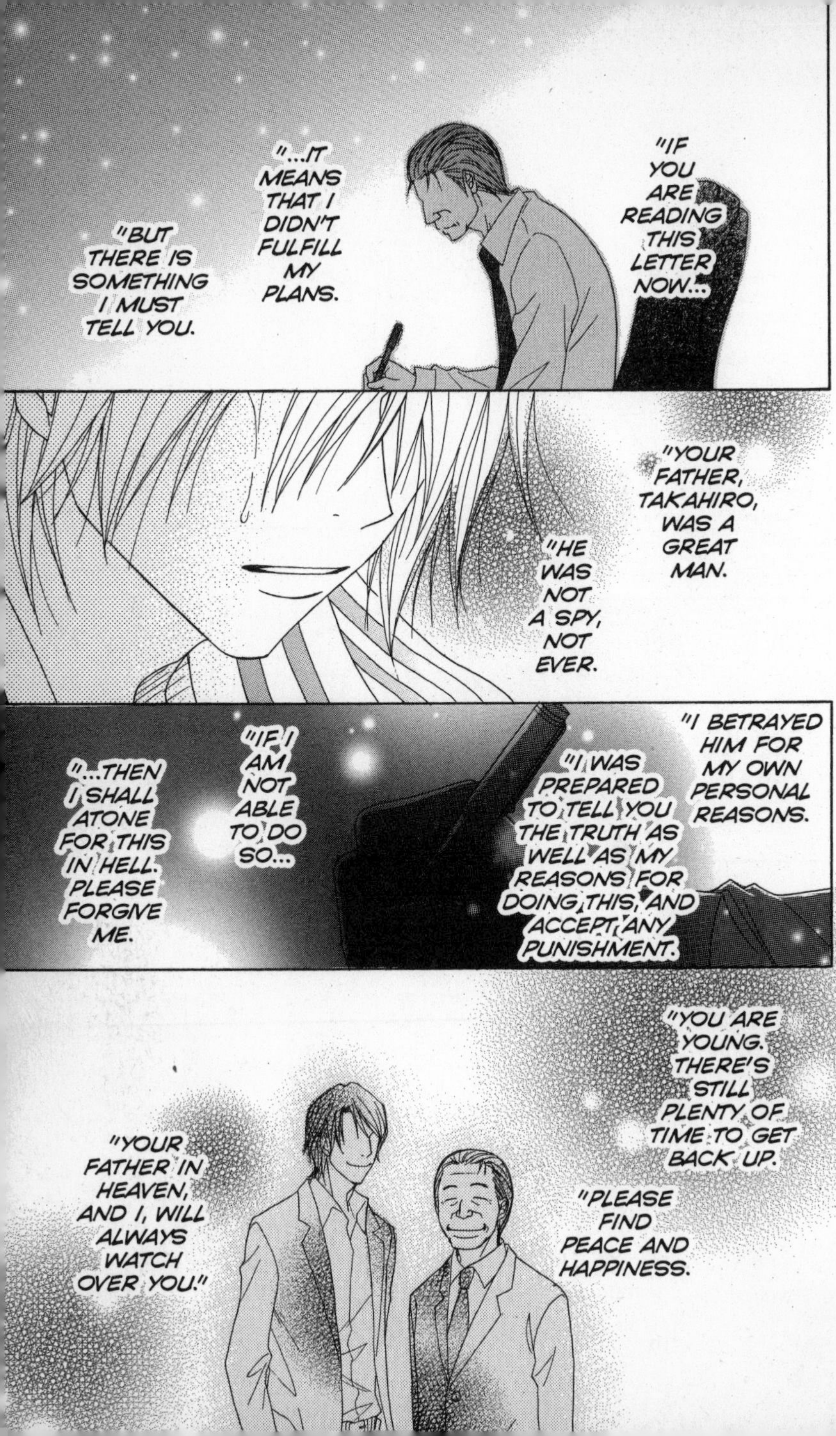
"IF YOU ARE READING THIS LETTER NOW...
"...IT MEANS THAT I DIDN'T FULFILL MY PLANS.
"BUT THERE IS SOMETHING I MUST TELL YOU.
"YOUR FATHER, TAKAHIRO, WAS A GREAT MAN.
"HE WAS NOT A SPY, NOT EVER.
"I BETRAYED HIM FOR MY OWN PERSONAL REASONS.
"I WAS PREPARED TO TELL YOU THE TRUTH AS WELL AS MY REASONS FOR DOING THIS, AND ACCEPT ANY PUNISHMENT.
"IF I AM NOT ABLE TO DO SO...
"...THEN I SHALL ATONE FOR THIS IN HELL. PLEASE FORGIVE ME.
"YOU ARE YOUNG. THERE'S STILL PLENTY OF TIME TO GET BACK UP.
"PLEASE FIND PEACE AND HAPPINESS.
"YOUR FATHER IN HEAVEN, AND I, WILL ALWAYS WATCH OVER YOU."

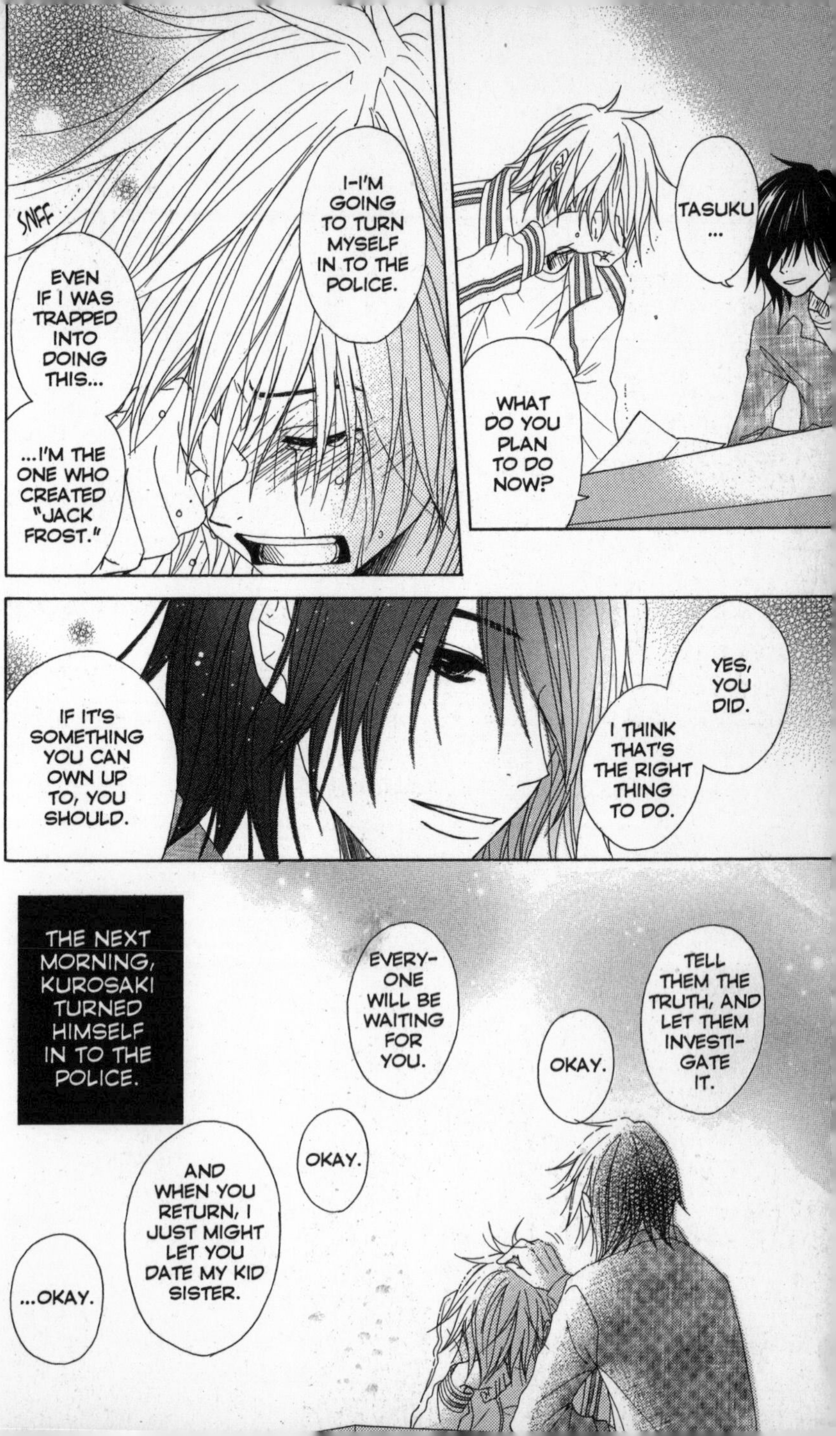
TASUKU ...
WHAT DO YOU PLAN TO DO NOW?
I-I'M GOING TO TURN MYSELF IN TO THE POLICE.
SNFF
EVEN IF I WAS TRAPPED INTO DOING THIS...
...I'M THE ONE WHO CREATED "JACK FROST."
YES, YOU DID.
I THINK THAT'S THE RIGHT THING TO DO.
IF IT'S SOMETHING YOU CAN OWN UP TO, YOU SHOULD.
TELL THEM THE TRUTH, AND LET THEM INVESTI-GATE IT.
OKAY.
EVERY-ONE WILL BE WAITING FOR YOU.
OKAY.
AND WHEN YOU RETURN, I JUST MIGHT LET YOU DATE MY KID SISTER.
...OKAY.
THE NEXT MORNING, KUROSAKI TURNED HIMSELF IN TO THE POLICE.

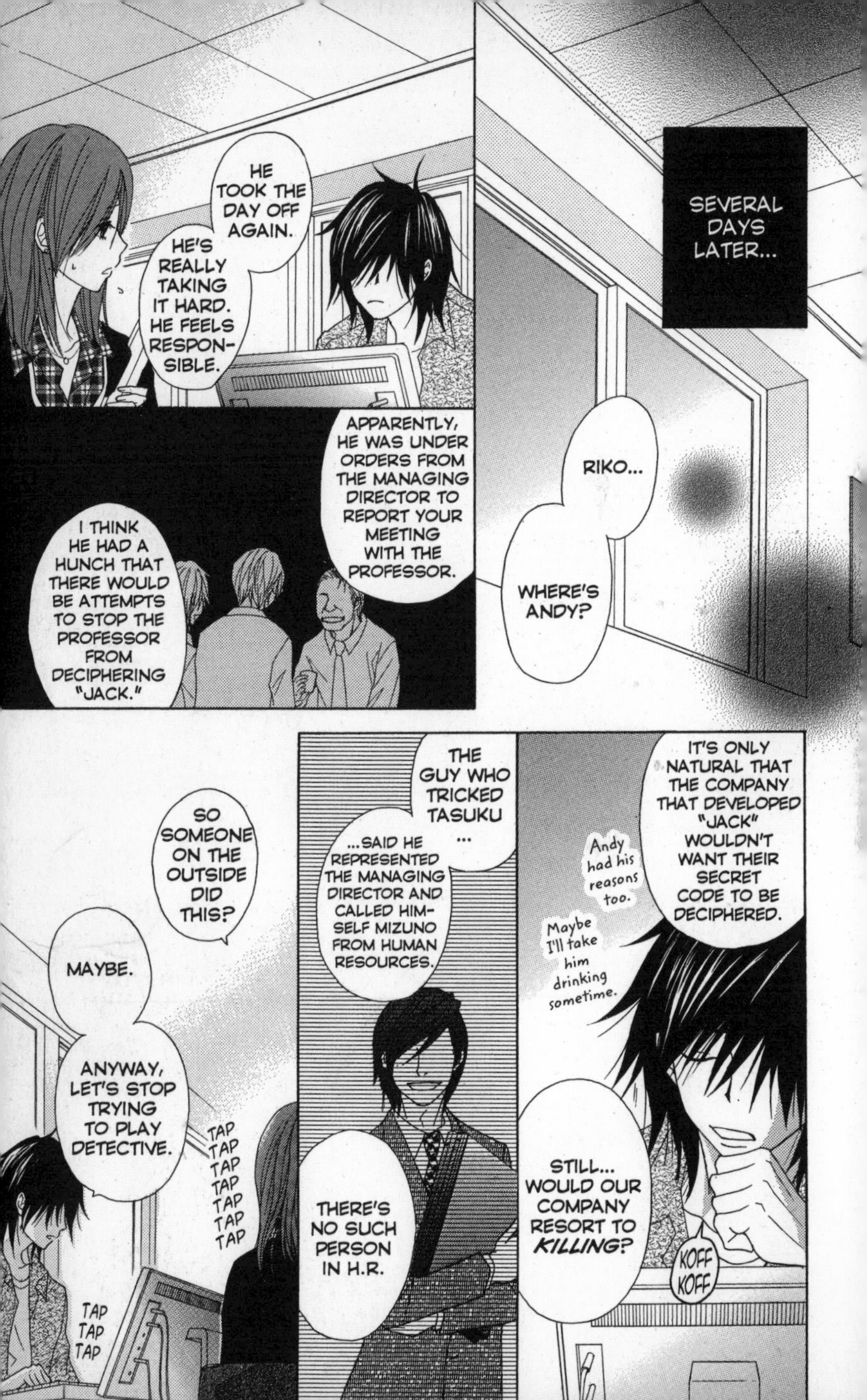
SEVERAL DAYS LATER...
RIKO...
WHERE'S ANDY?
HE TOOK THE DAY OFF AGAIN.
HE'S REALLY TAKING IT HARD. HE FEELS RESPONSIBLE.
APPARENTLY, HE WAS UNDER ORDERS FROM THE MANAGING DIRECTOR TO REPORT YOUR MEETING WITH THE PROFESSOR.
I THINK HE HAD A HUNCH THAT THERE WOULD BE ATTEMPTS TO STOP THE PROFESSOR FROM DECIPHERING "JACK."
IT'S ONLY NATURAL THAT THE COMPANY THAT DEVELOPED "JACK" WOULDN'T WANT THEIR SECRET CODE TO BE DECIPHERED.
Andy had his reasons too.
Maybe I'll take him drinking sometime.
STILL... WOULD OUR COMPANY RESORT TO *KILLING*?
KOFF KOFF
THE GUY WHO TRICKED TASUKU...
...SAID HE REPRESENTED THE MANAGING DIRECTOR AND CALLED HIMSELF MIZUNO FROM HUMAN RESOURCES.
THERE'S NO SUCH PERSON IN H.R.
SO SOMEONE ON THE OUTSIDE DID THIS?
MAYBE.
ANYWAY, LET'S STOP TRYING TO PLAY DETECTIVE.
TAP TAP TAP TAP TAP TAP TAP
TAP TAP TAP

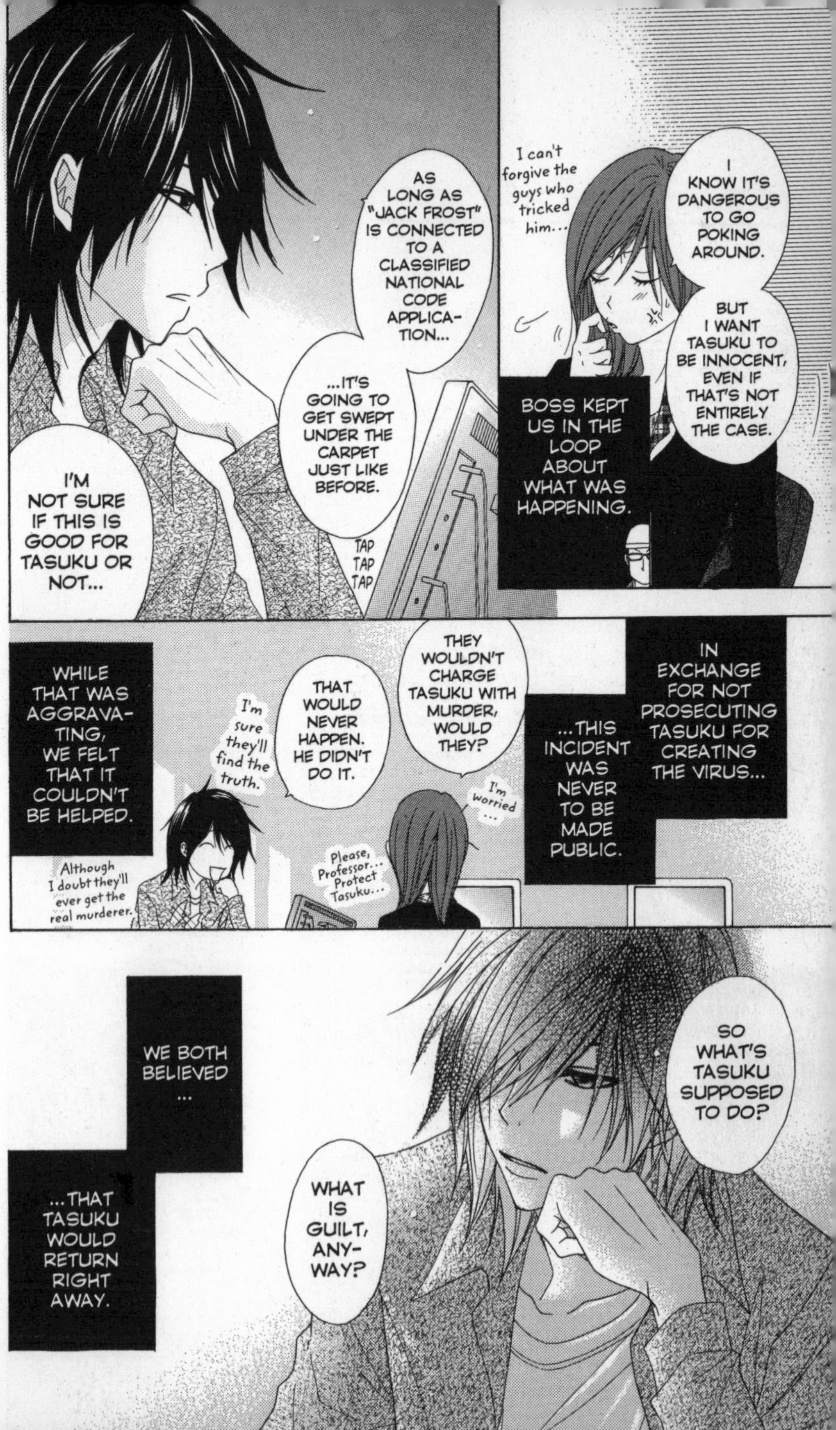
I KNOW IT'S DANGEROUS TO GO POKING AROUND.
I can't forgive the guys who tricked him...
BUT I WANT TASUKU TO BE INNOCENT, EVEN IF THAT'S NOT ENTIRELY THE CASE.
BOSS KEPT US IN THE LOOP ABOUT WHAT WAS HAPPENING.
AS LONG AS "JACK FROST" IS CONNECTED TO A CLASSIFIED NATIONAL CODE APPLICATION...
...IT'S GOING TO GET SWEPT UNDER THE CARPET JUST LIKE BEFORE.
TAP TAP TAP
I'M NOT SURE IF THIS IS GOOD FOR TASUKU OR NOT...
IN EXCHANGE FOR NOT PROSECUTING TASUKU FOR CREATING THE VIRUS...
...THIS INCIDENT WAS NEVER TO BE MADE PUBLIC.
THEY WOULDN'T CHARGE TASUKU WITH MURDER, WOULD THEY?
I'm worried...
THAT WOULD NEVER HAPPEN. HE DIDN'T DO IT.
I'm sure they'll find the truth.
Please, Professor... Protect Tasuku...
WHILE THAT WAS AGGRAVATING, WE FELT THAT IT COULDN'T BE HELPED.
Although I doubt they'll ever get the real murderer.
SO WHAT'S TASUKU SUPPOSED TO DO?
WHAT IS GUILT, ANYWAY?
WE BOTH BELIEVED...
...THAT TASUKU WOULD RETURN RIGHT AWAY.

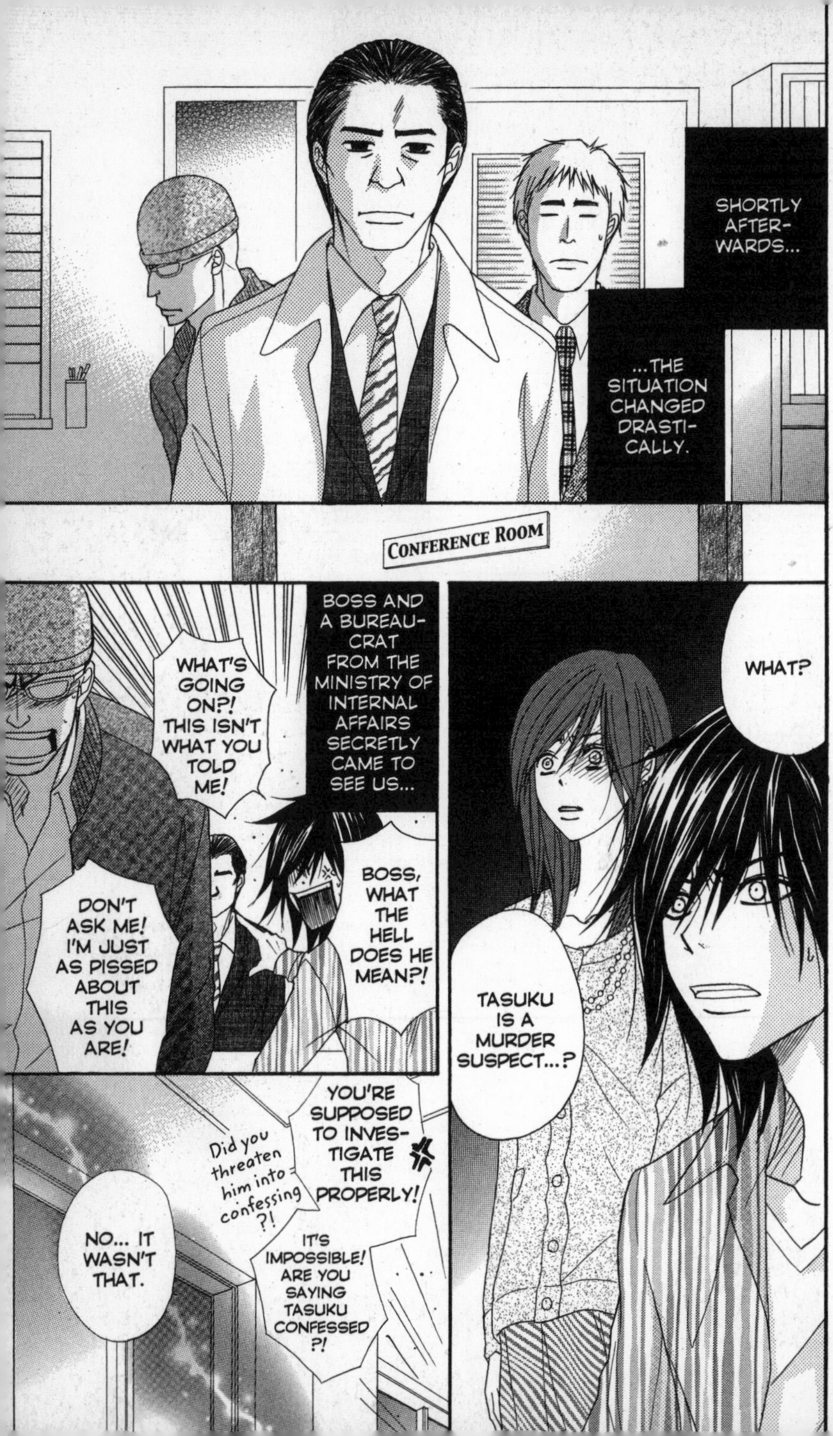
SHORTLY AFTERWARDS...
...THE SITUATION CHANGED DRASTICALLY.
CONFERENCE ROOM
WHAT?
TASUKU IS A MURDER SUSPECT...?
BOSS AND A BUREAUCRAT FROM THE MINISTRY OF INTERNAL AFFAIRS SECRETLY CAME TO SEE US...
WHAT'S GOING ON?! THIS ISN'T WHAT YOU TOLD ME!
BOSS, WHAT THE HELL DOES HE MEAN?!
DON'T ASK ME! I'M JUST AS PISSED ABOUT THIS AS YOU ARE!
YOU'RE SUPPOSED TO INVESTIGATE THIS PROPERLY!
Did you threaten him into confessing?!
IT'S IMPOSSIBLE! ARE YOU SAYING TASUKU CONFESSED?!
NO... IT WASN'T THAT.

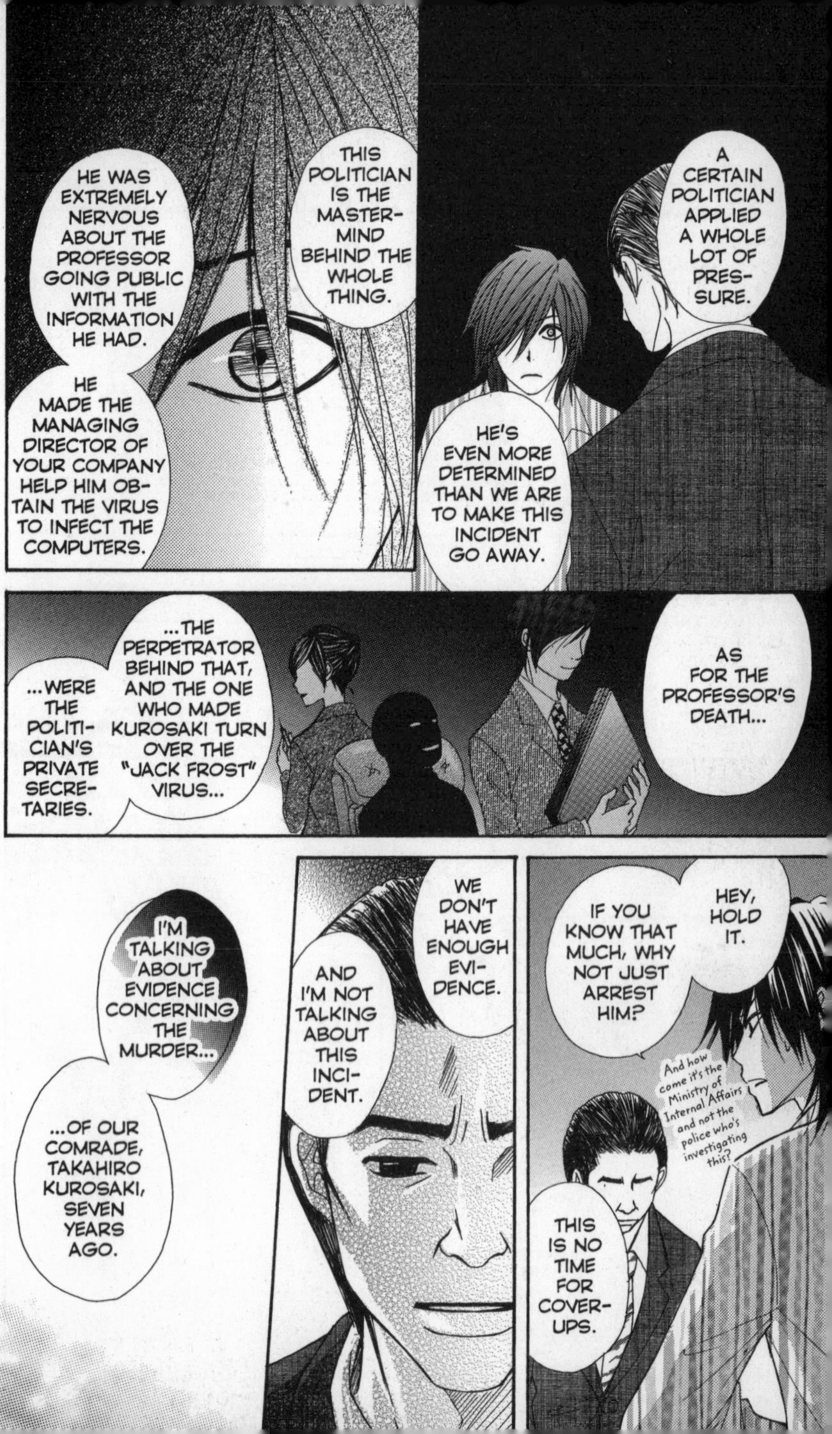
A CERTAIN POLITICIAN APPLIED A WHOLE LOT OF PRESSURE.
HE'S EVEN MORE DETERMINED THAN WE ARE TO MAKE THIS INCIDENT GO AWAY.
THIS POLITICIAN IS THE MASTERMIND BEHIND THE WHOLE THING.
HE WAS EXTREMELY NERVOUS ABOUT THE PROFESSOR GOING PUBLIC WITH THE INFORMATION HE HAD.
HE MADE THE MANAGING DIRECTOR OF YOUR COMPANY HELP HIM OBTAIN THE VIRUS TO INFECT THE COMPUTERS.
AS FOR THE PROFESSOR'S DEATH...
...THE PERPETRATOR BEHIND THAT, AND THE ONE WHO MADE KUROSAKI TURN OVER THE "JACK FROST" VIRUS...
...WERE THE POLITICIAN'S PRIVATE SECRETARIES.
HEY, HOLD IT.
IF YOU KNOW THAT MUCH, WHY NOT JUST ARREST HIM?
And how come it's the Ministry of Internal Affairs and not the police who's investigating this?
THIS IS NO TIME FOR COVER-UPS.
WE DON'T HAVE ENOUGH EVIDENCE.
AND I'M NOT TALKING ABOUT THIS INCIDENT.
I'M TALKING ABOUT EVIDENCE CONCERNING THE MURDER...
...OF OUR COMRADE, TAKAHIRO KUROSAKI, SEVEN YEARS AGO.

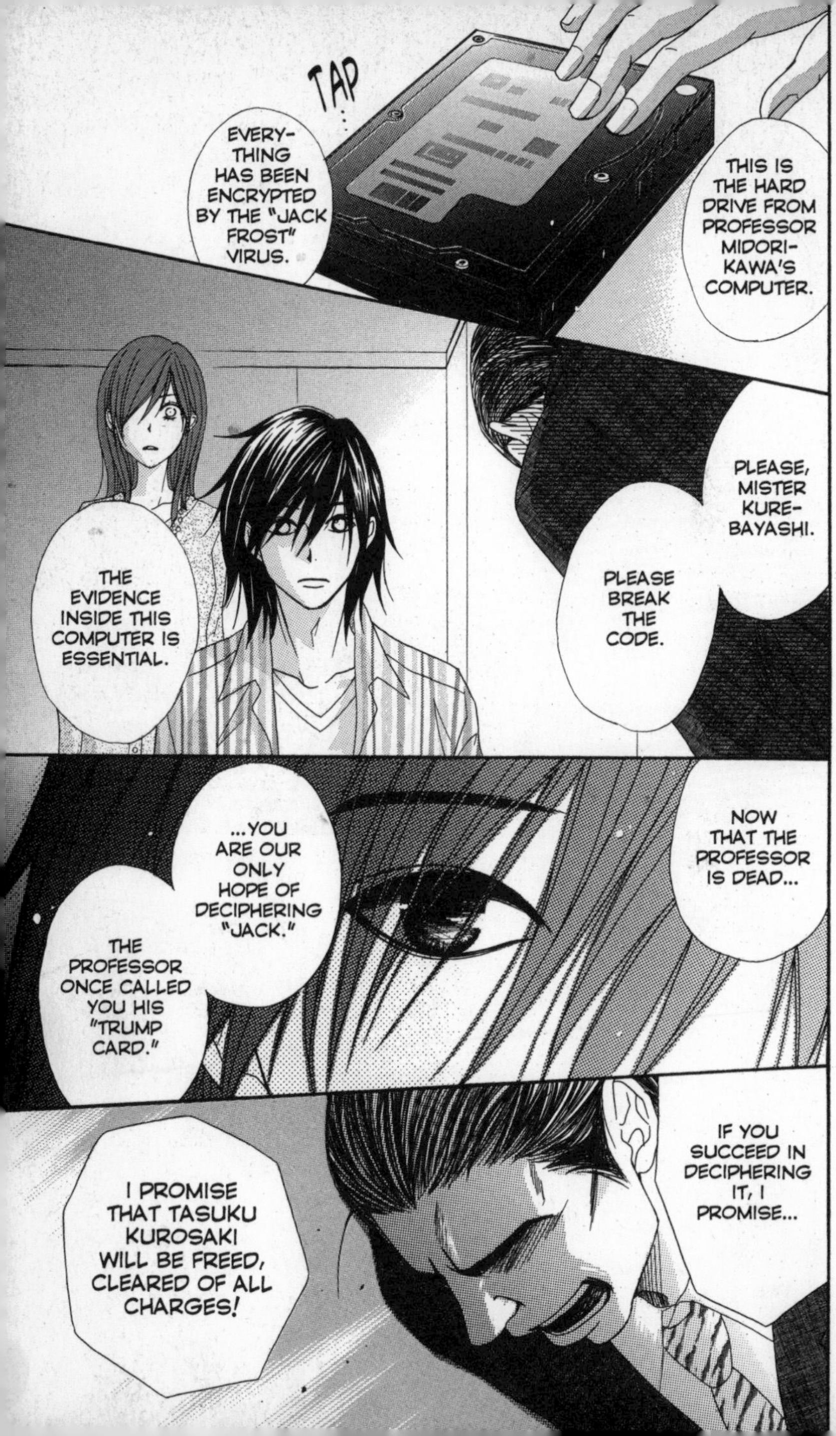
TAP
THIS IS THE HARD DRIVE FROM PROFESSOR MIDORI-KAWA'S COMPUTER.
EVERY-THING HAS BEEN ENCRYPTED BY THE "JACK FROST" VIRUS.
PLEASE, MISTER KURE-BAYASHI.
PLEASE BREAK THE CODE.
THE EVIDENCE INSIDE THIS COMPUTER IS ESSENTIAL.
NOW THAT THE PROFESSOR IS DEAD...
...YOU ARE OUR ONLY HOPE OF DECIPHERING "JACK."
THE PROFESSOR ONCE CALLED YOU HIS "TRUMP CARD."
IF YOU SUCCEED IN DECIPHERING IT, I PROMISE...
I PROMISE THAT TASUKU KUROSAKI WILL BE FREED, CLEARED OF ALL CHARGES!

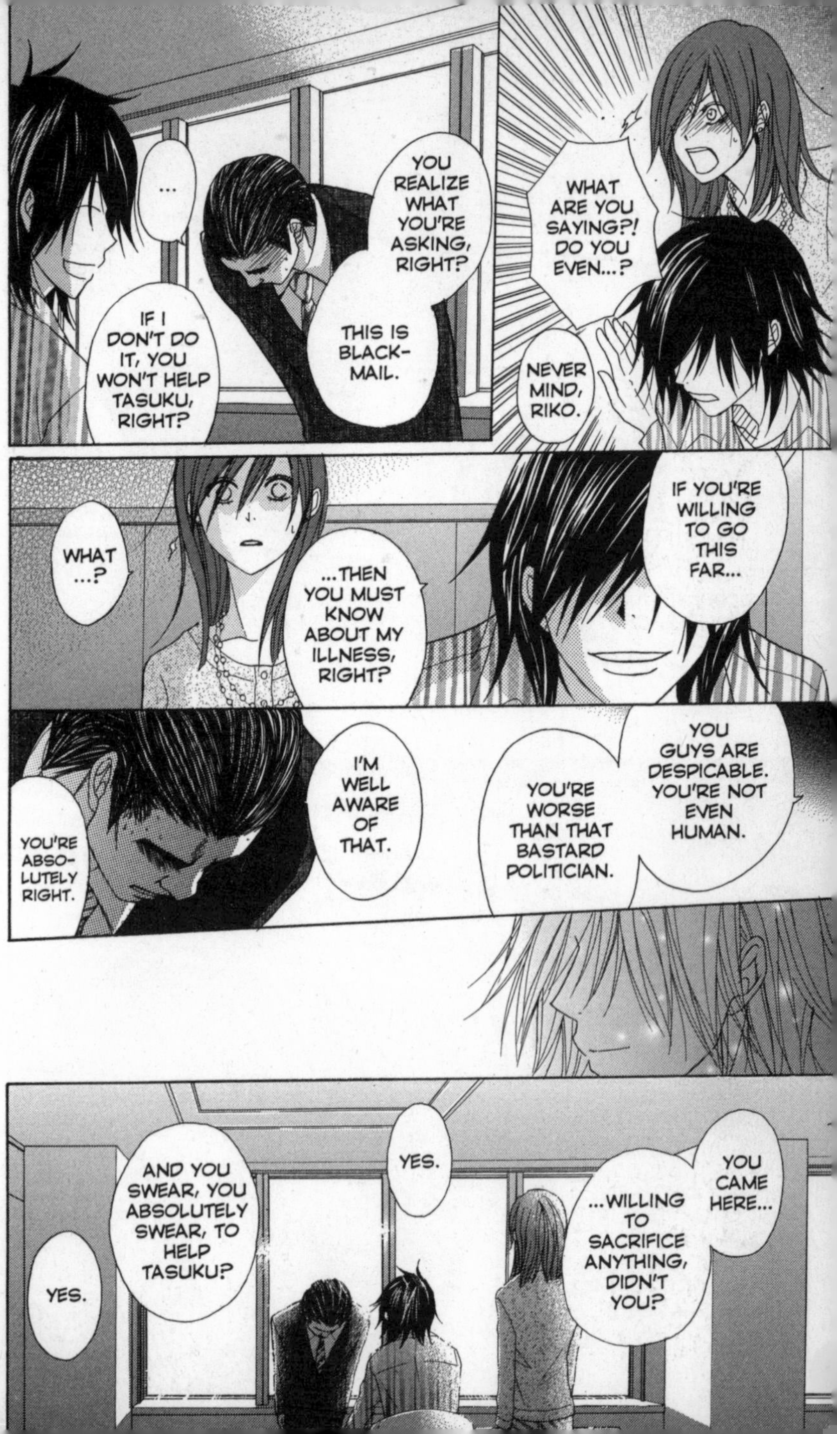
WHAT ARE YOU SAYING?! DO YOU EVEN...?
NEVER MIND, RIKO.
YOU REALIZE WHAT YOU'RE ASKING, RIGHT?
...
THIS IS BLACK-MAIL.
IF I DON'T DO IT, YOU WON'T HELP TASUKU, RIGHT?
IF YOU'RE WILLING TO GO THIS FAR...
...THEN YOU MUST KNOW ABOUT MY ILLNESS, RIGHT?
WHAT ...?
YOU GUYS ARE DESPICABLE. YOU'RE NOT EVEN HUMAN.
YOU'RE WORSE THAN THAT BASTARD POLITICIAN.
I'M WELL AWARE OF THAT.
YOU'RE ABSO-LUTELY RIGHT.
YOU CAME HERE...
...WILLING TO SACRIFICE ANYTHING, DIDN'T YOU?
YES.
AND YOU SWEAR, YOU ABSOLUTELY SWEAR, TO HELP TASUKU?
YES.

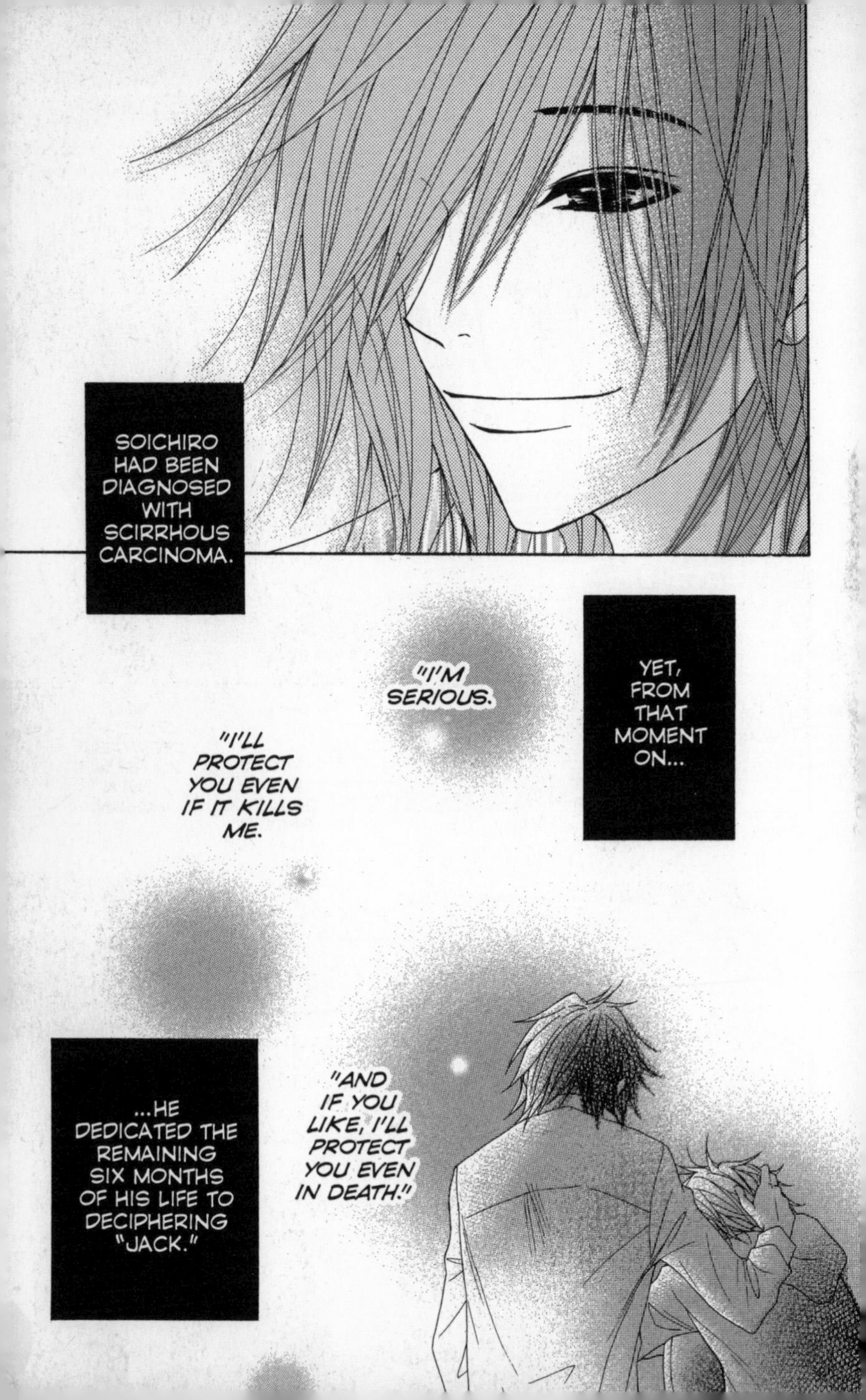
SOICHIRO HAD BEEN DIAGNOSED WITH SCIRRHOUS CARCINOMA.
YET, FROM THAT MOMENT ON...
"I'M SERIOUS.
"I'LL PROTECT YOU EVEN IF IT KILLS ME.
"AND IF YOU LIKE, I'LL PROTECT YOU EVEN IN DEATH."
...HE DEDICATED THE REMAINING SIX MONTHS OF HIS LIFE TO DECIPHERING "JACK."

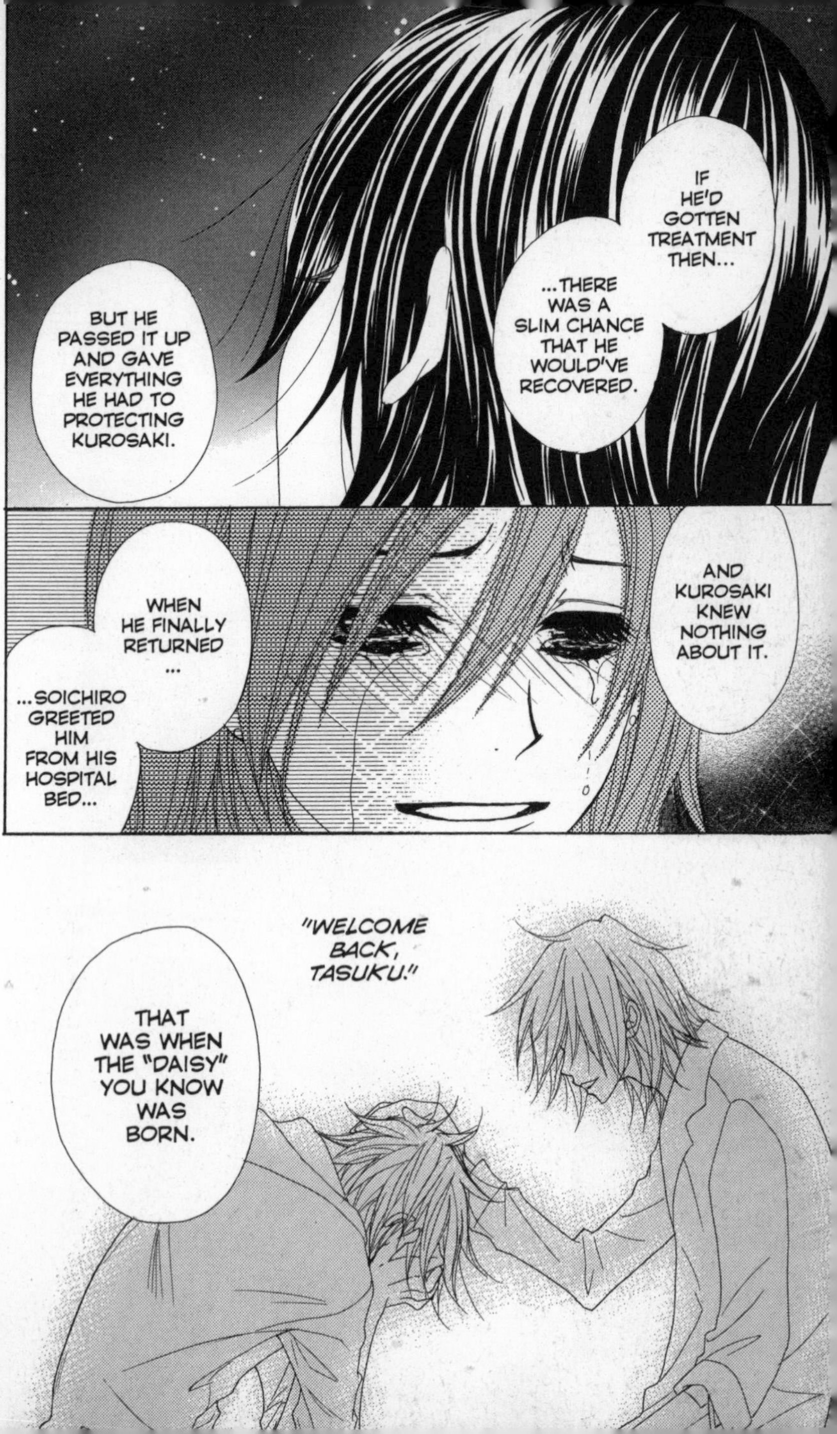
IF HE'D GOTTEN TREATMENT THEN...
...THERE WAS A SLIM CHANCE THAT HE WOULD'VE RECOVERED.
BUT HE PASSED IT UP AND GAVE EVERYTHING HE HAD TO PROTECTING KUROSAKI.
AND KUROSAKI KNEW NOTHING ABOUT IT.
WHEN HE FINALLY RETURNED ...
...SOICHIRO GREETED HIM FROM HIS HOSPITAL BED...
"WELCOME BACK, TASUKU."
THAT WAS WHEN THE "DAISY" YOU KNOW WAS BORN.

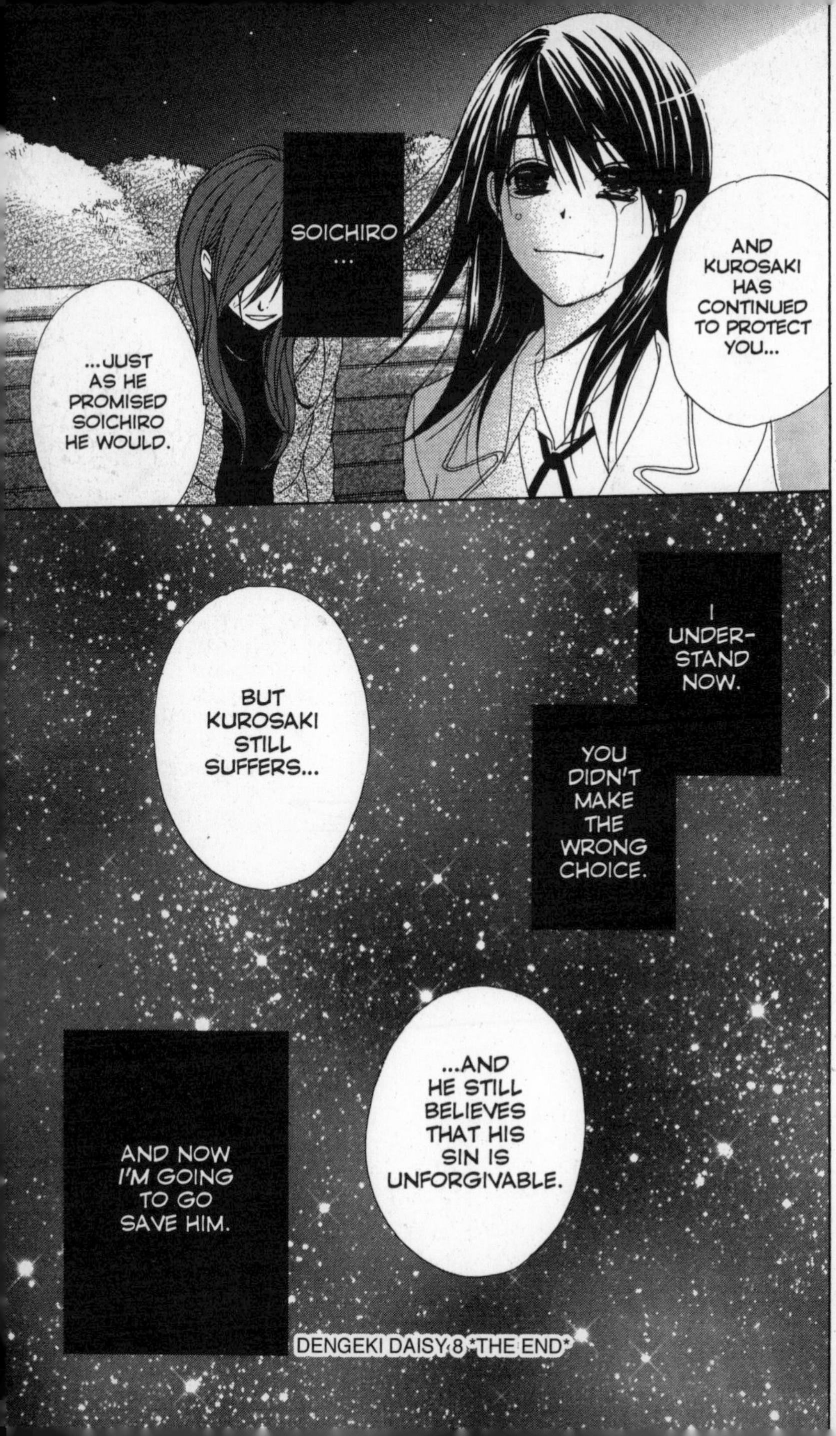
AND KUROSAKI HAS CONTINUED TO PROTECT YOU...
SOICHIRO ...
...JUST AS HE PROMISED SOICHIRO HE WOULD.
I UNDER-STAND NOW.
YOU DIDN'T MAKE THE WRONG CHOICE.
BUT KUROSAKI STILL SUFFERS...
...AND HE STILL BELIEVES THAT HIS SIN IS UNFORGIVABLE.
AND NOW I'M GOING TO GO SAVE HIM.
DENGEKI DAISY 8 *THE END*

AFTERWORD

Not being able to act silly...

Not being able to see her...

I expected this, but it's still hard...

I couldn't get rid of my cell phone...

...WELL... THAT'S IT FOR VOLUME 8.

AS I EXPLAINED AT THE START, THIS VOLUME WAS FILLED WITH A SLIGHTLY DIFFERENT MOOD. DUE TO MY SHORTCOMINGS, IT MAY HAVE BEEN SERIOUS AND HARD TO UNDERSTAND HERE AND THERE (IN SPITE OF IT BEING *DENGEKI DAISY*). I APOLOGIZE FOR THAT. STRANGE, RIGHT? I MEAN, IT'S *DENGEKI DAISY*, BUT IT HAD ALL THAT SERIOUSNESS IN IT.

DESPITE THE LACK OF HUMOR AND ROMANCE, THANK YOU SO MUCH FOR READING IT UNTIL THE END. IT'S BECAUSE OF READERS LIKE YOU THAT *DENGEKI DAISY* WILL CONTINUE FOR A WHILE. NOW THAT THE PAST HAS BEEN CLEARED UP, TERU AND KUROSAKI'S PRESENT STORY WILL PICK UP AGAIN. WELL, TERU GOES AFTER KUROSAKI. WILL SHE FIND HIM AND ~~MAKE HIM SIT ON HIS KNEES IN THE CORRIDOR UNTIL HE WAILS WHILE SHE LECTURES~~ RESCUE HIM?

I CERTAINLY WANT TO SEE YOU ALL AGAIN IN THE NEXT VOLUME. I'M LOOKING FORWARD TO IT.

DENGEKI DAISY
C/O DENGEKI DAISY EDITOR
VIZ MEDIA
P.O. BOX 77010
SAN FRANCISCO, CA 94107

← IF YOU HAVE ANY QUESTIONS , PLEASE SEND THEM HERE. FOR REGULAR FAN MAIL, PLEASE SEND THEM TO THE SAME ADDRESS BUT CHANGE THE ADDRESSEE TO:

KYOUSUKE MOTOMI
C/O DENGEKI DAISY EDITOR

...AND THAT'S IT. THANK YOU VERY MUCH!!

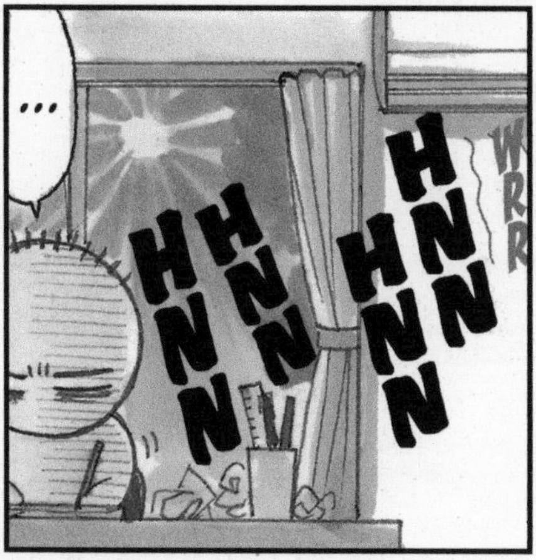
WRR
HNN
HNN
HNN
HNN
...

It was supposedly a scorching hot summer, but since I'm such a hermit, I really didn't notice. In fact, the last time I went to the beach was almost ten years ago.

-Kyousuke Motomi

Born on August 1, Kyousuke Motomi debuted in *Deluxe Betsucomi* with *Hetakuso Kyupiddo* (No-Good Cupid) in 2002. She is the creator of *Otokomae! Biizu Kurabu* (Handsome! Beads Club), and her latest work, *Dengeki Daisy,* is currently being serialized in *Betsucomi.* Motomi enjoys sleeping, tea ceremonies and reading Haruki Murakami.

DENGEKI DAISY
VOL. 8
Shojo Beat Edition

STORY AND ART BY
KYOUSUKE MOTOMI

© 2007 Kyousuke MOTOMI/Shogakukan
All rights reserved.
Original Japanese edition "DENGEKI DAISY"
published by SHOGAKUKAN Inc.

Translation & Adaptation/JN Productions
Touch-up Art & Lettering/Rina Mapa
Design/Nozomi Akashi
Editor/Amy Yu

Printed in the U.S.A.

Published by VIZ Media, LLC
P.O. Box 77010
San Francisco, CA 94107

10 9 8 7 6 5 4 3 2 1
First printing, January 2012

www.viz.com   www.shojobeat.com

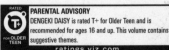

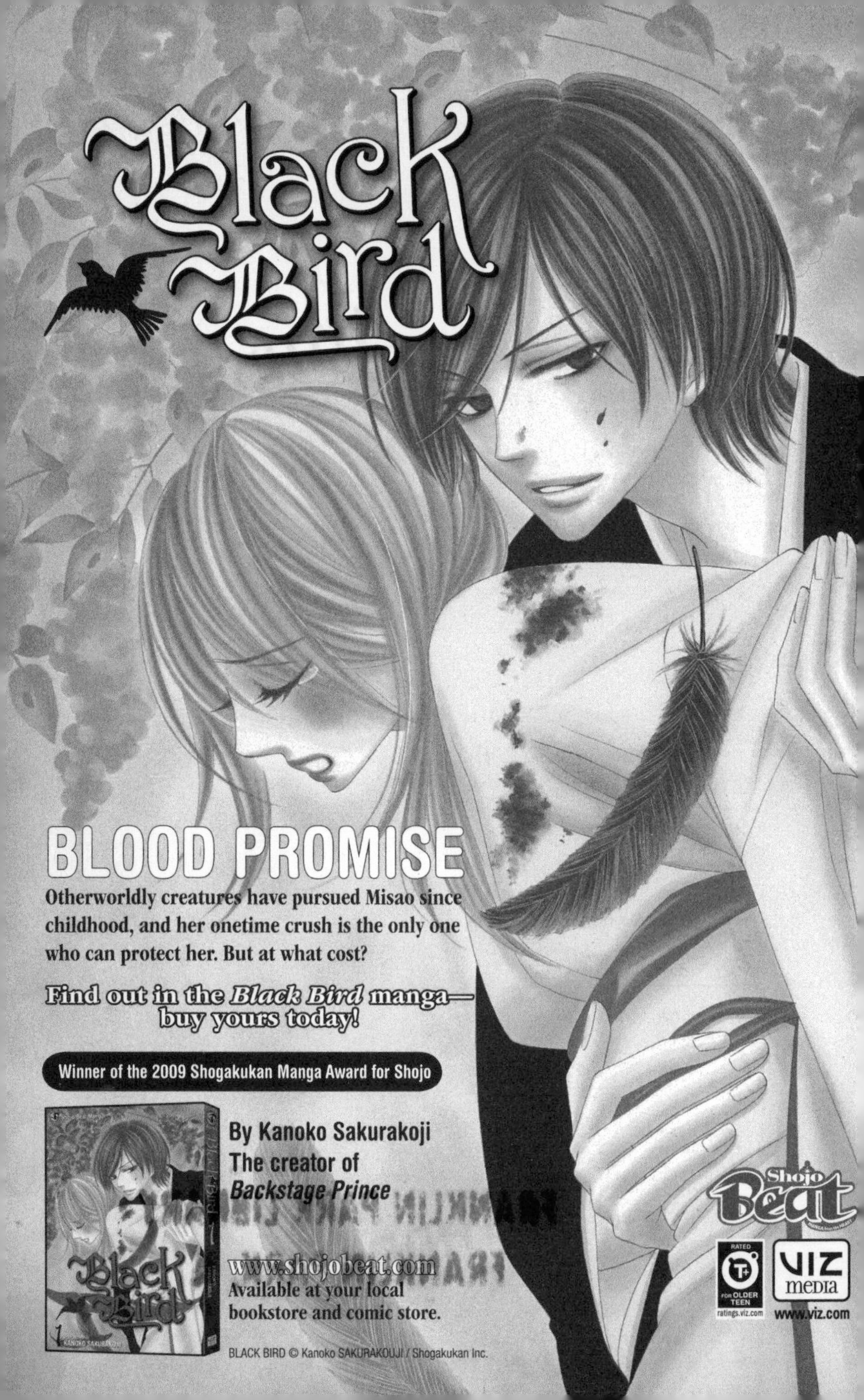
Black Bird
BLOOD PROMISE
Otherworldly creatures have pursued Misao since childhood, and her onetime crush is the only one who can protect her. But at what cost?
Find out in the *Black Bird* manga—buy yours today!
Winner of the 2009 Shogakukan Manga Award for Shojo
By Kanoko Sakurakoji
The creator of *Backstage Prince*
www.shojobeat.com
Available at your local bookstore and comic store.
Shojo Beat
RATED T+ FOR OLDER TEEN
ratings.viz.com
VIZ media
www.viz.com
BLACK BIRD © Kanoko SAKURAKOUJI / Shogakukan Inc.

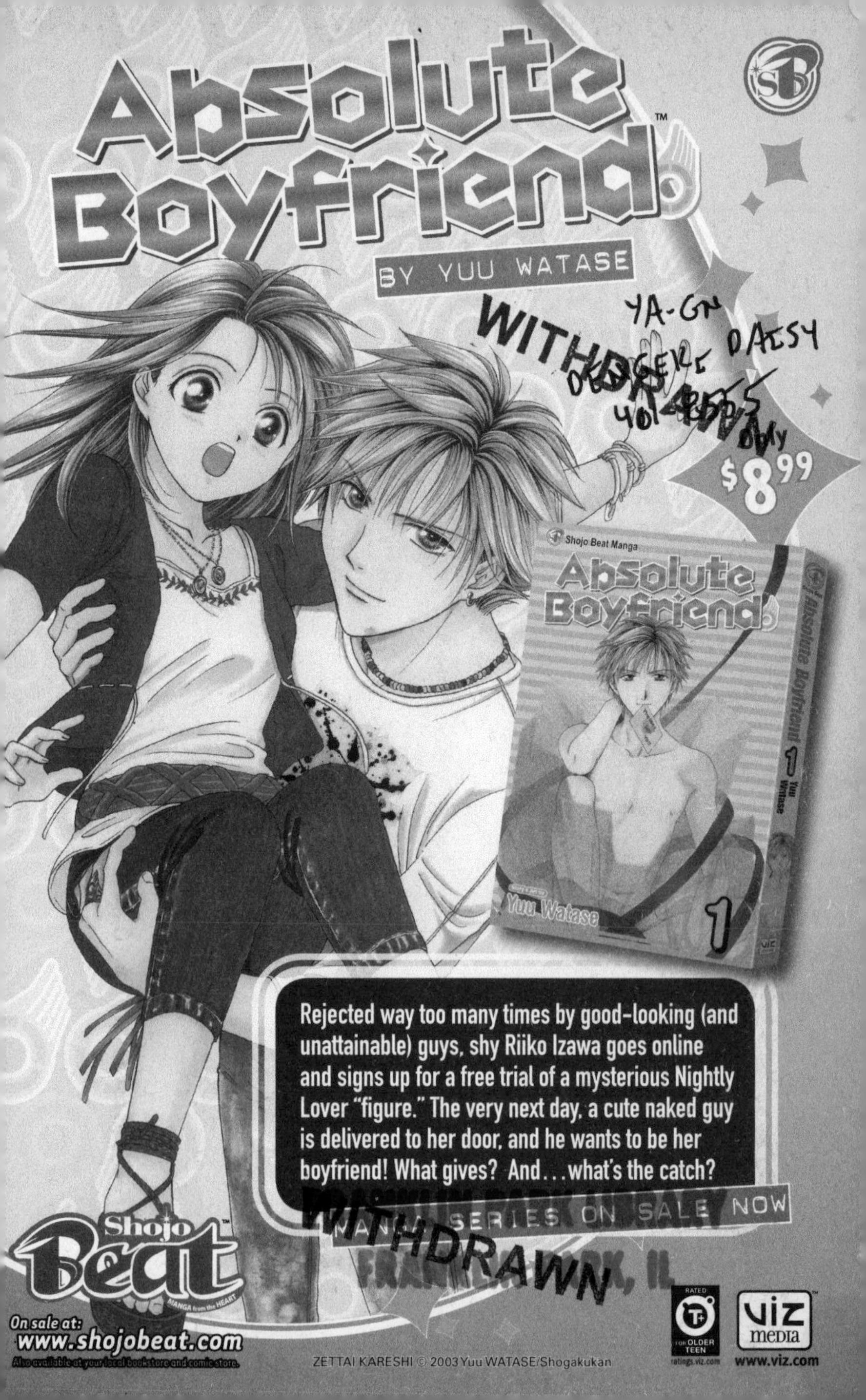

Absolute Boyfriend™
BY YUU WATASE
WITHDRAWN
YA-GN
ONLY $8.99
Shojo Beat Manga
Absolute Boyfriend
Yuu Watase
1
Rejected way too many times by good-looking (and unattainable) guys, shy Riiko Izawa goes online and signs up for a free trial of a mysterious Nightly Lover "figure." The very next day, a cute naked guy is delivered to her door, and he wants to be her boyfriend! What gives? And…what's the catch?
MANGA SERIES ON SALE NOW
WITHDRAWN
Shojo Beat
MANGA from the HEART
On sale at:
www.shojobeat.com
Also available at your local bookstore and comic store.
ZETTAI KARESHI © 2003 Yuu WATASE/Shogakukan
RATED T+ FOR OLDER TEEN
ratings.viz.com
VIZ media
www.viz.com

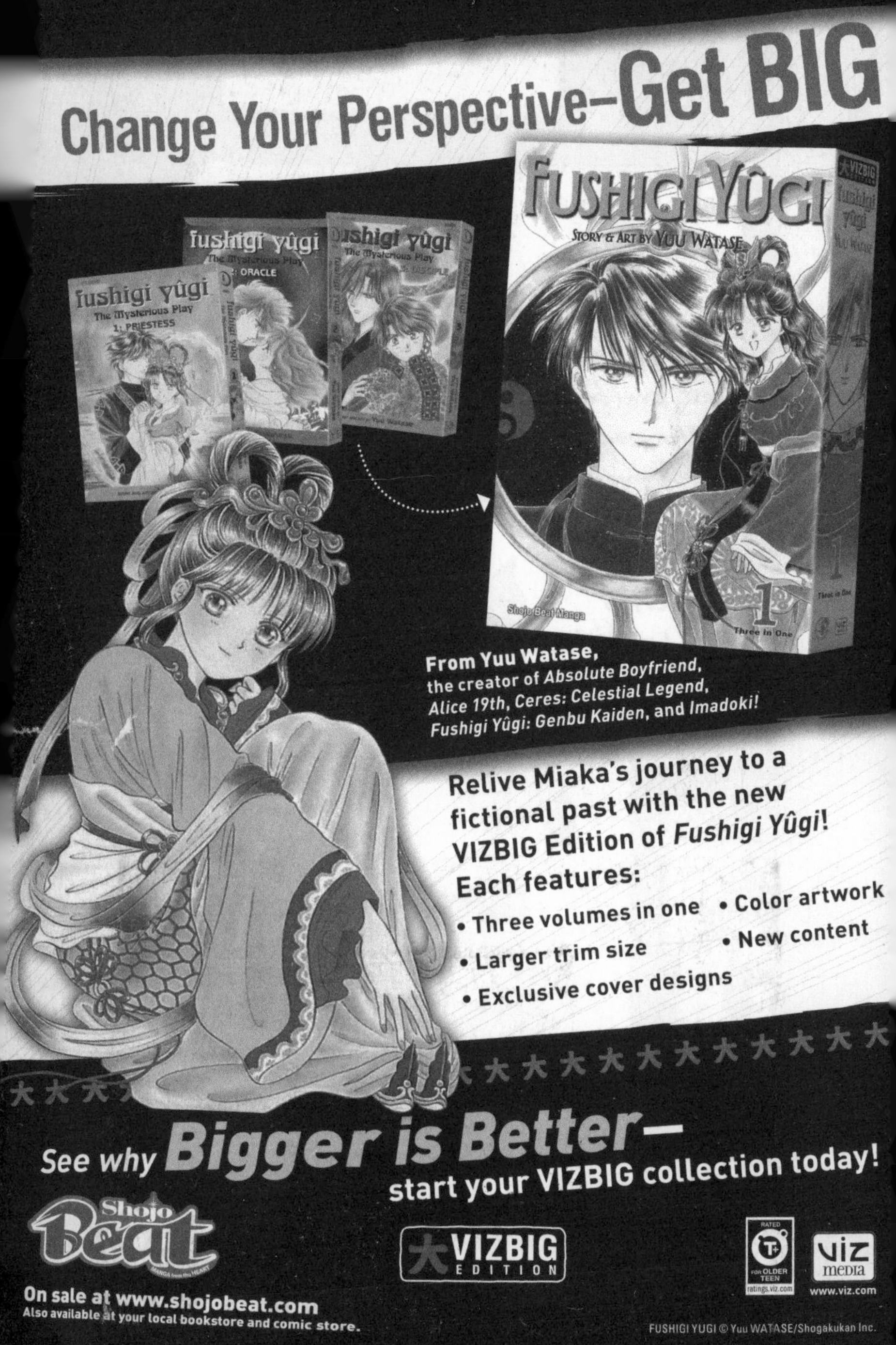
Change Your Perspective–Get BIG
FUSHIGI YÛGI
STORY & ART BY YUU WATASE
Shojo Beat Manga
Three in One
fushigi yûgi
The Mysterious Play
1: PRIESTESS
fushigi yûgi
The Mysterious Play
ORACLE
From Yuu Watase,
the creator of Absolute Boyfriend,
Alice 19th, Ceres: Celestial Legend,
Fushigi Yûgi: Genbu Kaiden, and Imadoki!
Relive Miaka's journey to a fictional past with the new VIZBIG Edition of Fushigi Yûgi!
Each features:
• Three volumes in one
• Larger trim size
• Exclusive cover designs
• Color artwork
• New content
See why Bigger is Better—
start your VIZBIG collection today!
Shojo Beat
MANGA from the HEART
VIZBIG EDITION
RATED T+ FOR OLDER TEEN ratings.viz.com
VIZ media
www.viz.com
On sale at www.shojobeat.com
Also available at your local bookstore and comic store.
FUSHIGI YUGI © Yuu WATASE/Shogakukan Inc.

4/12

Sand Chronicles™

By H

Used to t
anonymity
Ann Ueku
to the al
kindness
her moth

But will
that kind
personal

Find out in
Sand Chron
manga serie
AVAILABL

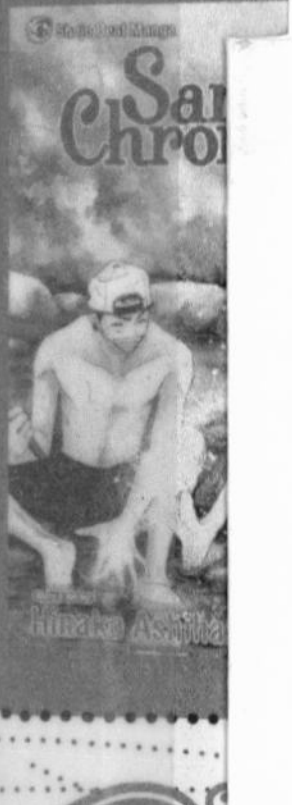
Sa
Chro

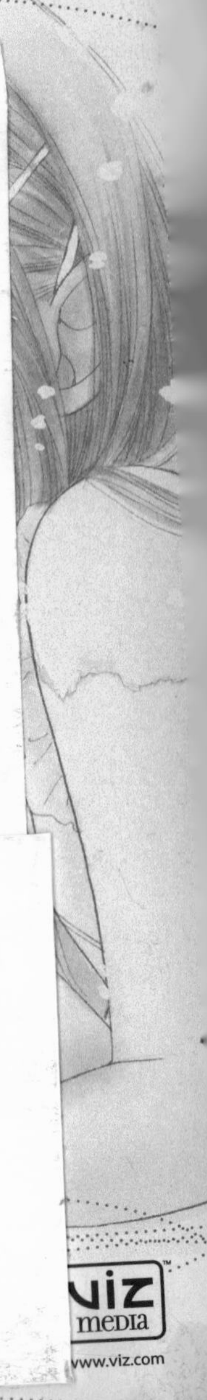

viz media

www.viz.com